A Jewish Life:

The Collected Writings of William Z. Spiegelman

Edited by William J. Brown

Colossal Books
New York, New York

Published May 2012

Colossal Books
POB 140041
Brooklyn NY 11214

www.american-colossus.com

Cover design: Susan J. Hull

ISBN: 978-0-615-61523-3

Printed and bound in the USA

Contents

III. Miscellaneous Essays (1924-1948)

IV. Introduction to *Bastions of Strength* (1940)

V. Unpublished Manuscripts (1927-1939)

Documents

Life

William Ze'ev ("Wolf") Spiegelman was born on August 28. Some of the official documents he signed say that he was born in 1893; others say 1894 or even 1895. All sources agree that he was born in the town of Mordy, in Sedlice County, in the nation once known as Poland, but then part of the Russian Empire. His father was named David Spiegelman (1828-1895), though some sources list his last name as Spzigelman. German for "Mirror Man," the name Spiegelman was – as William himself would point out, many years later, in a newspaper article about American Jews changing their names – no doubt "affixed by the decree of petty officials, whether the regime was Prussian, Russian or Austrian," and not chosen "by those who would have to bear them and transmit them to their progeny, but by the officials for considerations that were far from aesthetic, historic or euphonious."

William's mother was named Chava Kreitstein (1860-1944), though some sources list her last name as Ossinholtz. She was David Spiegelman's second wife. The first one, Chaya Ruchel Friedman, died in 1893. David Spiegelman died just two years later, at which time Chava Kreitstein took her son (her only child) and moved to Warsaw. There, it appears, she raised him in the household of Itzhak Meyer Spiegelman (1868-1940), who was one of ten children born to David Spiegelman and his first wife.

William's mother has been described as a devoted Hassid, indeed, as Hassid royalty. It is likely that she arranged for her son to be taught Hebrew, the sacred language in which the Torah and Talmud were written, as well as Yiddish, the "everyday" language of European Jews, and Polish and Russian, the languages of the authorities. William was probably an avid learner and brilliant child, with an obvious gift for languages; he would eventually learn German and English, as well.

But young William was also rather headstrong, even rebellious, and the reputedly stern and forbidding figure of his mother gave him plenty to rebel against. In one instance, he disobeyed his mother by walking by the neighborhood church during Easter. As she feared, he was harassed and attacked by anti-Semitic Polish youths. In another instance, he disobeyed his mother by going to a local Zionist meeting (no doubt illegal), which was held at the pickle-maker's shop. When she smelled the pickles on him, she knew that he'd gone, despite what she'd said – and she spanked him. But he was not deterred.

At the age of 14, William began studying at the Yeshiva in Lida, but left soon after, apparently because he was lonely. (Perhaps he'd been carried to Lida by his rebellion, which weakened somewhat after seeing what being away from home was really like.) Back in Warsaw, he was educated in the Torah, the Talmud, and Hassidic lore by Rabbi Poznanski, the Chief Rabbi of the Great Synagogue.

Sometime later, perhaps at the age of 16, William audited courses at the University of Krakow, where he developed a taste for contemporary Hebrew literature and the lyrical passages in the Torah. Perhaps, like C. B. Vladeck, somebody William wrote about later in his life, "he found [...] a greater appeal in the poetical cry of the Prophets, especially Isaiah, against the social injustice of the feudal system of ancient Judea, than in the hairsplitting and sharp-minded theorizing of the later exponents of abstract Jewish thought in the schools of Babylon and awoke, when yet a youth, to the problem of economic inequality in the country of his nativity."

In Krakow, William met Sarah Schenirer, who was a specialist in Samson Raphael Hirsch (1808-1888), the author of *Neunzehn Briefe unber Judenthum* (*Nineteen Letters on Judaism*). Written under the pseudonym Ben Uziel, the *Nineteen Letters* was a condemnation of the Reform Movement and its role in assimilating Jews into German society. Realizing that contemporary Jews couldn't "return" to traditional Judaism, Hirsch offered a third possibility: Torah, the study of Torah, plus *Derekh Eretz* (Hebrew for "the way of the earth"). For this *Haskalah* ("Enlightened") form of Jewish Orthodoxy, "the way of the earth" was the recognition of social injustice in the world and the duty to fight that injustice.

William was so impressed with Hirsch's book that he translated it from German into Hebrew. Perhaps he welcomed the alternative that *Haskalah* offered to Hassidism, which tended ignore both worldly injustice and the fight against it, and focus on joyful and uninterrupted study of the Torah. Perhaps, once again like C. B. Vladeck, William found that, "the tremendous chasm between the poor village population on one hand and the luxury of the small group of landowners on the other; [and] the limitless poverty of the city dwellers and the extravagant life of the then-powerful higher Russian officials, was too great a reminder of social difference for it not to set in motion a mind and a heart which had inherited a capacity for understanding and feeling."

According to the entry for him in *Who's Who in American Jewry* (1926), William began his career as a journalist in 1911, that is, at the age 17 or 18. Perhaps, like Peter Wiernik, someone William wrote an essay about, "he worked as a compositor for many years in various newspaper plants." And perhaps, once again like Wiernik, "the work of the composing room did not keep him from studying and taking an interest in the intellectual problems of life." In William's case – that is, if he did indeed work as a compositor – this experience came in very handy later in life, when he became the editor of his own newspaper.

Between 1911 and 1919, William lived in Warsaw and served as the city editor for the Yiddish-language paper *Der Fraind*; the city editor and parliamentary correspondent for the Yiddish-language paper *Der Moment*; a correspondent for the Polish-language paper *Nasz Przegland*; and a correspondent for two different Hebrew-language papers, *Hazefirah* (published daily in Warsaw) and *Haolom* (published weekly in Berlin). During this same period, he co-founded the Jewish Writers and Journalists Association of Poland.

In November 1918, William went back to Krakow to investigate and write about the anti-Jewish violence that had broken out there in the wake of the collapse of the Russian Empire and the establishment of a free and independent Polish State. It was in the course of this investigation that he met and became friends with Jacob Landau (1892-1952), who was covering the events for the Jewish Correspondence Bureau, which Landau and others had founded in The Hague in February 1917. It is possible, but not established, that William started contributing articles to the Jewish Correspondence Bureau at this point, or the following year (1919), when Landau moved the organization from The Hague to London and renamed it the Jewish Telegraphic Agency.

In July 1920, William traveled to London for the World Zionist Congress. Persistent family recollections and anecdotes about him leaving Poland in a hay wagon – with Polish soldiers sticking bayonets into the hay to see if anyone was hiding there – suggest that he traveled to London without proper authorization papers, perhaps in flight from anti-Jewish or anti-Zionist violence in his native country. In any event, after his Zionist work in London was over, William didn't return to Poland, but took Jacob Landau up on his offer to work as an editor for the Jewish Telegraphic Agency. It appears that he worked in London for two years.

In May 1921, William took a transatlantic trip to Montreal on company business, perhaps to see about opening a bureau of the Jewish Telegraphic Agency there. (In 1922, Jacob Landau would in fact move the agency from London and re-locate it in New York City.) In any event, when his business in Canada was done, William returned to London.

It appears that, early in 1923, William left England for good, and made his way to the United States. It seems that William first stopped in New York City for a brief period before moving to San Francisco, California, to stay with other members of the Spiegelman family. While in the Bay Area, he served as the Executive Secretary of the Jewish Education Association of San Francisco. Max Rudensky has claimed that William also "studied at the local University and edited the San Francisco Anglo-Jewish weekly" (*Land and Life*, Summer 1949), but both references have proved too vague – *which* local university? *which* Anglo-Jewish weekly? – to be substantiated. (The only Anglo-Jewish weekly published in San Francisco at the time was *Emanu-El*, later called *The Jewish Bulletin of Northern California*, but William was never listed on its masthead as an editor, nor did he ever publish any articles in it.)

In San Francisco, William met his future wife, Dora Moreiss (1899-1993), daughter of Morus Tekuchinsky. (There are a great many alternate spellings of both Moreiss *and* Tekuchinsky.) Like William, Dora was originally from Mordy, Poland and had immigrated to America, albeit much earlier in her life than he had (when she was only four years old), and had ended up in San Francisco via Montgomery, Alabama.

In March 1924, William moved to New York City because Jacob Landau had, once again, offered him a job with the Jewish Telegraphic Agency. The agency had grown immensely since William had last worked for it. There were now agency offices in Paris, Berlin, Warsaw, Jerusalem and London, and they received reports via telephone or telegram from approximately 150 special correspondents, who were stationed on all seven continents (but mostly in the United States and Europe).

In April 1924, William started publishing a syndicated weekly column for the agency entitled "Our New York Letter." Usually divided into three or four subsections, this column gave him the opportunity to write about a wide variety of topics and people, all from a strictly Jewish perspective. He would continue publishing "Our New York Letter" until 1929.

In October 1924, William became the editor of the Jewish Telegraphic Agency's *Jewish Daily Bulletin*, which, prior to his arrival in New York, had been a simple typewritten newsletter, apparently reproduced on the era's equivalent of a mimeograph machine. Under William's leadership, the *Jewish Daily Bulletin* suddenly became a truly professional affair, laid-out in columns, typeset by an experienced compositor, and printed by an offset press on high-quality paper. Apparently **the world's first English-language Jewish daily, the** *Bulletin* was originally four pages long (it quickly grew to eight), small (only 10.5 inches by 7.5 inches), and filled with dozens of short, concise and timely reports from all over the world. In a startlingly modern touch, the *Bulletin* boasted that it reported the news "within 24 hours" after it happened. It managed to live up to this claim by being open 24 hours a day: William did the day shift, while assistant editor Leo M. Grossman did the night shift.

According to family legend, William was one of the very first newspaper editors in the United States to take the rise of Adolph Hitler seriously. Indeed, the very first issue of the *Jewish Daily Bulletin* (October 15, 1924) contained a brief notice about the "leader of the German anti-Semites and defeated general of the Bavarian Beer Revolution" – then "imprisoned in Bavaria" – losing his Austrian citizenship. No doubt William had been aware of Hitler, and the threat he posed to Germany's Jews, ever since the publication of a report ("Hitler Threatens Jews, Americans, English") by the London branch of the Jewish Telegraphic Agency on January 30, 1923. By contrast, the *New York Times* only started paying attention to Hitler on February 28, 1925.

Sometime before November 1924, Dora Moreiss came to New York City, knowing that that was where William could be found. According to family legend, it was *Dora* who desired and proposed marriage, while William would have preferred to stay single. In any event, because the two of them were closely related (William was Dora's half-uncle), they couldn't get married in the State of New York. Towards the end of November 1924, they were married in Providence, Rhode Island, where a proper marriage license could be obtained.

In November 1925, while living in Brooklyn, the new couple welcomed the birth of their first child, Ruth Joy. A governess was employed to help raise her, which suggests that Dora was also working for a living and/or that William's job at the Jewish Telegraphic Agency was paying sufficiently well for the family to afford to hire one, and thus allow his young wife to do other things as well as be a mother.

In 1926, William became the Chairman of the Executive Committee of *Histadruth Ivrith* (the Hebrew Culture Organization of America), which had been founded in 1916 to promote the study of Hebrew culture, the teaching of the Hebrew language, and the use of Hebrew as a spoken tongue. It seems that William's involvement with *Histadruth Ivrith* lasted several years, at least.

On November 29, 1927, William wrote to Fraser Metzger, the Dean of Rutgers University, in response to reports that Rutgers was deliberately restricting the number of Jewish students it was admitting. "I will be brutally frank with you," an administrator was quoted as saying to a Jewish applicant. "You are rejected because you are Jewish." The next day, the President of Rutgers, John Martin Thomas, wrote a response to William. According to Michael Greenberg and Seymour Zenchelsky, authors of "Private Bias and Public Responsibility: Anti-Semitism at Rutgers in the 1920s and 1930s" (*History of Education Quarterly*, Fall 1993), that response was: "No discrimination such as you describe has come to my attention, nor could such action have been [taken] by authority of the President or the Trustees of the University."

In early August 1928, William wrote a letter to H. H. Martin, who'd published an objectionable article ("Adherents of Jewish Faith") in the August 2, 1928 issue of *United Presbyterian*. We know about this letter because Martin himself mentioned it in *United Presbyterian*'s October 11, 1928 issue. Unlike many other letters written to Martin in protest, "the beautiful letter from William Z. Spiegelman, editor of the *Jewish Daily Bulletin*, New York City" – also described by Martin as "a courteous letter and of a kind spirit" – managed to elicit from him an apologetic "amplifying statement" on the matter. According to Martin, William "printed it [the statement] in his paper in a generous spirit," and, at the conclusion of the affair, wrote a second letter to Martin that declared, "It is only human to err, but it is magnificent to admit the error in as frank and courageous manner as you have done."

In January or February 1929, William departed for Montreal, perhaps on assignment from the Jewish Telegraphic Agency. According to U.S. government records, William returned to the United States on March 14, 1929 and, on April 8, 1929, he officially declared his intention to become a citizen of the United States. (He would finally receive his official certificate of naturalization in June 1934.)

In March or April 1929, William – bolstered by a glowing letter of recommendation from Meyer W. Weisgal, the Secretary of the National Executive Committee of the Zionist Organization of America – was hired to be the Public Relations Director of the Jewish National Fund of America. Founded in 1901, at the First Zionist Congress in London, the Jewish National Fund (*Keren Kayemeth Leisrael*, in transliterated Hebrew) was the primary means by which Jews living in England and Western Europe could contribute funds that would be used to purchase and develop land in Palestine, then nominally under British control. Purchased in the name of the Jewish people as a whole, as the future location of the "Jewish National Home," this land would then be leased to Jews who emigrated there to work as farmers, foresters and other developers. Ideally speaking, those emigrants would come from Central and Eastern Europe, where the conditions in which Jews lived were (still) dark and desperate.

At the time William joined the Jewish National Fund *of America*, which had been created in Philadelphia in 1910, the methods by which the organization raised funds were the same ones adopted in the beginning: white-and-blue donation boxes, which were placed in synagogues and schools; donations towards the Golden Book, in which the names of supporters of the cause could be inscribed; sales of blue-and-white stamps and stamp books in which to collect them; sales of flowers on Flag Day and miniature Zionist flags on Flag Day; *dunam* land contributions; bequests and living legacies; and direct, written appeals by mail.

William certainly wasn't hired by the Jewish National Fund of America to invent new methods of raising money. Instead, he was brought in to widen the appeal of the existing ones. In the words of his essay, "From Cleveland to Cleveland," published in 1930: "Active interest in Zionism and in the Palestine work" had previously been "primarily centered in the upper-middle class and among the Jewish intelligentsia." But "to raise huge funds it was necessary to enlist larger numbers in the work," in particular, "the middle class," which was "a vast field whose resources and capacities have not yet been fully exploited."

One of the ways that William brought the message and activities of the JNF to the attention of the American middle class was the publication of American-style brochures. Well written and attractively and cleverly designed, each of these brochures contained a lot of illustrations (both drawings and photographs), and was reproduced in bright, clean colors. Even more impressive was the fact that these brochures were not created according to an overall format; in fact, none of them resembled another. Each brochure had a clever idea – a different size of paper or a different way of folding that piece of paper – that set it apart from the other JNF brochures.

On September 3, 1929, William sent a telegram to United States Secretary of State Henry L. Stimson concerning the Arab rebellion against the Zionist colonization of Palestine. We know about this telegram because Lawrence Davidson cites it twice in his book *America's Palestine: Popular and Official Perceptions from Balfour to Israeli Statehood* (University Press of Florida: 2001).

> "William Spiegelman, editor of the Jewish Telegraphic Agency, in a telegram sent to Secretary of State Stimson, suggested that the United States might consider taking over the Palestine mandate [from the British] because of its 'special significance to the American public since funds of American citizens have been and are expected to be the largest factor for the reconstruction and rehabilitation of the Holy Land'" (p. 101).

> "William Spiegelman, in his communication with Stimson, told the secretary of state that out of the crisis 'the Jewish National Home in Palestine will emerge with greater strength for the further spreading of Western civilization' and asked him for a statement about what the U.S. government was going to do to help" (*ibid*).

According to Davidson, who is a professor of history at West Chester University, the 1929 Arab rebellion "contradicted the 'progress means peace' theory of Zionist colonization" and yet "did not result in any critical reexamination of the Zionist venture in the popular press." Why not? In Davidson's analysis, the answer is that American Zionists were successful, on the one hand, in closely associating the Jewish National Home in Palestine with "the march of Western civilization," and, on the other hand, in characterizing the Arabs as "barbarians prone to fanatical violence." More particularly, "Zionist sources proved to be major ones for press pieces, and the stories they told followed consistently from the premises of the prevailing bipolar worldview." (In his article entitled "Zionism, Socialism and United States Support for the Jewish Colonization of Palestine in the 1920s," *Arab Studies Quarterly* Vol. 18, 1996, Professor Davidson gave an example of the phenomenon: "The *New York Times* also relied heavily on the Jewish Telegraphic Agency, run by the American Zionist William Spiegelman, for its Palestine reporting.") Meanwhile, Davidson writes in his book, "other points of view, such as those of Arab American activists, were too discordant to be taken seriously."

In October 1929, both William Spiegelman and Johns Simons resigned from the Jewish Telegraphic Agency to work with the Jewish Biographical Bureau, also located in New York. Their departures (Simons was the agency's business manager) were obviously amicable, because they were reported in amicable terms by the Jewish Telegraphic Agency itself.

Prior to the arrival of its new editors, who were also its new co-owners, the Jewish Biographical Bureau had published two editions of *Who's Who in American Jewry* (one in 1926, the other in 1928). As was mentioned earlier, there was an entry for William in the first edition. Like the other prominent Jews who were listed in it, he'd been sent a letter from the Bureau that informed him that he'd been selected. Once again like the others, he wrote his own entry. In 1928, William's brief autobiographical sketch was reprinted in the collection's second edition.

In November 1929, reunited in Brooklyn (no doubt for at least a year), William and Dora Spiegelman welcomed the birth of their second child, Judith Marcia.

In July or August 1930, William was forced to sue his business partner in the Jewish Biographical Bureau, John Simons, as well as a man named Hiram Elfenbein. William's allegation was that Simons had conspired to wrestle control of the Bureau from him (as well as steal William's financial stake in it) by falsely claiming that the enterprise had gone bankrupt and had been sold off (to Elfenbein, working in cahoots with Simons) to pay off its debts.

Aside from the obvious financial motive, Simons and Elfenbein might have engaged in this *alleged* conspiracy for political reasons. Unlike John Simons, who ended up bringing out the third edition of *Who's Who in American Jewry* in 1938, William was an ardent Zionist. Perhaps Simons didn't like the weight William assigned to his fellow Zionists or, conversely, Simons didn't like William's negative attitude toward his non-Zionist contemporaries. And unlike Hiram Elfenbein, who went on to publish *Socialism From Where We Are* in 1945 and *Organized Religion: The Great Game of Make-Believe* in 1968, William was both a committed anti-socialist and a firmer believer in organized religion.

On September 27, 1930, the Supreme Court of New York County ruled against William. The dismissal was based on the "insufficiency" of the evidence (no cause of action) against one of the two men. William appealed to the Appellate Division, but it upheld the lower court's decision in January 1931 (232 A.D. 651; 247 N.Y.S. 147; 1931 N.Y. App. Div.) It seems that William had been robbed, and there was nothing he could do about it.

In 1932, William and Dora Spiegelman welcomed the birth of their third child, Emanuel David.

For approximately eight months in 1934, William was an important executive member of the American Jewish Congress' Bureau of the Boycott Committee, which he helped form on February 21, 1934. (The American Jewish Congress itself was founded by Rabbi Stephen S. Wise, Felix Frankfurter and Louis Brandeis in 1918.) An attempt to make good on the Congress' intention to boycott all goods produced in Germany, which it declared in August 1933, the Bureau took action on a number of fronts. Not only did it publicize the existence and effects of the Nazi regime's recently enacted laws against Jews living in Germany through mass gatherings at places like Madison Square Garden, which were broadcast live on the radio, but it also did extensive research on the products (almost 30 in all) that the regime produced and on the ways and places that those products were shipped to and sold in the United States. Recorded on index cards and typescripts (not computers!), the results of all this research were made available to the public through the Bureau's "Information Service."

With William acting as the Director of the Economic Committee, and then as the Director of the Boycott Committee, the Bureau received confidential complaints from both whistle-blowers and ordinary citizens about non-compliant shipping companies and vendors, especially those that sold German goods to unwitting Jewish customers, and then – after acknowledging receipt of those complaints – sent out agents to investigate those claims fully. (William's personal investigator was an attorney from Long Island City named Charles Evers.) These agents generated confidential reports, which were then used to confront the confirmed offenders with facts, not mere allegations.

The Bureau sent out hundreds of letters – all of them typed up and signed individually, not churned out en masse by a mimeograph machine – to department stores throughout the New York City area. These letters, which explained the principles of the boycott ("Buy American, Boycott Nazi Goods") and asked for compliance with it, were then followed up upon by a second round of letters and, when necessary, personal visits by members of the "Vigilance Committee" to see if those who pledged compliance were actually being compliant. In those cases in which German goods were still being sold, but with their "Made in Germany" labels obscured by price tags or removed (both violations of the law), the Bureau worked with the New York Police Department and the District Attorney's office to bring the offenders to justice.

According to Rona Sheramy, the author of an essay entitled 'There are Times When Silence is a Sin': The Women's Division of the American Jewish Congress and the Anti-Nazi Boycott Movement" (*American Jewish History*, March 2001):

> The boycott of German-made goods was a multifaceted operation calling for the coordination of several branches, bureaus, offices, and individuals [...] Each chapter's boycott committee was subdivided into smaller units responsible for various aspects of the boycott's day-to-day operation. One of the most important of these subdivisions was the vigilance committee, which was responsible for collecting information on local consumer and business boycott observance. Vigilance committees were *first* proposed for New York City in 1934 as part of the boycott reorganization. Boycott organizers divided the metropolitan area into zones of surveillance corresponding to the principal Jewish populations. Vigilance committee members made daily visits to stores suspected of handling Nazi goods and submitted names of violators for investigation. [emphasis added]

Ms. Sheramy's footnote to this passage refers her readers to "Mr. William Z. Spiegelman to Dr. Joseph Tenenbaum, 4 April 1934, Joint Boycott Council Records, NYPL." The implication is that either Dr. Tenenbaum or Mr. Spiegelman, or both, can be credited with the invention of the Vigilance Committee.

The Bureau also engaged in lobbying efforts. In one instance, it attempted to convince the United States to terminate its commercial treaty with Germany (as had been done with Czarist Russia in 1911), and, in another, the Bureau contacted New York State Senator Lazarus Joseph in an attempt to get him to introduce a bill that would ban the wearing of "foreign military uniforms or insignia" and thus "counteract the spread of the Nazi movement in the State of New York" (letter from William Z. Spiegelman, dated April 13, 1934).

Knowing full well that many people would not support the boycott if they couldn't find alternate sources for the products they needed or relied upon to do their work, the Bureau did its best to locate and recommend alternate vendors. Between October 22 and October 27, 1934, the Bureau – in conjunction with the American Federation of Labor – organized an "International Merchandising Good Will Fair" at Grand Central Palace in New York. Its motto was, "Buy American, Don't Trade with the Enemies of Civilization, Foster Good Will Through Your Purchases."

It isn't clear why William resigned his post at the Bureau, an event that seems to have taken place in either September or October 1934. A lack of support from the American Jewish Congress is a possibility. In his report (dated April 16, 1934) to Dr. Joseph Tenenbaum, the Chairman of the Boycott Committee, William reported that the Congress had provided little or no material support to the operation, which was forced to raise funds, hire a staff, and rent an office on its own. Another possibility for William's resignation was the incompatibility of the boycott with the Zionist movement, or, rather, with the *Haavara* ("Transfer") Agreement that the Nazi regime had made with the Jewish Agency for Palestine in August 1933. Under the terms of this agreement, Jews could emigrate from Germany to Palestine, provided that they left without their possessions, which could then be purchased in Palestine as German exports. Technically speaking, such purchases were in violation of the boycott. Faced with a choice between anti-Nazism and pro-Zionism, William chose the latter.

In August 1937, William traveled to France to attend the Twentieth World Zionist Congress. Held in Switzerland, this Congress was convened to discuss the report of the Peel Commission, which had been dispatched to Palestine by the British government in response to the Arab uprisings of the spring of 1936. The Peel Commission had recommended a two-state solution (one Jewish, the other Arab); the decision of the Congress was to reject it.

In 1941, under the heading "Colonies, Agricultural: Palestine," the *Universal Jewish Encyclopedia* reprinted the entirety of William's 40-page-long brochure *Bastions of Jewish Strength and Hope: Brief Sketches of the Jewish Agricultural Settlements in Palestine: When They Were Founded, Where They Are Located and How They Have Progressed*, which had been published the prior year by the Jewish National Fund of America. Listed as a contributor to that particular volume (Volume 3) of the *Encyclopedia* ("William Z. Spiegelman, New York, Director, Public Relations, Jewish National Fund"), William added three new introductory paragraphs to his essay.

In 1942, William suffered his first heart attack, no doubt caused by overwork, years of cigarette smoking, and tremendous anxiety about the Nazis' advances on the Suez Canal, which, if successful, would have allowed them to attack Jewish settlements and installations in Palestine. By the end of the year, William had recovered and the Nazis had been defeated in Egypt.

Sometime during the early 1940s, William became the New York correspondent for the Hebrew-language daily *Haboker*, which was published in Tel Aviv, and continued his work as the editor-in-chief of the monthly magazine published by the Jewish National Fund of America, *Land and Life*, which started out as bilingual (Yiddish and English) in the early 1930s, and shifted to English-only in 1944.

In late 1945 or early 1946, William – through his work with the Jewish National Fund of America – began working with a team of married filmmakers, William and Ruth Zimmerman. With William Spiegelman serving as "research editor" or "special consultant," this team made four short documentaries about Palestine, all of them funded, produced and distributed by the JNF:

1). *Land of Hope* (23:30, 16 mm, color, Palestine/USA, 1946; narrator: José Ferrer; commentator: James G. McDonald) takes the viewer from the recently liberated concentration camps in Europe to the newly established Jewish settlements in Palestine;

2) *Behind the Blockade* (25:30, 16 mm, color and b & w, Israel/USA, 1947; narrator: David Carradine) concerns the British Navy's blockade of Jewish ports in Palestine;

3) *If I Forget Thee* (20:00, 16 mm, b & w, Israel/USA, 1949: narrator: Gene Kern) focuses on the agricultural settlements near Jerusalem established by Orthodox Jews; and

4) *A State Is Born*, (20:00, 16 mm, b & w, Israel/USA, 1949; narrator: Richard Tucker; Declaration of Israeli Independence: read by Abba Eban) compiles footage concerning Israel's declaration of independence.

In July 1946, William and Dora Spiegelman went on vacation to Quebec. Though it appears that the purpose of this vacation was to rest, William found it hard to do so. In the words of his letter to Ruth Spiegelman, dated July 18, 1946: "I have been doing nothing but relaxing and it was not an easy task. I had to work hard, with muscle and will power, to do so."

In 1947, William was offered a directorial position in the International Section of the JNF. He accepted and, accompanied by his wife, traveled to Palestine. Though he had spent his entire adult life as an ardent Zionist, he had never been in the Holy Land before, and no doubt he wanted to stay there. It appears that he was offered a top post at JNF headquarters in Jerusalem, but he declined, in part because Dora wanted to return to the United States, and in part because, while in Israel, he suffered his second heart attack and, in September, chose to recuperate from it at home in America.

Later in 1947, back in New York, William hid his weakened condition from everyone: his professional colleagues, his friends and even the members of his family. But, unlike Moses, William lived long enough to see his people (in the form of the State of Israel) return to the Holy Land and once again become a free and autonomous nation, an event that took place on May 14, 1948. In point of fact, William was healthy (or driven) enough to continue working, and so he himself both recorded and celebrated the great event that he had devoted his entire life to bringing about. One can only imagine how great his pride and joy must have been.

Exactly one year later, on May 14, 1949, William died from his third and final heart attack. There was an outpouring of sympathy and condolences from his friends, neighbors, and colleagues. Dozens of telegrams were sent to the Spiegelman household in Brooklyn and to the offices of the Jewish National Fund in New York. Countless obituaries were published in English, Yiddish and Hebrew by newspapers in both Israel and America.

On May 16, 1949, memorial services for William were held at the Flatbush Memorial Chapel, 1283 Coney Island Avenue, in Brooklyn. In attendance were members of a variety of

Jewish organizations, including the Jewish National Fund, the Zionist Organization of America, the United Palestine Appeal, and the Yiddish Writers Union. Morris Rothenberg, the President of the Jewish National Fund of America, gave the eulogy, which was soon after printed in the summer 1949 issue of *Land and Life*.

On May 22, 1949, William's body was buried at the Beth David Cemetery in Elmont, New York. In mid-April 1950, in response to the entreaties of Dora Spiegelman, who insisted that William desired to be buried in Israel, the Jewish National Fund of America made the necessary arrangements. His body was disinterred, loaded aboard the *Akko*, which was operated by the Israel-America Line, and transported to Haifa. Once in Israel, his body was brought to Tel Aviv, where special ceremonies were held in front of JNF Headquarters. In attendance were close friends and relatives, as well as members of the Israeli Journalists Association and the JNF. There was another ceremony at the Nahalot Itzhak Cemetery, where William's body was laid next to the graves of Israel's national heroes, most of them casualties in the War for Independence. J. Heftman, the editor-in-chief of *Haboker*, delivered a eulogy, as did M. Yinnon of JNF Headquarters.

At the same time, memorial services were also held at the offices of the Jewish National Fund in New York. Those in attendance included Mendel N. Fisher, the Executive Director of the Jewish National Fund of America; Sharon Weitz, the Forestry Director of the Jewish National Fund in Israel; and Mordecai (aka "Max") Rudensky, who had written an obituary for William in the summer 1949 issue of *Land and Life*.

Death

I never knew my grandfather; he died 10 years before I was born. But I was named after him, and I was born on his birthday. I grew up hearing a lot about him, about the funny things he'd said, half in English, half in Yiddish, when my mother (Ruth Joy Spiegelman) was growing up in a part of Brooklyn, New York, that is just a few blocks away from where I live now. Later on, when I was in high school, and began showing an interest in writing, editing, foreign languages, current events and politics, my mother told me how much I was like my grandfather and that I'd clearly inherited my "brains" from him.

Other facts suggested that I couldn't help but take after my father's side of the family, not my mother's. After all, physically speaking, I very closely resembled my father, Leon Brown, not my mother, nor the men on her side of the family. (It is my brother who looks like a Spiegelman.) But with the exception of my father, the Brown side of the family was not at all given to "brainy" pursuits, and so I had to grant that, though I was a Brown by nature, I was a Spiegelman by nurture.

Towards the end of her life, my mother told me about a box in which she'd stored all her father's writings. My curiosity was piqued; I'd never read any of them and very much wanted to do so. My mother said she *wanted* to show these writings to my brother and I, but she never did; she never got around to doing it. She wasn't exactly teasing us with these documents or withholding them, although I'm sure she sensed that, once out of that box, the memory of her father would no longer be her exclusive property. Other people would be able to lay claim to it; indeed, it might even take on a life of its own and decide it didn't want to remain cooped up in a cardboard box any longer. Eventually she decided – or announced what she'd decided long ago – that she was going to donate his writings to a prestigious library or historical collection, which is where she believed that they belonged and where the rest of us would, eventually, get our chance to see them.

My mother couldn't be persuaded to consider an alternative plan, even when it was explained to her that the materials within that box would have to be sorted through, examined, evaluated and catalogued *first*, *before* any reputable institution would accept it as a donation. Otherwise such an institution would have no way of knowing whether its contents were truly valuable or not. To prevent itself from becoming a repository for worthless papers that proud and sentimental people just couldn't bring themselves to throw away, such an institution would *have to* decline her offer, no matter how graciously, imploringly or convincingly it was presented. But my mother was so convinced of the greatness of her father – the greatness of his many accomplishments – that she believed that any institution worth its salt would be happy to accept the box, sight unseen, because of the great name that was attached to it.

There was another objection, equally unpersuasive. Even if a prestigious library or historical collection *would* accept her donation, despite not having a clear idea of exactly what was being donated, it might well take that library's archivists *years* to do all the cataloguing necessary to make those materials known and available to members of the public. In the meantime, no one would be able to see those writings for themselves, and that wouldn't be right. (According to someone who catalogues for the New York Historical Society, "cataloguing isn't a sexy job, you can't put your name on it, and no one wants to pay" to have it done. As a result, "the dirty little secret of most museums and libraries" is that "they have hundreds of thousands of things they don't even know they have.")

My mother died in February 2010, at the age of 84, before she got around to making the donation she'd planned. And so, ironically, perhaps, the box that she'd faithfully carried around with her and kept safe since 1950 didn't leave her family; it became the property of my brother and I. And we eventually did something with The Box that she hadn't done in decades: we opened it up, and looked inside to see what it contained.

Our first discovery was that, in addition to containing our grandfather's writings (all kinds of letters, manuscripts, proposals and published essays), it contained photographs of him, official documents, and publications in which his writings had appeared (whole newspapers, magazines, and glossy little brochures). All told, this memorabilia did a lot more than simply document the work of a prolific writer: it also offered a sketch of the life of a man.

Our second discovery was that little, if any, of this memorabilia had been saved with careful attention to preserving or documenting the original context. Some newspaper articles had been cut out in such a way that anything that might have identified when and where they were published was lost. A handful of clippings had in fact been cut out so carelessly that they were rendered partly or completely unreadable. Needless to say, none of these documents had been placed within an acid-free plastic sheath (or something like that), which would have kept each one safe from the air, from the damaging effects of cold, heat and moisture. In fact, it seemed that everything had been thrust into paper envelopes quite hastily, sometimes without making sure that all the pages had been located and included.

As a result, the passage of time – *sixty years* since the box was filled and sealed, and as many as *eighty-five years* since the items inside it were originally published – had been quite destructive. Every sheet or envelope that wasn't made of high-quality paper (and only a few were) had begun to disintegrate around the edges. If a piece of paper had been folded, it had broken into separate pieces along the line of the fold. Simply removing the upper-most items from the box caused flurries of small bits of dried paper to leap into the air and flutter to the ground like confetti. By the time everything had been lifted out and examined, this confetti was all over my clothes and the floor of my apartment. In most cases, the damaged clippings could be put back together again, like a jigsaw puzzle, and the text could be read. But in a few instances, the edges of the broken pieces had themselves disintegrated, which meant that, even when put back together again, the text was irreparably compromised. Whole words were missing in several places; in others, whole sentences, even whole paragraphs, were gone.

Needless to say, handling these fragile survivors from the previous century, once they were out of the box, was a delicate business. To figure out what each item was, I had to touch it, and touching it (not to mention unfolding it) only caused more damage to be done, more confetti to fly, no matter how gentle I was. Eventually I took to using a pair of tweezers and a magnifying glass, and wearing surgical gloves.

Over the course of the next month, working on the project for several hours every single day, I reclaimed (retyped) all of the printed material on my computer, and used a scanner to make permanent, digital copies of all the images. From these two strands of materials, I knew, this book would eventually be woven. But to make sure that all this wonderful stuff was immediately available to the other members of my family, I created a website and uploaded everything I'd digitized to it. Their appreciation was immediate, clearly expressed, and very gratifying to hear.

To make "my" website as complete as possible, I did a thorough search of the Internet. There wasn't very much, but it was good. The archives of the Jewish Telegraphic Agency contained about a dozen relevant texts: some of them articles he'd written; most of them references to things that he had done. The website known as YouTube, thanks to Hebrew University in Jerusalem, contained copies of two *films* that my grandfather had helped make – which came as a total surprise to everyone, because no one, not even my mother, had known that he had helped make movies.

In response to the existence of "my" website, my aunt hunted around in her apartment and managed to locate *her* box of memorabilia, which she kindly made available to me. It, too, was full of a wide variety of clippings, manuscripts, photographs, letters, and official documents, most of it in good condition, some of it in the process of turning into dust. Though there was some overlap between what the two boxes contained, they complemented each other nicely, and, when taken together, constituted a significant and very impressive amount of material. All of it was digitized and uploaded.

Not everything in the boxes was in English. There were two newspaper articles, obviously obituaries, in what looked to be Hebrew. I consulted a professional translator, who informed me that while one of the newspaper articles was indeed in Hebrew, the other was in Yiddish. (This was news to me: I didn't know that Yiddish, when written down, uses Hebrew letters, not German or Slavic ones, to form non-Hebrew words.) As the reader will see, translations were made of both obituaries, and they are included in this book.

There were also two handwritten letters or, rather, one complete letter and one letter of which only the last two pages remained, both written by the same person, who was a family member (a Spzigelman) still living in Poland. It wouldn't be easy to have them translated. Both were written in Yiddish *and* had "real" Hebrew words mixed in. To make matters worse, they were written in a cursive script that was very hard to read. I was told that the cursive Yiddish would first have to be "translated" into printed Yiddish; only then could the printed letters – read as words – be translated into English. As an experiment, I had the incomplete letter translated by a specialist. If its contents proved interesting, I would then get the complete letter translated as well. Unfortunately, the first letter, once translated, yielded nothing of interest or value. Unlike my grandfather, the writer was not educated; indeed, he or she was illiterate and discussed nothing other than routine family matters. ("I wish to let you know we are all, thank God, well, and everything is alright," William summarized such letters in his "Our New York Letter" column for August 15, 1924. "Second, it grieves me to tell you that I do not feel very well and things have not been going at all well with us.") And so I never tried to get the complete letter translated into English.

Once I exhausted the contents of the boxes, I turned my attention to finding other articles and essays that my grandfather had written. Towards this end, I spent two solid months searching through the archives of the Dorot Jewish Collection at the New York Public Library. Because neither the *Review of Periodical Literature* nor the *Jewish Review of Periodical Literature* covers the period in question (1923 to 1949), I sometimes felt that I was looking for the proverbial needle in a haystack. All I had to go on were the essays already in my possession; all I could do, under the circumstances, was locate one of those essays and then search the issues that came out before and after the essay in question was published, hoping to find others.

Mind you, these searches weren't conducted through printed volumes or on a computer, but on *a microfilm machine*, something I hadn't used since I was in high school back in the 1970s. Learning to work the machine properly, and to get it to print out legible copies of the articles I'd found by scrolling through reel after reel, was a time-consuming business. It also was very taxing on the eyes. Some days I found nothing on those old, brittle celluloid reels, or found that the original filming had begun a few years after the articles I was looking for were published, which meant that the articles I was searching for were never put on microfilm, and are now irretrievably lost. Other days I found the full versions of essays that I only possessed in pieces; and on a few fortunate days I turned up dozens of essays, "new" or at least previously unknown to me, which could then be printed out (as best as could be managed, given the way some of the originals had been photographed) and retyped, and thus rescued from oblivion.

As a result of all this research, I've come to know as much, if not more, about my grandfather's professional life than his wife and his children did. He didn't talk about his many accomplishments with them. And yet, even though it is comparatively deep, my knowledge of my grandfather's writings is also rather limited. I know nothing of his unpublished manuscript, *History of the Development of Jewish Sects*; nothing about the many books he translated from German; and nothing about the newspaper articles and essays that he wrote in Yiddish, Hebrew and Polish between 1911 and the end of his life (there might be dozens of articles in each one of these languages).

But, given the richness and interest of what I've discovered and reclaimed so far, the very breadth of what I *haven't* been able to document suggests the true magnitude of the man's accomplishments. It's too bad that my mother isn't alive to hear this, for it surely would have pleased her immensely. *She was absolutely right about her father; he was in fact a Great Man, worthy of posthumous study, admiration and praise.* And he was a Great Man by virtue of the fact that he was, to use an expression he himself favored, "a great Jew." Everything he did was devoted to the wellbeing of the Jewish people, wherever they lived, but especially in the "dark" places were Jewish lives were made miserable, threatened or cut short by prejudice, hatred and violence. Though he had studied and had great respect for and knowledge of the Jewish past, for tradition and for those who had gone before, his emphasis was always on the Jewish present and the future, on the living, on life itself.

In what spirit should his writings be collected and published (again) *today*, more than 60 years after his death? Note well this remarkable passage, which comes from his uncompleted manuscript about Mary Fels.

> We have stony hearts toward the living and we erect monuments of stone to the dead. A living memorial is the only kind worthy of living beings, whether they are with us here or have gone Beyond. Better name after him the street in or near which he lived than to erect some obstruction in stone, for the one

comes into our life and the other we pass by carelessly. But better still to work the noble ideas which he had and do, as far as we may and can, that which he longed to do. Thus he remains in our lives, the living factor that he was, and the memory of him does not become part of a tombstone or a static statue.

In answer to these suggestions, I have titled this collection "A Jewish Life," which is a phrase that often reoccurs it in: my grandfather lived a Jewish life; it was to Jewish life that his life was totally devoted; and it is now *back to life* that I deliver his long-dead words.

* * *

It is not surprising to me that this particular Great Man is unknown in our times. As he himself wrote about Dr. Isaac A. Hourwich, **"We are accustomed to judge men by their achievement in material wealth or by their popularity; we often overlook those scholarly, quiet workers whose efforts make a deep impression on the environment in which they live without causing much noise outside it."** My grandfather was always the executive secretary, never the president, of the organizations he was part of. He wrote the speeches, but rarely gave one himself. He never became as famous as the people he worked for, wrote about, or socialized with. Why? My guess is that fame was available to him, but that a combination of factors (modesty, prudence, insecurity and fear, among them) kept him from taking advantage of the opportunity. (One of his favorite mottoes was "Don't volunteer information.")

Good examples of this would be his essays about the Jewish Telegraphic Agency (one was written in 1924; the other in 1929). Both essays provide good solid answers to *three* of the basic journalistic questions (why is the JTA needed, what does the JTA do, and where is the JTA active), but say nothing in answer to the *other* three basic questions (who runs the JTA, when did they found the JTA, and how does the JTA actually work on a day-by-day basis). Because of these lacunae, the reader learns nothing about *William Z. Spiegelman,* who, in addition to being the author of the essays in question, was also the author of a weekly JTA column entitled "Our New York Letter," the founder and editor-in-chief of the JTA's *Jewish Daily Bulletin,* and the head of the JTA's office in New York.

The same thing takes place in his pair of essays about the Jewish National Fund ("America's Response to a Vital Appeal," published in 1936, and "Four Decades of *Geulath Ha'Aretz,*" published in 1947). Though he himself had joined the JNF in 1930, and was still with it, seventeen years later, he doesn't mention himself or his contributions to its success, even though the circumstances clearly called for it.

My grandfather's tendency to avoid fame can be seen (literally seen) in the photograph that ran in the February 11, 1934 issue of the *Jewish-American Forward.* Though he had every right to appear on equal footing with the seven other people who were photographed for the occasion, which was a celebration of the composer Arturo Toscanini, my grandfather chose to situate himself *behind* the others and peak out from between the shoulders of B. Shelvin and Rabbi Wolf Gold. Perhaps the photographer who took this picture was in a hurry or didn't care about the way his or her subjects positioned themselves; perhaps the lack of equal footing was pointed out by the photographer to the man who chose to allow *only his head* to be visible and was told, "Don't worry; it will be OK the way it is."

My grandfather had a name for this self-deprecating little fellow: "Z. Alroy," which seems to be a combination of his own middle initial ("Z" for Zev) and the last name of David

Alroy, also known as Menachem ben-Solomon, a self-proclaimed Jewish messiah of the 12th Century. (My grandfather would have known about David Alroy through Benjamin Disraeli's *The Wondrous Tale of Alroy*, published in 1833, as well as through his own research: his entry in *Who's Who in American Jewry* lists *History of the Development of Jewish Sects* as an "unpublished manuscript"). He first used Z. Alroy as a pseudonym when, fearing reprisals, he wrote about controversial subjects for Yiddish publications in Poland. Later, after he moved to America, he signed himself Z. Alroy on an odd assortment of occasions: when he published in Canada; when he had cause to refer to an effective headline he'd written; when he publicly questioned powerful anti-Semites who might seek revenge (the Queen of Romania and Henry Ford); and when he authored more than one article in a single publication. In other words, he used his pseudonym on precisely those occasions when another person – someone intent on becoming famous at all costs – would have *insisted* on using his or her real name.

My guess is that this is why Ernest E. Barabash could note in his obituary for my grandfather than "a collection of his writings would constitute a valuable contribution to contemporary Jewish literature," and yet neither he nor anyone else stepped forward to put such a collection together and get it published. Perhaps the creation of a posthumous anthology wasn't seen as appropriate for such a self-effacing writer, "an introvert by nature," in Barabash's words, even if he had been a Great Jew.

* * *

A few editorial notes. For the purposes of clarity, I have divided this collection into eight chronologically ordered sections. The first section contains my grandfather's writings *about* the Jewish Telegraphic Agency and the *Jewish Daily Bulletin*, and the second section contains "Our New York Letter," the syndicated weekly column he wrote *for* the Jewish Telegraphic Agency. The third section contains the essays he wrote for various publications in Canada and the United States. The fourth section consists of the introduction to his book-length brochure about agricultural settlements in Palestine, which was entitled *Bastions of Strength*. The fifth section contains his proposals and unpublished manuscripts. The sixth section is devoted to his correspondence: letters received and letters sent out. The seventh section contains the references that were made to my grandfather while he was alive and the obituaries that were written after his passing. The eighth and last section contains photographs, facsimiles (the entirety of the first issue of the *Jewish Daily Bulletin*, as well as selections from a few of the many brochures that he produced for the Jewish National Fund), and reproductions of key official documents.

I have corrected obvious typographical mistakes; altered a few spellings to fit modern usage ("Tokio," for example); inserted parenthetical remarks [thus] when necessary; changed "which" to "that" when the former was used incorrectly; and added commas and hyphens when necessary. All footnotes and translations are mine, except where noted.

My love and deepest thanks go to my brother, David, who not only assisted in the research, but who was also a constant source of appreciation, encouragement and good advice. This book is dedicated to his honor, and to the memory of our mother, Ruth Joy Spiegelman.

William J. Brown
Brooklyn, New York, May 2012

Articles and Essays in English

"A Century in Retrospect: Survey of Trends and Events in the Course of the Hebrew Calendar Century Closing on Rosh Hashanah," *The New Palestine*, September 12, 1939

"A Prince Has Fallen in Israel," Jewish Telegraphic Agency, 12 September 1929

"America's Response to a Vital Appeal," *The New Palestine*, October 8, 1936

"Announcement of the Observance of the Fiftieth Anniversary of Prof. Albert Einstein," Jewish National Fund, 1929

"At the Mayflower: A Jewish National Home in Palestine," Jewish Telegraphic Agency, January 29, 1932

"Brandeis Looks at Us: His Analysis of and Approach to the Jewish Problem and Zionism Show Incisive Logic and Breadth of Vision; An Interview with Brandeis On-Record," *The New Palestine*, November 13, 1936

"Builders of American Cities: Isaac Meister, Founder of American Venice," *The Sentinel*, July 2, 1926

"Changing Values in American Jewish Fraternities," *The Canadian Jewish Chronicle*, July 31, 1925

"Colonies, Agricultural: Palestine," *Universal Jewish Encyclopedia*, Volume 3, 1941

"Dr. Thon, Philosopher and Political Realist," *The New Palestine*, November 20, 1936

"Four Decades of Geulath Ha'Aretz: Program, Achievements and History of the Jewish National Fund Briefly Described," Pittsburgh Tri-State Pinkas, 1947

"From Cleveland to Cleveland: American Zionism from 1921 to 1930 in Review," *The New Palestine*, June 27, 1930

"High Noon at Kfar Etzion: Leaves from a Palestine Traveler's Notebook," *Land and Life*, February 1948

"Is Poland Balancing Her Budget and Soul? Some Thoughts and Facts on The Polish-Jewish Agreement," *The Reform Advocate*, August 8, 1925

"Is the Orthodox Jew in America Re-Awakening? An Interview with Rabbi Herbert S. Goldstein, President of the Union of Orthodox Jewish Congregations of America," *The Canadian Jewish Chronicle*, October 9, 1925

"Jewish Men in the Public Eye: Nathan Straus," *The Sentinel*, 1926?

"Jewish Telegraphic Agency," *The Chicago Chronicle*, June 13, 1924

"Josef Pilsudski, Poland's Strong Man," *The Jewish Tribune*, May 21, 1926

"Land for Victory," *The Jewish Post*, September 25, 1941

"Menachem Ussishkin," Pittsburgh Tri-State Pinkas, 1947

"Molders of Jewish Public Opinion: Their Biography, Their Work, and Their Views on the Future," *The Chicago Chronicle*, June 6, 1924

"Molders of Jewish Public Opinion: Their Life, Their Work and Their Views (II): Peter Wiernik, Historian and Editor," *The Chicago Chronicle*, August 22, 1924

"Molders of Jewish Public Opinion: B. Charney Vladeck, Jewish Labor's Tribune," *The Chicago Chronicle*, September 5, 1924

"New York Topics," *Canadian Jewish Chronicle*, October 14, 1927, *The Sentinel*, November 18, 1927, *The Jewish Post*, July, 1929

"Our New York Letter," *The Chicago Chronicle*, April 18, 1924, *The Chicago Chronicle*, July 11, 1924, *The Chicago Chronicle*, July 25, 1924, *The Jewish Criterion*, August 1, 1924, *The Chicago Chronicle*, August 8, 1924, *The Sentinel*, August 15, 1924, *Jewish Transcript*, August 22, 1924, *The Chicago Chronicle*, September 12, 1924, *The Chicago Chronicle*, September 26, 1924, *The Chicago Chronicle*, December 26, 1924, *The Australian Jewish Herald*, February 26, 1925, *The Chicago Chronicle*, March 6, 1925, *Jewish Transcript*, March 13, 1925, *The Jewish*

Criterion, March 20, 1925, *American Jewish World*, April 3, 1925, *The Ohio Jewish Chronicle*, July 24, 1925, *The Sentinel*, April 30, 1926, *The Sentinel*, June 4, 1926, *The Sentinel*, September 17, 1926, *The Sentinel*, October 29, 1926, *The Sentinel*, November 5, 1926, *Canadian Jewish Chronicle*, December 31, 1926, *The Sentinel*, April 29, 1927, *The Sentinel*, January 22, 1928

"Peter Wiernik: Scholar, Historian, and Editor," *The New Palestine*, December 18, 1925

"Review of an Eventful Year," *B'Nai B'Rith Magazine*, October 1929

"The Chair for Jewish History and Philosophy at Harvard University," *The Jewish Tribune*, February 5, 1926

"The Jew on the Stage and Screen," *B'Nai B'rith Magazine*, January, 1929

"The Jew on the Stage and Screen," *B'Nai B'Rith Magazine*, February 1929

"The Man Who 'Desired Life'," *The Jewish Spectator*, September 1933

"The Scramble for 'Elbow-Room': International Drama Centering Around The Soil Question," *The Jewish Standard*, November 14, 1930

"The Year's Events in Diaspora Jewry: A Review of the Highlights of 5696," *The New Palestine*, September 11, 1936

"What's Happening in New York," *Canadian Jewish Chronicle*, February 3, 1928, *Canadian Jewish Chronicle*, June 15, 1928

Articles and Essays in Yiddish

"Briv fun Polyn" [Letter from Poland], *Der Id*, September 23, 1920

"Di Yidische heym in Ertsisroel" [The Jewish Home in Eretz Israel], *Der Moment*, April 29, 1920

"Notitsen: Di 'milderne umshtenden'" [Notes: The 'Modern Condition'], *Yudishe Folk*, April 11, 1918

"Notitsen: Ven es vet noytik zayn" [When the Hardship is Yours], *Yudishe Folk*, April 25, 1918

"Yidish-Polyische unterhandlungen in London un Zsheneve: an intervyu mit Lusien Volf" [Jewish-Polish negotiations in London and Geneva: An Interview with Lucien Wolf], *Der Moment*, January 21, 1921

Books

The Jewish Telegraphic Agency: Its Function, Its Importance, and Service to American Jewry (New York: Jewish Telegraphic Agency, 1929)

Bastions of Jewish Strength and Hope: Brief Sketches of the Jewish Agricultural Settlements in Palestine: When They Were Founded, Where They Are Located and How They Have Progressed (New York: Jewish National Fund, November 1940

Brochures for the Jewish National Fund

Orthodox Pioneers on the People's Land (no date)
David's Dream (no date)
Good Wishes Raised This Forest (no date)
Land for Survival (no date)
The Great Day in His Life (no date)

Announcement of the Observance of the 50th Anniversary of Prof. Albert Einstein (1929)
An Appreciation of the President's Great Humanitarian Act for the Refugees (1938)
JNF Quiz: 75 Questions & Answer about Eretz Israel & the JNF (1939 1940)
On Our Land Front (1943)
Land for Victory (1943 or 1944)
The Stranger of Mount Carmel (1945)
The Jewish People's Roll of Honor (circa 1946)
The Mountains of Israel Call for Trees (circa 1948)
This is Israel (circa 1948)
Land for Homes (1948)
Presenting the Golden Book of the Jewish State (1948)
Give the Jewish State Jewish Land (1948)
Land in Defense (1948)
Land for Jewish Settlement in the State of Israel (1948)
Look See and . . . Do! (1949)

Documentary Films (Research Consultant)

Land of Hope, directed by W. Zimmerman (Palestine/USA, 1946)
Behind the Blockade, directed by W. Zimmerman (Israel/USA, 1947)
If I Forget Thee, directed by W. Zimmerman (Israel/USA, 1949)
A State Is Born, directed by W. Zimmerman (Israel/USA, 1949)

Translations

Samson Raphael Hirsch, *Nineteen Letters on Judaism* (from German into Hebrew, circa 1918)

Meier Dizengoff, *Im Tel Aviv ba-Golah* (from Hebrew into English, published in *The New Palestine* in three parts: September 25, 1936; October 7, 1936; and October 16, 1936)

Y. Ostrovtzer, "I Believe, I Believe: The Story of the Jewish Martyrs' Hymn Which Is An Expression of faith in the Return to Zion" (Hebrew into English, *Land and Life*, May 1946)

Unpublished Manuscripts

History of the Development of Jewish Sects (circa 1926; lost)
Mary Fels: A Study in Jewish Womanhood (circa 1927; incomplete)
"Your Will: A Potent Factor for Preserving Jewish Learning; A Suggestion to Men of Vision; A Guide for Legal Advisors" (October 1927)
"A Survey of American Jewry During the Last Five Years" (circa 1930) "Kosher Food: A Suggestion for Talk on Radio Station WOR" (January 1933)
"I Saw *The Eternal Road* Ten Times: A Review of Audience Reactions to the Themes and Characters in Reinhardt's Production of Werfel's Biblical Drama and Spectacle" (1937)
"Address to Fellow Members of the American Zionist Guild" (circa 1939)

"Jewish Telegraphic Agency"
The Chicago Chronicle, June 13, 1924

Every studious reader has in the last four years frequently come across, be it in the Anglo-Jewish weeklies, in the Yiddish or in the general American press, some news items of Jewish interest that attracted his attention from time to time. Preceding every such item he was always bound to read the three words "Jewish Telegraphic Agency." I imagine many have asked themselves what these three words meant, why a Jewish telegraphic agency, why an agency, and if an agency why a telegraphic agency. I think a few words of explanation at this moment would not be out of place.

There is not a single businessman who takes his business seriously who would form his opinion about any matter concerning his business or private affairs without making an attempt to get the best available information on the subject. Information, in our days, is the underlying principle of that constant endeavor, toil and speed, which, for convenience and brevity's sake, we call "life." All of us have our interests. Our interests are dictated first of all by our natural inclinations. One cannot be interested in the country if one's interest in one's own city has not yet been aroused. One cannot have a deep concern in the affairs of a community if one's heart has not been opened to the affairs of his own family. One cannot have a real broad view of the world's affairs if one is not sensitive to the needs and demands of his own race.

Whether one is a Zionist, a non-Zionist or an anti-Zionist, a Reformed Jew or an Orthodox Jew or even a radical, one's attention is eagerly caught when mention is made of an event of a Jewish nature. We are affected when we hear of atrocities committed against Jews, no matter how distant the place of their occurrence may be, if only we preserve our sincerity and are truthful to ourselves. We are glad to learn of any change for the better that takes place in any of the persecuted Jewish communities. We have an interest, pro or con, in that tremendous effort that is now being made to rebuild Palestine. We are, above all, deeply concerned when we notice that some American papers carry an item concerning Jewish life, which is represented in an improper form or with the usual lack of accuracy and knowledge of conditions. What is all this? It is our desire for proper and reliable information.

It is not more than half a century [ago] that the most outlandish problems in Jewish life in nearly all the countries with a Jewish population was the question. How and what to do [so] that our neighbor may know more about us? It was thought at the time that salvation would come if this information could be imparted.

The writer of these lines knows a fact that will well illustrate this. It was during the stormy period at the end of the war, and during the armistice. Numerous Jewish communities in Eastern and Central Europe were constantly threatened with terror and violence, the result of tremendous changes of regimes and social orders. A desperate cry for help reached the Western European countries from the devastated regions. It seemed that only a few lines – a few truthful and impressive lines – in the press of the civilized world would suffice to relieve the situation. However, those who were charged with this task found it very hard, if not impossible, to accomplish it, because of the fact that Jewish news was considered as mere propaganda.

To disseminate Jewish news items amongst Jews, and to keep the Jewish press of the world informed of what is going on in Jewish life all over the world, to have the general press posted on Jewish happenings and problems – this is the task to which the Jewish Telegraphic Agency has set itself and which it has been carrying out for the last five years.

Some labor under the impression that specific Jewish news items must imply either pogroms or sufferings or misery of another nature in some distant lands. But Jewish life, like the life of all other peoples, is manifold and is rich both in tragedy as well as in happiness, in pathos as well as mirth. In fact, it is even still richer. Those radio fans who "listen in" on those evenings when news of the Jewish Telegraphic Agency is being given (its news items are broadcasted twice a month from station WEAF, New York City) have had a splendid opportunity to convince themselves of the many amusing and instructive aspects of the knowledge thus imparted. When one is well posted on Jewish life, as understood in a broader sense, one gets the breath of all climates under the sun, the effects of all governmental regimes, the workings of all kinds of social orders, and the changing pressure of civilization and culture according to the degree achieved by that particular place of settlement on the globe's surface.

A tremendous effort is required in order to keep in constant touch with these changing conditions in that moving Jewish world. Misrepresentation that is in other cases, and to other people, harmless is in the case of the Jews, very harmful and even dangerous. Constant study of the political, economic and social conditions in the various countries is necessary in order that information may be disseminated. The position of the Jews should be properly and accurately represented for our own knowledge and for the knowledge of the general press. The Jewish Telegraphic Agency, believing in the usefulness of the work and the tremendous amount of good that could result from it has taken upon itself this responsibility. It has established offices in New York, London, Warsaw, Berlin, Paris and Jerusalem, and maintains correspondents in every important Jewish center of the world. An event of Jewish interest that occurs in New York, for instance, comes to the knowledge of the Jewish community in Shanghai; an incident that takes place in Vladivostok is reported in Paris; an occurrence in Jerusalem is communicated to San Francisco; a happening that takes place in Jewish life in Moscow is commented upon [by readers] in Winnipeg. In transmitting this news, the Agency has preserved the line of the golden mean, not bending towards any of the conflicting parties, submitting only the facts, leaving the rest to those who are ready to form their opinion. The Jewish Telegraphic Agency is not affiliated or bound to any of the tendencies fighting for supremacy in Jewish life. It takes an interest in everything that is Jewish, in everything that relates to Jews and may affect them, directly or indirectly.

The service of the Agency during its five years of activity was recognized to be of great value not only by those public institutions that deal with matters of international concern and need authentic knowledge of facts, but also by those institutions that are mainly concerned with local affairs. Its value as a news-gathering and -transmitting agency was appreciated also by the general American press that considers it the proper and reliable source for information concerning Jewish events and activities.

A glance at the editorial pages of the numerous and influential Anglo-Jewish publications of this country will readily prove that nearly all editorial comment is based upon the dispatches of the Jewish Telegraphic Agency. The Jewish Telegraphic Agency has been the source of many references in the general press concerning the Jewish situation in one or another country.

There is one more point that deserves the attention of our educational leaders. The amount of knowledge among the younger generation of current Jewish history is, as is well-known, very limited. In some cases their ignorance is simply amazing. A few of these leaders of education have found it extremely valuable to make use of the news gathered and issued by the Jewish Telegraphic Agency for educational purposes.

Arthur Brisbane, perhaps the leading American journalist, says of the Agency: "I am delighted to say that I consider the Jewish Telegraphic Agency of very great value to

American newspaper workers and newspaper readers. You have representatives able to recognize news when they see it and to express it clearly."

The *Interpreter*, published by the Rockefeller Foundation, has this to say: "A very important factor in the life of the Jewish group of immigrants in the United States is the Jewish Telegraphic Agency, which specializes in the transmission of news events and general information of interest and importance to its patrons. The news agency was organized four years ago and now maintains principal headquarters in New York and London. One hundred and fifty newspapers printed in Yiddish are served directly by the service, while the non-Jewish press of the United States and other countries is served indirectly with its material through the large general news agencies. Special correspondents are maintained at present in Jerusalem, Jaffa, Constantinople, Rome, Paris, Washington, Chicago, Boston, Pittsburgh, Detroit, San Francisco, Moscow, Vienna and other important centers.

"The Jewish Telegraphic Agency functions not only as a bearer of news to Jews concerning Jews, but as an informative intermediary between that group and the rest of the public. The importance of its work is recognized by statesmen as well as publishers. 'Most hearty interest in the Agency and hope for its increasing efficiency and usefulness' was voiced by President Coolidge in a recent message to the organization, on the occasion of its annual dinner. 'The Agency is engaged in real public service,' Secretary Herbert Hoover announced. Secretary of Labor Davis expressed his pleasure that directors of the organization 'seek to serve the best interests of your immediate patrons and that of the country as well,' while the former ambassador to Germany, James M. Gerard, referred to 'the splendid and patriotic work' performed by the Agency."

"Statement of Purpose"
Jewish Daily Bulletin, October 15, 1924

The *Jewish Daily Bulletin* will be the conveyor of the World's Jewish news. It will report impartially, concisely and authentically, all Jewish facts. It will be a connecting link between the Jewish communities of all states in the Union. Today, the Jewish Community of Chicago does not know what the Jews of Boston are doing and the Jews of the West are uninformed of what is happening in Jewish life in the East.

The *Jewish Daily Bulletin* will fill the much-felt need of a proper disseminator.

By subscribing to the cable and telegraphic news service of the Jewish Telegraphic Agency, the *Jewish Daily Bulletin* will be enabled to present to its readers accurate reports of Jewish events from all parts of the globe within 24 hours of their occurrence.

The *Jewish Daily Bulletin* will serve as a stimulating guide and will arouse a great many, who are now indifferent, to a larger interest in Jewish affairs.

The *Jewish Daily Bulletin* will be independent. It will not propagate any particular philosophy or theory or tendency. It will limit itself to the presentation of facts, leaving to its readers the forming of their opinion.

The *Jewish Daily Bulletin* will offer its readers a daily survey on Jewish and non-Jewish public opinion throughout the world on Jewish topics.

The *Jewish Daily Bulletin* will be the clarion to the young American Jew, who is growing up uninformed on contemporary Jewish life to proper understanding and consequently consciousness and responsibility to the Jewish community.

The *Jewish Daily Bulletin* will be the Jewish mouthpiece and interpreter.

The *Jewish Daily Bulletin* will acquaint its readers with the manifold activities and undertakings of Jews throughout the world. By giving Jewish news in the right proportions it will enable all thinking non-Jews to perceive Jewish conditions in their true perspective.

The *Jewish Daily Bulletin* will accurately report all developments in Palestine and in the surrounding mid-eastern countries.

The Jewish Telegraphic Agency: Its Function, Its Importance, and Service to American Jewry (1929)[1]

"A Jewish News Service: Is It Necessary?"

Every reader of the press in America, whether the large metropolitan dailies, the Anglo-Jewish weeklies or the newspapers published in Yiddish, has encountered three initials preceding many news items that were of special interest. The three letters, J.T.A., as the reader will recall, preceded such news dispatches as dealt with occurrences in Jewish life or with such events and situations that affected large or small Jewish groups and communities, or pertained to the doings and achievements of Jewish individuals. Frequently one must have wondered what these letters stand for and who stands behind them.

The letters J.T.A. are the initials of the Jewish Telegraphic Agency, a news gathering and distribution enterprise, just as AP stands for Associated Press, UP for United Press and the like.

To those who are familiar to some extent with the subjects dealt with in the Jewish Telegraphic Agency dispatches in the press and in the *Jewish Daily Bulletin*, the question of whether or not Jewish news is necessary needs no answer.

Before a proper understanding of the work of the Jewish Telegraphic Agency can be reached, however, a correct definition of what constitutes Jewish news and why it is necessary are important.

"News is news without regard to the subject or who is involved or affected by it." This would be the average reaction to the question. A closer examination, however, will convince the reader that the common notion is far from the actual fact.

The problem may be debated as to what the Jewish community is: Is it a religious sect? Is it an ethnic minority? Is it a cultural group? Is it a remnant of a nation that aspires to regain its former status? Is it a special economic class?

No matter what one's answer may be to these perplexing questions, the fact remains that Jewish life goes on. The very fact that Jewish communities in whatever forms they may be found are in existence, the very fact that Jewish families are adhering to a Jewish mode of life, the very interesting phenomenon of the persistence of the age-old traditions of ancient faith, the existence of synagogues, the various communal, charitable and cultural interests created and maintained by the effort of Jewish initiative, in all climes and under all conditions, the very fact that the Jewish population in the various countries are easily and voluntarily recognizable, prove that there is a distinct Jewish life that, in the course of its unfolding, produces Jewish news.

The logical consequence of this situation is the following: If one takes seriously his affiliation with the Jewish community, in whatever form he chooses, or if one simply follows his natural inclination to know what is happening to his family, kin and group; if one is interested in the trend of affairs of the group at large, if one pursues a special study of one

---

[1] Excerpts.

or another phase of this development, if one is interested in promoting a special activity distinctly Jewish, or finally, if one is interested in the interrelations between the community at large and the Jewish community in particular, such a person is and must be interested in "Jewish news."

Is a Jewish news agency necessary? The very fact of its existence would prove its necessity. However, the necessity is proven when one turns to conditions that existed years ago, before the Jewish Telegraphic Agency was established.

Jewish news has always [been] filtered through the columns of the general press. But in what form and on what kind of background? With what attitude was it approached, explained and presented to the uninitiated reader? The answer to this question caused much concern to every Jew who cared for the fate of his people and for its good name among the nations.

"An Urgent Need For Jews and Non-Jews: How the Problem Is Met"

Frequently the Jewish reader of the general press used to be startled when he came across items describing what was understood to be "Jewish news." "Jewish news" pertained to crimes committed by Jews, to business failures, divorce scandals and fires. Such individuals who happened to be Jews and who were involved in such news items were specified as Jews. However, prominent Jewish scientists who enriched the heritage of mankind by their contributions, leading Jewish philanthropists who gave their wealth and substance to relieve human suffering, outstanding Jewish leaders who achieved success and fame by promoting the best interests of their countries at personal sacrifices, Jewish soldiers who gave their lives for their countries' sake, Jewish writers, musicians and artists who contributed toward the world's spiritual treasures – were credited to their countries without the additional information of their Jewish origin, which was so eagerly affixed in cases that were of doubtful credit to the Jewish community.

The Jew in this procedure obviously got the worst of the bargain.

There was another angle to the situation. When a legitimate item of Jewish interest reached the desks of the city editors by the play of chance, it was frequently presented only in so far as the knowledge of the writer extended. The wider aspect of the events was lost, the inference totally excluded. When important Jewish news "broke," such as anti-Jewish violence, anti-Jewish legislation in European countries, cases of social ostracism or of economic discrimination, it was often distorted and no clear picture of the event could be gained.

This was a natural consequence of the entire situation. Jewish news cannot be properly understood without a thorough knowledge of the conditions in which these events occur.

Many worthy Jewish activities, which might appear insignificant to the uninitiated, were totally ignored at a time when a projector that would throw light on Jewish events would depict them on the background of their natural conditions, would present them in their proper proportion, would take the blame when blame was due and claim the credit when credit was deserved, was an urgent one.

To meet this need the Jewish Telegraphic Agency was established.

"The Jewish Telegraphic Agency: Its Scope, Policy and Aim"

The Jewish Telegraphic Agency, when established, set out to fill this need. Founded on purely journalistic principles, its prime purpose was to serve the press of the world in a field that until this time had been neglected.

As a prospector going out into a new region, convinced of the existence of precious metals and willing to undergo the hardships and difficulties of the pioneer, the Jewish Telegraphic Agency started its work firmly convinced that the field of Jewish events had a tremendous wealth of news values that are of absorbing interest not only to Jews but also to non-Jews.

Jewish life, revolving around the Bible traditions that are sacred to all nations, struggling under most perplexing and difficult conditions, marching ahead with the progress of the world, suffering and hoping with humanity, cannot remain obscure to the world at large. Its survival in the countries of persecution, its emergence in countries where progress is dawning, its valuable contributions in democracies that are flourishing, is a tale of human endeavor, joy and sorrow, which is fascinating and must be told to Jew and Gentile alike.

Much of the prejudice that has accumulated throughout the ages, much of the dust that has fallen upon the name of the Jew throughout generations of misinformation, much of the malice that has grown on the fertile ground of ignorance and bigotry, will be brushed aside and disappear as the rays of light and truth are turned toward them.

With this conviction, the Jewish Telegraphic Agency established its journalistic apparatus.

"Here is a fountain of stirring events, the original cause of which is obviously traceable to a drama that has stirred and puzzled the world for centuries. It is not propaganda, it is Jewish news, but news, hot off the wire, having occurred today, within the last twenty-four hours. It touches upon a subject that is certainly of interest to your Jewish readers, but may also be of interest to your non-Jewish readers who want the truth."

To prove this contention, the Jewish Telegraphic Agency has had to establish a world-wide apparatus that would meet this requirement, to adopt a policy that would protect it against the charge of propaganda and bias or its own Jewish prejudice, and to set for itself a goal toward which all enlightened men aim.

In going to the depths of Jewish life to gather Jewish news items, the Jewish Telegraphic Agency has adhered to a line of strict impartiality, no matter where its search has led.

In the conflict of parties into which Jewish life is divided, just as in non-Jewish life, in the play of factions whose number in Jewish life is greater than in that of any other group of people, in the record-breaking speed in which Jewish events are marching on the background of political, economic and social conditions throughout the world, on controversies between east and west, north and south, so distinctly accentuated in the lives of Jews, in the struggle between doctrine and theory, between the practical worker and the visionary, the work of a news agency such as the Jewish Telegraphic Agency aimed to be, a neutral attitude toward all and a passion for the truth, was an unavoidable necessity. In attempting to break through the indifference of a world press that had been accustomed to view "Jewish news" differently, this quality had to be of so sterling a character that no doubt could be cast upon it.

In this effort the Jewish Telegraphic Agency has met with a great measure of success. This success is evident by its penetration into the Jewish press throughout the world in all languages in which newspapers are published and into the non-Jewish press of America, Europe, Asia and Africa.

"Around the Globe: How Jewish News Is Gathered"

The gathering of Jewish news and distributing it to the Jewish and non-Jewish press takes the Jewish Telegraphic Agency to all parts of the world, to all countries where Jewish communities are to be found – around the globe.

The process of gathering Jewish news is as intriguing as the varying political, social, cultural and economic conditions of the communities in which the search is made. Six offices of the Jewish Telegraphic Agency, located in New York, London, Paris, Berlin, Warsaw, and Jerusalem, and 152 correspondents in the smaller centers are engaged in this task. The search is made and the light is flashed – through the modern mediums of communication – not on what is usually termed daily occurrences but also on such events that could not be seen except through the eyes of trained observers. Attention is given to decisions, changes, happenings and situations that directly or indirectly affect the economic, political, cultural and religious situation of the Jewish communities. Attention is also directed to the field of intellectual endeavor and the world of letters where Jews are active. The inter-relation between Jews and Christians, whether it be in the field of economic, political or social life, or whether it is in the field of theology, is traced.

When President Coolidge, in a memorable addressed decrying the evils of bigotry and prejudice, recalls Lecky's observation that "Hebraic mortar cemented the foundations of American democracy," the ear of the Jewish Telegraphic Agency is there to pick it up and the apparatus ready to bring this message to those who should know it.

When the Council of the League of Nations meets in session to consider the protest against the Hungarian *numerus clausus* limiting the number of Jewish students in the universities, in contradiction to the basic laws of the country and its international obligations, the Jewish Telegraphic Agency is there to accurately report the proceedings and the action taken.

When Romanian students, in a fit of "national ecstasy," engage in anti-Jewish violence; when Soviet authorities in their determination to raise a Communist paradise on the debris of the ruined present order confiscate property and arrest Jewish petty traders; when small-town Poles, still under the influence of Middle Age barbarism, revive the ritual murder agitation, threatening the position of an entire Jewish community; when the Norwegian parliamentary committee decides to prohibit the Schechita, thus making it impossible for Jewish families to partake of meat; when anti-Jewish feeling rises high in Persia; when Jewish refugees enlist in the citizens' militia to maintain peace in war-torn China; when new Jewish communities spring up in the distant islands of Japan; when German racial anti-Semites begin advocating the abandonment of Christianity because of its Jewish origin and urge a return to Teutonic paganism; when the new Macabees of modern Palestine meet the sport representatives of modern Greece on the soccer field and the former emerge victorious; when Professor George Foot Moore, the famous American scholar of Harvard, in a life study of Judaism, comes to conclusions giving the lie to assertions of German Bible critics; when the Pope orders a Novena to be recited for nine days for the "speedy conversion of Jews to Catholicism"; when the Ku Klux Klan rises and falls in America; when the United States Court hands down a decision in a legal action that is picked up by German anti-Semites and used to advocate the annihilation of the Jewish race through measures that apparently have legal sanction; when Palestine, the cradle of world religions, is shaken by an earthquake; when Jewish work to rehabilitate the land makes considerable progress, laying the foundations for the national home provided under the terms of the Mandate under the protection of the League of Nations, or when it meets with obstacles attending such development –

When an attempt by ignorant men is made, as occurred in Massena, New York, to plant the barbarous and long-disproved anti-Jewish libel of ritual murder on American soil and public opinion is speedily reacting to banish this remnant of the Middle Ages –

When Zionists and Non-Zionists after protracted negotiations in a solemn session, under the leadership of Louis Marshall, enter a pact to join all forces of Jews for the rebuilding of Palestine – and to disregard the differences of the past for a common work in the future –

These, in addition to all the daily events in the march of life, are carefully observed and broadcast through the channels of the Jewish Telegraphic Agency within twenty-four hours of their occurrence.

It is an intricate, highly complicated process, to which the highest measure of responsibility is attached. The discharge of this responsibility necessitates a thorough familiarity with conditions, changing as in a kaleidoscope, a knowledge of languages as diverse as the linguistic families into which humanity is divided. To this task the Jewish Telegraphic Agency has devoted its labors.

The Jewish Telegraphic Agency was originally established February, 1917, by Jacob Landau in The Hague, with the help of Jacques Buchenholz, Elias Chanania, Sylvain Birnbaum and Sylvain Russ. It was reestablished in 1919 by Jacob Landau and Meer Grossman. The Jewish Telegraphic Agency in New York and its associated companies in London, Paris, Berlin, Warsaw and Jerusalem, are under the direction of Jacob Landau. William Z. Spiegelman is the editor of the New York JTA. B. Smolar is editor for the Yiddish Service. Joseph Leftwich is editor of the London office. The Paris office is under the management of A. Herenrot; the Berlin office under M. Wurmbrandt; the Warsaw office under M. Moses; and the Jerusalem office under S. Schwartz.

How the News Is Distributed

The service of the Jewish Telegraphic Agency is distributed by cable, radio, telegram and mail, through the six offices functioning in New York, London, Paris, Berlin, Warsaw and Jerusalem. The service reaches 38 Jewish dailies in Yiddish, Hebrew and the various languages of the countries in which they are published; 91 Jewish weeklies [in as many] cities of the world.

In addition to the Jewish newspapers, the Jewish Telegraphic Agency reaches, through its arrangements with general news agencies, more than 4,000 newspapers in every part of the world.

The service to the dailies goes over the wire. The service to the various weeklies is rendered in the form of mimeographed bulletins issued in the language of publication. The head office for receiving and distributing the cable service to the various offices is located in London.

In addition to the cable and telegraphic service, the Jewish Telegraphic Agency maintains a regular feature article service that consists mainly of news letters, complementary information and topical articles written by the local correspondents and special experts.

The J.T.A. Bulletins

In addition to the service rendered to the press directly, the J.T.A. offices are issuing daily bulletins in the language of the country. A daily bulletin is issued by the London [and New York] office[s] in English, by the Paris office in French, by the Berlin office in German, by the Warsaw office in Polish and Yiddish, and by the Jerusalem office in Hebrew and English. These bulletins are also available to private subscribers who are permitted to use the information only for private purposes.

Many of the outstanding leaders of the Jewish and non-Jewish communities in the respective countries are eager subscribers to these bulletins.

"The *Jewish Daily Bulletin*: Smallest Yet Most Effective Newspaper"

An outstanding achievement in the history of the Jewish Telegraphic Agency is the publication in New York of the *Jewish Daily Bulletin*.

The *Jewish Daily Bulletin*, established by Jacob Landau, October 15, 1924, was the first Jewish daily newspaper published in the English language, devoted exclusively to the dissemination of Jewish news. William Z. Spiegelman has been the editor of the *Jewish Daily Bulletin* since its inception. In newspaper-ridden America, in the hustle and bustle of American life, the publication of a specially Jewish daily newspaper in a field totally unexplored was distinctly an undertaking of pioneers.

With the big metropolitan newspapers, splendidly equipped, as apparent rivals, the *Jewish Daily Bulletin* made its way to a successful reception and to a position of influence in the Jewish community despite its being the smallest newspaper in the world.

Issued daily with the exception of Saturdays and Jewish high holidays, 10½ x 7½ inches in size, containing matter that requires only 10 minutes for perusal, the *Jewish Daily Bulletin* succeeded in filling every inch of its space with items of information of distinct interest, available through no other source, and of a brevity and precision that was widely approved and commended.

A glance at the date lines in one issue of the *Jewish Daily Bulletin* brings to its readers a roll call, as it were, not only of the capitals of the world's busy life, but also of the smaller centers where Jewish life is pulsating, where the struggle for existence is hardest and where Jewish contributions to the economic, cultural and political life of the world are being made. A glimpse into the contents of the *Jewish Daily Bulletin* brings the reader into contact with the various climes, political, social and economic conditions where Jewish life unfolds itself on the varying backgrounds of the different countries, all ringing out their messages in such varied tones.

The *Jewish Daily Bulletin*, in its nine years of existence, in addition to bringing the world's news from foreign countries in a nutshell, was a pioneer in directing daily the attention of its readers to American Jewish life. Through its news service it has established daily contact between the leaders of the Jewish communities scattered throughout the Union. Its accurate and speedy reports of the achievements of the various Jewish communities in their religious, communal, cultural, social and philanthropic activities has served as a stimulus for the leaders of other countries to do likewise.

In the many fundraising activities of American Jewry during recent years, in the lively discussions on American Jewish issues, in the presentation of the specific needs of the Jewish group, in portraying the progress of the good will movement between Christians and Jews, in following closely the march of events in the various communities and in American Jewry as a whole, the *Jewish Daily Bulletin* has proven itself to be of great service to the community at large.

Almost all of the leaders of the Jewish communities throughout the Union, all men of affairs occupying key positions in their groups and communities, are constant readers of the *Bulletin* and are eager for its continued success.

The *Jewish Daily Bulletin* is incorporated under the laws of the State of New York. Its officers are: Jacob Landau, President; John Simons, Secretary; S. Bienstock, Treasurer. Leo M. Grossman has been a member of the editorial staff since the beginning of the paper.

The list of subscribers to the *Jewish Daily Bulletin* reads like a "Who's Who of American Jewry": Dr. Cyrus Adler, Daniel Alexander, Louis Bamberger, James H. Becker, John L. Bernstein, David A. Brown, Fred M. Butzel, Rabbi Edward N. Calisch, Alfred M. Cohen, James Davis, Hon. Abram I. Elkus, Dr. H. G. Enelow, Mrs. Mary Fels, Bernard Flexner, A. J. Freiman, Felix Fuld, Harry Guggenheim, Rabbi Max Heller, Michael Hollander, Otto H. Kahn, Prof. M.M. Kaplan, Mrs. Rebecca Kohut, Max J. Kohler, Samuel C. Lamport, Herbert H. Lehman, Adolph Lewisohn, Louis Lipsky, Jacob M. Loeb, Hon Julian W. Mack, Louis Marshall, Henry Monsky, Henry Morganthau, Adolph S. Ochs, Hon. Jacob Panken, Dr. David Philipson, Julius Rosenwald, Mrs. Jacob Schiff, Mortimer L. Schiff, Rabbi Schulman, Ben Selling, Rabbi Abba Hillel Silver, Judge Horace Stern, Nathan Straus, S.W. Straus, Miss Henrietta Szold, Isaac M. Ullman, Ludwig Vogelstein, Felix M. Warburg, Dr. Stephen S. Wise, Rabbi Louis I. Wolsey, etc.

"A Lighthouse for Israel: Education – A Striking By-Product"

The service of the Jewish Telegraphic Agency, important as it is in reporting Jewish events and conditions to the non-Jewish world, is perhaps of even greater importance to the Jewish communities themselves. "Know thyself" is, in truth, not one of the Ten Commandments given to Moses at Sinai, but as a maxim of life and as a guide to determining one's own position and direction, it is as important and might well be classified as the Eleventh Commandment.

It is not long since the knowledge of one community of what was taking place even in communities not so remote met with so many obstacles that almost complete confusion and disturbing misconceptions arose. In the nature of things Jewish, an occurrence in one community has an effect upon the rest of the Jewish communities. The responsibility of the Jewish community as a whole for the actions of individuals affiliated with it, or for smaller groups within it, though never fixed in a legal sense, is none the less a fact, the implications of which have to be taken cognizance of. Apart from this, when one community acts in its own behalf, trying to grapple with its problems, if no information is available, it may often waste its labors in solving the very problem that is common to all and in the solution of which must experience has been gained in other localities. The division along religious lines within American Jewry and the more aggravating division along lines of origin, east or west, north or south, add to the confusion.

The dissemination of news concerning the activities of the Jewish communities, no matter what their type of religious affiliation, the reporting of the events within and outside these communities, the presentation of new ideas devised by one group to cope with this or that particular problem, the form of organization adopted by one or another group for any particular purpose, the change in approach that arose out of the necessity of spiritual or cultural adjustment, is a valuable help to these communities in their efforts to continue Jewish life, to enrich it, to normalize it, and to perpetuate it.

Linking the Scattered Communities

Take, for instance, the question of Jewish education. Education and Judaism are almost synonymous. It was not long ago that one of the wittiest students of mankind's history observed that the Jews are the only people living on the globe today who have not stopped reading or writing for the past two thousand years. Nonetheless, the question of

Jewish education as it presents itself to American Jewry today is a grave one. It is no longer a question of securing secular education for Jewish children who are thoroughly imbued with their Jewish knowledge, but rather to secure, choose if you please, a maximum or minimum of information that is to make the child's Jewish education and thus train it for affiliation with the Jewish community, or to muster it as a guardian for the continuity of Jewish life in the United States.

Education

Whatever view one would take of this Jewish education, whether it be ultra-orthodox, consisting of the study of the Talmud and the Codes; or Zionistic, insisting on the national aspects of the modern movement; whether it be Conservative and insists on the cardinal principles of catholic Israel or it be liberal or Reform, limiting the Jewish education of the child to a Sunday School instruction in Bible stories and an explanation of the monotheistic doctrine of Judaism and the moral teachings of Prophetic Judaism – all are agreed that a knowledge of the Jewish present is of inestimable value to this effort.

The interest of American children, who are used to an active life, cannot be held merely by the recitation of dates and details of events that occurred in history. Their interest and attention are rather engaged by a contact with present-day Jewish life and an observation of the workings of Judaism in the trials and tribulations, successes and failures of today.

In this respect the service of the Jewish Telegraphic Agency in gathering and distributing the news of Jewish life and presenting it in an attractive form has been recognized as of the greatest value. For instance, a number of schools for Jewish children have adopted the reading of the *Jewish Daily Bulletin* in the current events clubs. The Commission on Religious Education of the Union of American Hebrew Congregations and the Bureau of Jewish Education recommend the use of the *Bulletin* for this purpose.

"During the past ten years," Dr. S. Benderly, Director of the Bureau of Jewish Education, writes, "the study of Jewish current events has taken its place in the curriculum of many schools. Teachers, however, have found considerable difficulty in obtaining material for this study. They had to spend considerable time in looking over many periodicals before they could find the appropriate news. This difficulty, however, has been removed since the beginning of the publication of the *Jewish Daily Bulletin*.

"The Bureau of Jewish Education has made an experiment in the teaching of Jewish current events with the help of the *Jewish Daily Bulletin* and found the *Bulletin* exceedingly helpful."

Palestine

A distinctive service to the Jewish community is rendered by the Jewish Telegraphic Agency in its information service from Palestine.

Palestine is to Zionist and non-Zionist alike a place of inspiration, hope, devotion or cultural, political or religious interest, in accordance with the views held by the section of the Jewish people to which the individual belongs. The problem of rebuilding Palestine in accordance with the Mandate of the League of Nations and with the international peace treaties is emerging from the stage of a disputed theory and is becoming a task above discussion.

Since the early stage of this development and particularly following the close of the World War, the interest of Zionist and Non-Zionist, Jews and Gentiles alike, has been centered in the ancient country that by force of events has been transformed from the distant, unknown and mysterious Holy Land into a country closely connected with present-day civilization and interest where a pioneer movement is at work struggling against difficult odds. In cutting this distance and in spreading accurate information day by day on the conditions in Palestine, the successes as well as the failures, the progress as well as the setbacks, the Jewish Telegraphic Agency is rendering a service that is much needed.

To accomplish this task, the Palestine Telegraphic Agency, an associate company of the Jewish Telegraphic Agency, was formed. Its task is of a two-fold nature: to inform public opinion at large and Jewish public opinion in particular, throughout the world of what is going on in Palestine, to throw light on the new economic and cultural values that are evolving in the process of a Jewish rebuilt Palestine and, on the other hand, to inform the inhabitants of Palestine and neighboring countries on world events and on the happenings in the Jewish world that are the closest in its interest in the Palestine development.

In Palestine, the service of the Jewish Telegraphic Agency is not limited to the gathering of Jewish news in the strict sense of the term but to the gathering and distribution in Palestine and the Near East news in all fields of life, the conception being that all events and all phases of life that pulsate in that region of the world affect the foundation upon which the Zionist builds his aspirations, the non-Zionist pins his interest, the devout Jew his prayer, the politically minded his calculations.

Another aspect of the Jewish Telegraphic Agency work in Palestine is that which brings out there, in a calm way, the general principle underlying the J.T.A. work all over the world. It is the principle of international fellowship and understanding among the races. In bringing to the Jewish community of Palestine authentic information on events in the Arab and Muslim world and, on he other hand, informing the Arab and Muslim press of the true facts and the significance of the events in Jewish life in Palestine, it facilitates the establishment of a cordial understanding between the two peoples of the Mandated territory.

To this task the telegraphic service available to the Hebrew and Arab press and the *Palestine* [*Daily*] *Bulletin*, the only English daily published in Palestine, is devoted.

"Carrying America's Name to Distant Corners: East is East and West is West – But They Meet"

One aspect of the work of the American branch of the Jewish Telegraphic Agency is of particular interest to American Jews.

A superficial knowledge of Jewish history suffices one to know that the centers of Jewish life in the past two thousand years have been shifting from empire to empire and from state to state as the trend of mankind's history proceeded. Observers of Jewish life in the Post-War period have reached the conclusion that the cultural, religious and philanthropic center of Jewish life has been transferred to America.

The American Jewish community today, numbering over four millions, emerging from the initial stages of adjustment to the environment of the New World, is the leading Jewish community in the world. All projects, all plans, all ideas, depend in their success or failure on the support of American Jewry. The eyes of the Jews of the world are focused on the Jewish activities of American Jews. The precarious position in which many Jewish communities in Europe, Asia and Africa have found themselves following the World War is due to the fact that they could not discover, as speedily as necessary, the formula of adjustment that became essential due to the fundamental changes in the structure of the commonwealths with as a result changes wrought by the cataclysm.

The strides in the direction of cultural, economic and social adjustment made by American Jewry in the past decades is of tremendous constructive value to the Jews of the world.

The manner in which American Jews have coped with the problem of social service, their incomparable contribution toward social welfare through the Federation system, their helpfulness introducing into American life the Community Chest idea, their unparalleled per capita contribution to philanthropic causes, their world-wide interest in humanitarian effort, their attempt at solving the Jewish education problem, their contributions to the economic upbuilding of the Republic, their leadership in civic affairs – are an outstanding example to Jews and non-Jews the world over, which, if properly known and emulated, would solve many perplexing problems of the so-called national, religious or ethnic minorities.

Since the principle of religious and personal liberty was incorporated into the Declaration of Independence, America has become the world's leader not only in reiterating this ever-true principle, but in including it as an integral part of the basic law and by making the government the guardian for its application.

Max. J. Kohler, prominent New York attorney, in a conclusive study submitted recently to the Judeans, showed in detail how America influenced Europe in embracing this principle. The spirit of equal opportunity to all men, the principle of fair play, the total lack of discrimination against Jew as far as the branches of the government are concerned, the atmosphere of American life comparatively free of anti-Semitism – equipping the Jew with freedom in all branches of life and receiving in exchange most valuable contributions in all fields of human endeavor – is an inspiring tale that is daily broadcast to all parts of the world by the service of the Jewish Telegraphic Agency.

This service brings the name of America into every distant corner of the world. Jewish leaders in all countries eagerly absorb the description of events in America, the achievements of American Jews, their large-scope plans to alleviate human suffering, their cooperation of non-Jewish Americans in these endeavors, the attitude of the United States government in this matter, the growth of the Jewish communities, the results of Jewish research, the conclusions of Jewish studies, the spirit of helpfulness and understanding that prevails.

Due to the effort of the effort of the Jewish Telegraphic Agency, no detail of this absorbing story, standing out unique in the history of the Jews, is lost to Jewish readers in all parts of the world. In the service of the Jewish Telegraphic Agency, it is not subjected to the perchance picking up that must unavoidably be marked by inaccurate translations, distortions and misunderstandings.

The American branch of the Jewish Telegraphic Agency tells the majestic story, daily, through trained, efficient writers and observers of life, thoroughly familiar with international conditions, thus preventing the possibility of American events being viewed through "European" eyes and European events being viewed through "American" eyes, guarding the proportion and the color of the occurrences described.

"A Medium for International Understanding: Misconceptions Disappear When Light Is Shed"

Much of the blame for the calamities that befall the world is often placed by the semi-informed on the press of the world. The press, instead of being seen as a reaction to the life of the people and nation, is often presented as the cause that shapes the life. Generally it is unjust to blame the press for events that it records. There are, however, cases in which the press is not free from blame. This pertains to international, inter-racial and inter-group relations in which the guilt of the press lies not so much in promoting hatred, but rather in its lack of effort to prevent or limit it as much as possible by the spread of exact information.

Unlike other news agencies, the Jewish Telegraphic Agency has no political axe to grind. Its purpose in inter-group and inter-racial relations is to disseminate truth and to prevent, as far as is humanly possible, the spread of false reports that give rise to unjustified hatred, to bigotry and misunderstanding.

No group has suffered as greatly as a result of these failings of human nature – prejudice, hatred, bigotry and malice – as have the Jews.

However, prejudice and malice are not necessarily synonymous. A spirit of kindliness might dictate the opinion that prejudice is possibly due to ignorance. Ignorance of the law, it is true, is not an exonerating circumstance before a court of law. However, ignorance of fact is an exonerating circumstance before a court of public opinion, particularly when this public opinion is based on what is supposed to be facts. When no opportunity is afforded to present the facts properly without bias, without fear and without favor, how can the court of public opinion be constituted?

In certain sections of the globe where discerning judgment is not as highly developed as might be desired, and in certain portions of many nations in which strata education has not reached the level to which many are aspiring, not WHAT HAS HAPPENED matters, not the FACT is important, but what is said to have happened or what is believed to have happened matters.

This circumstance is of particular interest to the Jew, who has many a bitter experience because of it. Many a misconception concerning the Jew has been floated in the mind of humanity, many a prejudice has been deeply rooted due, a spirit of kindliness might say, not to malice, but to prejudice resulting from misinformation or from the total lack of information.

The situation with regard to the Jew among the nations is still more aggravated, in addition to the natural lack of information and the natural suspicion of the unlike, by the existence of clearly defined factors that are interested in spreading misinformation and are active in multiplying confusion so that prejudice might be created.

In this situation the service of the Jewish Telegraphic Agency is of particular value and falls in line with the intentions and the plans of the best representatives of human thought and human aspirations. It lends direct assistance to those great leaders of the enlightened Christian churches and societies who have initiated the goodwill movement, which had its noblest expression in the memorable meeting for Jewish relief held December 5, 1926, in the cathedral of St. John the Divine under the leadership of Bishop William T. Manning, General John J. Pershing, Louis Marshall, Major General John F. O'Ryan and Dr. S. Parkes Cadman.

"Can Anti-Semitic Propaganda Be Neutralized? Yes, Indeed, When Facts Drive Out Bias"

Also, in this regard, the Jewish Telegraphic Agency is not engaged in the propaganda of counter-action. It limits itself to a presentation of the facts, which indirectly neutralize the propaganda disseminated by the anti-Semites. In this the Jewish Telegraphic Agency must guard itself against any taint of a suspicion that it presents the facts with a Jewish bias. One outstanding example would be of interest here.

In the beginning of the Bolshevik Revolution in Russia when the simultaneous international concert of anti-Semitic propaganda was started, the charge was frequently made in the anti-Semitic press that Jews and Bolsheviks were synonymous, alluding probably to the participation of several Jewish Communists in the Soviet Government. When the Jewish Telegraphic Agency reported daily the actions of the Soviet authorities in persecuting Russian Jews en masse for engaging in merchandising, when the Jewish Telegraphic Agency reported the continued confiscation of synagogues by the Soviet authorities, the charge that "Bolshevik" was synonymous with Jew obviously became ridiculous.

A Factor for Protection

Another phase of this situation should be not overlooked: the protective character of the existence of such a service.

A public opinion armed with facts as they really are is the strongest weapon against the commission of unjustifiable acts of malice or violence. On the authority of James N. Rosenberg, vice-chairman of the American Jewish Joint Distribution Committee, who spent some time in Europe for the Committee, the following incident was publicly related.

One of the governments in Eastern Europe had issued a decree ordering several thousand Jewish refugees, who had no place to go, to leave the country within three days. The calamity that would have pursued them and the lament with which this decree was received by the Jews were indescribable. The correspondent of Jewish Telegraphic Agency, who was there, as Jewish Telegraphic Agency correspondents are to be found on every spot where Jewish news is breaking, cabled these facts to the American branch. The report of the threatened expulsion, giving the correct number, exact location, quoting chapter and verse of the decree, was published in the American press. The reaction to the publication of this report was the immediate "change of mind" of the government concerned. It was unwilling to incur the disfavor of public opinion in the United States and relinquished this plan for the "disposition" of the Jewish refugees.

On the other hand, the responsibility resting on the J.T.A. in such emergency cases cannot be overstressed. It is obviously responsible to both the government concerned and to the Jewish and non-Jewish public.

A striking demonstration of the possible result of an inaccuracy in such an emergency case was recently related by Louis Marshall, who was largely responsible for the clauses included in the Treaty of Versailles for the protection of the national minorities in Europe. The incident Mr. Marshall speaks of occurred prior to the existence of the Jewish Telegraphic Agency service.

The report reached the Jewish leaders who had come to Paris to plead with the statesmen of the world for the protection of Jewish rights, that several hundred Jews were killed in an anti-Jewish massacre in Vilna. Alarmed, the Jewish leaders appeared before the responsible statesmen. How weakened was their position when it was learned that the number was not several hundred but only a score or more. This gave the government the opportunity of denying flatly the entire report, without stating how many were really killed.

Another example of the far-reaching importance and the protective value of the Jewish Telegraphic Agency's news service was demonstrated recently by an occurrence in Yugoslavia.

In that country an attempt to revive the ritual murder accusation was made by a group of benighted and malicious persons. An entire Jewish community was thrown into jeopardy. The speedy action of the Jewish Telegraphic Agency in dispatching its Belgrade correspondent to the spot of the outbreak and the swift publication of all details proving the groundlessness of the rumor in the West European and American press contributed in no little measure to the energetic action taken by the local authorities to squelch the agitation and protect the innocent Jewish community.

The Jewish Telegraphic Agency has made it a point to report not what is believed to have happened but what actually happened.

The Chicago Chronicle, April 18, 1924

Welcome the Swastika!

It has crossed the ocean and has been permitted to land at Ellis Island without any difficulties. Was it admitted in the quota? In excess of the quota? Or, perhaps, above the quota? Do not ask. It is a real Nordic [saga], and has hurried its arrival in expectation of a generous welcome present in the form of the 1890 census. It has even gained considerable publicity for itself. In Europe it is quite famous, but, perhaps, you do not know what the Swastika looks like, and what it stands for? Its pedigree, therefore, must be given to the best of our knowledge.

Scholars are in doubt whether the cross as a religious symbol originated in the Golgotha. Some claim its origin was in Persia; others that it was in India. Whichever claim is correct, Jewish history has grown accustomed, since the time of the Gregories and the Crusades, up to the present time of modern "Christian Socialists," to see all kinds of anti-Semitic movements find shelter under the sign of the cross. It has been, indeed, the tragic-comism [sic] of Jewish, as well as of Christian history, that all anti-Semitic movements should be directed under a sign upon which a Jew was supposed to have suffered and died.

However, the blonde nature of Nordic races, which for generations have "suffered" under the yoke of Jewish moral teachings – although diluted and modified – has broken out in revolt. A primal revolution is taking place and attempts are being made to dejudaize the New Testament. At this time when in the churches the cry of "Down with Jesus the Jew" can be heard, the German anti-Semites have found conditions ripe to make their radical change.

They have taken from the prehistoric archives the old Pagan – not exactly Nordic – sign of the Swastika, two hooks crossing each other, and have made it the emblem of the anti-Semitic movement.

The first to introduce the Swastika was the Fascist army of Hitler and Ludendorff. This sign was to be used as the symbol of those who had taken upon their shoulders the task of saving Germany from the Jewish influence. In a short time the Swastika became so popular that it began to be used as a new kind of jewelry. Monarchists, aristocratic ladies and anti-Semites wore, as adornment, gold, silver and bejeweled Swastikas, demonstrating that they were really Nordics and absolutely free from anything Jewish. The Swastika became the "bogeyman" for Jews and Republicans alike. At the houses of Republicans and Jews in Central Europe, where formerly the old-time cross could be discovered as a warning and threatening sign, can now be found the new symbol of terror – the Swastika.

With the sign of the Swastika on its cover, there has appeared a twenty-page booklet, many thousand copies of which have been circulated. The booklet contains a plan "to make peace prevail in the world." The author, Ernst Goerner, probably, an American-German, submitted this plan to the Bok Peace Award Committee with full expectation of receiving its prize of $100,000. The Bok Committee did not consider this plan the best, however, and the disgruntled author now raves at the Committee, claiming that it is no more than a Jewish contrivance to win America for the League of Nations idea, in order that the "Jewish Treaty of Versailles" may be maintained. You, probably, would think that this [person] is a crank. You would misjudge. He has a well-known program – the program of the Swastika.

"The cause for the world's unrest is the fact that during the time of the war, Russia, Germany, Austria, England, France and America were represented, not by Aryans and Nordics, but by Jews. The trouble with the Versailles Treaty is the same: the nations and states were not represented, but misrepresented by the Jews, especially [in] America, which was misrepresented by Colonel House, the evil spirit of President Wilson, 'The all-powerful

Jew at Versailles.' He was not the representative of the United States, but of world Jewry. It is possible to make peace prevail in the world only when the nations will understand and consent:

"That men of another race have grown fat, rich and enormously powerful through this war, have taken the places and enriched themselves at the expense of those who were honestly fighting – that those men of another race have usurped the governmental power of the nations of the Aryan people and in the fact have enslaved and tyrannized them and enforced a most brutal policy of starvation.

"That each and every nation participating in the discussion shall consent, promise and bind itself, to have in all their affairs, internal and external, only men of their own kind, only men of the Aryan race, and to withdraw and eliminate, without exception, all men of non-Aryan races and all those who have even a minimum of non-Aryan blood. Also all those of the Aryan race who have intermarried with non-Aryan blood and those who are economically or socially under non-Aryan influence shall be called non-Aryan.

"That where a country is dominated by non-Aryan influences as is the case in Germany and Russia, then Aryan representatives shall be approached instead of non-Aryan official government.

"The 'Plan' having been either approved by the U.S. Senate or the Aryan public of this country, shall be submitted to the different governments or 'TRUE REPRESENTATIVES' of the several nations."

Together with the new symbol of the Swastika, America has been granted a new name, Usania (U.S. ania). The booklet is being circulated by an organization that calls itself the Nordic-Aryan Federation of Usania, and its headquarters are in Portland, Ore., and Milwaukee, Wis. An investigation has revealed that this Nordic-Aryan Federation of America is a German-American organization that publishes also a monthly German journal, under the same name in Portland.

Who has imported the Swastika into America? How great is the danger, if any? Is there going to be a putsch made in its name? Who is backing this movement – supporting it?

Concerning the author, Ernst Goerner, we are in a position to say as much as he himself has been willing to tell. During the war he was *persona non grata* with the Wilson Administration, on account of his pro-German propaganda. The government even started proceedings to annul his citizenship.

When we read over his program for the approaching presidential elections, giving twelve reasons why the future president must be a "man racially conscious," a "successful businessman," and one "who would not sell himself for money and to the Jews," it becomes evident that, if in the ancient and medieval times all roads used to lead to Rome, they lead now, under the sign of the Nordic Swastika, to Detroit.[1]

The Chicago Chronicle, July 11, 1924

Unobserved, a date of great historical importance has been inscribed in the history of American Jewry. On the first of July the new quota law, based on the 1890 census, reducing the possibility for Jewish immigration to the United States to almost nothing, went into effect. After the stormy protest meetings, pleading committees, individual appeals and aroused public sentiment, there came a lull. With one stroke of the pen, history was made.

A period of thirty years of Jewish immigration to the New World, averaging about 100,000 yearly, has come to a close. It can safely be said that this period will be recorded as

---

[1] That is to say, to Henry Ford.

the most remarkable and outstanding in the age-old and complex process of Jewish transformation. Upon the thin layer of the original Spanish and German Jewish settlers in the United States have come layers of Jews from all corners of the world, merging slowly into one American Jewish community, creating new forms of Jewish life, opening new avenues of Jewish thought and even making new Jewish customs and traditions.

What course will American Jewry take now that its reservoir of vitality has been cut off? This question has been correctly answered by one who has seriously thought on the matter. While the new change is to be regretted, there is no reason for despairing. American Jewry has already developed a sufficiently strong element of spiritual leadership and communal responsibility to assure its further inner growth.

Jewish history has seen the development of a distinct Arabian-Jewish type, succeeded by a Spanish-Jewish type, which has in turn been transformed into English-Jewish, French-Jewish, German-Jewish, Polish-Jewish and Russian-Jewish types. Jewish history is now preparing for the emergence of the distinct American-Jewish type.

* * *

That there is no need for worrying over the future of American Jewry is also the belief of the champion of the doctrines of our Bible, the always-original democrat, William Jennings Bryan.

While the Democratic Convention, in the City of New York, was floundering between the deep sea of innumerable ballots and the evil spirit of the Ku Klux Klan, inspiration came to it from that ancient source of salvation, the Bible. Are the progressive and democratic elements of America to come out in an open fight against the hooded knights of religious prejudice and racial discrimination, endangering perhaps the outcome of the presidential campaign, or are they to compromise? The forces of American democracy were split into two distinct halves. These halves must be welded together again. How can it be done? Who can do it? It was William Jennings Bryan who then pleaded:

"The Jews do not need this resolution. They have Moses. They have Elijah. They have Elisha, who was able to draw back the curtain and show upon the mountain tops an invisible host greater than a thousand Ku Klux Klans."

And so it happened that the spirit of Moses, Elisha and Elijah rested upon a woman, who decided the outcome; it was recorded that the resolution against the Ku Klux Klan, condemning it by name, was lost by a majority of less than one vote, cast by a woman delegate.

* * *

That the spirit of Moses, Elijah and Elisha will be perpetuated – and again through the efforts of the women – can be safely predicted when we forget for a while the noise and fanfare of the political conventions and stop to listen to another kind of convention.

I have in mind the convention of the Jewish women's organization of America, Hadassah, which has just opened in Pittsburgh. 17,000 Jewish women are quietly organized for the carrying on of a splendid humanitarian and Jewish work. The organization, under the able leadership of Miss Henrietta Szold has, in the last year, gained over 5,000 new members, an increase of almost 50% over its previous membership. For its special work, aside from the contributions that its members make to various Jewish communal undertakings, the organization has been able to collect $250,000 during the last year.

The organization has to its credit the remarkable progress in sanitary conditions in

Palestine, and the curative and preventive work among the inhabitants of that country. It intends, according to the plans outlined by its president, to assume even greater responsibility. Its immediate intention is to help maintain the newly proposed hospital in Tiberias. Another and more distant plan is to take over the entire medical work in Palestine.

Surely the spirit of Moses, Elijah and Elisha rests with the work and efforts of this unique Jewish women's organization.

The Chicago Chronicle, July 25, 1924

One of the most interesting figures in American Jewish life, perhaps not so well known to the country at large but nevertheless of dynamic influence, passed away suddenly in the City of New York.

Dr. Isaac A. Hourwich, Doctor of Philosophy, lawyer, American immigration expert, statistician and defender of labor's rights, died at the age of 64. We are accustomed to judge men by their achievement in material wealth or by their popularity; we often overlook those scholarly, quiet workers whose efforts make a deep impression on the environment in which they live without causing much noise outside it. Brought to America by the wave of Russian Jewish immigration 34 years ago, Isaac A. Hourwich's activities and sudden departure mark an epoch in American Jewish life. Through his work in fermenting [sic] a new life-forming period of Russian Jewish immigration, he made his contribution not only to Jewish life in America, but to America as a whole.

When the mass of mostly unskilled Russian Jewish immigrants found refuge from economic barrenness and political oppression and had to adapt themselves to their new environment, they found economic potentialities for applying their labor power, a Bill of Rights to protect their civil liberty, and charitable institutions, perhaps, to help those who were in need. To the American Jewish community of German origin must be credited the building up of great industries that created the possibilities for the new arrivals to be easily digested and assimilated in the economic system of their country. This same American Jewish community has on the other hand provided a splendid system of institutions to extend philanthropic aid to those who were either unfit for the new kind of endeavor or who were victims of the new industrial regime. It was left, however, for those intellectual leaders who followed the wave of Jewish immigration from Russia to start a movement that would remedy the evil at its root.

No matter what our attitude may be towards the doctrines of socialism as a remedy for the evils of the world, one cannot help but admit that the movement started and pursued with so much energy and idealism – perhaps exaggerated idealism – resulted in much good for the large class of immigrants. The betterment of the conditions, in this respect the introduction of organization in these ranks, the abolishment of the sweatshop system, was not only a contribution towards improvement of the situation of the Jews in America but also a contribution towards the general standard of living in America. In this movement Dr. Isaac A. Hourwich was in the lead.

Russian Jewish intellectuals of the type of Dr. Hourwich, when fleeing to America, did not bring with them a burning desire for individual liberation alone; they carried with them the care and thought of the group. In the service of the United States Government as statistician, Dr. Hourwich devoted his time not to the achievement of a personal career but to the securing of correct and enlightening figures on Jewish immigration. Immigration, especially Jewish immigration, on which opinions differ so much, always required the dissemination of correct information presented in the proper light.

Fighting for liberal immigration policies, his last days saw this country being closed to immigrants; fighting for socialism all his life and at one time reaching the heat of communism, he went to Russia, to return a convinced anti-Bolshevik.

It was a tragic figure, significant of his generation, that passed away.

Russia will for a long time hold the attention of those who have either their materialistic or idealistic interest before their eyes. Will the present regime continue in Russia, and if not what is going to happen when it falls? This question was repeatedly asked and with especial anxiety by those who are interested in the fate of a great number of Jews in the former Russian Empire. This question was asked as many times as there arrived in this country some new anti-Bolshevik mission or delegation.

A new Russian delegation has arrived, representing quite a new kind of Russia. It is "Green Russia." M. A. Moskwinow, who is a representative of the All-Russian Peasants Association, is here in this country to advocate the support of a Green Russia, claiming to represent the Russian peasant. The Russian peasant is still the puzzling unknown quantity. Russia consists mainly of peasants. Were they to be properly organized, brought to the point of literacy, they would be the rulers of Russia. And they will some day no doubt be the rulers of Russia. What would be the attitude of this Green Russia towards Russian Jewry at that dreaded moment when one regime falls and another rises? M. Moskwinow, speaking on behalf of the Russian peasantry, advocates the ideal of a democratic Russia whose form of government should be determined by a Constituent Assembly. His statement in the general press in connection with this plan was, "To be honest, we are not anxious to include (in the Constituent Assembly) the Jew. We believe he makes trouble in Russia."

I do not know how successful an organizer M. Moskwinow is, how many millions of peasants of the Russian steppes have already joined the banner of the future Green Russia. One thing is certain: that he knows how to get out of a bad situation. When asked for an explanation, the similarity in sound and difference in meaning of one of the words came to his rescue. M. Moskwinow says that, speaking in German to one of the American journalists, he said, "*Wir haben keine Angst, die Hebraer miteinzuschliessen, denn Unruhen koennen nicht entstehen, falls die Andersstaemmigen (inorodtsi – in Russian) auf demokratischer Wahlgrundlage die moeglichkeit haben ihre nationalen Interssen zu verteidigen.*"[2] The American journalist then made a "slight mistake." He thought the German word *Angst* (fear) is equivalent to the English "anxious [about]." M. Moskwinow assures us that he has no fear of Jewish participation in the proposed Constituent Assembly of the future Green Russia.

From the representative of Green Russia this is not a bad explanation.

* * *

Mr. Samuel Untermyer, one of America's most prominent lawyers, President of the Keren Hayesod,[3] Vice President of the American Jewish Congress, and great Democrat, was "out of luck" at the recent National Democratic Convention. Already at the very start nature revolted against him. Desirous of extending a warm welcome to the Democratic delegates, he proposed giving a lawn party at his home in Yonkers. But a terrific thunderstorm prevented his acting the generous host to his guests and holders of Democratic votes. No

---

[2] "We have no fear of Hebrew participation, unless riots originate among other ethnic groups (in Russian: foreigners) who defend their national interests upon democratic electoral foundations."

[3] The Colonization Department of the Jewish National Fund.

less a storm was caused by another revolt, not the elements this time, but against the elementary right of secrecy of political advices.

Mr. Untermyer was a McAdoo man. Rumor had it a long time ago that in his McAdoo devotion he was the one to advise McAdoo to accept the support of the Ku Klux Klan, even though he dumped it later. There was an inclination to treat the rumor as mere gossip. Along came the *New York World* and in its enthusiasm for Smith threw the stone into the water. It published what was apparently authentic correspondence between Mr. Untermyer's nephew and Mr. Julius Peyser, which seemed to confirm the long-suppressed rumor. Since Mr. Untermyer denies that his nephew has any access to his political convictions and advices we may believe him. But since the advice was not effective, we need not worry about the possible consequences. The question, however, to which this incident gave rise still remains to be clarified.

The American Jewish Congress, having been anxious to have both parties take a definite stand on the Klan question, appointed a committee to wait on the Democratic convention for the purpose of pleading for an anti-Klan plank. The committee appointed by the President, Dr. Stephen S. Wise, was to include the Vice President of the American Jewish Congress, Mr. Samuel Untermyer. Mr. Untermyer, however, refused to serve on the committee and in refusing, after the revolt against secrecy was made, put forth the principle that American Jewry does not have to fight the religious intolerance and racial discrimination advocated by the Klan. Urging a purely Christian policy of non-resistance by Jews, Mr. Untermyer puts his entire trust in the Protestants in the Klan matter.

It is hard to think that this policy of non-resistance is consistent with the courageous readiness for self-defense expected of organizations like the American Jewish Congress and the Keren Hayesod, of which Mr. Untermyer is Vice President and President, respectively.

However, Mr. Untermyer agrees to disagree on this policy.

The Jewish Chronicle, August 1, 1924
The Ohio Jewish Chronicle, August 1, 1924
The Jewish Criterion, August 1, 1924

The Klan question again. Are the Jews of the United States as such to take the burden of battle against the Ku Klux Klan, or shall they leave this matter to the leaders of the Protestant church? The question that sprang up in the heated atmosphere of pre-election campaigns has first caused an agreement to disagree between Dr. Stephen S. Wise and Samuel Untermyer. However, it seems that they are not the only prominent American Jews to disagree on the matter. An inquiry sent out by the Jewish Telegraphic Agency to various leaders of American Jewry in all parts of the country brought quick returns. In substance, they seem to travel over two parallel lines, which because of their very straightness, never meet, as our geometry tells us.

American Jews, as free men and free citizens, have the right, nay, are obliged to fight openly and courageously against any appearance of racial discrimination and religious bigotry, not waiting until someone else at some future time will come to the conclusion that his generosity to his fellow-men calls for his taking up the fight for them, one line of thought argues.

American Jews, as free men and free citizens, are obliged to uphold and defend the principles of the Constitution, guaranteeing religious liberty, equality of opportunity without racial discrimination, but in the case of the Klan it is not a matter for the Jews alone to wage battle against – it is rather the work of the Protestant church, urges another trend of thought.

Anti-Semitism has always existed and will exist for a long time to come; the Jewish people in all countries and under all conditions have survived antagonism, remaining true to their traditions of justice and fair play, pleads another resigned call for adaptation and survival.

The eternal volume of Jewish history could produce enough evidence for and against these three lines of thought.

Parallel lines that never cross each other and never meet.

* * *

M. B. Mammonas, Charge d'Affaires of Greece in Washington, has a deep resentment against the Jews of Greece, especially the entire Jewish community of Salonica. Salonica, with its important Jewish population, as will be recalled, was a part of the Turkish Empire until the World War. It was incorporated into Greece as a result of the events that followed the World War. True to the principle adopted by those who determined the political fate of the world in the new era, Greece, as all other newly created or enlarged countries with new populations, pledged itself to an international treaty guaranteeing the national minorities the free exercise of their religion and the fulfillment of their cultural needs.

Now, however, the Greek Parliament has passed a law of compulsory Sunday rest for the entire population. The Jewish community of Salonica protested against it, arguing that if it be compelled to rest on Sunday it would either have to abandon its religion or go out of business, as it would be unable to stand competition if it is compelled by the law to have a two days' vacation every week.

M. Mammonas, answering an inquiry of the Jewish Telegraphic Agency, resents the protest of the Jewish community of Salonica. He says:

"The Jews of Greece enjoying all the political and religious rights must not ask to be exempted from the general measures and to have distinction and privileges granted them apart from the other citizens." M. Mammonas claims that justice is on the side of Greece in this case. "The law of Sunday rest in Greece was voted in favor of the working and industrial classes in order to limit the number of working hours. Inasmuch as this is the aim of the law, it could not contain any exemption, but ought to be general for all those residing in Greece, independently of their nationality and their religious beliefs." He also refers to England where a similar law exists and the Jews never protested against it.

M. Mammonas is entirely wrong. Granting that it is just for the state to assure one day of rest of the working and industrial classes, is this sense of justice really violated if the group of workers concerned choose to rest, not on Sunday, but on Saturday in conformity with its religion? Obviously not. M. Mammonas is also wrong when he cites England as an example. Broad-minded Britannia, in spite of its Blue Sunday Law, permits its Jews, especially the small businessmen, artisans and workers who maintain their orthodox religion and who resemble in type the Jewish community of Salonica, to rest one day in the week, on Saturday if they so please.

The Jewish community of Salonica, which dates back to the days of the Apostles, having observed its day of rest on Saturday through the centuries, will not violate any principle of justice if they continue to do so, especially since international law has given them the guarantee for it.

* * *

A tribe of Bedouins in the neighborhood of Safed has applied to the Chief Rabbinate of Palestine for permission to return to Judaism, a report from Palestine states. Judaism, in its long and varied course of development, has never been a proselytizing religion. At least it never sent out "missions" to bring non-Jewish communities into the fold. Neither was it in a position to organize warfare expeditions for conversion purposes. An ancient proverb of the race, which has survived as a historical document, speaks in rather disparaging terms of proselytes. It says that, "proselytes are burdensome to Israel like a growth." It is not known what the Chief Rabbinate has or will decide in the matter, but the application of this small tribe of Palestinian Bedouins is more than significant.

The Bedouin population is nothing else than the descendants of the "people of the land" (Am-Haaretz), records of which have been preserved in the Jewish literature of the time telling of their backward cultural condition, that pleasant class that was not particularly active in the Roman-Jewish warfare and that remained in the country even after the destruction of the temple and underwent all the changes of religion, of political and social upheavals through which Palestine passed.

Intense Jewish colonization work in the country, coupled with the revival of a strong and all-embracing Hebrew culture – who could predict how the seemingly hard Arab-Jewish problem in Palestine will be solved?

The application of the small Bedouin tribe for return to Judaism is indeed a significant indication.

The Chicago Chronicle, August 8, 1924

Metropolitan newspapers told American readers of an importance piece of work that was finished in Jewish life. The announcement was made that the American Jewish Relief Committee, under the leadership of Louis Marshall, Cyrus L. Sulzberger and Felix M. Warburg, would close its activities on Thursday, July 31st, 4 o'clock in the afternoon, with a record of hundreds of thousands of lives saved, more than 4,000,000 children fed and clothed and the distribution of close to 1,000,000 tons of food in Central Europe – and a total of $63,137,562 raised for that purpose.

This event was given wide publicity in the press. As usual, publicity writers are inclined to exaggerate, so it was claimed that the sum of $63,137,562 was raised by the American Relief Committee, and that the credit for this tremendous achievement of American Jewry, in the work of reconstructing Jewish life in the war-stricken countries, was due to Henry H. Rosenfelt, now affiliated with the La Follette campaign.

Mr. Rosenfelt, in a communication to the Jewish Telegraphic Agency, wished to make the following corrections:

1. That he did not personally raise the tremendous sum as stated in the press report; that he having been the National Director of the American Jewish Relief Committee for four years, is in a position to know that it is Mr. Jacob Billikopf to whom credit is due for organizing the great work.

2. That the American Jewish Relief Committee has not finally closed; that only its campaign for money had closed, but that the collection of unpaid pledges will still go on at the offices of the Joint Distribution Committee, 64 Water Street.

These corrections are certainly well taken. There is, however, another correction that ought to be made and that, when overlooked, lessens the significance of the great period in American Jewish life that is apparently coming to an end.

The closing of the campaign for funds for the American Jewish Relief Committee, as officially announced, and the final liquidation of the activities of the Joint Distribution

Committee, in Europe, mark the quiet end of an heroic demonstration of self-sacrificing generosity and big-hearted giving on the part of the American Jewish community. It is a romantic chapter that will gloriously be inscribed in the annals, not only of American Jewry, but of America as a whole. It is since the day when a group of immigrant Jews, by their social status and adherence to tradition, belonging to none other than the orthodox group, assembled in an East Side meeting room, a few months after the outbreak of the World War, that this romance was been woven.

The longer the war continued – and at first it was expected that it would not last more than three months – and the greater the misery among the Jews in the war-stricken countries of Europe, the greater grew the spirit of generosity and the ranks of those who felt the responsibility of coming to the aid of the suffering. It was originally the orthodox Central Relief Committee that was organized. There was then organized the American Jewish Relief Committee. These two were followed by the People's Relief Committee, composed of such Jewish elements as were usually in principle opposed to any benevolent or philanthropic action. It was through the cooperation of all three committees – and due recognition must be given to the dominant role of the American Jewish Relief Committee – that the sum of over $63,000,000 was raised and disbursed by their Joint Distribution Committee.

When the epoch-making donation of $1,000,000 of Julius Rosenwald to that fund was under touching circumstances announced, it was President Wilson who stated, "Your donation, while it furnishes inspiration, puts on us an obligation."

The $1,000,000 donation of Rosenwald certainly introduced a new style, not only in Jewish America, but in American war-relief activities. This inspiration, no doubt, served as a constant reminder to American Jews of their obligation to their brethren in war-stricken Europe. The obligation was honorably fulfilled. Over $63,000,000 was raised and efficiently spent. The prestige of American Jewry, and with it of America, was elevated to an incomparable height.

But this effort did more than raise millions of dollars. It awakened a feeling of responsibility, created Jewish communal leadership in the remote hamlets of America, brought the Jewish social service, in the person of Jacob Billikopf, to its present prominent place in Jewish communal life, generated enthusiasm and laid a basis for a real united American Jewish community.

It is announced that the work of collecting money for war-relief activities will stop. Will the enthusiasm and communal responsibility created in the course of this work end?

* * *

The wheel of Jewish history is turning with its hub seemingly placed in Palestine. In addition to the Bedouin tribe, which has made an application for permission to return to Judaism, there has appeared another group, which has made a similar application to the Chief Rabbinate of Palestine. This application is reminiscent of a tragic period and gives food for thought to those who are accustomed to thinking in historical terms.

A group of Maranos, the descendents of Jews in Portugal and Spain who were compelled by the Inquisition of Torquemada, Ferdinand and Isabella to embrace Christianity, desire now to return to Judaism. A number of these Maranos are experienced farmers in Portugal, and there is an intention to help their settlements in the land of Palestine. It seems as though the Biblical prediction of the return of the "scattered of Israel" is beginning to be realized. However, the Chief Rabbinate has decided not to take any definite steps concerning the application of the Bedouins and the Maranos before consulting the national Jewish organizations, and before a thorough investigation is made from the standpoint of Jewish law.

In a conversation with the writer of these lines, Rabbi A. J. Kook, Chief Rabbi of Palestine, who is now visiting the United States – [and] the one who is to decide the matter – had many doubts on the matter. With regard to the Bedouins, who are considered by reason of their language as Arabs, it is a very delicate political question. Unless sufficient historical proof is found establishing the Hebrew origin of this wandering tribe, the incorporation of the tribe as a group, with deeply rooted beliefs and modes of life of its own, into the growing Jewish body of Palestine is hardly to be recommended. It is different with the Maranos, who are, undoubtedly, of Jewish origin. But here again there are obstacles from the standpoint of Jewish law. Jewish law, particularly concerning marriages and divorces, represents a highly accentuated tendency towards legalism. Any shortcoming in the observance of the marriage and divorce laws are a grave transgression of the principles of traditional Judaism. In some cases the offspring of such marriages are under a question mark, which makes their incorporation into the Jewish religious community an impossibility. And these Maranos, though they clung tragically to the faith of their fathers, inwardly could not obviously be very particular.

The Sentinel, August 15, 1924
The Jewish News, August 21, 1924

Readers of letters, especially family letters, occasionally have an opportunity for a good laugh. In the days when the public school system had not yet produced the average grade of intelligence that is so common now, the average family member was not able to compose a letter on his own accord. An enterprising publisher saw an opportunity to accommodate this public need and issued a *Briefensteller* (book of form letters). Since that day most of the family letters usually began with "I wish to let you know we are all, thank God, well, and everything is alright. Second, it grieves me to tell you that I do not feel very well and things have not been going at all well with us. . . ."

One is almost tempted to begin a "New York Letter" reporting the activities of the Jewish family in these hot and dull days [of summer] in a similar fashion. It seems, first, that we are, thank God, well; and second, that we are grieved to note that we are not so well, and this and that, of a not too cheerful nature, is happening.

* * *

Harold Bolster, a promoter of an exclusive Country Club in Tarrytown, N.Y. that was to occupy a part of the estate of the late William Rockefeller, brings suit against Frank H. Hitchcock, former Postmaster General and now in charge of that exclusive club.

There is something wrong somewhere, and a difference of opinion is brought to court. But one of the reasons that caused the difference of opinion is a fact of interest to us. Frank H. Hitchcock refused to issue life membership in that fashionable country club to several members "because the Board of Governors will not tolerate in its club anyone of Jewish extraction as a member of Rockwood Hall." It is revealed that those persons who were refused life membership in that club were the very ones who took a financial interest in the enterprise and contributed largely towards the club.

Among the members of the Board of Governors of the Club are Vincent Astor, Robert W. Chambers, Bainbridge Colby, Edward L. Doheny, T. Coleman du Pont, Charles Dana Gibson, Frank A. Munsey and Melville E. Stone. Who were the ones to whom membership was refused, we are not in a position to say. However, Supreme Court Justice McGoldrick sees no reason to appoint a receiver as the plaintiff demands, probably following what is called the "logical line of thought" that any group of members who form a fashionable country club have the right to decide whom they want to have as life members, and whom they wish not to have as such.

Are we not, first, thank God, well; and second, not so well?

* * *

The Ku Klux Klan has "modified" its policy with regard to the Jew. This was made known by none other than the Grand Kleagle of the Ku Klux Klan in Atlanta, and the news was given to none other than Mr. E. Milton Altfeld, Assistant State's Attorney of Baltimore, author of "The Jew's Struggle for Religious and Civil Liberty in Maryland." The new literature of the Klan, mailed hurriedly to Mr. Altfeld, if party literature means anything, marks a sudden turn in the Klan's tactics. It announces that Jews who served in the army during the war could be accepted as members of the KKK and that the chief platform of this organization will from now on be the fight "against the reign of Catholicism in America."

I do not know what other 100% Americans may think or do, but Mr. Altfeld proudly refused this invitation.

Is not this another sign that we are well, and perhaps not so well?

* * *

"The entire refugee problem, besides being a specifically Jewish one, is what may be termed an American issue as well, and must be solved by American Jewry, since the relatives of these emigrants are in this country. Here is the situation. The relatives of these emigrants live in America. These relatives sent to the prospective emigrants money, the necessary papers, the native government's issued passports, and the American Consuls visaged these passports, and the Steamship tickets for the United States had been purchased and the people were all in readiness to come to this country. If the Consuls had not issued the visas, the problem of these stranded emigrants might not have arisen. It is a Jewish problem from the point of view of relief, because these emigrants are Jewish. Politically and diplomatically, it is an issue that has to be taken up with the American government."

This is in substance the conclusion that was reached by the delegation of the Hebrew Immigrant Aid Society upon its return from investigating the situation of the Jews stranded in various parts of Europe. It is reported that not less than 8,000 refugees find themselves in this position. More than 50 percent of them are women and children. It is certainly a Jewish and an American question. Not long ago an important conference took place, called by Louis Marshal and Dr. Stephen S. Wise, at which representatives of many Jewish organizations participated. It will be recalled the conference decided to create an American Emergency Committee on Jewish Refugees. Owing to the unpreparedness of the leaders, the conference was not in a position to elect its executive body and left it to the originators to form the committee "within ten days." Ten days and more have elapsed. No one was ever informed that this committee was formed, or is ever going to be formed. It is true the heat drives everyone out [of the city] for a vacation, but does it also remove the emergency of the situation for which the American Emergency Committee for Jewish Refugees was to be created?

We are well. We are having a deserved rest. Are we really so well?

Jewish Transcript, August 22, 1924

What has been an engaging problem to the authorities in the various embarkation ports, to government officials and to relief organizations – the problem of the stranded refugees who were granted visas to be admitted to America but were detained not of their own fault – found no expression, so far, in any official record of the State Department or even the Labor Department. The authorities upon whom the refugees have placed their trust and as a result of that trust have disposed of their property, left their homes and started journeying with the encouraging hope of finally reaching their opportunity in the land of opportunities, lost track of these originally hopeful emigrants in the moment of their despair. Commissioner General of Immigration Husband has made the statement to the Jewish Telegraphic Agency that outside of newspaper reports, the immigration authorities of the United States have no official record as to the number of American visa holders classified as "stranded refugees." Will the lack of record, however, solve the problem and remove the responsibility?

That the authorities who have issued these visas and encouraged the hopes of these refugees have to some extent a responsibility towards them is indicated by the fact that the State Department has issued instructions through the Consuls abroad to give preference in the issuing of new visas to those stranded refugees who hold previous visas. There is, however, very little salvation in this instruction of the State Department. The quotas according to the new law for the Eastern European countries, from where the majority of the refugees come are, as known, very limited. Out of this meager quota only a half of each quota can be allotted for preference to the stranded refugees, in as much as the other half of these quotas are to be reserved for a certain class of near relatives of American citizens and agricultural laborers that has gained preference by the provisions of the very same immigration law. Besides, according to the same law only 10% of the annual quota could be admitted monthly. Even those refugees who would prove to belong to the "preferred stock" would have to continue in their trying and exhausting position of anticipation. What is then to happen to these eleven thousand stranded immigrants toward whom a certain measure of responsibility has already been admitted?

Congress at its very last session, before adjourning, passed the resolution that will remain in the immigration annals as an act of human mercy, decided to admit those who have already embarked for the United States and would become victims of the new law when they would see land again. Will Congress take up and deliberate in the same spirit on the question of these stranded refugees when it convenes?

* * *

General Plutarco Elias Calles, President-elect of Mexico, leader of the Mexican working classes, influenced by an organization that would correspond more to the tendencies of a labor party than to an extremely socialistic party, left a cheerful message during his stay in New York before his departure for Europe.

When he assumes the reins of the government in Mexico, he stated he would be prepared to ask his government to grant a large tract of arable land to Jewish settlers, with proper facilities and concessions. The Mexican solution of the Jewish immigration problem is not a new proposal. It has been taken up, discussed and even abandoned already two years ago. However, Mexico is the typical land of changes and the sudden arrival in power of what is termed to be a Mexican Labor Party may offer some new aspect to the problem. General Plutarco Elias Calles is not only interested in Jewish colonization work in Mexico, he has also a "good eye for business." According to the interviewer of the Jewish Telegraphic Agency, the Mexican President-elect stated that Mexico under a labor regime, where a system of cooperative guilds could provide employment for tens of thousands of Jews in various branches of industry, offers a great possibility.

"It would be at the same time," the President stated, "a distinct benefit to Mexico to manufacture within its own boundaries many articles and products that it is compelled today to import from other countries. A sum in the neighborhood of $2,000,000 could give a start to this movement and furnish employment possibilities for Jewish immigrants, a start that is similar to the beginning of the large Jewish industries in the United States."

An invitation to Jewish industrial workers with an allowance for a possible drifting of a certain percentage into individual enterprises is a new and sensible proposition. It ought to be taken up and first of all thoroughly investigated. The nearness of Mexico to the large American Jewish community, with its possible connections and credit facilities, would no doubt present an incentive to the home-seeking class of Jewish workers and artisans in the devastated regions of at-present economic barrenness.

Here I think the work of the Independent Order of B'nai B'rith carried on in Mexico in recent years could offer good material for the forming of a sound judgment on the matter. Just recently this benevolent Order appropriated a sum of $20,000 for the purpose of establishing a branch office in Mexico City and the enlargement of the activities [there]. Those who have experience in that country will have to be consulted first.

* * *

Hans Herzl, the little son of his great father, after a week's search in the populous metropolitan city of London, came out from his hiding place. In a letter to the *London Daily Telegraph* he confirms the sad news that was reported about him.

"It is true that I was baptized into the Christian Church on July 20 in Vienna," Hans writes.

But Hans is resentful. He denies the correctness of all the other particulars reported by the Jewish Telegraphic Agency. What could be incorrect, since his principal incorrectness was unfortunately correctly reported?

It is incorrect that his action was a result of a mental depression? But was it ever recorded that anyone else under similar circumstances admitted his mental depression? You certainly would not expect Hans to admit that! Necessarily this must be left to the judgment of those who know more about it.

If you will search through the pages of the histories of all peoples, you will not find the names of great men's sons being as brilliant as their fathers. We do not know anything of the sons of Moses, Maimonides, Plato, Aristotle, Caesar, Luther, Spinoza, Copernicus or Newton. The majority of great men had no sons. Those who were born did not live up to their names. It seems as if nature takes a rest for a few generations after it has exerted itself at the heights of genius.

How painful it is, however, to recollect the [following] entry in Herzl's diary: "June 10, 1904, was the 7th birthday of my Hans. I make a date out of the birthday of my good Hans. May he, healthy and happy, grow to be a strong man and continue my work!"

The Chicago Chronicle, September 12, 1924

His Serene Highness, Nicholas Horthy de Nagybanya, Regent of Hungary, willed, on the 8th day of February, to confer upon Felix M. Warburg the Cross of the Hungarian Red

Cross Decoration. On August 29th, Louis Alexy, Hungarian Acting Consul-General in New York, presented the Insignia and Statutes of the decoration to the President of the American Jewish Joint Distribution Committee.

The President of the American Jewish Joint Distribution Committee, decorated by Admiral Horthy?! Were the news to be made known in Hungary, the Hungarian Jews would read it with amazement.

Admiral Horthy, since the collapse of the Austro-Hungarian Empire, the Revolution and the Reign of Terror, is quite a familiar name, but it has an unharmonious sound to Jewish ears. The amazement would be a natural one. The protector of the "awakening Magyars," the head of a government that has to its "credit" one of the most devitalizing policies with regard to the Jewish population of Hungary, an element that was state-building and responsible for a large portion of native Hungarian commerce, industry and culture, bestowing honors upon one of the greatest Americans and Jews, Felix M. Warburg, the protector of all needy victims of the same government and many others.

Hungary has recently obtained a loan from the International Monetary Market. Felix M. Warburg is the head of Kuhn, Loeb & Company. Is there any connection? Those who look for the motive of every action would form such a suspicion. Some of us are inclined to sense politics in any government will or decision. However, the decoration was granted, not [to] Felix M. Warburg of Kuhn, Loeb & Company, but to Felix M. Warburg, President of the American Jewish Joint Distribution Committee. Has the government of the "awakening Magyars" awakened to the great benefactory role that the American Joint Distribution Committee has played in all the war-stricken and devastated countries where Jews were victimized by the resurrected nations and most of all Hungary? Nothing of the kind.

American public opinion, including American Jewish public opinion, knows very little of a great action undertaken by many American organizations, including the Joint Distribution Committee, in favor of a great number of war prisoners. At the head of this great humanitarian work stood Felix M. Warburg. It is for this reason that his Serene Highness deemed it fitting to bestow distinction upon the President of the Joint Distribution Committee.

It's a pity that so little is known of that work. I believe that a few details ought to be told now.

Those who had occasion to find themselves in the fatal years of 1914 and 1915 on the fertile plains along the Rivers Prut and Vistula, witnessing the struggle of the Austro-Hungarian and Russian armies, knew how great was the number of Austro-Hungarian soldiers who were "taken" prisoners. These prisoners, fortunate in the eyes of their [dead] comrades, were hurriedly shipped off into the distant and snowy plains of Siberia. Thousands were their number. The collapse of the Russian Empire, followed by the ruin of the Central Powers, the signature of the Versailles Treaty and the chaos in Russia, sealed the fate of those war prisoners. The spoils of the Russian army were abandoned in the snows of Siberia, with no one to take care of them and no one to repatriate them, doomed to death through starvation and typhus.

A portion of these prisoners were privileged. They belonged to the same Austro-Hungarian Army, but they were Czechs and the allied governments have provided means of transportation for their return to their homes or again to the front of battle. Different, however, was the lot of the nationals of Turkey, Austria-Hungary and others whose governments were unable to either take care of them at their place of exile or bring them home to their families. Thousands perished.

Echoes of this misery reached America. Fifteen American organizations with the American Red Cross and the American Jewish Joint Distribution Committee formed a

Siberian Repatriation War Fund. This fund assumed the task of rescuing these prisoners and fulfilling the obligation that rested upon their bankrupt governments. Besides the American Red Cross, which contributed to that fund $500,000, the American Jewish Joint Distribution Committee headed the list of contributors with its $25,000.

Felix M. Warburg was elected Chairman of the fund and, together with Lewis L. Strauss and Capt. Rosenbluth in Siberia, performed the major portion of that tremendous task. The main beneficiaries of this American generosity were Hungarians. Not less than 8,000 Hungarian war prisoners were repatriated on a route encircling almost the globe at a cost of nearly $1,000,000, after prolonged negotiations with the various governments, with almost unbelievable efforts and difficulties.

"We have sent an ambassador of the best American ideals into Europe in the person of each of the men whom we have been privileged to help and we have left an ineradicable testimonial of American Good Faith in the troubled Far East that will be more enduring than a thousand diplomatic declarations of our honest intentions," said Felix M. Warburg in speaking of this work.

In the person of Felix M. Warburg both American and Jewish generosity was recognized and honored by the Hungarian government.

Will this marvelous humanitarian work remain long in the memory of the "awakening Magyars"?

The Chicago Chronicle, September 26, 1924

The Skehinah Wanderers – as early as 1,700 years ago one of the Jewish chroniclers recorded with both pride and resignation the wandering of the Skehinah to and from ten successive centers.

What is the Skehinah? Every generation has had its own Skehinah, representing in the final analysis the genius of the nation. Since the Kabbalah, beginning with the twelfth century, became deeply rooted in the Jewish mind, the Skehinah grew into a conception of the all-embracing, supreme intelligence of the universe. So it happened that the Skehinah was not satisfied with ten changes of its center: it continuously accompanied the Jewish people in their wanderings. Jerusalem, supplanted by Baghdad, Baghdad by Cordoba, followed by Montpelier, Wurms, Lublin, Vilna and again the German Jewish communities.

If Skehinah is to be taken as the expression of the thing that is peculiar to the Jews, it is nothing but the study of the nation's genius, the search into the past, the understanding of its literature.

German Jewry has to its credit the creation of a modern system of Jewish research, the clarification of the darkest corners in Jewish history, the rendering accessible of the sources of old inspiration. It produced men like Geiger, Zunz and Jost, who laid the foundation for the *Wissenschaft des Judenthum*. It is owing to the scientific efforts of German Jewry that the monumental building of Jewish history could be erected and that the romance of Jewish transformations and adaptations could be retold in a precise manner. Much criticism has been voiced against those who occupy themselves with historical research and confine their interest wholly to the past. However, no real understanding of present-day Jewish life and no possibility for a continuation of Jewish thought is imaginable if this work is neglected.

It would seem that in the last few years this has stopped. The war, with its attending impoverishment, uprooted the old established Jewish centers. Scientific research into Jewish learning stopped; publications of this nature were suspended.

The Skehinah of Jewish research has now landed in America through Cincinnati. It should be sincerely welcomed by American Jews.

The first Hebrew Union College annual, containing many valuable contributions towards Jewish lore and philosophy, has appeared under the editorship of David Philopson, K. Kohler, Jacob Z. Lauterbach, Julian Morgenstern, David Neumark and William Rosenau. The nature of the newly issued annual cannot better be expressed than in the words of the chairman of the board of editors: "It offers convincing testimony to the universality of Jewish learning. Here all diversions of opinion and party merge in the friendly fellowship of true scholarly endeavor, and all geographical and national lines are obliterated."

Indeed they are.

* * *

Both Reform and Orthodox seem to be determined to make rapid steps in the advancement of American Judaism.

The Rabbi Isaac Elchanan Seminary, a strictly Orthodox rabbinical seminary, now located on the East Side of New York, with very poor accommodations, has bought a site for the erection of a modern college building for its students. It is stated that the Seminary intends to construct a building that will be large enough to accommodate 1,000 students, with classrooms, study rooms, an auditorium, a senior high school, a library and a dormitory. There will also be a campus with playgrounds. This should be encouraged. A Yeshiva with a campus and playgrounds adapted to the tastes and aspirations of American Jewish youth is a promising innovation.

Perhaps the time is not distant when the prediction of many close observers of Jewish life in America will come true. American Jews are perhaps approaching the period when, besides dollars for the material relief of distressed communities, it will send to other Jewish communities spiritual encouragement and highly learned leaders as well.

The Chicago Chronicle, December 26, 1924

The American press carried the names of four Jewish men who passed away within a fortnight: Samuel Gompers, President of the American Federation of Labor; Julius Kahn, Chairman of the Committee on Foreign Affairs in the House of Representatives; August Belmont, millionaire subway builder and sportsman; Dr. David Neumark, Professor of Jewish Philosophy at the Hebrew Union College, Cincinnati; and a fifth, a stranger within our gates, Rabbi Isaac Friedman, exalted king of the Sadagora court.

That August Belmont, although not a Jew in name was a Jew in origin, is known. When the provisions of his will, disposing of a fortune of from twenty to forty million dollars were made public, it was clear that his interest in racing surpassed all other interests. No sum of any considerable importance was bequeathed by him to any public fund.

The line of demarcation between the Schoenberg family, from which he descended, and the Rothschild family, whom his father represented in America, is distinctly drawn by the provisions of this will.

The sportsmanship of August Belmont was much spoken of in the metropolitan press. The sportsmanship of Rabbi Isaac Friedman is less known. A few paragraphs on the subject will be of interest.

A drama of deep human concern came to a tragic conclusion with the death on East Broadway of the young Sadagora Rabbi.

In the history of the Hassidic movement, the name "Rabbi of Sadagora" is an outstanding one.

Hassidism, originally a movement of the common people with many elements of revolutionary attempt and protest against the stagnation of form and content in Jewish life of the eighteenth century, based its conception on simplicity of life and insisted on once again introducing enthusiasm and love into Jewish life. God has to be worshipped not in fear of punishment, but in admiration of his majesty, out of love for the Creator, out of the feeling of nearness of the omnipotent and omnipresent Supreme Power.

Insisting on freedom of social intercourse, on real fellowship and brotherhood and joint, joyous worship, Hassidism, at the time, introduced the cult of the leader, the power of personality. The struggle that the leaders of the Hassidic movement had with the old established Rabbinical authorities soon brought about with the Hassidic leaders a drastic change: they drifted from simplicity to asceticism.

Israel Ryschiner, grandfather of Rabbi Isaac Friedman, and descendent of the founders of the Hassidic movement, then revolutionized Hassidic life. Asceticism is not necessary for gaining happiness in this world, or nearness to the omnipotent power. Luxury is conducive to joy, joy is the state of mind necessary for real nearness to God, was the theory he introduced into practice.

A palace, surpassing the castles of the Russian and Polish nobility in the vicinity, was erected in Ryschin, a little town in Podol. A court in royal grandeur was maintained. When the "Ryschiner" had to journey, a courtage of sixteen horses was employed, a luxury enjoyed by only the richest landowners and nobility in Imperial Russia. The period being the time immediately after the French Revolution, the Russian Government, in fear of a revolutionary movement, sensed danger in the "royal behavior" of the Hassidic Rabbi. Arrested, released and again arrested, the royal Rabbi succeeded in transferring his court and establishing his grandeur in Sadagora, then Austria.

Sadagora, a small town, was soon famous as the seat of the Sadagora Court. The fate of many Jewish communities in Galicia and the provinces near the Austro-Russian frontier was dependent upon the orders of the Sadagora "court." Attacks of great intensity were made against the prestige and power of the Sadagora Hassidic ruler, but Sadagora remained in power. In fact Sadagora, on the death of Rabbi Israel, branched out into several sections, growing with the number of descendants of the dynasty. The World War checked this unique development of Hassidic royalty.

Ten years after Austria's ultimatum to Serbia, the Rabbi of Sadagora dies on East Broadway in poverty, and congregations seek arbitration before a Rabbinical court as to which should be permitted to bury him, so that a number of high-priced graves might be reserved.

The Australian Jewish Herald, February 26, 1925

The fact that the crossword puzzle, which requires at least a fair knowledge of spelling and something approaching an average intelligence, became so popular is in itself a great puzzle that could be explained only by the wizards of American newspaperdom. This puzzle is particularly difficult of solution when one remembers the result of the intelligence tests during the War.

Those who look at every matter for its Jewish angle were not disappointed also in the crossword puzzle problem, which, thanks to the epidemic nature of the puzzle, crossed the ocean, where it was discovered that the crossword puzzle was originally a Jewish invention made by none other than our old acquaintance, Abraham Ibn Ezra, poet, astrologist, world trotter and epigramist.

However, here there is another puzzle that awaits solution. Why was it necessary for the crossword puzzle to travel across the ocean to find its Hebrew origin is really difficult to explain. Why America, with its great number of rabbis, Jewish journalists, scholars, having among its treasures the best Jewish libraries and manuscripts, could not find the Hebrew origin of the [crossword] puzzle is to be wondered at.

A superficial knowledge of medieval Hebrew literature, nay, even a knowledge only of the prayer book for the High Holidays, would indicate that the form of crossword puzzling was quite familiar in Hebrew literature and liturgy.

As a matter of fact, the majority of the special hymns and songs for the principal holidays have a crossword puzzle, at least one way down. The first letter of every line is always to be connected with the following letter from the beginning to the end of the song or hymn, and preserves a complete record of the name, surname and city of the author. The main evidence for the existence of the first Hebrew Paiton, Eliezer Ha-Kalir, was preserved chiefly through this cross-wording of his few and beautiful hymns.

In fact, most of the Hebrew poetry written in Spain during the Hispano-Jewish Golden Epoch was based, similarly to the Arabic poetry of that time, not so much on rhythm as on the number of letters contained in the verse, coupled with cross-wording at the beginning of the line. The Cabalistic literature developed subsequently had a particular fondness for the playing with words, and it claimed that the entire universe was merely the result of a combination of certain letters. The playing with letters went so far that the belief was held that with certain new combination of letters, [whole] worlds – spiritual and material – could be made and destroyed. Many a letter-enthusiast, it is reported, fasted for years in order to be privileged to learn some mysterious combination of 72 letters expressing the name of the Omnipotent Power.

The Notarikon (the Hebrew development of the Latin "Notaricum") and the Gematrioth were another, much earlier and much more serious manifestation of the crossword fad.

It does not, however, seem too safe to go into the history of cross-wording and letter puzzles, as is evidenced by the fact that the brilliant crossword puzzles of the 12th, 13th, and 14th centuries were not altogether appreciated even in the prayer books, and it took some scholar from overseas to bring to the attention of American Jews the Hebrew origin of the almighty Crossword Puzzle.

* * *

Lord Robert Cecil, British statesman, champion of the League of Nations idea, winner of the Wilson Peace Prize of 25,000 dollars, in an address at the Hotel Astor, relating the achievements of the League of Nations, credited it with the securing of rights for national minorities in Eastern Europe. That the protection of the rights of minorities should be taken into consideration and cared for after the conclusion of a war is not a new international practice. The latest precedent that existed before the War in this regard was Article 44 of the Treaty with Romania signed at the Berlin Congress. In this Article, Romania had pledged itself to secure citizenship rights to its Jewish population, but it never fulfilled its pledge.

The commonly called "national minority treaties," in the actual text of the supplement to the Versailles Peace Treaty, speaking of the national minorities in the various countries, resorted rather to a long term. In the treaties, the national minorities are described as "religious, language, and cultural minorities," [which is] rather a vague and diplomatic term for such a burning question as the national-minorities-question represents in the various countries of Central and Eastern Europe.

In this regard, the League of Nations has really an achievement to its credit. As to the execution of rights, it seems that it has not gone any further than the Berlin Congress. The situation of the Ruthenian-Lithuanian minority in Poland, and the discrimination "enjoyed" by the Jewish minorities in Latvia, Lithuania, Poland and Romania is, just because of this achievement, a constant challenge to the League of Nations.

The Chicago Chronicle, March 6, 1925
The Ohio Jewish Chronicle, March 6, 1925

A small item slipped through the metropolitan press, probably unobserved by many readers.

The Young Men's Christian Association in the City of New York, incorporated about fifty years ago, caused the introduction of a bill into the New York State Legislature to permit the amendment of the incorporation charter of the institution.

Those connected with the management of the New York Y openly stated that in the future, when the charter is amended, they would allow non-Protestants to become members of this institution, not exceeding thirteen percent of the general membership.

One might say that the incorporation charter of any charitable or social institution is a matter of concern only to those who are interested in it. I believe, however, that in the circle of those who should be interested in this seemingly unimportant application for an amendment, a great number of our own folks ought to be included.

The Young Men's Christian Association and the Young Women's Christian Association are not unfamiliar names in the households of American Jews. The numerous Jewish membership applications in the YMCA and YWCA, in the early stages of development, had no doubt their justification and were even desirable. It was the desire of mingling in the American environment and a not-to-be-suppressed wish to engage in wholesome sport and social entertainment conducted along spiritual lines. Although the Young Men's Hebrew Association, modeled after the similar Christian association, endeavored to create the same environment with a Jewish background, only a small group at first heard the delicate call that is dictated by the maxim that the best social interests of the various communal and racial groups, although they may be a part of as fair-minded and great a nation as the American nation, is best served by an institution that bases its social activities and educational efforts on the heritage of that particular group and in conformity with its traditions on the proper background.

The delicate, but not less determined hint of the New York City Young Men's Christian Association ought to be taken in its proper light. It would be a misunderstanding to see in it a kind of social ostracism. It is only just that the religious and racial groups serve the interests of their members. The Jewish communities are sufficiently equipped at present to take care of their own. The Jewish Community Center movement, which is a more proper aim and natural consequence of American Jewish development along the line of social and educational endeavours, will only benefit by it.

Although not listed as a Jewish contribution, the American Jewish Community may with pride read of the many interesting details of the Three Million Dollar scholarship foundation established by Simon Guggenheim, President of the American Smelting and Refining Company and former United States Senator.

All the characteristics attached to the establishment of this great endowment fund point to the Jewish tradition from which it emanates.

Simon Guggenheim's son, when he was eighteen years of age, prepared for Harvard University and intended to undertake scholastic studies in European universities. Unfortunately, premature death destroyed this plan. This tragic event in the Guggenheim family prompted the establishment of a fund that is to enable no less than fifty scholars, without distinction of race, color, or creed, without distinction of social status, without distinction to subject of study, to go abroad for the purpose of continuing and perfecting themselves in their particular branch of study. The sum of $2,500 is to be given annually to each of the appointees for this purpose.

No people cherishes the memory of its departed dear ones as do the Jewish families. Three times a year Yiskor services are held. No people attaches as much importance to life under every circumstance as the Jewish people and no one feels more intense tragedy when a promising life is prematurely cut off.

Both the deeply human motive and the broadly human purpose of the foundation indicate its Jewish origin, although the Guggenheim family have contributed little towards specifically Jewish philanthropies.

The provisions of this endowment, destined as they are to further scholarship, will no doubt be of assistance also to those scholars who devote their lives to Jewish scientific subjects.

Jewish Transcript, March 13, 1925

The fourth visit to America of Dr. Chaim Weizmann, president of the World Zionist Organization, is a matter of intense interest not only to Zionists, but also to non-Zionists.

The reception rendered to him this time, and the messages delivered on this occasion, differed from those on his previous visits. Little was left of the pomp, grandeur, and high phrases so frequently used in the effort to enlist the cooperation of the most important Jewish community in the world – American Jewry – in the process of rebuilding Palestine as a Jewish center.

Enthusiasm has played a great role in the history of all nations, when these nations had to lay the foundations for their existence or to start out on the road of cultural development. It is the driving power that gives the start. Soon, however, the actual realities of human life, the complex problems of hardships, disabilities and obstacles have to be faced and calmly dealt with. Since the war, Zionism has passed its enthusiastic flame of youth. It has grown to manhood and is facing immense tasks.

Dr. Weizmann, in delivering his message on the occasion of his fourth visit to the United States, could do no better than to state the facts. And stating facts of Jewish realities in Europe means reviewing the economic, cultural, political and ethical conditions prevailing on the vast space from the Rhine to the Volga, where nine million Jews are on the verge of economic destruction.

* * *

Leaders of men, as the recent record of the stormy period during the world war has amply shown, often depend upon their ability to summarize the situation confronting them and coin one phrase that would bring home the command of the hour.

"Taxed out of existence" is the remarkably well-coined statement made by Dr. Weizmann at the Carnegie Hall meeting in describing the situation of the Jewish communities from the Volga to the Rhine, particularly in Poland, Latvia, Lithuania, Romania and Soviet Russia. A feeling of security has developed lately owing to the fact that reports of severe anti-Jewish excesses have begun to arrive with less frequency than in previous times, or owing to the fact that we have stopped reading such reports.

There is, however, a stronger machinery of extermination directed against the large Jewish communities at work. The difference is only that the wheels of this powerful machine, frequently operated by the states, is well-oiled and its grinding is not so loud that it can be heard across the ocean.

* * *

A report of the Bureau of Immigration of the United States Department of Labor for the period of July to December 1924 states that of a total of 147,737 new immigrants to this country, 4,975 were Jewish. Of a total of 28,098 immigrants to the United States during the month of December, 1151 were Jewish. The total growth of the Jewish community in the United States for this period through immigration, counting those who left the country, amounted to 5,835.

The National Bakers and Confectionery Workers Union in the City of New York called a conference of kindred organizations for March 1st to consider the critical situation that has arisen in the Jewish bakery industry in the City of New York.

Is there any connection between these two news items?

You will no doubt be inclined to say most emphatically "No."

Upon close examination and through a study of the undercurrent in American economic and social life, the connection will become more than apparent, even highly instructive and characteristic.

The story revolves around a loaf of rye bread.

Among the many contributions of the various immigrant groups to the manifold forms of American life, the loaf of rye bread remained an epic that awaited telling: rye bread, the favorite food of the Jewish middle classes in the various East and Central European countries, was introduced into American city life as a non-quota immigrant. Pardon – there was no quota as yet dreamed of.

Baking as an industry, relieving the American housewife of this trying task and laying the foundation for her higher social status, paving the way for her political equality and suffrage, was introduced by immigrants fifty years ago. These were the Germans who were the best bakers on the European continent. Upon their heels followed the Jewish baking industry in New York City. Galicia, the poor strip of land that had not enough corn to make bread salable to a poverty-stricken population, exported to these shores great numbers of bakery hands who felt it their duty to feed the hungry ones. Not only hands were sent – also some heads arrived and a great industry developed.

One of the foundations of this industry was the novelty of rye bread, the favorite food of the Jewish immigrant masses. In the European countries where the Jews occupied a central position between the peasants (the lower class that fed itself upon black bread) and the nobility that was fed on French rolls or German "Kaiser rolls," the economical Jewish housewife chose the golden mean. A compromise was brought about in the shape of the rye bread loaf, a kind of bread that neither entirely black nor entirely white.

Since the closing of the gates to immigration and the shifting of the second generation into professional and business occupations, the rye bread is about to make its exit. The rapidity of the Americanization process of the Jewish immigrant groups in New York City can be ascertained by this phenomenon, affecting a sphere of dietary habits that are the least susceptible to change.

The annals of Jewish cookery and baking have witnessed the ascent and descent of

Egyptian bread, the Hamantaschen, the Challah and the Kreplach, and many other kinds of foods and dishes with the change of times, tastes and customs. Further developments concerning the rye bread can be watched quite calmly.

Has not the Bible said, "Not on bread alone the man liveth"?

The Jewish Criterion, March 20, 1925

It was during the last session of the Permanent Mandates Commission that examined the execution of the Palestine Mandate, that one of the distinguished members rose to ask of Sir Herbert Samuel, High Commissioner of Palestine, an explanation of a subject that he thought was most important and needed enlightening.

During the discussion, mention was made several times of the Jewish "Back to [the] Land Movement." There is an obvious misstatement in this expression, the distinguished member claims. So far as is known, the Jews are not very fond of engaging in farming and therefore there cannot be any back to the land movement.

Sir Herbert Samuel, who was thoroughly cross-examined by the Commission on all phases of Palestine development, and on more than one occasion during the meeting served as an expert on Jewish life, furnished an explanation to the Commission.

The Jewish people is a reminiscent people and its memories date back many centuries to when agriculture was the main basis of Jewish existence in Palestine and elsewhere, he stated.

What a pity that the report of the Jewish Agricultural Society of America, covering its twenty-five years of activities had not yet, at the time of the Commission meeting, been published.

According to this report the number of Jewish farmers in the United States has increased in the last twenty-five years from several hundred to 75,000. The amount of land cultivated by Jewish farmers in the United States is no less than one million acres. The products produced by Jewish farmers in all parts of the Union include all branches of agriculture: wheat, corn, oranges, tobacco and poultry.

Petaluma, the "World's Egg Basket," the pride of California farmers, contains a considerable number of Jews. One witty observer, upon returning from California, stated that if the author of the "Song of Songs" (whether it was King Solomon or not), had he seen the poultry industry on the sun-kissed hills of Petaluma, would easily have compared his beloved bride, not to the "Sheep flocking down the Gilead," but to the poultry feeding on the Jewish farms.

Perhaps the distinguished member of the Permanent Mandates Commission in Geneva would have been spared the anxiety over the correctness of the Jewish "Back to the Land Movement." Another twenty-five years' activities of the Jewish Agricultural Society in America may be helpful in removing many other anxieties in different directions.

Fifty thousand Jews in the United States are adherents of what is commonly known as Christian Science. That people who are in mental and physical distress should be willing to accept a doctrine that offers relief is and should not be surprising. The history of religion shows that all religious sects had their beginning in offering relief and healing.

Dr. Albert Einstein, the author of the relativity theory, once was asked to summarize, in a scientific manner, the relativity of Jewish life to the life of other nations. He put it in a very descriptive and convincing way. It was, he said, the well-known phenomenon of mimicry. Birds living in tropical forests usually grow feathers the colors of which are identical with the leaves and grass of the surrounding landscape.

Dr. Clifton Levy, although not as famous as Einstein, has apparently set out to give additional proof to Einstein's definition of the mimicry. Since there is a powerful Church of Christian Science, and since there are many persons of Jewish origin seeking, in distress, relief from what they believe to be religion and science combined, why should there not be a Jewish Science?

Well, there is a Jewish Science, Rabbi Levy claims, and has found a number of followers.

There is no harm in this and no one can resent it. The only resentment that might be voiced is his reference to Maimonides, the clear thinker, philosopher and physician of the Twelfth Century.

What Maimonides attempted to do was reconcile the Greek philosophy dominant in his time and the natural science advanced by the Jews and Arabs in Arabic Spain with the Bible. To declare him as authority for a Jewish Science can only be equaled with an attempt to prove that Copernicus paved the way for the League of Nations idea.

American Jewish World, April 3, 1925

A change of tremendous dimensions seems to be taking place in this country. From the worship of the idol of Success, attention seems to be concentrated more and more on education in all its shapes and forms.

If all signs are not misleading – and they cannot be misleading since the matter is gaining the attention of such practical men as members of the various state legislatures, belonging to the national political parties – the supreme question in American life today is the problem of education. From California to New York, and from New Jersey to Oregon, the best minds are occupied with this problem.

* * *

Representatives of Catholics, Episcopalians, Congregationalists, Methodists and Jews in New York City, at a meeting held at the office of the City Superintendent of Public Schools, resolved to launch a movement that could be termed "Back to the Ten Commandments."

For this purpose they propose that the Ten Commandments be read every day in the New York City public schools. The difficulties that they meet are two-fold: first, it interferes with the principle of the public school being non-sectarian, and although the Ten Commandments are common to all sects, the interpretation might become sectarian. Secondly, the reading of the Ten Commandments to minors without comment is a service that cannot be sufficiently appreciated by the children and cannot make much of an impression on them. To be sure, several of the Commandments are not explainable to children.

* * *

In New Jersey, the matter had advanced a little further than a pious desire for the mere reading of the Ten Commandments. There, a bill pending in the legislature would introduce religious instruction in the schools, which is presently non-sectarian. However, New Jersey Jews at present don't worry about it, since the measure has been postponed for the next legislative session.

* * *

In California, the matter stands a little different. There, a bill introduced by Assemblyman Miller would introduce a system of excusing school children three hours a week from regular school work to attend religious instruction outside the school building. The bill, opposed by the Western Board of Jewish Ministers and the Seventh Day Adventists was, as is reported, pleaded against on behalf of the homogeneity of the public school system and the constitutional principle of separation of church and state. Joyfully it is reported that the bill has been tabled.

* * *

In Wisconsin, the educational committee of the assembly introduced a bill that would require the obligatory recital at the beginning of every school day of the Lord's Prayer. Although nothing in the prayer could be objected to by any religious denomination, the fact of its being obligatory might be unwelcome to those parents who not be affiliated with any religious congregation and by orthodox Jewish parents since its text is taken from the gospel according to Matthew.

* * *

Altogether different stands the matter in Oregon. There a law enacted in 1922, and, as was alleged, sponsored by the Ku Klux Klan, makes the attendance of any child in the public schools obligatory to such an extent that the existence of all private and parochial schools would be unlawful.

The Sisters of the Holy Names of Jesus and Mary, a Catholic institution, led the fight against the bill. When the federal district court declared the measure unconstitutional, the battle, which as it seems will be of a decisive nature, began. Governor Pearce and Attorney General Van Winkle appealed to the United States Supreme Court in Washington. To the defense of the decision of the federal district court came the Sisters of the Holy Names of Jesus and Mary, the Hill Military Academy, an Oregon institution that has attacked the validity of the anti-private school law, the North Pacific Union Conference of the Seventh Day Adventists, the Domestic and Foreign Missionary Society of the Protestant Episcopal Church, and Mr. Louis Marshall on behalf of the American Jewish Committee. The legal talent engaged holds the promise of an interesting constitutional battle.

The interest, however, of the Jewish public opinion in America is, no doubt, not in agreement with the idea of establishing Jewish parochial schools. Expressions to this effect have been made on more than one occasion. On the other hand, however, the prohibition of the existence of any private or parochial school would be a serious attack upon the principle of liberty and even on the principle of free education. Students of educational systems in various countries have for a long time given considerable thought to the question whether the general public school system does not bring more harm than good.

The law of the public school system frees from attendance every child who is abnormal or subnormal or ill, but it does not free from attendance those children who are super-normal and it is just those [students] whose education needs particular care so that they may not be retarded by the average mentality of the class. However, the question could not be more clearly and forcibly represented than it has been done by Louis Marshall, that vigilant spirit of American Jewry, in his brief filed in the case with the Supreme Court of the United States. Louis Marshall says:

"This legislation is clearly calculated to confer upon the public schools a monopoly of education. That would tend with absolute certainty to the suppression of all religious instruction, the importance of which cannot be minimized. Under our system of government the state is powerless, as it should be, to give religious instruction. That is a right and a duty that rests upon parents, upon the churches and the synagogues. If private, parochial and denominational schools are, however, to be deprived of the right to educate children, and parents are forbidden to send their children to such schools, then we shall be in precisely the same situation as that which now prevails in Russia. There it is strictly forbidden under severe penalties to impart religious instruction of any kind to children until they reach the age of eighteen years.

"Fundamentally, the questions in these cases are: May the liberty to teach and to learn be restricted? Shall such liberty be dependent on the will of the majority? Shall such majority be permitted to dictate to parents and to children where and by whom instruction shall be given? If such power can be asserted, then it will lead inevitably to the stifling of thought. If the will of a temporary majority may thus control, then it is conceivable that it may prohibit the teaching of sciences, of the classics, of modern languages and literature, of art, and of nature study. A majority might reach the conclusion that the teaching of the Darwinian theory, of the philosophy of Spinoza or the ideas of Montesquieu, or of Jeremy Bentham or of John Stuart Mill, or of Emerson, should be prohibited. Today a majority may seek to eliminate the private or parochial school. Tomorrow it may attempt to compel parents to send their children to such schools. In some parts of this country, a majority, if it possessed the power, would unquestionably limit instruction in the public schools to the Three Rs. New York has recently witnessed an attempt to eliminate from the handbooks of history used in the public school any reference to England that is not to its discredit, and any reference to America that, although truthful, did not assert that it had at all times attained absolute perfection and was thus immune to criticism.

"Recognizing in the main the great merit of our public school system, it is nevertheless unthinkable that public schools alone shall by legislative compulsion, rather than by their own merits, be made the only medium of education in this country. Such a policy would speedily lead to their deterioration. The absence of the right of selection would at once lower the standards of education. If the children of the country are to be educated in accordance with an undeviating rule of uniformity and by a single method, then eventually our nation would consist of mechanical robots and standardized Babbitts.

"Proceeding on the theory that seeks to eliminate private parochial schools, the Legislature might as well compel all of the inhabitants of the land to subscribe to the same newspaper, to attend the same church, to become members of the same political party, and to join the same lodge. Indeed, it would be less of an invasion of liberty to do any of these things than to say to parents that, regardless of their ambitions and aspirations for their children, regardless of the love and affection that they bear for them, regardless of their conscientious beliefs, respecting the duty that they owe for the ethical, moral and religious rearing of their children, the State may come in and take away from them that sacred right that involves the performance of that high duty that they themselves regard as owing to their children and to future generations, that of zealously caring for their education. Our children do not belong to the State, nor is their future to be shaped according to the will of any casual majority of the electorate. As a rule the poorest of parents are better qualified to rear children than the best politician or professional agitator could possibly be."

The Ohio Jewish Chronicle, July 24, 1925

An ancient custom in the ancient synagogue has it that, when the reading of the weekly portion of the Bible is concluded and the last verse of the final chapter read, immediately the reading of the first verse of the first chapter of the Pentateuch follows. This is a formality that at the moment makes no particular impression but that has a greater significance. It is a pledge that the reading, or the unity between the people of the Book with the Book, must continue.

More than several years have elapsed since the last $14,000 campaign for Jewish relief work was successfully concluded under the management of David A. Brown. The ancient custom of the synagogue was at that time not observed, and it seemed for a while to the American Jewish public as if the "reading" of the Jewish plight and needs would not be resumed.

Here we are, however, witnessing the first steps of the necessary preparations for the second "reading," by the same "reader," David A. Brown.

This time the chord touched is not merely the sentimental appeal of a piteous situation but reconstruction.

* * *

Following what could be termed a flying trip to Russia in the midst of a tour around the world, David A. Brown had occasion to obtain an inside glimpse of the real situation of Russian Jewry under the regime of the Soviet Government, which promised with thunder and stone the arrival of not a "heavenly kingdom on earth," but an earthly kingdom under a Communist heaven. In this process the bulk of the Jewish masses in the territories comprising the former Russian Empire were, in the nature of things, not only ruined by war, massacred by pogromists and crushed by the social upheaval, but they became a mass of people who no present and with no hope for the future. The economic aspect of the Jewish problem in Russia that had been "burning" since the days of Alexander the First presents itself now, after the death of Lenin the First, in its real acuteness.

What is to be done?

The answers come from Russian Jewry itself. It began to "move" and to transmigrate, to avoid the sharp pointed rays of the Communistic sky, into more stable and protecting shadows of the all-blessed earth. They wished to become farmers.

And although many may object to this plan for one reason or another, the enthusiasm, magnetism, dynamic energy and invigorating optimism of David A. Brown dispels the objections and holds a promise of success.

* * *

There could have been no better demonstration than at the last luncheon given by David A. Brown to representatives of the Jewish press in New York City.

* * *

Of the many strange words that became popular before and after the war, the pure king's English word "pledge" gained its full significance in the process of Jewish war relief collections.

Many a man and woman responded to appeals. Many found it in line with their sentiments and status in the community to attend public meetings where one or another famous speaker addressed the audience on the plight and needs of Jews in other countries. Many readily made pledges. Now it is interesting to know that no less a sum than $1,500,000 of unfulfilled pledges was recovered by the American Jewish Relief Committee in the last two years through civil action. A decision of the Appellate Division maintained the opinion that the maker of a pledge is legally obligated under the laws of contract. It is reassuring to know this in view of the forthcoming $15,000,000 campaign.

Reassuring also is the news coming from Paris by cable that the question of the stranded Jewish refugees in various European countries will finally be settled. The American Jewish Emergency Committee on Refugees, the Jewish Colonization Association and the United Jewish Emigration Committee of Berlin will create one agency to deal with this problem. A fund of $5,000,000, of which the American Jewish Emergency Committee on Refugees will subscribe $340,000.

* * *

Count Alexander Skrzynski, Polish Minister of Foreign Affairs, has an excellent reputation in his own country and not an altogether bad one in other countries. He is unique among statesmen in having a "good press." No matter what government was in power in Poland, Count Skrzynski remained in the foreign office. He is credited with the new orientation in Polish politics, the new aim to create a better feeling with neighboring peoples to make friends. He is credited with having concluded no less than five arbitration treaties.

On his arrival in the United States, he made extensive but not complete statements on the recently concluded Polish Jewish agreement. As a result of this, much space was devoted to him in the American Jewish press, but it cannot be said that Count Skrzynski had a "good press."

Perhaps final judgment is to be reserved until more light is thrown on the subject.

* * *

Newspapers charge that the Polish Government "talk" about the Polish Jewish agreement is merely an attempt to pave the way for a Polish loan in America. At the same time, financial reports state that the Jewish banking firm of Speyer & Co. of New York has concluded negotiations with the Hungarian Government for a loan of $10,000,000 to be floated in the United States with the approval of the League of Nations Commissioner, who is supervising Hungarian finances.

Has Hungary, the country that openly enacted the *numerus clausus*, abandoned her discriminating practice?

Has the Horthy regime changed?

The Sentinel, April 30, 1926

Passengers in the subways, elevated trains and surface cars, as well as the motorists and pedestrians within the metropolitan area of Greater New York, cannot help seeing everywhere a sad-faced woman with distinctly Jewish features, who looks on them from posters and billboards. On her face is an expression of limitless pain and suffering. On her lips there is a challenging, hidden smile.

The leaders of the United Jewish Campaign, who have taken upon themselves the task of arousing the sentiment of American Jews to give in order that this suffering people may be helped, have furnished the following text to this, which is understood to be an authentic picture.

"Tired of giving? You don't know what it is to be tired!"

One must credit the author of this poster with genuine ability and insight into human nature. It adequately describes the situation on both sides of the ocean. When the Joint Distribution Committee decided, several years ago, to discontinue its activity and persisted in going on with the liquidation of its work, it was done not on the theory that all that was ill in Jewish life in European countries had been remedied, but that American Jews had grown tired of giving. When the misery of the situation was again unfolded and focused attention, action was not undertaken before it was ascertained that American Jews, tired as they may be of giving, are, after all, American Jews. The spirit of the Philadelphia conference, despite its dramatic episodes, resting on a fundamental difference of opinion as to the outlook of Jewish life, brought out this fact.

New York is entering upon its United Jewish Campaign with a quota of $6,000,000. It is expected that the outcome will prove that New York Jewry is [in fact] not tired of giving. That it is not tired of giving for a worthy cause was also proven by the successful conclusion of the United Palestine Appeal, which sought to raise the amount of $1,500,000 in New York City for 1926.

* * *

Jewish education is again coming to the fore. On the initiative of the Zionist Organization of America, a national conference on Jewish education will take place in May. A league for Jewish Education in America is to be the outcome of the call for the conference.

Education is not a new Jewish problem. It was only a hundred years or so ago that, when the question of Jewish education was discussed, it was understood to mean general education for Jews. With the setting in of the Emancipation period and its accompanying changes in Jewish life, Jewish education has come to mean just the reverse, that is, providing a specifically Jewish religious, cultural or ethical background for what is accepted to be the general standard of education, according to the standards of culture and learning in the respective countries. What a complete change these hundred years in Jewish history have wrought!

There was no difference of opinion at that time as to what comprised Jewish education. Jewish education in the United States is a name into which every group and tendency reads its own definition. To the ultra-orthodox rabbinical group, Jewish education might mean an extensive study in Talmud; to the liberal tendency, it might mean religious training of the Sunday school content; to the distinctly Zionist mind, it might aim at acquaintance with modern Hebrew literature; to the less informed, it may mean the ability to recite the Bar Mitzvah prayers at the age of 13 and, of course, the accompanying "speech," and "after 20 years," the recital of the Aramaic Kaddish.

What the national conference on Jewish education will decide to define as Jewish education will determine its own success or failure. Should it succeed in handling the problem that affects not only the synagogue and the temple, but also the home and the status of the Jewish community, if judged from a broad viewpoint, and [if it] should succeed in directing its activities toward the provision of a Hebraic background, which is common to all the tendencies and not alien to America, it will make American Jewish history.

* * *

Interest in Jewish sport has been increased with the arrival of the soccer team of the Viennese sport club, Hakoah, and their matches with picked teams of professional players in the United States.

Jews in sport are still a novelty, although since many American Jews have taken their place[s] as leaders in American sport, this should not be so new. Nevertheless, the opinion prevails that Jews are new participators in sports.

Some time ago a well-known writer went to the extent of constructing a theory that the difference between Jew and Gentile is that the Gentile lives for the purpose of sport and play, while the Jew lives his life earnestly. This contention is not entirely based on facts or on historic conception. When the original meaning of the word "sport" is consulted, it is found to mean "amusement." One can search the early Jewish literature from Aleph to Tav and find not a single injunction against wholesome amusement. The misleading impression that Jews are opposed to sport gained ground due to the recorded fact that the Jews opposed the athletic sports of the Greeks in Palestine during the scission between Hellenism and Judaism. This, however, was due to the fact that it was an hour of national danger. Just as the fact that many countries introduced prohibition during the war cannot be used as a basis for the argument that these countries are permanently in favor of prohibition, so it cannot be argued that the Jews are opposed to sport.

If, however, by sport is meant that the game is to be played fairly, ancient Jewish lore might provide some argument proving the existence of this conception.

The fact in the Bible that Jacob was renamed Israel, following his gallant, singlehanded fight with the unknown "man" who injured him, tells the story. Jacob was named Israel because he "fought with God." The many references in the Bible to the Book of Yashar, always mentioned when poems concerning the life and achievements of heroes are given, is, in the opinion of many scholars, an indication of the existence of a special "Book of Heroes," giving thus new meaning to the old name of Israel: Israel-Yashar El, or the Knight of God.

The Sentinel, June 4, 1926

The resignation of Al Jolson, famous Broadway comedian, from membership in the Westchester Biltmore Country Club at Rye, N.Y., is quite a bit of first-class American Jewish "social news." Al Jolson, the son of a cantor, has never made any secret of his Jewish origin and faith. He could not, out of respect to himself, his friend and his people, remain any longer a member of the exclusive country club, which reprimanded him for bringing undesirable guests to the club, referring to Harry Richman, nightclub entertainer and proprietor, whom Mr. Jolson had brought to the Club as his guest.

"If you want it straight, I'll tell you. Mr. Richman is undesirable for the simple reason that he is a Jew," Mr. Jolson was told by the manager of the club when he asked the reason for the objection to Mr. Richman. On asking whether it was not known that he, too, was a Jew, Jolson was told, "Of course, but you are an exception."

"You are an exception" has been the mask under which rabid anti-Semitism sailed everywhere. Self-respecting Jews everywhere have always refused to be accepted as an exception. This "social event," in itself insignificant as it may be, carries a lesson to many of our golf-playing co-religionists. It also should be a reminder to those who look to Great Britain for standards and comparison.

This American Jewish "social event" coincides with the conferring upon the former Mr. Isaac Rufus and the former Alice Cohen of the title of Marquis and Marquise of Reading. The Court of St. James and the British Nordic aristocracy do not treat outstanding Jews as "exceptions."

They could, if they sought, also find standards here. As the New York $6,000,000 drive of the United Jewish Campaign is nearing its successful conclusion, along comes John

D. Rockefeller, Jr., with a $100,000 contribution "for the relief of the Jewish people in Poland and Russia."

Are there many of these exclusive country-club members who would applaud John D. Rockefeller when he says [the following] in the letter accompanying the gift?

"In a matter of this kind, there ought to be no barriers of race or creed. Therefore, although my participation in the movement has not been solicited, I hope you will allow me to enclose herewith my check for $100,000 toward the fund, which I do with the best wishes for the successful consummation of the campaign."

Many throughout the country will no doubt applaud the decision of the National Conference on Jewish Culture and Education that was called by the Zionist Organization of America. The conference, which formed the association for Jewish Education and Culture, has succeeded in eliminating from its program those edges that would be most likely to create friction on the question of Jewish education.

In addition to its purely Zionist activities, of which the new Association makes no secret, it also intends, according to its program, to encourage Jewish educational work on a larger scale, on the need of which there seems to be no division.

There can be no objection to "fostering in American Jewish life an appreciation of Jewish cultural values; to create a better understanding of Jewish traditions and aspirations; and the cultivation and dissemination of the Hebrew language and literature."

The fears entertained by those who are interested in religious education, in the various Sunday schools and Talmud Torahs, either of Orthodox or reform, were allayed by the fact that direct interference in the work of the various religious and educational institutions will not be attempted by the new association.

The Sentinel, September 17, 1926

Bialik, the Hebrew poet who received such a warm welcome from American Jews, is far away from these shores. Dispatches state that a similarly warm reception was accorded him in Paris last week. His impression of American Jewry and particularly of the Zionist public, with whom he came in closer contact, as summarized in his interview before his departure, was not very complimentary. The public, which is usually extremely sensitive to criticism, however, has its own way with poets. It was not long ago that the artist, particularly the man of Jewish letters, was a total stranger within the gates. The artist of old would have been grateful for even being noticed, be it with criticism, let alone applauded and welcomed.

But times have changed. The artists are overwhelmed with attention and the limelight of publicity. They have a hard time escaping to the seclusion so necessary for their creative work.

Perhaps it was in this sense that the American Jewish public did not deliver the "consequences" of Bialik's criticism. Besides, Bialik, as the quintessence of the Hebraic aspiration, is entitled to ask for more and to aspire to a higher level, the level that he probably knows so well.

However, even Bialik was not entirely spared from the consequences of controversy, with which Jewish life in America was so rife during the recent heat wave. In the noise of New York metropolitan life, of public banquets and money-raising gatherings, to the accompaniment of subways, elevators and streetcars, Bialik found a moment of seclusion in which to pick up a thread of his creative genius, which has been silent for a number of years. He wrote a poem of the Great City. . . .

The great American metropolis under whose pressure of life the poem was written did not fare better at Bialik's pen than did American Jewry.

"Yenasser Lo Chilvavo" is the name of the beautiful poem that is the center of discussion in New York's Hebrew literary circle.[4] The burden of the poem is the arrival and penetration of spring through the asphalt, brick, iron and steel structure of the Great City and the perpetual superiority and beauty of the smallest blade of grass over the huge and powerful structures of modern civilization.

> "Let the noise of the metropolis roar as it passes,
> "Let the exploiter and exploited perish in the stench of their exploitation,
> "Let the smoke of its chimneys darken the blue of the seven skies,
> "Spring in its eternal law, sweet, pure and tender,
> "Will come through millions of cracks and will flourish."

Thus Bialik begins his description of spring in the Great City.

> "And I said in my heart, Nest of Satan
> "The source of all mankind's plagues, the bosom of all horrors, the city that God's grace has despised and where God's eye will not rest,
> "Your end is the end of Sodom and Nineveh.
> "When the Day will come, the Day of Judgment,
> "When you will have grown very high,
> "And your burden will be too heavy,
> "When your yoke will become too irksome,
> "You will fall to pieces
> "Like a straw hut."

Here are a few of the poet's visions of the Great City. Those who read poetry with prosaic eyes resent these visions. "New York has not treated the poet so badly that he should predict for it the end of Nineveh," they mutter. The lovers of poetry laugh at the resentment and are happy that New York, with its splendor and hugeness, has awakened in the Hebrew poet his harp and has brought out tones reminiscent of those of the Hebrew prophets of old.

* * *

The "national minorities" or the "minority rights" with which American Jewish leadership had much to do in the post-war days are again on the agenda. They came up for discussion in connection with the act of the seventy Turkish Jewish notables who met in what was termed a "Jewish national assembly of Turkey" to renounce the claim of Turkish Jewry to the national minority rights guaranteed to it under the terms of the Treaty of Lausanne. This step of the Turkish notables was taken under the pressure of Kemal Pasha's dictatorial government and under promise of stopping the reprisals and returning confiscated property. The right of the Turkish Jews to arrange their internal religious affairs, [and to] maintain their educational and communal organizations, is now left to the mercy of the all-powerful Kemal Pasha government.

---

[4] The translation from the Hebrew original into English seems to have been done by William Z. Spiegelman himself.

Have the Turkish Jewish notables done well? ask some. Was it expedient? Will the deal bring beneficial results? others ask. There is confusion and misunderstanding on the subject. The other day I was surprised when an otherwise learned gentleman displayed great astonishment when he heard that Jews were fighting for minority rights. Why, he said, "minority rights"? Do they fight for *less* rights? What is the idea of guaranteeing them minority rights?

That is the point. The minority rights were intended to prevent a situation where Jews who are citizens of East European countries would have less rights than were coming to them and less than the rights guaranteed to every American by the United States Constitution. They were written into the international peace treaties, and America, as well as American Jews, had a whole lot to do with it.

It was under the influence of Wilson's fourteen points and his theory of the self-determination of small peoples that these clauses were made a part of international law. European Jews were then grateful to the leadership of American Jews, headed by Louis Marshall, who, in Paris, worked indefatigably toward that end. It is tragic to see that now, eight years later, disappointment with the slow realization of these treaties has led to this action of [the] Turkish Jewish leaders and to a growing misunderstanding of the original intentions of these clauses. It is reassuring to again hear the voice of Louis Marshall thundering powerfully to instill confidence and self-respect in the hearts of the Jewish minorities.

"I would rather die ten thousand deaths than to show myself so lacking in manly courage as to sell my birthright of liberty and equality for temporary safety."

His words will be heard throughout Europe.

The Sentinel, October 29, 1926[5]

A clever New York headline writer is to be credited with the sentence "Orthodox Jews and Henry Ford Agree on One Point."[6]

It concerns the introduction of the five-day industrial week. From the discussions in the press and the attempts in various parts of the country to test this proposal, it appears that the five-day industrial week, although the American Federation of Labor at its recent convention in Detroit did not come out for it as fully as it might have, is within the realm of possibility. It is true Henry Ford in introducing the five-day system in his Detroit plant has, reports say, gone no further than a five-day weekly payment, but the move to shorten the working week and allow additional time to the working classes for recreation and educational development is a great step forward.

Incidentally, it is balm to the heart of Orthodox Jewry in America, which has been sighing under the burden of the problem of the observance of the Sabbath. There is a pathetic note in the statement made by Dr. Bernard Drachman, president of the Sabbath Alliance of America, when he says, "Although Mr. Ford, to our sorrow, can hardly be classed as a friend of our people, we must in justice divorce his present action from his otherwise narrow-minded policy, and trust that his example in adopting the five-day week will be followed."

Rabbi Drachman and Henry Ford agree.

* * *

---

[5] Attributed to Z. Alroy.
[6] Cf. *Jewish Daily Bulletin*, October 21, 1926.

It was on the deck of the *Leviathan* that 200 American newspapermen assembled to greet Her Majesty, the Queen of Romania, on behalf of the American reading public. In the wayward light that has accompanied Queen Marie on her route from Bucharest to the Statue of Liberty, the highest point was reached at that moment. It was a conspicuous moment; it was a crucial moment.

The Queen, a guest of the American nation; the Queen, ruler of a country where not all is well, not only with the Jews but with many other peoples. Among the many questions of the American newspaper representatives, sandwiched in between a question on her manner of eating corn on the cob and on the New York skyline, the Jewish question was hurled at her by a zealous Jewish newspaperman.

Was it right? Was it proper?

Opinion may be divided, but it is difficult to condemn the action.

That this sentiment is shared not only by American Jews, but also by American Christians, there is ample evidence. On that very day, when the Queen returned from the glorious reception accorded her by the Chief Executive and stopped at Baltimore, the 91st annual convention of the Maryland Baptists Union Association was in session there. And what did the Baptists do? They framed a set of appeals in the form of resolutions, which were submitted to the Queen. In these resolutions attention was drawn to the situation of intolerance in which Baptists and Jews in Romania find themselves.

Those who need non-Jewish support before every move can be justified have it now in the action of the Maryland Baptists. Queen Marie, who is so liberal in quickly conveying to the public her impressions of America, may also find occasion to comment on this circumstance.

The Sentinel, November 5, 1926

Dr. Chaim Weizmann, president of the World Zionist Organization, has arrived on his fourth visit to the United States, cheered by Zionists, received cordially and with interest by non-Zionists.

Dr. Weizmann's visit to the United States is an event in Jewish life. It makes Zionist history and also Jewish history.

The echoes of the recent controversy between Zionists and non-Zionists in this country having subsided,' the irritation caused by the friction having been appeased, the situation in Palestine being, as it is, fraught with many problems, the course of action that will be chosen by the Zionist leader is a matter of interest to Zionists and non-Zionists [alike].

Of course, the outstanding problem facing the Zionists at present is the unemployment situation and what is termed the crisis that followed in its wake. When the facts in the situation are considered, when the human side of the problem is looked upon, the matter is of deep concern not only to affiliated Zionists but to all American Jews. No doubt this will be the dominant note in the discussions and the public receptions that will be given "from now on." It should be recalled that it was Dr. Weizmann who, months ago, before the crisis in Palestine reached its present state, with his usual courage and vision, analyzed the situation and, as it were, predicted events.

"It is true that not all of the human material that has attempted to find refuge in agriculture in Palestine was fitted for it. We take note of this certainly with regret and deep sorrow. But we have no right to close our eyes to the fact that a certain part of the new settlers will be compelled to leave their places. This happens not because those settlers don't want to work. The contrary is true. They have shown, and are still showing, a sacred devotion to the ideal of work and the national resettlement. But there are physical and psychological obstacles over which no effort can avail." He described the situation upon his return from Palestine in the early spring.

"We were all glad to observe the large immigration of last year and we were inclined to see in it the beginning of the redemption, a symbol and a proof of the realization of the Zionist ideal. At the same time we did not give sufficient consideration to the possibility that such an overwhelming immigration can also bring disaster, if we do not simultaneously increase in the same measure our own efforts in order to increase the capability of the country to absorb the incoming masses."

"If we do not increase our efforts." "If" is one of the shortest words in the dictionary, but it is like many other monosyllables – the fate of a man, of a nation, of a movement, of a country, of an ideal, depends not on the large words, but on monosyllables. The Palestine situation has exercised a tremendous appeal for Jewish public opinion in the last ten years. If there was a time when Dr. Weizmann was called upon to bring the influence of his personality to bear upon conditions, it is now that he has before him one of the most difficult situations he has ever faced. However, Dr. Weizmann, a chemist by profession has, during his Zionist work, developed a new kind of chemistry. It is the chemistry of the public mind, the secret of international success, the blending of a variety of colors into the Blue and White. His new formula in the chemistry of shaping the American Jewish public mind, to be applied to remedying the Palestine situation, is looked forward to with more than interest.

* * *

History does not belong to the popular subjects; Jewish history much less. American Jewish history is in its infancy as yet. It is not surprising, therefore, that the American Jewish Historical Society is not heard of frequently. It is a pity, however, that the facts brought out at its last annual convention in Philadelphia were not more widely broadcast. I believe that they are of interest even to those who have no particular inclination for the study of history.

American Jews were the principal backers in the development of the West. Philadelphia Jews were the prime movers in the settling of the early West and were employers of Col. George Grogham and Daniel Boone. They owned the sites of Chicago and St. Louis. So says Dr. A. S. W. Rosenbach, president of the society, on the basis of extensive research work in the early records of the expansion of the West. The fact that many American Jews have succeeded so well as realtors is merely a reversion to type. This is interesting and instructive. What a fine thing it would be if prominent American Jewish realtors would make it possible for the accomplishment of "their ancestry" to be more widely known! They can certainly take pride in it.

By the way, those early backers of the development of the West were in partnership with Benjamin Franklin, George Washington and Robert Morris.

* * *

Dr. Chaim Tchernowitz, professor of Rabbinics at the Institute of Jewish Religion, finds fault with all three types of Jewish congregations in the United States. He is satisfied neither with Orthodoxy nor with Reform; not even with the Conservatives, who are in between. He objects particularly to the deviation from the substance of Jewish law. He cannot agree to the enthronement of the cantor, instead of the scholar. He cannot submit to the rule of the congregational president, instead of the leadership of the Rabbi. He is not attuned to the melodies sung in the present-day synagogues. He wishes that the center of Jewish life would be directed from the synagogue, the house of prayer, and return to the Beth Ha'Medrash, the house of learning.

How can all this be accomplished?

To Professor Tchernowitz it is a simple matter. He proposes that a Rabbinic Council, composed of recognized scholars, well-versed in the Jewish law and lore, be endowed with the authority to revise whatever is necessary in the Jewish religious laws in accordance with the requirements of the time. This Council would, he believes, bring about the fusion of the now disagreeing elements. A sort of "Council of Forty-Eight States" instead of the olden Council of Four States.

While some may agree with his criticism, it is difficult to see how a Rabbinic Council can remedy it.

Canadian Jewish Chronicle, December 31, 1926

The colorful American Jewish life has been enriched by the addition for a time of the Hebrew performances of the Habima[7] on the Broadway stage. Strange are the ways of development in Jewish life. The usual procedure with other races or groups is that at first the material foundations of life are firmly laid and then, on their strength and economic and social structure, is erected the spiritual stratum. The Fine Arts are the latest arrivals in the development of society. They require, in addition to the natural process of development, the cultivated mind and understanding spirit of the patrons of the Arts. America, the youngest of nations, constituted, perhaps, in this respect, the happy exception.

Through the unique circumstances of "one nation, indivisible," subject to the influence of one language and one culture, served by a unified system of communication, facilitated by modern devices for conquering space and time, raised to a higher standard of living by the means of mass production, America has the distinction that a greater part of the population is in a position and does [in fact] enjoy the benefits of the Fine Arts. This circumstance, while it has no doubt the advantage provided by democracy, has also its setbacks.

The Habima, a forerunner of specifically Jewish art, coming to America, was borne on the wings of the imagination. With an audience to be recruited from the greatest Jewish community in the world today, the expectations of the Habima were high. It is a unique product in Jewish life. Springing up in Russia under the most adverse circumstances, where every influence is diametrically opposed to the very essence of Hebraic thought and form, the Habima developed, grew and preserved its treasure. When listening to their interpretations of human life in Jewish forms, one, being aware of their triumphant wanderings, is reminded of the ancient band of prophets, going to and from the land and proclaiming their message.

There may be some difference of opinion as to this or that detail in the performance of the Habima, as to the propriety of this or that influence on their part, but there is unanimity as to the superb character of their playing and there is no doubt of their distinct contribution to art in general and to Jewish art in particular.

---

[7] Founded in 1917 in Moscow by Nahum Zemach, and at first affiliated with the Moscow Art Theatre, the Habima ("Stage," in Hebrew) was one of the first Hebrew-language theater companies. In 1926, the company left the Soviet Union and toured extensively for several years before settling in Palestine in 1931.

* * *

One can never tell what the outcome of a word spoken [aloud] may be. Those who attended the Palestine conference in Boston hardly expected the dramatic developments that followed the challenge issued by Nathan Straus to Henry Ford. Nathan Straus, in his address, in criticizing the Jewish rich for their indifference to Palestine and other Jewish causes, said a word or two about the beneficial activities of the non-Jewish rich. A comparison to the activities of the Rockefellers was made. The tremendous difference between the way the Rockefellers use their wealth and that employed by Henry Ford suggested itself. Then, the challenge to Ford came. As the situation is now, through the energetic activity of Congressman Sol Bloom, the United States Congress may have to investigate the charges of Henry Ford.

The chronicle of Jewish events, public disputes and trials on anti-Jewish accusations are not at all as much a novelty as some may imagine. It was with great endurance that Jewish leaders in centuries gone by agreed to appear at the famous disputes, usually arranged between a church dignitary and the rabbi or the *Judenmeister*. Convictions cannot be subjected to the outcome of an oratory debate, nor can general accusations be refuted by words. Unless the charge is specific, unless the time, place and names are given, the effort to clear oneself of the wildest charge is bound to be futile.

If the Congress pleases to have the investigation, the defense will not be a single Jew, nor the Jewish race, nor the Jewish religion. It is an accusation directed against the United States Federal Reserve System. And the plaintiff will be Henry Ford. Incidentally, Henry Ford will be given the opportunity to substantiate all of his charges, to explain the reasons for his maligning propaganda against the Jews, who are not a legal personality and cannot, therefore, sue him for libel. It will be a unique spectacle from which anti-Semites all over the world will have much to learn.

* * *

George Cretziano, Romanian Minister to Washington, also has to learn something about the situation in this country. He, as well as his comrade, the Romanian Minister in Warsaw, has found it diplomatically wise to flatly deny all the reports about anti-Jewish excesses in Romania.

"There is no trouble anywhere, everything is being completely quiet. All rumors to the contrary which have been spread in foreign countries are, like the rest, 'tendentious' and malicious," the honorable George Cretziano, with the dignity of his office, declared in a public statement in response to reports specifying the time, the place and the names of the persons attacked, the houses demolished, and the leaders responsible for the wave of anti-Jewish excesses.

American public opinion has, at present, an aversion to reading reports of anti-Jewish excesses in Europe. Several years ago, these reports came in such rapid succession and with such abhorrent details that they exhausted patience and belittled belief. When one reads of a violent death or an atrocious attack at infrequent intervals, one's feeling of righteousness is outraged, but when one continues to read repetitions of the same attacks, the only variations being the date and the place and the names, the effect is lessened. Nevertheless, these atrocities are as real today as they were several years ago. One's feeling of protest is more outraged today, in view of the fact that this lawlessness comes seven years after the Armistice and after many solemn promises, declarations, assurances and royal compliments. One's feelings are more outraged when, in the face of all these continuous atrocities, cold-blooded denials are issued on the assumption that they will appease someone or they will prevent any protests.

The Sentinel, April 29, 1927

On May 2 a national conference of Orthodox Jewish congregations in the United States and Canada will be opened in New York City. The initiative in calling this conference came from the Yeshiva Building Fund, the organization that has raised over two million dollars for the erection of a Yeshiva college to house in eight magnificent buildings the Yeshiva, named after Rabbi Isaac Elchanan, for the training of Orthodox rabbis, and a College of Liberal Arts and Sciences. The step was taken in connection with the festive ceremonies on the occasion of the laying of the cornerstone for the first group of buildings of the Yeshiva on May 1.

These festivities are a significant event in American Jewish life and indicate a tremendous change in the component elements of the Jewish community. It was not long ago that the terms "Orthodox," "immigrant," and "poor Jew" were considered synonymous. Now, in every Jewish community in this land there are considerable groups of Orthodox Jews whose capacity for leadership in economic, civil and cultural life is admitted. When the leaders of this movement decided to use the occasion when Orthodox leaders will meet for the ceremonies attending the laying of the cornerstone, as an attempt to unite Orthodox congregations into a national body, it is an effort that has to be followed with arresting interest. Word has gone abroad that this effort may result in the creation of an opposition of Orthodox Jews to the so-called "rule" of the liberal element in American Jewry.

Whether the fight between Orthodox and Reform will be renewed under present conditions is highly doubtful. The days of the early conflicts are, it seems, gone, never to return. The liberal movement has had a long time to prove its worth and it can now be judged not in the heated atmosphere of fanaticism on one side and revolt on the other, but in the light of historic facts, achievements or failures.

Whatever one's view may be on Orthodox Judaism under present-day conditions, the fact remains that there is a vast number of Orthodox Jewish congregations, with a membership not accurately recorded, which are continuing Orthodox traditions. Whether the trend common to these congregations is one of militancy, as claimed by some of their leaders, or one of passive resistance to all assaults of changing times, a feature characteristic of Judaism in past ages, is a matter that cannot be determined with any measure of accuracy.

The claim has been made that there are between two and three thousand Orthodox Jewish congregations on the North American continent. When these groups are united and express their will with regard to things Jewish, what will this will be? It is a matter that leaves room for interesting speculative thought. The fact is that, according to the latest figures, the Union of American Hebrew Congregations, representing the Reform congregations in the United States, has a membership of 279 congregations that have in turn an individual membership of 53,960 people. The United Synagogue of America, which represents the so-called Conservative trend in American Judaism, has a membership, it is stated, of 226 congregations with a total membership of about 33,000. The union of Orthodox Jewish Congregations, an organization started about 30 years ago, but whose development has been rather slow, also has a membership of 150 congregations. This leaves a margin of several thousand congregations, unaffiliated with one another and unorganized, each group confined to the interest of its local importance and totally unguided in matters of national interest and significance, such as Jewish education.

To endeavor to organize these bodies is a herculean task. It is perhaps an attempt to move a slumbering giant. Those of the Yeshiva College Building Fund who have undertaken it deserve praise for their courage and vision.

The proceedings and decisions of this conference ought to be watched with abiding interest by all who take an active part in the life of the Jewish communities throughout the country.

Canadian Jewish Chronicle, October 14, 1927[8]

Jewish life in western countries cannot be measured on the basis of everyday observation. Should it be subjected to such a scrutiny, it would justify a dark, pessimistic view. Loosely organized communities, weekly functioning organizations, divergences of opinion, splits, currents and undercurrents that seem to destroy the totality of the picture.

What a different view one may obtain when the High Holiday season comes around. The seating capacity of the permanent synagogues is overtaxed, an intense building activity reaches its climax where operations were started before and new plans are formulated for the future, halls are hired, even though for pecuniary purposes, where the traditional tunes are heard again and where multitudes come to pray and to take stock of individual as well as group interests.

The sudden growth is ascribed to the "one-day synagogue Jew," usually spoken of in derision.

He is a familiar type, that "year-end Jew." You cannot find him all year round. It seems as if he had lost his identity and the hope is small of gaining his re-affiliation with a group in whose membership few privileges are apparent but many duties are expected. All the efforts and all the ingenuity of the campaigners for all Jewish organizations hardly suffice to reach that proverbial "year-end Jew."

As the year turns, the synagogue accomplishes this task miraculously. It needs no campaign, it needs no ingenious means, it offers no inducements, it accords no privileges except the one of a response to a call of conscience. And it works. So much so that New York City, whose Jewish population is perhaps the most disorganized and the hardest to reach in any concerted effort, changes its aspect on Yom Kippur. Traffic is lessened by half. Stores, offices, amusement places that seem never to close lock their doors as if by the touch of a magic wand. The sidewalks of New York, the subject of song, are partly deserted when the age-old Hebrew prayers are being recited either in their original or in the latest translation.

The ingenious campaign directors of the various national and local Jewish organizations who, it seems, have at times outdone themselves, may still learn a lesson or two from the Fathers of the Synagogue.

The "year-end" Jew is usually spoken of with scorn. It is a wrong attitude to take. There are great potentialities in this type of Jew, whose interest and devotion is there, but it is latent. One must agree with the learned editorial writer of the *Jewish Morning Herald* when he points out that the traditional Jewish view of the "one-day" Jew was not as severe as one might be inclined to believe. Judaism is complacent with all those who awaken to the call of their conscience, even when it is only once in every 365 days.

---

[8] Published under the title "New York Topics."

The fact that the Yom Kippur services are not begun until an improvised Court of Three issues permission for the Avaryanim to participate in the services is evidence that, although the "one-day Jew" is not admired, he is not barred.

* * *

Dr. Judah L. Magnes, Chancellor of the Hebrew University on Mount Scopus, has again returned to America.

That an American Jew is at the head of the Hebrew University is and should be a source of pride to American Jewry. It would be doubly pleasing to American Jews that this post is occupied by as popular and beloved a figure as Dr. Magnes is among Jews and non-Jews in America. He brings the glad tidings of considerable progress made by that Jewish institution for higher learning. During the past year, although it was badly affected by the earthquake, the University has made considerable strides forward. In all of its departments – the Department of Mathematics, the Department of Chemistry, the Department of Microbiology, the Department of Hygiene, the Department for Oriental Studies, and the Department of Palestine Topography – research work was continued and considerable contributions to these sciences were made.

More apparent and of greater appeal to American Jews, however, must be the work of the Institute for Jewish Studies, which was begun by the magnificent fund of Felix M. Warburg, and the contribution of Mrs. Sol Rosenbloom, who donated $500,000 for the erection of a building to house the Institute. This Institute is fulfilling a dream of many an enlightened Jewish mind. Its publications of research work in Jewish history and literature are real treasures to scholars and laymen interested in the subject.

The second volume of *The Publications of the Hebrew University in Jerusalem*, recently off the press, is a testimony to the spirit of scholarly research that handles Jewish values with piety and understanding. The work of this department in editing the ancient texts and in shedding light upon [the] phases of Jewish cultural development in its various branches encourages one to hope that a real *Wissenschaft des Judentums*, based on the authentic sources and pursued without the bias so frequently observed in the writings of non-Jewish scholars, will be developed on Mount Scopus.

The University, Dr. Magnes reports, is now introducing several departments for undergraduate instruction. The University that is dear to all shades of Jews, Zionist and non-Zionist, Reform and Orthodox, has a building program that will require the expenditure of $800,000 during the next two years. It is to be hoped that the American Advisory Committee for the Hebrew University and Dr. Magnes will meet with a ready response to continue and expand this real, vital work among all classes of Jews, even among the "year-end Jews."

* * *

Twenty-three Yiddish theatres have opened their doors to Yiddish theatregoers in New York and elsewhere this season. Those who predicted the demise of the Yiddish stage with the enactment of the Johnson Immigration Law seem to have been premature in their prognostications. The native Yiddish stage, which has produced so much talent, continues to hold out its attraction to the New York Jew. As the years progress, the Yiddish stage comes closer to the adjustment that it so sorely needed. In a way, the survival of the Yiddish theatre is an indication of the inherent Jewish love for his original drama, without regard to the form in which it is presented.

Things have progressed to such an extent that the Yiddish stage and the Broadway stage are in closer relationship than ever before, the latter frequently borrowing talent from the former. The adjustment that threw many into extreme pessimism and others into unwarranted hilarity is making headway.

A new note into this variety of tones will be introduced this season by the Habima, the Hebrew players of Moscow, who came here last year as a guest troupe.

Following internal changes, the troupe has now been reorganized on an American basis and will venture forth with new courage in the Neighborhood Playhouse, where an interesting repertoire, including new and old plays in Hebrew, is promised.

* * *

The Zionist movement at the beginning of the season seems still to be sailing in the waters of uncertainty. The members of the American delegation to the Fifteenth Zionist Congress are divided in their view as to the completeness of the decisions taken there.

The election of Miss Henrietta Szold to the Jerusalem triumvirate gave expression to the importance in which American Zionist participation is being viewed by the Zionist constituents all over the world. The policy of economy and retrenchment was the last of the evils that were made necessary by the existing situation. The movement seems to have reached a turning point. It is obvious that retrenchment and economy in themselves will not advance the goal toward which true Zionists aim. Something more than efficiency and the cutting of the budget will be necessary to further the development of the Jewish National Home. In previous years, as the season of activity began, the plans for Zionist efforts were mapped out and were well under way. At present nothing except rough outlines are visible.

Those who follow the affairs of the Zionist movement closely unanimously agree that the movement is now passing through a transition period that will require the bending of all energies to make the turn safely.

The first group of American experts of the Joint Palestine Survey Commission, with Dr. Elwood Mead at its head, has returned. Their report will be completed soon, paving the way for the Jewish Agency, with the cooperation of Zionists and non-Zionists, to step into the Palestine situation.

The Sentinel, November 18, 1927[9]

Some enterprising news editor in the Middle West [of the USA] in search for the unusual made a great discovery. Upon the large American continent, populated as it is with talent and genius, he has discovered the Average American. A close scrutiny was made of the unicum and it was discovered to the surprise and amusement of the reading public that the average American is quite a normal man. The find was made in the state of Iowa. He is a small businessman. He owns his own home, drives a car, cares for his family, goes to church, is a good, congenial neighbor and is all around all right. Because of these unusual qualities he was on exhibit and all his actions, opinions and reactions to the world and its affairs were scrupulously recorded and interpreted.

To summarize his outlook not a very large vocabulary is necessary. It would range between a complacent "all right" and satisfaction with what exists.

---

[9] Published under the title "New York Topics."

Notwithstanding the harpings of the highbrow intellectuals, if it is true that the average American is indeed what he is claimed to be in his exemplary personification, there is nothing wrong with him.

It is to be wondered that there was not an ingenious editor of a Jewish newspaper, daily or weekly, to attempt to find his counterpart in the American Jewish community. Not wishing to anticipate the finding of such a search, the following qualities might be suggested as a clue to the discovery.

The average American Jew corresponds more or less to the average American. He is a businessman, he owns his own home, drives his car, cares for his family and is a congenial neighbor.

The only difference that might exist is that he goes to synagogue at least once a year. He is not a member of many social clubs but instead has hands full and his pockets empty with the payment of all kinds of dues to charitable organizations, societies and lodges. Another difference is that he is either a "driver" or is being driven in the various consecutive [fundraising] drives for every imaginable good, uplifting cause.

* * *

A trial of unusual interest will take place next week in the city of Cleveland. As a preparatory step for providing the legal guns for the parties concerned theological advice on the background of the conflict was sought from the leaders of the respective branches of American Jewry in New York.

The crux of the matter on which light was sought in the depositions taken was the answer to the question: What is orthodoxy? A minority group of the Cleveland Jewish Center is responsible for instituting the suit against Rabbi Solomon Goldman, spiritual leader of the Center. The minority claims that the Rabbi, a graduate of the Jewish Theological Seminary, has deviated from the constitution of the congregation that provides that, as long as ten members will insist on the Orthodox ritual, the congregation must remain Orthodox. To prove that the Rabbi's deviations are un-Orthodox it is first necessary to establish what Orthodoxy is. To bring out the answer to this question a great volume of questions were prepared to be submitted to the experts. Many of the questions framed by the attorneys for both sides who are, by the way, both non-Jews, contain the danger of turning this essentially necessary battle into a Jewish edition of the Dayton trial. Many of the questions and answers during the taking of the depositions brought in the entire mass of religious lore that, when transferred into the secular atmosphere of a court, might tend to create a kind of ridicule similar to that which attended the "monkey trial" in Dayton. When questions concerning Baalem's Ass are asked and answered, or when the perplexing problem is presented as to whether or not kissing a bride by the officiating Rabbi is in accordance with Orthodoxy or whether the reading of this or that book on present-day social problems is or is not in accordance with Orthodoxy, the entire matter is reduced to the level of vaudeville that will certainly do no good for the dignity of Jewish religious life in the United States.

This, however, has nothing to do with the question itself. There seems to be no doubt that in the present transitory period through which American Jewry is passing, the friction between the traditional synagogue and the modernized synagogue is at its height.

Orthodoxy is generally a misnomer when Jewish religion is spoken of. It is a word new in the use of the synagogue. It came into use only after Reform Judaism made its entrance. With Reform Judaism the traditional synagogue has no quarrel. Friction of which the Cleveland case is typical is in existence and the dignified settling of the matter in the Cleveland court will have a wholesome influence and lead to a clarity that is much needed.

* * *

Life has its tragic and comic sides. Dispatches from Budapest conveyed the indignation of the highly cultured Magyar students who objected to performance of "Abie's Irish Rose" in the Metropolitan Theatre.

The refined Magyar students objected to the play not because it did not measure up to their artistic appreciation but because they believed that "Abie's Irish Rose" represents American Jews in too favorable a light. Here is one point where many an American Jew whose eye has grown weary for the past six years of seeing "Abie's Irish Rose" blossom among the bright lights of Broadway agrees with the Magyar youths – but obviously not for the same reasons. "Abie's Irish Rose" is as far from being complimentary to the Jew as it is far from the truth; it is also as far from proving the public's knowledge of the Jew as of its artistic appreciation.

* * *

A chair for the instruction of the Yiddish language and literature will be created at the Hebrew University on Mount Scopus. This is another achievement that Dr. Magnes has added to his brilliant record as chancellor of the University.

The Hebraist zealots in Jerusalem and elsewhere will not, strange as it may seem, derive any too great satisfaction from the accomplishment. In the struggle for the cultural dominance among the Jewish masses, Hebrew and Yiddish have fought many a battle that was certainly injurious to both. The renaissance of Hebrew is of too recent a date to have instilled in its followers the feeling of security that is necessary for a proper appreciation of the academic necessities of an institution like the Hebrew University, which must unfold its activity in an impartial, scientific and serene atmosphere.

Hotheaded Hebraists will visualize an attack of the Yiddishists on the Hebrew integrity of the Scopus institution. Dr. Magnes, however, has to be complimented on the achievement that will bring renown to the university as it will do much good for the prestige of the vernacular of a large section of the Jewish people and as it will furnish new living material for the study of Jewish life and institutions.

Dr. David Shapiro, publisher of *The Day*, and his associates on that New York Yiddish newspaper who are responsible for the idea and its execution by establishing a $100,000 fund, the income of which will secure the maintenance of this department, have made a valuable contribution both to the Hebrew University and to the study of Jewish literature.

The Sentinel, January 22, 1928

The republic of Poland is to receive a new loan, estimates of which vary from $25,000,000 to $50,000,000, the financial pages of the metropolitan newspapers announce. These announcements come simultaneously with the information that Dr. Edwin Kemmerer, financial expert of Princeton University, the "money doctor" who went to Poland for the purpose of inquiring into the causes of the difficulties that the republic has to face, is one his way back to the United States. The full report is not yet known. Some newspapers quoted him very optimistic, others, less. One report, however, is of special interest to American Jews.

The "money doctor," looking for a cure for Poland's financial difficulties, touched upon a subject that, on the surface, has nothing to do with it. He advised his hosts to remove the legal and economic disabilities of the Jewish merchants in Poland. The "money doctor" diagnosed the situation properly.

A Cure for Financial Troubles

Had not the policy of "nationalizing" commerce and industry in Poland been interpreted to mean that only Christian Poles are to engage in commerce and industry and, had the state machinery not been employed to help these Christian Poles to forcibly take the place of the merchants and workers who have generations of experience and craft tradition behind them, perhaps the crisis would not have occurred or, at least, not in such an acute form. The anti-Semitic branch of the Polish press is reported to have severely criticized the American expert for this advice. The truth does not seem to be a welcome guest to these gentlemen.

Yes, the Polish Jewish agreement, that unknown and puzzling creation that was heralded as the beginning of a new era, the words of the present Polish Prime Minister, Count Skrzynski, is still talked of. But that is as far as it has gone. The New York Jewish bankers, however, are prepared to go a step further. Kuhn, Loeb and Company are reported to be one of the backers of the Polish loan.

Agreements, Words and Loans

This winter will be recorded in the annals of American Jewish history as an extremely interesting and lively season. Beginning with September 13, public men who take the Jewish interest to heart, be it philanthropic, cultural, religious or political, were given no opportunity to rest and look at matters calmly. One controversy followed upon the heels of another. No sooner had the Crimean controversy, involving, as it does, the fate of millions of Jews, quieted down, than there arose the Wise controversy, touching, as it did, the very fundamental principles about which the history of Europe and the history of the Jews revolved. The latter seems to have died out as quickly as it came up and this is fortunate. The former seems to be losing its sharp edges as it is being put to the test in the heart and pockets of American Jewry.

The crux of the situation apparently was, in the minds of those who engaged in the Crimean controversy, whether the Palestine reconstruction or the East European relief, with its admixture of a colonization plan in Russia, has or is to have the "right of way" to the heart and pockets of the American Jew. As the two campaigns progress into action, it appears that there was too much ado over such a flexible and uncertain thing as the public mind.

At a state conference of the United Jewish Campaign for the State of New Jersey, the quota of $750,000 for the three-year campaign was enthusiastically accepted and simultaneously a resolution was adopted foreseeing the possibility of uniting efforts with the United Palestine Appeal.

Michael Hollander, a New Jersey leader and one of that fine type of Jew discovered during the campaign years, is applauded when he says: "Fifteen million dollars is a mighty small sum for the work of aid we must do in Europe; fifty million would be nearer right. Russia or Palestine, I am interested in Jewry everywhere."

All's Well That Ends Well

A third issue is expected to come up before American Jewry. It is the question of the much discussed and long delayed Jewish Agency, the body that is, under the mandate of the League of Nations, to be formed to succeed the Zionist Organization in assisting in the Jewish resettlement of Palestine and advising the Palestine administration in all matters concerning the establishment of the Jewish National Home in that country.

The conferences that have deliberated upon the question, the negotiations that have been carried on, the heated disputes among Zionists and non-Zionists, have apparently come to an end. So far as the legal side of the original plans are carried into effect, it can become the first universal Jewish body, inclusive of Zionists and non-Zionists, devoted to the task of rebuilding Palestine.

Will it? Will all this preparatory diplomatic work materialize? That is the question that was, admittedly, in the background throughout the Crimean controversy. Dr. Chaim Weizmann, President of the World Zionist Organization, the father of the Jewish Agency idea, its negotiator in the ranks of the non-Zionists and its champion in the ranks of the Zionists, is expected to arrive in New York shortly. There may be another interesting episode in this very interesting season.

Canadian Jewish Chronicle, February 3, 1928[10]

Changing Names

Justice Aaron J. Levy, who reprimanded Everett Levy, a young electrical engineer, when he applied to the court for permission to change his name to Lehoy, was applauded by many as having done and said the right thing, though the decision was obviously contrary to the argument.

In granting its permission, the court expressed an opinion that represents the sentiment of many with regard to those who abandon their inherited Jewish names to be substituted by those more in vogue in the environment.

It is indeed a pathetic case of a man who believes that the economic discrimination that he met in his upward struggle toward success was due to his Jewish name. It is a kind of mimicry observable among the weaker tribe of birds that assume the color of the trees in which they live in order to protect themselves against the eyes of birds of prey. The stronger fowl retains its colors and puts up a fight when called upon. It is a pitiful plight of the man who believes that ostracism will disappear when the sound of his name is changed.

An episode is current in well-to-do circles of a man who was once stranded in the mountains and, seeking shelter overnight in a fashionable hotel, was told by the clerk that no room was available. He endured the hardships of a night in the open, being fully conscious that this was due to his Jewish-sounding name. In due process of law the name was adapted to sound as pleasant as is required to be a free and accepted guest in fashionable resorts. He then took off a special week from his work with the intention of going to the same fashionable hotel and, being given accommodations, to have his "revenge" on the clerk by a hearty laugh in the privacy of the best suite of the house.

How great was his disappointment when upon arrival, after registering his new name with a flourish, he was told that there was no room available. An excursion into the other directions of mimicry seemed to be the inevitable thing to do.

---

[10] Published under the title "What's Happening in New York."

Still greater is the pity that essentially there is nothing wrong in the changing of a name. That this is even the opinion of the learned judge can be seen from a subsequent ruling, acting upon the application of a Mr. Goldberg, who changed his name to Goulding. Mr. Goldberg, a member of a numerous and ingenious tribe, presented the case from an altogether different angle. He had, he said, so many namesakes on the island of Manhattan that he finds it difficult to establish his identity in his business and social relations. The telephone directory of Greater New York contains not less than 2,000 of his namesakes, he declared in his petition. Justice Levy granted the petition without comment. Perhaps the judge has intended to differentiate between a Goldberg and a Levy.

Indeed, there is a difference. Jewish family names, particularly those of German and Slavic origin, belong to a period in Jewish history that is not most pleasant. Many of the names that were affixed by the decree of petty officials, whether the regime was Prussian, Russian or Austrian, were often chosen not by those who would have to bear them and transmit them to their progeny, but by the officials for considerations that were far from aesthetic, historic or euphonious. However, the case is different with those names that have their origin in the true Jewish history of the Biblical and post-Biblical times. Those names like Levy, which are of Hebraic origin and sound, carry with them a tradition of nobility, character and distinction that has been tried and time-honored. To abandon the Slav or German ending of a name does not seem to indicate an intention of denial of Jewish origin and affiliation; the rejection of a Biblical name is a different matter.

Justice Levy in expressing his opinions frankly gave food for thought to thinking men who are anxious for the future of the emerging American Jew. After all is said and done, this problem of the changing [of] names is only one that attends the changing conditions in the huge and unparalleled process of adaption that the largest Jewish community in the world today is going through in these United States.

Are American Jews Tiring of Giving for Palestine?

It was a good service that Louis Lipsky, President of the Zionist Organization of America, rendered to the cause of Palestine and to the belief of American Jews in the final success of the effort to rebuild Palestine when he took the opportunity to speak his mind to Col. Leopold H. Amery, British Secretary for the Colonies, during his present visit to the Dominion of Canada.

The President of the Zionist Organization, in drawing attention to the grievances held by American Jews against the government of Palestine for its inadequate cooperation with the Jewish endeavors to rebuild Palestine, stated frankly that this attitude "undermines the confidence of American Zionists in the British policy in Palestine," a circumstance that is the more deplorable because it affects the campaign for funds that are necessary to continue this work. One may safely say that, without regard to party, affiliation, or adherence to one another faction, there is unanimity of opinion as to the necessity at present of a frank presentation of the case against the British policy in Palestine.

Equally applauded will be the statement made by Col. Amery of how deeply he realized "how much the task of the Zionists in America in raising funds was made more difficult by the fact that at the very moment when these funds are most needed, they could only point to a difficult and anxious situation in Palestine."

Not that one could say that, if the British policy in Palestine would be definitely set against the Jewish endeavors, American Jews would discontinue their interest in Palestine. There is, however, a difference between the sentimental desire for seeing Palestine rebuilt and the degree of enthusiasm that has been raised to a high pitch by the alluring promise of a nearing and gradual fulfillment. To maintain this degree of enthusiasm and active interest, a definite understanding of how the powers that are inclined to treat the aspiration and to assist it actively is imperative.

Very reassuring was the statement of the Minister for the Colonies when he declared that the work already achieved in Palestine was sound and enduring, and that the British government had no intention of going back on its undertakings. In a small country like Palestine, depressions might not only come quickly, but also go quickly, he said.

Success of the United Palestine Appeal this year will help the depression to go more quickly.

A Noted Guest Has His Say

A distinguished visitor has just left these shores. Rabbi Benzion Uziel, the Chief Rabbi of the Sephardic community in Palestine, who spent several months in this country as a member of the Mizrachi delegation, sailed for home on the *Aquitania*. Many American audiences who had occasion to listen to the fluent, euphonious Hebrew accents of the Sephardic Chief Rabbi of Palestine, dressed in his Oriental garb, with a countenance resembling Maimonides, will not forget him soon. In his work of enlisting the interest of American Jews of Sephardic stock and in his endeavors to intensify the interest of Orthodox groups of Ashkenazi origin, he has had occasion to study the mood of large groups of American Jews in relation to the Palestine problem.

The writer had occasion to attend a farewell reception for the Chief Rabbi. He explained the reasons that compelled him to leave the post to visit the United States. The reason, he stated, was that when he visited Paris several years ago, one of the anti-Zionists of France endeavored to argue him out of his Zionist convictions. "You know, Grand Rabbi," the French anti-Zionist said, "that [the] success of the Palestine work depends on the generosity of American Jews in their contributions to the Keren Hayesod. Do you not think that American Jews in a couple of years will grow tired of giving money, even for Palestine?" The opponent argued.

These were saddening words to the Chief Rabbi. He came to the United State to test the strength of this argument. Upon leaving he stated that he was convinced that the French leader of the non-Zionists knew as much about the mood of American Jews as he knew about Zionism. American Jews are willing to open their purses for the Palestine work as long as they see the need and provided that they see that the seed bears fruit.

The distinguished ecclesiastic seems to take a long view of the situation. The impression is generally current that the Keren Hayesod is only seven years old. Though this may be true technically speaking, it is not essentially true. One can well say that the Keren Hayesod or the annual offerings for Palestine date back eighteen hundred years. Since the fall of Bethar, the Jewish communities have been responding to calls for funds for Palestine in all lands and under all conditions. Of course the forms were different as were the methods, the sums and those who presented the call – at one time, collections were known as the Kuppath, the Ramban, another as the Rabbi Meir Ball Ha'Ness, then there came the Kollelim, until these sentiments were embodied in the modern Zionist funds. What the modern Zionist movement has done was merely to crystalize the sentiment, direct it along political channels, and give it organized form and method.

Nathan Straus on His Eightieth Birthday

That the sentiment for Palestine continues in its strength was proven by Nathan Straus, the leading benefactor of the Palestine cause among American Jews. Celebrating his eightieth birthday on January 31, he announced his contribution of $100,000 towards the United Palestine Appeal. It is Mr. Straus's first contribution directly to the Appeal and will no doubt serve as a strong stimulus.

The eightieth birthday of the Grand Old Man of American Jewry is a red-letter day in the annals of American Jewish philanthropy and constructive endeavor. Many have succeeded in passing the Biblical three-score-and-ten, but not many can say they have lived to celebrate their eightieth birthday, calling for the tributes of leaders and spokesmen throughout the world. This is a life that has shed glory not only on the man who lived it, but [also] on the people to whom he belongs.

Canadian Jewish Chronicle, June 15, 1928[11]

The five-day week, the latest word in social and industrial adjustment, the demand and dream of many, has become a reality for 35,000 workers in the garment industry in New York. This week the industry in which a majority of the employers and workers are Jewish, mainly of immigrant stock, went [to work] on a forty-hour five-day week basis.

When compared with the sweatshop system of 30 years ago, when the influx of Jewish immigration from Eastern and Central Europe had just started, the five-day week appears as an undreamed of millennium. Outside of New Zealand, whose industrial and social legislation stands alone, the Jewish workers in New York's clothing industry may claim the distinction of having arrived at an amicable understanding with the captains of the industry, both in the interest of the industry itself and the vast number of families whose livelihood and cultural status is affected by the arrangement.

It should be particularly pleasing to those who have the feeling of [illegible] as lately defined by [illegible] G. Montefiore as being peculiar [illegible], not only to one branch of Jewry but to all, regardless of synagogue [illegible] affiliation, that the worth of the idea concurred in theoretical discussions, not only by labor leaders but also by captains of industry, such as Henry Ford and others, is being experimented with by the untiring Jewish worker who only a generation ago was considered the least desirable.[12]

The Forty-Hour Week

Labor leaders give the assurance that the five-day workweek will perform miracles for the economic and cultural standards of the working class as a whole. At present they assure [us] that the five-day week does not lessen the average earning capacity of the workers. In addition, it does away with the slack season, the frequent interruptions of work that have been the plague of the industry.

En passant, one may recall that among the early advocates of the five-day week were none other than the Orthodox rabbis of the United States. As long ago as twenty-five years ago, an Orthodox Rabbis' convention went on record as being in favor of such an

---

[11] Published under the title "What's Happening in New York."

[12] The illegibility of several words in this paragraph is due to damage to the original newspaper, which was reproduced in the microfilm made of it.

arrangement. It goes without saying that the rabbis were not motivated by socialistic tendencies. They were, rather, anxious to provide the opportunity for those Jewish workers who considered the violation of the Sabbath as detrimental to their peace of conscience to comply with the dictates of their religious conviction. But then, the institution of the Sabbath as defined in the Mosaic Law is perhaps the first great radical social reform that humanity has had. Now we can see that the *Wall Street Journal* welcomes the five-day week.

Merit Recognized

Many members of the Jewish community, outstanding in the field of industry, commerce or philanthropy, are nowadays being honored by the educational institutions of the land. The reports of the graduation exercises of many colleges unfailingly contain reports of honorary degrees conferred upon outstanding American Jews for their contribution to one or another branch of American life. New York University has conferred the degree of Doctor of Commercial Science upon Daniel Guggenheim, founder of the Daniel Guggenheim Foundation for the Promotion of Aeronautics; the degree of Doctor of Hebrew Letters was conferred upon George Alexander Kohut by the Jewish Institute of Religion; Dr. Lee K. Frankel and David A. Brown were given the degree of Doctor of Hebrew Law by the Hebrew Union College; the degree of Doctor of Hebrew Literature was conferred upon Dr. Solomon Solls-Cohen by the Jewish Theological Seminary; and the degree of Doctor of Law was conferred upon Jacob Billikopf by the University of Richmond. This week Western Reserve University of Cleveland will confer the degree of Doctor of Letters on Dr. Abba Hillel Silver, and Moses J. Stroock will receive the degree of Doctor of Law from St John's College, Brooklyn. Who is it who said merit is not recognized?

American Jewry Enriched

The Jewish Theological Seminary graduates eight rabbis and 23 teachers; the Jewish Institute of Religion graduates eight rabbis; the Hebrew Union College graduates 14 rabbis; [and] the Yeshiva is about to graduate a number of Orthodox rabbis.

With the conclusion of the academic year, American Jewry finds itself enriched with a number of rabbis who are ready to become the public servants of the community, to propagate its ideals, to continue its traditions, whether these are Orthodox, Conservative or Reform, to teach its youth, and to attend to the social service needs.

Pessimists may brood over the future of American Jewry. Critics may indulge in recriminations against one branch or another on the grounds of theology or in reminiscences and comparisons with the ancient type of rabbis and leaders in Israel. As the midsummer approaches, one is rather inclined to ignore the doubts and see nothing but the gradual emergence and progress of a unified American Jewry that is confident of its future and is determined to continue, in the main, a three-thousand-year-old tradition, notwithstanding the minor points of difference.

Tempests in a Teapot

A Citizens' Committee of prominent New York Zionists has taken upon its shoulders the difficult task of attempting to restore peace within the movement.

Dr. Louis I. Harris, Commissioner of Health in New York City, who has his hands full with the milk problem and other issues of public welfare; Professor Mordecai M. Kaplan, the theoretician of Conservative Judaism, the father of the Jewish Center idea, busy with finding a more accurate definition of Conservative Judaism; and Israel Matz and others who have the good repute of the movement at heart have united to attempt to solve the crisis.

The writer finds it difficult to recall a single Jewish conflict in recent years that seemed at the beginning to threaten a "catastrophe," on which peace did not descend suddenly. When looked at from some distance, it then appears that the controversy and the impending "catastrophe" were merely a tempest in a teapot. It is premature to predict with what measure of success the Citizens Committee will meet in its attempt to untangle the Zionist situation. Will they succeed in bringing about reconciliation between Jacob de Haas and Louis Lipsky? Will it clarify the issues? Will it prevent the Zionist convention in Pittsburgh from becoming another Cleveland or at least a magnified Atlantic City? Will it at least succeed in confining the fire within the three-mile limit and save, until the next Zionist congress, the Weizmann regime from a continuation of criticism and attacks? Will it make the commission form of government as the basis for negotiations? Or will it retain the President's office without the sacrifice of personal reputations?

These are questions that Zionists and even neutrals will be interested to see answered. If this Citizens Committee succeeds in bringing about a solution that will be satisfactory to all and will not contain the germ of a new opposition a few months later, it will see the gratitude of many.

Convention Time is Here

It is convention time. Groups and organization of which the public at large hears nothing or comparatively little during the year appear on the scene in convention halls to make their vow to the public.

The Rabbinical Assembly, the organization of the Jewish Theological Seminary Alumni and such rabbis as may be classified as Conservative; the Central Conference of American Rabbis, the Independent Order of B'rith Abraham, the Order [of the] Sons of Zion, the Avukah, the Histadruth Ivrith, and others too numerous to be named, are about to call together their members to listen to the achievements of the year before they retire for a midsummer nap.

Those who think in terms of community responsibility are frequently complaining of the lack of unified action on the part of American Jews. They point to conditions under other climes and under other circumstances where Jewry has its fixed organizational forms and its appointed or elected spokesmen. In a way the summer bows of the various organizations are as near a substitute as is possible to a community feeling. The organizations and groups as they appear in a convention assembly present themselves for judgment to the public. The *summa summarium* of these convention proceedings represents the total of our group assets and sometimes liabilities.

Luxurious Cemeteries

New York's Attorney General, Albert Ottinger, lately spoken of with great certainty as the forthcoming Republican candidate for the governorship of the State of New York, has instituted an investigation into charges presented by the Hebrew Religious Protective Association of Greater New York with regard to conditions that seem to prevail in some Jewish burial associations.

The Jewish Post, July 1929[13]

Thirty thousand garments workers, mostly Jews, are on strike since July 3. The Manhattan district from 23rd Street to 40th Street, called the Garment Center, is the scene of daily unrest. Nothing fundamentally dangerous, to be sure. Those who have witnessed revolutionary labor struggles in other world centers, with their direct threat to society as now constituted, will be inclined to view these events as a rather mild occurrence. The fights develop, not between the State and labor as a class, but between organized labor as a social force, constructive and state-building in the fight against this social plague, [the] antisocial forces of the sweatshops on one side and the left-wingers on the other.

The sweatshop was the enemy that stood at the cradle of the Jewish labor movement a generation ago.

The individualism and the innate sense of justice of the Jewish worker waged a fierce battle against it. Due to the energy and intellect invested in the fight against this social plague, it was by and by recognized that the abolition of the sweatshop is not only in the interest of labor but perhaps more to the benefit of the State, of industry as such, and of business in general. Under the influence of these labor struggles, social legislation was placed on the statue books[, an] example of a fair and humanitarian approach toward a solution of the problems under modern conditions.

As a result of the unfortunate 1926 strike under the left-wing leadership, the ladies' garment workers, who were in the forefront of progress, seem again to be threatened with the sweatshop menace. The war declared against it is significant in more than one direction. It certainly has the sympathy of the enlightened New York public, who think in social rather than in narrow class terms.

The appointment by Gov. Roosevelt of our Lieutenant Governor, Colonel Herbert H. Lehman, who was Chairman of Governor Smith's board during the 1924 strike, augurs well for a speedy and just settlement. It has a particular meaning from a Jewish point of view when it is remembered that the welfare of almost 30,000 Jewish families directly affected and about as many indirectly interested, is at stake.

A housecleaning in the New York needle industry has even greater importance from a Jewish political point of view. The outstanding feature in the Jewish mass immigration to the United States during the beginning of the twentieth century was the compulsory, rapid transformation of a large number of our people from the "Luft menschen"[14] class into a healthy and productive factor in the economic fabric of American life.

Of late, alarming signs of an increasing exodus of many workers and their children into the ranks of the lower-middle classes were beginning to be noted. This fact not only tended to undo the work of the first generation of pioneers, but also to raise many weighty economic and social questions.

The elimination of the sweatshop evil and the raising of the standard [of living] in the needle industry may be a step in a direction perhaps beyond the program of the

---

[13] Published under the title "New York Topics," this essay appears to have been edited "for style," and thus doesn't resemble the writer's other essays. It also doesn't make sense and/or makes odd, unsubstantiated claims in places, which suggests that it was hacked up so that it could fit the space that was available.

[14] Yiddish expression ("air people") for people who have no apparent means of support.

International Ladies Garment Workers' Union and the American Federation of Labor which lends to it its support.

"Molders of Jewish Public Opinion: Their Biography, Their Work, and Their Views on the Future"
The Chicago Chronicle, June 6, 1924

It is the general opinion that with the passage of the new immigration bill, American Jewry is entering a new epoch in its history. With immigration severely restricted, American Jewry will from now on have to depend for its spiritual development on its own resources. The Jewish Telegraphic Agency considers this moment opportune to portray to the Jewish public these figures in American Jewish life who are at the head of Jewish public affairs and are responsible for the molding of Jewish public opinion through the medium of the Jewish press of this country.

Herman Bernstein

What is Journalism? Is it merely to write of things that happen through the will of other people, or is it rather writing that influences other people and creates in them the will to do? What is the inner force of a man who has enriched the globe, come in contact with kings, presidents and diplomats, discovered secret treaties and unearthed the most intimate letters of Emperors?

Is it merely the journalistic search for "good newspaper stuff," or is there in back of it a central idea that employs these methods in order that some higher ideal may be achieved?

With these questions in mind I went to see Mr. Herman Bernstein. I had met him several years before. It was in the city of Warsaw during the Versailles Peace Conference. The prestige of President Wilson and America was at its height. Rumors were afloat in Central and Eastern Europe that President Wilson was determined to see to it that his fourteen points, including the point, introduced for the first time in the history of the world, of self-determination for small nations, should be carried out. Reports had been circulating in the Polish press that the "anonymous power" (meaning Jewish representatives at the Paris conference) had set all forces in motion to influence the contracting parties to guarantee, in a special international treaty, the rights of small nations whose fate it was to live on territories ruled by other nations. It was merely rumored, but not believed; and here is Mr. Herman Bernstein, who on a shortcut from Paris to Moscow, stopped over in Warsaw and brought with him the actual text of the treaty, before it was intended to be published.

He came armed with a letter of introduction from the then-powerful Prime Minister Paderewski to Minister of the Interior Wojciechowski, now the President of the Polish Republic. Surely a document brought by him is authentic. However, when the document was published, the Polish press poured out its wrath on the "anonymous power" and most of all on the wandering Jew, Herman Bernstein.

But the Wandering Jew did not stay long enough in the capital of the resurrected Poland to see these attacks upon him. In pursuit of his mission, he proceeded . . . north, or west, east or south? Who could tell?

When I sat down in his apartment in New York for the purpose of interviewing Mr. Herman Bernstein, I thought I had a very hard task before me. To interview a president or a minister is not a hard thing. If you concentrate on your subject, you will "catch him." But to interview an interviewer, one who knows the ins and outs of the interviewing game, seemed to be rather a difficult task. However, Herman Bernstein, the great interviewer, proved to be not so terrible after all. On the contrary, he seemed to have decided in advance to make up for all the suspense that he must have caused in others by repaying with kindness those who come to interview him. As I looked at the amiable, smiling countenance and listened to his fluent conversation, a most interesting tale of a life started in Russia, developed in New York and exercised in Tokyo, Petrograd, Paris and Vladivostok, unfolded itself.

* * *

Born in 1876 in Neustadt-Shervint, raised in Mogilow in a well-to-do, enlightened Jewish family, he received a thorough religious training combined with a sound secular education. As early as at eleven years of age, his interest in the affairs of his people manifested itself in his attempts to become the correspondent of the then-influential and widely read Hebrew daily paper *Ha' Meilitz*, in Petrograd. While learning by heart Talmudic volumes, he endeavored to write Russian poetry, his heart having been captured by the poetry of Pushkin and Lermontov. However, the life of the promising lad was destined to undergo an important transformation and all the pain of a transplantation into a new and entirely strange environment. It was his uncle, Hirsch Bernstein, the family's first "discoverer of America," who having found in the '80s a refuge in New York, proceeded immediately to prepare the ground for a large settlement of his race in the New World. He was the first to establish a Hebrew newspaper in this country, under the name *Hazopheh B'eretz Ha'Khadacha* (The Observer in a New Land). Soon the entire family came over and the young Herman had to assume part of the family's responsibilities.

Changing jobs and professions as many times as is imaginable in the course of five years, he finally landed on Division Street, New York, in a clothing store, where the position of bookkeeper seemed to offer him a livelihood with the possibility of continuing his education and his literary work. Having mastered the English language, his old literary ambition found expression in continuous attempts at Russian poetry, translations into English from the Russian and numberless short stories in English. While some of his poetry and translations were published in weekly Jewish magazines, his short story offerings were always returned to him; until one day, a quarter of a century ago, the young Bernstein found to his own surprise that a story of his pen had been published in the literary section of the then-widely read *New York Evening Post*.

The name of the story was "Sareh Rivke's Vigil." It was a sad story of a Jewish mother watching over her son who, in her brooding, seemed to be in danger of being led astray. Herman Bernstein has been ever since vigilant of the important problems in the life of America and in the life of his people all over the world. Although an immigrant of not more than five years' residence, Bernstein's stories, which had been sent back to him time and again, were now in great demand by American editors and publishers. Although unrecommended and unsponsored, Herman Bernstein's journalistic work won success on its own merits and placed him in a short period of time in the rank of those who form American opinion on international affairs, and one of the molders of Jewish public opinion in this country and many others.

* * *

It is hard to choose from the multitude of problems that attracted the attention of Herman Bernstein's pen, those that are of greater significance. In fact, they were all significant and all important in their day. It is the tragedy of the journalistic profession that the greatest amount of intellect and skill, invested in "burning issues," is of no longer duration than Jonah's gourd. With the difference, however, that while the leaves of the journalistic Jonah disappear as soon as the sun rises and a new day is marked on the calendar, the work of the Jonah in journalism, the one who in his sea-crossings is driven by an inner search for truth and has at the point of his pen a message of real value, endures. Because of his literary activities, particularly the translations from the Russian into English, Mr. Bernstein found one day a short story in the Russian magazine *Viestnik Europy*, under the name of "S. Witte." Being anxious to translate the story into English, he wrote to "S. Witte," in care of the journal, asking for permission to do so. In return, Mr. Bernstein received a letter from Mlle. Sofia Witte, enclosing an entire volume of her stories that she thought would prove to be as interesting as her first story. However, some of the stories were ink-spotted in a manner that indicated censoring. The censored spots proved to be unpleasant references to the Jews. Without being personally known to each other, author and translator engaged in a heated correspondence concerning the Jewish question in Russia. The somewhat bitter controversy ended, however, in a sincere friendship that was to lead to a great change in Herman Bernstein's activities.

Sofia Witte proved to be none other than the aristocratic sister of the then-powerful Count Witte, the Prime Minister of Russia, who at the time was due to arrive in the United States, at the invitation of President Roosevelt, to negotiate the Russian-Japanese peace treaty of Portsmouth.

Startling revelations of an international character, probably still remembered by devoted newspaper readers, were the result of this correspondence, and Bernstein rose to be the feared and fearless American journalist, exposer of international intrigue and corruption.

* * *

What is the outstanding problem in American Jewish life at the present time, was the question that I put to Mr. Herman Bernstein in conclusion. "There are two questions that are of interest to leaders of American Jewry above everything else," he answered. "The first is the question of securing Jewish education for our youth. It has been the evil of our life in this country that in exchange for the material blessings that our people have received here, many of us, in our anxiety to become fully American, have overdone it. Many have become 110 percent American, crushing entirely their Judaism, and losing thus their rich racial and cultural heritage, the things that make for their individuality. It is evident that if Jewish life in America is to continue it must have a sound foundation in a proper Jewish education. There is no conflict between real Americanism and the ancient teachings of Judaism.

"The second problem that ought to get the attention of our people in this country is the problem of rebuilding Palestine. With the other relief work stopped, the work of rehabilitating Palestine is the only great task, the fulfillment of which is rightly expected from us."

"What is the future of the Yiddish press in this country?" I ventured to ask the founder and former editor of the great Yiddish daily *The Day*, "and what tendency is likely to predominate in Jewish life in this country after the complete stoppage of immigration?"

"While it is true," Mr. Bernstein said, "that the Yiddish press has already seen its best days in this country, there is no ground to hold any pessimistic views regarding the future of American Jewry, which has already sufficiently strong elements of communal vitality, learning and leadership."

"Do you think that the passage of the anti-immigration bill, together with the talk about the superiority of the so-called 'Nordic' [people] may create a ferment of racial discrimination in America, affecting the Jewish people first of all?" I asked in conclusion.

"America, as well as the rest of the world, has not yet demobilized its spirit of unrest and the wave of chauvinistic madness. The anti-immigration bill is one expression of this general unrest that is still prevailing. America will sooner or later free itself from it. But while we need not be alarmed, we should not follow any longer the course of the 'Great Non-Resistant,' as Tolstoy named us. We ought to combat anti-Semitism openly and vigorously at any time it makes its appearance."

"Molders of Jewish Public Opinion: Their Life, Their Work and Their Views (II): Peter Wiernik, Historian and Editor"
The Chicago Chronicle, August 22, 1924

The advocate of the conservative tendency – no, I should say, [the] fact in Jewish communal life is the *Jewish Morning Herald.* It is distinguished by its age, circulation and sphere of influence. It has been in existence for over 20 years, and has not only brought information and strength to the older Yiddish-speaking generation, but also to a large part of a younger generation of Jews who adapted themselves to the American environment and did not at the same time abandon their interest in Jewish affairs.

The living force of thoughtful conservatism, a combination of modern knowledge, based on the wisdom and experience of [the] ages, is given to this publication by its venerable editor, Peter Wiernik. Readers of the Jewish press, when looking for the purely Jewish view of any matter that happens to occupy the minds of men, have necessarily to look to the editorial comment of Peter Wiernik. His pen finds interest not only in matters purely religious; his attention is devoted to matters of politics, Democratic or Republican, social reform, political appreciation of any given complicated situation in any country, and to the latest expression in modern philosophical thought, naturally comparing it with the inexhaustible sources of the Jewish philosophical school of Maimonides, Yehuda Ha'Levey, Ramban, the mystic self-seeking and self-expressing reflections of an Ari and Baal Shem Tov.

Peter Wiernik represents an entirely new type in Jewish literature and journalism. Although born in the midst of the heated fight that went on in the middle of the 19th century between the dominating tendencies in Jewish life, "Haskalah" and "Hassidism," he was never caught in the whirlwind of this struggle. The course of his life marks a departure from the then-usual routine. He did not spend his youth in study alone; did not fight against the "darkness"; did not cherish high ambitions for saving the world from its troubles. He simply sat down to work from the very beginning.

The son of a traveling Magid (preacher), having the privilege of seeing his father only at rare intervals, perhaps once a year, he did not have to resist parental education, go through the usual conflict between "fathers and sons," and could not naturally indulge in theorizing on account of material abundance. Being harnessed at hard work at the age of 13 in Riga, he found the joyful and enthusiastic attitude of the Hassidim on Saturdays and holidays a great redeeming feature. Being welded to the prose of everyday life, experience[d] in the poetry of a Hassidic Rabbi on the Sabbath.

Peter Wiernik is positively not a Socialist. But immediately upon his arrival in America he plunged into the field of productive labor, working as a compositor for many years in various newspaper plants. However, the work in the composing room did not prevent him from continuing his interest in the intellectual problems of life and did not limit his capacity for absorbing more and more knowledge of the world's history, the history of his people and its literature.

When I came to visit Mr. Peter Wiernik at his home I found the American Jewish historian in most excellent spirits. Place a chemist in a well-equipped laboratory with all facilities for his work: what more will he require for his happiness? I asked a few questions of Mr. Wiernik and his replies came with such ease and familiarity that one would not feel like arguing any longer since they are the result of a lifelong process of thinking, based not only on historical study, [but also] an outcome of mature judgment, brightened by an optimistic view of the future.

"What is the main motive of the history of the Jewish people?" I asked Mr. Wiernik.

[He responded:] The basis of the development of all races and peoples is, as no one can deny, the economic motive. No development or advancement of any race or any people would be accomplished were not the very natural needs of the individuals and their collective striving as a group forcing them towards expansion and conquest. This is true of all the races and of all peoples. It is equally true of our people. To put the purpose of making in a nutshell, one could say it is an elemental longing and striving for salvation of the world. It was the slow process of development, the first step of which was necessarily the establishing of a reign of justice of one individual towards another, and one group of individuals, call them peoples or nations, towards another. In this respect our people have made, one can say, the greatest of all contributions, proclaiming that principle and putting itself as a sacrifice on the altar of this ideal. This tendency made itself evident beginning from the period of the Prophets and ending with the latest developments in attempting to solve the social problems. There are principally two tendencies in history. The one described above, represented by us; the other represented by those who oppose it. When the struggle for the dominance of one of these tendencies is to be ended there is no way of knowing. All we can do is record the things that have already happened.

"What is the central tendency in American Jewish life that is likely to gain dominance?" I asked Mr. Wiernik.

"Parallel with the pushing ahead of this tendency for justice and equity, aiming at the salvation of the world, the fight for the emancipation of the Jewish people has been going on. It was not until the French Revolution and the German Revolution of 1848 that the Jews were in principle given equal rights. The existence of the American Jewish community in its present form and numbers is the first fact of this kind that was ever recorded in the history of the Jewish people and the history of the world. America represents a unique experiment in this respect. It is for the first time that a great number of Jews are incorporated into the body of a great and free nation under the protection of a democratic and liberal government and given the possibility of enjoying full citizenship rights and religious liberty. This state of affairs certainly has its advantages, but it also has its dangers. Here again Jewish history can furnish us a good reason for optimism. It was not earlier than the date when the Jewish settlements began to grow and the development of the Slavic countries [took place] that the type of Jew that we are now accustomed to look upon as the only representative of traditional Judaism, characterizing him as [an] Orthodox Jew, began to make his appearance. We are always inclined to think of this type of a Jew, whose Jewishness is expressed by his difference in language, dress and external custom, as different from the other inhabitants of the land. But let us take a lesson from history. The Jewish community in Arabic Spain was highly cultured, highly developed and certainly highly Jewish, since it would produce such a basically Jewish literature as the one that has inspired our historians to name that period 'The Golden Epoch.' Nevertheless, a leader and intellectual genius like Maimonides was not any different from his countrymen in his language, external custom and culture than any other leader of that country and time. The essentials of Judaism do not depend upon such external appearances. There is no ground for pessimism in the prediction of the approach of a similar type of American Jew who, enjoying the to the full measure his political rights, cultural and economic opportunities, should remain true to his specific Jewish culture, line of thought and religion. The time is not far off, in my opinion, when America, the youngest of Jewish communities, will be in a position to supply with intellectual and religious leaders all the other, older and now seemingly decadent Jewish communities of the world. In this respect, Orthodox Judaism is a valuable protection and a veritable armor, as it has proven to be in the course of our long and varied historical development."

What is your opinion with regard to the lately much talked of theory of the superiority of the Nordics in connection with the anti-immigration bill, and is there any danger that America will become susceptible to the doctrines of anti-Semitism?

Here, again, Mr. Wiernik concluded, "History could furnish us valuable service. The fate of the Jewish communities in the Anglo-Saxon countries that we could rightly call biblical countries is sufficient proof that anti-Semitism, at least so far as its sharp and violent forms are concerned, never could root itself very deeply in these countries."

"Molders of Jewish Public Opinion: B. Charney Vladeck, Jewish Labor's Tribune"
The Chicago Chronicle, September 5, 1924

There is a romantic touch of heroism in the life of B.C. Vladeck, general manager of the *Jewish Daily Forward*.

Born in an orthodox Jewish family in Dukov, Gov. of Minsk, Russia, he has received together with his older brother, the well-known literary critic S. Niger, the usual Jewish religious training. Studying in a Yeshiva in Minsk his mind, at an early stage, underwent the exercises and discipline of Talmudic scholasticism. He found, however, a greater appeal in the poetical cry of the Prophets, especially Isaiah, against the social injustice of the feudal system of ancient Judea, than in the hairsplitting and sharp-minded theorizing of the later exponents of abstract Jewish thought in the schools of Babylon and awoke, when yet a youth, to the problem of economic inequality in the country of his nativity. White Russia, the place where Vladeck grew to maturity was, it seems, particularly fit to cause such an awakening. The tremendous chasm between the poor village population on one hand and the luxury of the small group of landowners on the other; the limitless poverty of the city dwellers and the extravagant life of the then-powerful higher Russian officials was too great a reminder of social difference for it not to set in motion a mind and a heart that had inherited a capacity for understanding and feeling. But Vladeck is not a mere dreamer. When obsessed with an idea he strives to turn it into a fact. The immediate need of the Jewish city population in that region of the former Russian Empire was the attaining of a secular education. Vladeck, a young boy, joined the staff of some private library in the city. His first conflict with the Russian government was on account of his activity, for which he had to repent in jail.

Class Distinctions Faint at Start of Movement

At the early stage of the labor movement among Jews, the Jewish masses represented a unique spectacle. The bulk of Jews in the former Russian "Pale of Settlement" consisted of one large middle class. Although divided by the degree of possession, there was no such distinction as bosses and workers (although they were nothing else but wage earners, with the difference that wages were paid to them not by any employer, but by their small enterprises). The Jewish labor movement, creating a labor consciousness had at the same time to create a workers' class. It had when "selling" the idea of a Jewish workers' organization, at the same time to "sell" the status of such a class. The "Bund," Marxian and international in principle, but granting concessions for the peculiar cultural needs of the Jewish masses, was the first and most important of Jewish labor organizations of Russia in promulgating this doctrine and in spreading the idea of class consciousness. B.C. Vladeck joined this organization, which was not a small factor in the Russian revolutionary movement of 1905. But "selling" an idea in former imperial Russia, not to speak of any distinctly revolutionary or socialistic idea, was a dangerous undertaking.

Vladeck, stirred by the idealism and attracted by the practical task that this movement offered, devoted himself to the "selling" of this dangerous article. Traveling to and from the cities and villages on the plains of White Russia, Lithuania and Poland, Baruch Charney had to conceal his identity in order to escape the inquisitive eyes of the Russian secret police. Vladeck, a Polish name in common usage, correspondent to that of Jim or Jack in America, was the safest pseudo[nym] to sail under. Charging somebody to find Vladeck in Poland would be as trying a task as the finding of Jim in America. But the mysterious Vladeck, who appeared at meetings and gatherings in towns where the Russian secret police expected him the least, many times fell into the hands of his adversaries. When it was not [any] longer possible for "Vladeck" to carry on his work, he immigrated to America and became B.C. Vladeck. Here the stream of immigration of previous years has performed the metamorphoses, urged, preached, expected and almost prayed for by the Jewish labor leaders. The transplantation of the large mass of unskilled men into America has within a comparatively short period performed their almost miraculous transformation into a class of hard-toiling workers with a sound beginning of unions and organizations. Here Vladeck found the place for the development of his energies. In a short period of time we see him assume responsibility after responsibility and become the spokesman of New York's Jewish laborers, defending their rights, not only in [the] settlement of strikes, but representing [them] as aldermen in the board of aldermen.

Believes Large Professional Classes Cause of Anti-Semitism

When you look at the stern features of Vladeck and meet his penetrating eyes, you immediately get the impression that you talk to a man who has the great gift of preserving cool-mindedness under all circumstances. He has also the ability of dealing with problems in a detached way, so to speak. When he speaks to you, you feel that he does not think about himself. In a leisurely hour, during a busy day, he presents to you in a forcible and convincing way his views on any question that you choose to take up.

"What is the greatest problem in Jewish life in America?" I asked Mr. Vladeck.

"The strength of Jewish life in America was the place that our fellow workers have occupied in the life of producing America. This place has been earned by hard toil, skill and intelligence. Its rights and privileges were fought for and acquired in a way that could be expected from any group of thinking and well-led working class [people]. The problem that arises now in the life of the Jewish working class is, strange to observe, the drifting away from that principle of labor that wrought strength and economic position to the first generation of workers. There is too great a tendency in the younger generation towards the so-called intelligent professions, a drifting that might create again in the life of the Jewish working masses the problem of a middle class that depends upon external conjectures and is exposed to envy, criticism and call it, if you like, anti-Semitism."

"What is your opinion about the signs of anti-Semitism that came sporadically to expression in this country?"

"America, which bases its pyramidal structure on enterprise welfare and governmental institutions, on the principle of successful endeavor, cannot very well abandon this sound course and follow the sickly doctrines of racial divisions and prejudices. A government that derives its power from the polls, depends for its continuity upon public opinion and the way it manages to enlarge the circle of those who enjoy prosperity, cannot be influenced in its actions by racial prejudice."

"Does the Jewish working class in America feel in any way the present need for some action on the part of American Jewry towards relieving of the situation of those parts of the Jewish people who suffer in other European countries, or [in other words] do you admit the existence of a Jewish problem with the result that some action ought to be taken?"

"The fate of Jewish people in Eastern Europe and in other countries who are subject to persecution on one hand and locked up in certain countries in groups that have no opportunity for developing their natural energies [on the other], is no doubt a question that interests the Jewish working class in America. There is a responsibility resting upon us and I would venture to say that some action ought to be taken in this respect."

"Changing Values in American Jewish Fraternities"
The Canadian Jewish Chronicle, July 31, 1925[1]

The wave of tropical heat that [recently] descended upon the northeast gave way to a lower temperature. People were relieved. However, a new wave has descended. It is the wave of conventions.

The convention is a product "made in America." Conferences are known everywhere. Conventions, with their large attendance, [a] combination of business and pleasure, politics and amusement, are typical of a great democracy.

"The fatherhood of God and the brotherhood of man" – a Jewish idea that has remained an ideal through the centuries – would justify one to believe that brotherhoods, fraternities and orders were an important factor in Jewish life. However, Jewish history has only one record, and that an incomplete one, of the existence of a Jewish fraternal order: the Essenes, a product of Palestinian soil, which left to posterity only an unexplainable name.

The Essenes, as described by Josephus Flavius, were, perhaps, the first fraternity that gathered its membership with caution and held it in a strong common bond of brotherhood, social justice and religious purity. It was, perhaps, also the first effective teacher of hygiene, imposing the duty of cleanliness upon its members. The "sunrise bathers" is the vague expression that they left upon the Jewish mind, giving rise to the movement that preceded the birth of Christianity and precedence to the various Orders of the Bath.

Since then, however, Jewish history represents a "tabula rasa" with regard to fraternities. Perhaps it was due to the environment that prevented such organizations. Perhaps it was due to the common fate that created, as it were, a Jewish fraternity at large.

---

[1] This essay, it seems, was heavily edited, if not rewritten, by its publisher, and thus barely resembles the author's other texts.

And it was not until the glorious chapter in American Jewry was added to Jewish history that Jewish fraternal orders came into existence.

Perhaps in no other country is the social life of its citizens so colorful as in the United States. The color introduced by the fraternities is particularly radiant against the grey background of the democracy. This is also perhaps one of the motives responsible in this country.

But there were many more and much deeper reasons. Critics of Jewish life have frequently indulged in an accusation, which on the surface might appear true, that when Jews form a community, the first care of the community is to purchase a cemetery. When non-Jews form a settlement, their first care is to create a park. On examination this accusation is only half-truth. Physicians in Jewish districts know better. The Jewish people consider life above everything. "And you who are united in God, you are all alive today" was the commandment of optimism and encouragement that has sounded in Jewish ears since the days of Moses.

But life is not eternal and must be followed by death. The practical Jewish mind cares for both, life and death.

When the wave of immigration to America brought on its crest thousands of newcomers who needed assistance in life and were subject to sickness and death, the fraternity was formed to take care of the sick and the burial of the dead. Numerous orders were in operation. Rituals were composed, by-words created, [and] forms laid down for their increasing membership.

Some of the older fraternities, such as the [Independent Order of] B'Nai B'rith, swiftly abandoned their primate form and ascended to greater heights of social service. Others, with greater individual numbers, underwent a slower process. Large bodies move slowly, but the process is going on with its attending difficulties, obstacles and trying situations.

Observers of Jewish life in America have often given expression to the fact that only a small minority are affiliated with any kind of congregational life, whether it be reform, conservative or orthodox. An observer at the Thirty-Ninth Convention of the Independent Order of B'Nai Abraham, a fraternity with a membership of 135,000, could find a reply to this comment. While the bulk of the membership is apparently of the type that is termed "unaffiliated," the proceedings of this gathering proved beyond doubt how deeply tradition, and Jewish tradition at that, holds them in its grip.

Not objecting to the new and progressive ideas of widening the scope of the fraternity, and introducing social membership lodges, the convention persistently objected to all attempts of the leaders to do away with the old-fashioned post-mortem assessments and to introduce a modern, scientific system of mutual insurance. With only a $2,000,000 reserve fund and 135,000 members, and with an increasing rate of mortality, the financial situation can be saved by nothing short of a miracle. However, the majority voted for optimism and tradition. "We have existed for thirty-nine years on the post-mortem assessment system; we will continue to do so," they argued. More than this, adherence to tradition came to the surface when the convention preferred to delay the transaction of business on the agenda to listen to a well-known cantor sing religious songs.

"From dust does man come and to dust doth he return." There could be no better expression of the spirit of this type of Jewish fraternity in this period of changing values in American Jewish life.

"Is Poland Balancing Her Budget and Soul? Some Thoughts and Facts on the Polish-Jewish Agreement"
The Reform Advocate, August 8, 1925

On a July evening in Brooklyn, the city of homes, the "tired American businessman," the manufacturer and the worker seek refuge from the oppressive heat in that quiet and peaceful corner – the home.

The radio is the window to the world, maintaining contact and furnishing possibilities for amusement, entertainment and instruction.

We were assembled in a typical home of an American Jewish family. All questions of the day disposed of, the host opened the "miracle box" for entertainment and, perhaps, casual information.

A heavy but fluent voice announced: "Honorable Count Alexander Skrzynski, Polish Minister of Foreign Affairs, will address the American people following a 'Polish hour.'"

* * *

The "Polish hour" consisted of musical selections by Chopin, Paderewski and Wieniawski. The gathering, mainly American born, all Americanized, enjoyed the tone of the classical selections that are in such striking contrast to the half-negro jazz.

Atavism apparently is a great factor. Almost all of the assembled, looking back in historical and geographic terms, could trace the reason why the music of Polish genius had a special appeal to them. One's father or grandfather, another's mother, lived at one point in some part of God's world that was somehow connected with Polish territory or under the influence of Polish culture.

Atavism was not, however, necessary to explain the intense attention with which the further announcements were listened to.

"We will now have the honor of listening to the Honorable Count Alexander Skrzynski in his first address to the American people over the radio," the announcer's voice resounded.

Aha. The noble with that unpronounceable name who comes from a country where millions of Jews have lived and suffered. Is it true that conditions there are to be better now? Let us listen.

The loudspeaker was placed in the center of the room. Everybody lent an ear. A proud voice that seemingly attempted to be mild issued forth.

"Poland will never forget its gratitude to the United States. Poland will never forget that it was Wilson's thirteenth point that raised the stone from its tomb.

"Poland, a democratic country, has in the last seven years built up a state. We have opened schools, spread education. Our country has difficulties, but Poland has balanced not only its budget but also its soul.

"One of the main questions is that of the national minorities. One of the outstanding features of the national minority question is the Jewish question. There is no reason why the Jews in Poland should not be able to live together and derive their livelihood in a country as rich in opportunities as Poland is. The agreement recently concluded in Warsaw is an important step in that direction."

All ears were eager to hear more. When the hour struck eleven the voice that came from the distance ceased.

An impression remained. Poland is balancing not only its budget, but also it soul.

An agreement has been concluded.

* * *

In the course of many centuries Jews have lived in Poland. As long ago as the time of the almost prehistoric King Mieszko, the first coins that were issued on the banks of the Vistula had Hebrew inscriptions. In the course of centuries a golden chain of Jewish work, of Jewish development of commerce and building of towns, continued in what were "Polish forests."

Through the various crises, misfortunes, wars and the three partitions, the poem of a Polish Jewish idyll went on. Rabbi Meisels marching with the Catholic priests at the head of the Polish legions, fighting desperately against Russian invasion. Berek Yosselovitch forming a special Jewish legion for combating the Russian invasion, the Jewish members of Pilsudski's liberty legion, the blood and flesh embodiments of Mickiewicz's "Yankel Cymbalist" and Eliza Orzesko's "Meir Josephowicz."

The influence of the Kabalah took root. Towjanskism was the forerunner of Polish Messianism that, after prolonged struggle, suppressions and sufferings, attained what seemed to be a victory.

* * *

December 11, 1918. Wilson's Fourteen Points hang over Europe like fourteen challenges. Under the pressure of these challenges, Europe tottered. The heavens seemed for a moment to open and resurrected Poland sprang forth with the desire of a Poland from sea to sea.

The star of Pilsudski rose on the horizon.

At the same time, however, there appeared the dark clouds of Dmowski, Glonbinski and Grabski, the pillars of that party that had, before the war, proclaimed militant anti-Semitism as its program and a boycott against Jews as its weapon.

The internal struggle for power in the new republic started. The road to political and economic power lay over the Jew. The popularity of a party depended upon the intensity of its anti-Semitism. A loud auction where the highest bidder on anti-Semitism was the winner was a continuous performance. In seven years, ten governments succeeded each other. The Bolsheviks came as far as the Vistula and receded; Czechoslovakia was indignant; Germany murmured; the millstones of history turned and the Jews of Poland were crushed.

* * *

Suddenly, strange dispatches began to come forth from Poland's capital. The Polish government, represented by its Minister of Foreign Affairs and Minister of Education, are "negotiating" with the Jews concerning an agreement. Conferences and negotiations continued for long weeks. Concessions, declarations and exchanges were talked of. Finally, a Polish Jewish "agreement" was concluded with proper ceremonies at which the following declaration was, as demanded, submitted by the Jewish leaders.

"Adhering continually to the standpoint of the immunity of the frontiers of the Polish Republic and the defense of Poland's policy as a great power, adhering to the view of the necessity for an internal consolidation within the Republic, the Club of Jewish Deputies in the Polish Sejm establishes that its policy in the Sejm with regard to general matters, as well as concerning Jewish national questions, was conceived and conducted in conformity with the aforementioned principle for the purpose of protecting the interests of the Jewish population in the Republic."

The Polish constitution is, one can safely say, a most liberal one. So far as the letter and spirit of the law goes, it guarantees equality before the law to all citizens, freedom of speech, freedom of worship, freedom of the press, and even goes further, as if to meet the international obligation incurred by Poland through its signature to the supplementary treaty on national minorities attached to the Treaty of Versailles, and guarantees the rights of "religious, racial and ethnographic minorities to foster their national characteristics and language."

Were there a desire to fulfill the constitution, other laws or concessions would be utterly unnecessary.

However, the fact is that negotiations, conferences and concessions were necessary in exchange for which a declaration of the Club of Jewish Deputies was submitted. A list of demands was submitted, only part of which was published.

* * *

Count Alexander Skrzyski, a tall gentleman of Polish aristocratic family, born in Galicia, educated at the University of Krakow and trained to diplomatic service in the school of the former Austro-Hungarian empire, presents an imposing figure of a man who can without difficulty meet the most difficult situation and smile it away.

The initiator of the Polish Jewish agreement, who is described as a man of courage, had great reserve when approached at the Hotel Pennsylvania in New York for more details on the circumstances and conditions of the agreement.

The declaration by the Club of Jewish Deputies to the Prime Minister that was, as is understood, a *sine qua non* for the agreement, contains a phrase in which the Club states that it "adhered continually to the standpoint of the immunity of the frontiers of the Polish Republic and the defense of Poland's policy as a great power," and also "to the view of the necessity for an internal consolidation within the Republic." This creates the impression that an oath of loyalty was asked of the Jewish deputies. Why was such a declaration of loyalty necessary? Have the Jews in Poland ever been disloyal to the Polish Republic? the minister was asked.

"Just as by inference one could form a charge against the Jews, basing it on this phrase of the declaration, so a similar charge could be formed against the Polish government that, by concluding an agreement, proved that it was not previously fair toward the Jews. While it is true that Polish Jewry was as a whole not disloyal, one might say that at least the impression prevailed that the Jews in Poland were not enthusiastic or, in the best of cases, were indifferent to Poland as a state," the count replied.

Press dispatches stated that the government has issued twelve ordinances concerning the democratization of the Jewish communities in the Polish Republic and recognizing the use of Hebrew and Yiddish at public meetings, as well as some concessions concerning school matters. Is this the only result of the agreement and if so, why were these concessions issued as government ordinances and not as legislation that would insure their permanency?

"The questions dealt with by the government ordinances are basically within the rights guaranteed in the constitution to all citizens of the Polish Republic. No special legislation is necessary. Until now any government that was in power could, as long as no change in the law was made, interpret the law in its own way. A few points that affect the economic status of the Jewish population may be objects of legislation at a later time. What was necessary was to give the lead. The government gave the lead to the agreement and its further development is, of course, a matter of time and of gradual adjustment based on a better understanding between the Jews and the Poles that requires a psychological change."

Did the government, when it concluded the agreement, act in this matter with the knowledge and consent of the Polish parties represented in the Sejm? Has your government a permanent majority in the present Polish parliament?

"So far as the present government is concerned, it has the largest support that any government has had. The mere fact that it is in existence for two years when, during the last seven years, ten governments have changed, proves its stability."

Is it true that the parliamentary club of the National Democratic Party has passed a resolution stating that the negotiations between the government and the Club of Jewish Deputies took place on the government's own responsibility?

Count Skrzynski seemed not to be aware of this resolution that was probably adopted after he left for America. He stated, however, that a guarantee that no opposition will come from that quarter lies in the fact that the Minister of Education, Stanislaw Grabski, who is one of the leaders of that party, conducted the negotiations and concluded the agreement.

Will steps be taken that the anti-Semitic press cease its fierce propaganda, which, in the opinion of many, was mainly responsible for the conditions created for the Jews in Poland?

"Here I must again refer to the Minister of Education who is himself an owner of several national dailies. I cannot imagine that the Minister of Education, who is a recognized leader of the National Democratic camp, would be criticized by his own press."

How would you explain the fact that the agreement was concluded at a time when the Jewish leaders from Little Poland, formerly Galicia, succeeded the leaders of former Russian Poland?

"I am from Galicia myself," the count smiled in answer.

* * *

The purpose of Count Skrzynski's journey to America was not a diplomatic mission but, as was stated, to lecture at the Williamstown Institute of Politics. In his address at that Institute, Count Skrzynski dwelt on the security pact that is now being negotiated between Great Britain, France and Belgium and Germany. In the draft of this pact, which is considered almost *a fait accompli*, mention of the security of Poland's western frontiers and its corridor to the sea, running through Germany, is omitted. Count Skrzynski, while stating that Poland was in favor of the security pact, declared that Poland would support the full provisions of the Treaty of Versailles in the delimitation of the Polish borders.

"Poland is seeking to preserve peace with all its neighbors, but until the nation feels secure it will not think of reducing its armaments," he declared.

The loan that was floated by American bankers for $50,000,000 has brought only $35,000,000. Poland needs funds for private industries and negotiations are now pending for an official government loan.

"Is the Orthodox Jew in America Re-Awakening? An Interview with Rabbi Herbert S. Goldstein, President of the Union of Orthodox Jewish Congregations of America"
The Canadian Jewish Chronicle, October 9, 1925[2]

When the first symptoms indicating that immigration to the United States would be restricted, a feeling of uncertainty and even anxiety manifested itself in various Jewish quarters. Both Orthodox and Reform seemed to be fearful of the fate of the American Jewish community in the United States. The impression prevailed that Judaism in America can be sustained only if immigration continues. Should the doors of America be closed, should the influx of new Jewish masses with their fresh Jewish traditions and adherence to Jewish forms of life cease – what might happen?

Those who were seized with these feelings had some justification. From early days there was a remarkable situation prevalent in those religious organizations that formed the background of American Judaism. As the membership of the Reform congregations and temples decreased, it continually drew fresh recruits from the Orthodox. Viewed from this experience, anxiety had its justification.

Enactment of the quota laws and the practical closing of America's doors to Jewish immigration are only of recent date. Developments within American Jewish life in this short period, however, carry sufficient evidence to show that this fear has no justification. The opposite has been proven.

The consolidation of the American Jewish community is taking place. One of the forces of this consolidation was the rise of the influence of Orthodox Jewry in America.

When, twenty-seven years ago, a small group of immigrants from Eastern Europe heard of the death of Rabbi Isaac Elchanan, the dean of the Yeshiva in Kovno, they decided to honor his memory by fulfilling a rabbinical dictum: "When a great man dies, an academy is set on his grave." They formed the Isaac Elchanan Yeshiva in America that was an attempt to imitate the Yeshiva of European fame. Now a $5,000,000 Yeshiva college, which is to be the exponent of traditional Judaism under modern conditions and methods of instruction[, is going to be built]. The Union of Orthodox Jewish Congregations of America is about to hold its twenty-seventh annual convention in New York City with a large number of delegates representing hundreds of congregations. The long latent forces of Orthodox Judaism in America are awakening. What is their direction and what power do they represent?

Dr. Herbert S. Goldstein, president of the Union of Orthodox Jewish Congregations of America, belongs to this school of American Orthodox rabbis who are both American and Orthodox. The writer of these lines was eager to hear Rabbi Goldstein's views on the present situation of Orthodox Jewry and the tasks that it confronts and that will be the subject of profound deliberation at the forthcoming convention.

[He said:] "In recent years it has become fashionable in American Jewish ranks to speak fervently and almost religiously about the need of 'Jewish education' and 'Jewish culture.' Something is seeking expression, but it seems to me that those who feel this inner wedge are afraid to be consistent. They speak of the need of Jewish education and Jewish culture, fervently, religiously, but avoid saying 'Jewish religion.' Until the close of the eighteenth century, there was only Orthodox Judaism. Jewish life meant Jewish religion. In fact, the difference between Jewish and non-Jewish life was the religious discipline under

---

[2] Attributed to Z. Alroy.

which the Jews lived. Human society, organized government and even industrial and commercial progress are inconceivable without the principle of self-discipline. This was in essence the doctrine that Judaism from its very outset proclaimed and that has, as 1,500 years of history has proven, been the driving power in the maintenance of orderly life and the progress of the world. True, this influence went through a variety of channels, but its source is, without denial, unmistakably Orthodoxly Jewish. If this influence is to continue and exercise its power for good, the source must be guarded and kept alive. This is the duty of the Orthodox Jew. Judaism was the first religious doctrine to recognize the importance of the forms of everyday life for impressing the higher principles. An occasional hearing of even an inspiring sermon [is] sufficient to bring about the required results. It is Orthodox Judaism that has created the guarantees for the realization of the high principle by the creation of a set of rules of conduct that must be observed if the belief is adhered to."

What is the present situation in Orthodox Jewry in America? I asked the President of the Union.

"Those who are trained to observe things in the making cannot fail to admit that the reawakening of the Orthodox Jew in the American Jewish community is not far off. Gone are the days when the religious affiliation of American Jewry was determined by commercial success or failure. You must not labor under the false illusion that those members who have left the Orthodox congregation to join the Reform temples did so after a profound study of the principles of Orthodox and Reform Judaism that was followed by a recognition that the principles of Geiger and Lindon were better than those of traditional Judaism. This was only natural in the first years of the forming of the American Jewish community. The Jewish community was divided into two distinct groups: a minority of settled families who were acclimated and successful; the other, recent arrivals who lacked the feeling of certainty and stability both in their material and spiritual status. The majority of the individuals being of a progressive nature, as evidenced by the fact of their immigration to this country, when [they were] a little more settled, joined the minority. This condition has undergone a fundamental change. Given time, applied thought has performed this change. The intuition of the Jewish masses in America and their desire for self-preservation, not to speak of the strength of family traditions that are age-old, directed the return to Orthodox Judaism. Speaking of a return is misleading. There was, in fact, no departure. The present moment marks only a full-power reawakening. Twenty-seven years ago, almost at the dawn of the present American Jewish community, the principles of Orthodox Judaism were re-proclaimed on American soil by the founders of the Union of Orthodox Jewish Congregations."

"Do you think, Rabbi Goldstein, that Orthodox Judaism in America can continue the old forms of orthodoxy as lived in other countries?"

"It has been the contention of many of the enemies of Orthodox Jewry that its source is European, implying, thus, that it would be un-American. What a great mistake this is. The spirit of America is essentially religious. It is on the precepts of the Bible that the fundamental laws of this country are based. The living of a real Orthodox Jewish life in America cannot be impaired by living in America. Take for instance the dietary laws that are one of the fundamentals of Orthodox Jewish observance. Not only is this not an impossibility, but, as is well demonstrated by the New York State Kosher Law, a desirability. The observance of the Sabbath is also not contrary to the trend of modern industrial life in America," Rabbi Goldstein concluded.

"Peter Wiernik: Scholar, Historian, and Editor"
The New Palestine, December 18, 1925

"Peter Wiernik, editor and historian, celebrates his 60th anniversary." This short notice slipped through the columns of the American Jewish press this week.

With the modesty characteristic of scholars, the fact of this holiday was withheld from the public large. The occasion was celebrated by only a small group of friends and those initiated – the *Yodei Chein*.

It is not surprising that this celebration was limited to a charmed circle. A peculiar charm of reserve, the result of profound knowledge, has always accompanied the life and work of Peter Wiernik.

The birth of the Yiddish press in this country was simultaneous with the birth of the Jewish labor movement and the school of radical thought under which it developed. This fact resulted in the impression, prevalent in certain influential quarters even today, that the Jewish press in this country is devoted mainly to the advocating of more or less radical doctrines. Jews as a rule are considered, if not precisely sponsors of radical ideas, at least sponsors of liberalism. Due to these developments conservative Jewish thought unfolded with greater strength and found expression in the publication of a conservative Jewish press. In this press, the *Jewish Morning Journal* played a leading role.

The moving force of thoughtful conservatism, a combination of modern knowledge coupled with the wisdom of ancient sources, was and is Peter Wiernik. Readers of the Jewish press, when looking for the specifically Jewish view of any event that happens to occupy the minds of men, look to the editorial comments of Peter Wiernik. His pen finds interest not only in matters of purely religious or Jewish national character; his pen is devoted to matters pertaining to politics, social reform and science. Any complicated situation in any country finds his mind attentive. His comments, while based on the latest information, always possess a Jewish "punch," which can be explained only by his being steeped in Jewish philosophic thought and in traditional Jewish expression.

Peter Wiernik thinks in terms of tradition. Nothing that has any material, moral or aesthetic value can spring from a vacuum; all matter has a beginning and an origin; its duty lies in its continuity. The new must have its roots in the ancient. For these reasons history is not only Wiernik's hobby but, one might say, his viewpoint.

Peter Wiernik represents an entirely new type in Jewish literature and journalism. Although born in the midst of the heated fight that went on in the middle of the 19th century between the two dominant tendencies in Jewish life, the "Haskalah" and "Hassidism," he was never caught in the whirlwind of this conflict. In fact, the course of his life marks a distinct departure from the then-prevailing routine.

He did not spend his youth in study alone; he did not fight the "darkness," did not cherish high ambitions to save the world from its ancient troubles. He simply settled down to work from his early youth.

The son of a traveling Magid, having the privilege of seeing his father only at rare intervals – perhaps only once a year – he did not have to resist paternal education and go through the usual conflict between "fathers and sons." He was also spared the luxury of indulging in theorizing on account of too great material abundance. Harnessed to hard work, at the age of 13, in Riga, he found, unlike all his contemporaries, great relief in the joyful and enthusiastic attitude of the Hassidim on Saturdays and holidays.

Though not a Socialist, Peter Wiernik, on his arrival in America, plunged into the field of productive labor immediately; he worked as a compositor for many years in various newspaper plants. However, the work in the composing room did not keep him from studying and from taking an interest in the intellectual problems of life.

Setting up the articles of others, in the course of many years he grew and developed into one of America's most prominent and widely educated Jewish editors. Before his eyes the great wave of Jewish immigration from Slavic countries unfolded in the new environment. Observing it closely and dispassionately, he was, logically, destined to become the historian of this important, many-sided and restless period in the life of American Jews. His *History of the Jews in America*, the only one of its kind so far, is naturally, in its greater part, devoted to the history of the recent past. It contains an invaluable amount of information and documents embracing the Jewish history of America that could be preserved only by a man of Wiernik's intellect and serene attitude towards the problem. Despite his personal bias toward tradition, he devoted his attention not only to the moving chapter of what may be termed "Congregational development" in the life of the first Jewish immigrants from Slavic countries, but also to the numberless attempts to organize the Jewish labor union movement, the movement that was rightly characterized as the "constantly changing army under unchanging leaders."

There is something strengthening and refreshing in the views that form the background of the work that Mr. Wiernik has performed. They can be formulated as follows.

The basis of development of all races and peoples is, as no one can deny, the economic motive. No advancement of any race or of any people would be accomplished were not the natural needs of the individuals and their collective effort as a group striving towards expansion and conquest. This is true of all races and of all peoples. It is equally true of our people. To put the purpose of mankind in a nutshell, one might call it an elemental longing for the salvation of the world. It is the slow process of development, the first step of which was necessarily the establishing of a reign of justice of one individual towards the other, and one group of individuals, call them peoples or nations, towards another. In this respect our people has made the greatest of all contributions. This tendency made itself evident from the period of the Prophets and till the latest attempts to solve social problems. There are principally two tendencies in history. The one described above, represented by us; the other represented by those who oppose it. When the struggle for the dominance of one of these tendencies is to be ended there is no way of knowing. All we can do is record the things that have already occurred.

Parallel with the advance of this tendency for justice and equality, aiming at the salvation of the world, the fight for the emancipation of the Jewish people has been going on. It was not until the French Revolution and the German Revolution of 1848 that the Jews were, in principle, given equal rights. The existence of the American Jewish community in its present form and numbers is the first fact of this kind that was ever recorded in the history of the Jewish people and the history of the world. America represents a unique experiment in this respect. For the first time a great number of Jews are incorporated into the body of a great and free nation under the protection of a democratic and liberal government and given the possibility of enjoying full citizenship rights and religious liberty. This state of affairs certainly has its advantages but it also has its dangers. Here again Jewish history can furnish us with a good reason for optimism. It was not earlier than the date when the Jewish settlements began to grow and the development of the Slavic countries [took place] that the type of Jew that we are now accustomed to look upon as the only representative of traditional Judaism, characterizing him as Orthodox Jew, began to make his appearance. We are always inclined to think of this type of Jew as one whose Jewishness is expressed by his differences in language, dress and external custom from the other inhabitants of the land. But let us take a lesson from history. The Jewish community in Arabic Spain was highly cultured, highly developed and certainly highly Jewish since it could produce such a basically Jewish literature as the one that inspired our historians to name that period "The Golden Epoch." Nevertheless, a leader and intellectual genius like Maimonides was not different from his countrymen in his language, external custom and culture. The essentials of Judaism do not depend upon such external appearances.

There is no ground for pessimism in the prediction of the approach of a similar type of American Jew who, enjoying to the full measure his political rights, cultural and economic opportunities, will remain true to his specific Jewish culture, line of thought and religion. The time is not far off when America, the youngest of Jewish communities, will be in a position to supply with intellectual and religious leaders all the other older and now seemingly decadent Jewish communities of the world. In this respect, Orthodox Judaism is a valuable protection and a veritable armor, as has been proven in the course of our long and varied historical development.

Jewish life is safe in America.

The fate of the Jewish communities in the Anglo-Saxon countries that we can rightly call biblical countries is sufficient proof that anti-Semitism, at least so far as its sharp and violent forms are concerned, never can root itself very deeply in these countries.

These, briefly summarized, are the dominant features of Peter Wiernik's philosophy. These are the views that shaped his policy and made him one of the leading figures in contemporary Jewish journalism and Jewish thought.

"Jewish Men in the Public Eye: Nathan Straus"
The Sentinel, 1926[3]

A small house with no furniture except a broken table, one baby chair, three straw-filled sacks lying on the floor, four children between the ages of three and eight – half starved, more undressed than dressed, sitting on the floor, not playing, but on the verge of crying, as if something very unpleasant were going to happen. A woman not over thirty-five, holding in her arms a dying baby of three. Her features could tell the story: A life wrecked through no fault of hers. The care and worries of a helpless, lonesome mother, destroyed all semblance of what was once great feminine beauty. Her husband taken to the army, left in a small city overshadowed by the depressing skies of the Pina Plains through which armies were marching; without supplies, no chicken to be procured, not even a glass of milk to be obtained.

"The little one dies because I could not nourish it," she cried in despair.

All the horrors of the war, the misery and the suffering of the adults, the struggle for freedom, democracy, independence and the idea of the future ideal state appeared to me as worthless things, if there were only something that could save the life of this little innocent baby.

It was during the summer of 1917 when the great struggle went on, spreading on one hand, death, misery and suffering, and on the other, strengthened faith and renewed hope for some kind of a better future, which is, after all, to be the result.

The result? For whom?

Under the brightest of circumstances and the most consoling and quieting beauty of the ever-changing landscapes that travel affords, I could never forget that apparently insignificant dying baby.

---

[3] The exact date of publication in 1926 is not known.

The physician who was, after many hours, brought with great difficult from a distant city on a wagon drawn by oxen, diagnosed, too late, the case in the words, "Death resulted from under-nourishment and contracted tuberculosis."

* * *

On a Sunday noon, several years later, I found myself in a crowded train bound for Mamaroneck – the residence of Nathan Straus.

In the colorful and overwhelming pyramid of American life, there is hardly a feature that carries a greater appeal to the human heart and mind of all humanity than the picture of that grand old man who spent his life and his energy for the sake of the world's babies. How I did regret that the influence of his work did not reach out in time to prevent the death of the little one under the Pina skies.

In 1891, out of every thousand babies born in New York City, 241 died before they were a year old. This means that one-fourth of all the newly born babies did not have even a chance to live. It was in this year that Nathan Straus set out on the mission of his life. Not a scientist, merely a successful and wealthy businessman, a devoted father, he made it his ambition to call the world's attention to the fundamental principle of lifesaving.

"The future of the nation and of humanity lies in the cradle." This is so simple and obvious that one really must have great courage to proclaim it as the Shibboleth. This, one would think, plain, self-explanatory and obvious sentence required the fortune, energy, foresight, determination and good-heartedness of a man of the caliber of Nathan Straus to translate it into the economic system and bring it into the realm of questions that deserve attention. Millions of babies were born, fed with the unclean and disease-carrying milk of tubercular cows, died in the best of cases; in the majority of cases continued to live as crippled, tubercular beings, filling the hospitals, jails and institutions – a burden to themselves and a burden to the community.

Nathan Straus conceived, one might say, the inspiration to remedy the evil at its root. How was it to be done? Simply. Not to give the babies unclean milk.

Since modern society in the great cities has been organized on principles of a commercial regime, leaders have awakened to the existence of various problems. There is a meat problem, a fish problem, an unemployment problem, an employment problem, and many other problems. Nathan Straus has added to this multitude of problems one fundamental one – the milk problem.

Out of every 1,000 babies born in the City of New York now, instead of 241, only 75 die. Out of 54 larger cities in the United States, 48 now follow the advice and system of Nathan Straus, by supervising or encouraging the supply of pasteurized milk.

Since the time of the great Greek philosophers, the discussion has never ceased as to what is the motive and nature of philanthropy. The word in itself, which would seemingly give the best definition – love of mankind – has acquired, in the course of the dispute, a particular meaning.

Love of mankind? Love for beauty, youth, happiness and perfection is natural. Philanthropy – the love for imperfect humanity, for victims of nature or social regimes – is a state of mind that is not easily understood and appreciated. What is the motive of the giver? Is it pity? The moral injury imposed upon the beneficiary is equal or perhaps greater than the amount of temporary relief. Is it egotism? Is it prompted by the feeling that accentuates at the moment the gap between the giver and the receiver? One way or another, philanthropy in the old-fashioned style, under the influence of modern tendencies, still leaves room for a heated difference of opinion.

Yet the world is far from perfection; the human race is to a large extent handicapped; the social evils are still numerous. True, present-day philanthropy remedied the situation by introducing the system of organization, removing thus the personal contact between those who give and those who are compelled to take. Here, again, the sharpened points of "organized" charity are oft-times not less painful.

The life work of Nathan Straus, although the dictionary has not provided another term, is more than philanthropy. Nathan Straus has the distinction of having enriched the English language with an expression that could easily be translated into many other languages and transplanted into many other spheres of human endeavor. It is the word "preventorium." What he really has accomplished or, better, given an indication of what can be accomplished, is how to prevent philanthropy. But to prevent philanthropy, it takes a philanthropist, a great fortune, a big heart, an open purse, an open mind and boundless energy.

* * *

There has not been a single idea of principle worthy of its name, destined to become a utilizing power, that has not met with resistance and struggle. But it always took the personality of its originator to being it to victory. What did Nathan Straus have that enabled him to carry on his fight for the babies' sake? His army, the number of which is legion – the world's babies – were mere infants. All he has are the most resourceful qualities when they are in existence: his personality, and his desire and determination to help. The elemental opposition to every innovation, the resistance of organized interests, was the great obstacle.

Pasteurization, the precept suggested, demonstrated and advocated by Nathan Straus, is a process named after one of the greatest scientists, Louis Pasteur. It was he who suggested heating below the boiling point as a means for destroying bacterial organisms in fluids.

However, his experiments had nothing at all to do with milk. Said Nathan Straus, "Pasteurization destroys all the germs of disease that may be in the milk, but does not impair the taste, digestibility or nutritive qualities of the milk. Cow's milk, pasteurized, is then a perfect food for adults; but cow's milk needs something further to make it an ideal food for infants. Their immature organs are capable only of digesting the ingredients in such proportions as they are found in mother's milk. A process called 'modification' makes cow's milk all that the baby's system and condition require.

"Milk, then, in order to be suited to a baby's needs, must meet with these three requirements: It must be as pure as possible; it must be pasteurized; and it must be properly modified. The Nathan Straus Pasteurized Milk Laboratory solves these problems."

His famous milk stations, maintained at an enormous expense for a quarter of a century, in spite of opposition and, not seldom, even of ridicule, demonstrated in an unmistakable way how easily human lives can be saved, how much disease and misery can be prevented, if the proper care is given and the right method is applied. The health departments of American cities have already learned to value and apply the precept of Nathan Straus. Other large cities and other governments still have to be convinced, and this great American Jew does not, at the age of 76, shrink from the task. The Straus enlightenment work concerning pasteurization is now being extensively carried on in England, France and other countries. There is no record available as to the amount of money spent by Mr. Straus in his charitable work, but it can be safely said that for every day of his useful life, many thousands of babies owe their life and health.

* * *

How does a father of so many babies feel at his advanced age? A man whose main care was not only his own and his family's welfare, but also the welfare of his race and the happiness of mankind?

In his palatial home, the grand old man with so many recollections of work and deeds that could justify an air of self-satisfaction and pride, simplicity is the striking note; the oneness of the individual life, no matter to what imaginary height it may have reached, is the conception here.

With understanding and forgiveness Nathan Straus tells the story of the conceited successful lawyer who reached the goal of his am- [rest of article missing]

"The Chair for Jewish History and Philosophy at Harvard University"
The Jewish Tribune, February 5, 1926

"The Nathan Littauer professorship of Jewish literature and philosophy has been established, thanks to a gift from Lucius N. Littauer, Harvard '78, of New York, in honor of his father, who died in 1891. The gift of Mr. Littauer will be completed in 1928, on the fiftieth anniversary of his graduation from Harvard University. It is the confident hope of the donor that the establishment of this chair will be a force of far-reaching service in the cause of higher education, of scholarly research, of enlightenment, appreciation of Jewish ideals, and a contribution throughout the ages by the Jews to the humanities."

In these few words, the Information Secretary of Harvard University announced to the reading public the establishment of the first chair for Jewish literature, history and philosophy at Harvard, the oldest institution of higher learning in America. This announcement, although properly regarded by the American press, is more than a record of the establishment of a chair. It is, one might say, an epic of Jewish life in general, American Jewish life in particular, and the culmination of a long and deeply rooted desire that found expression in so modest a fashion. Those who are familiar with the growth of the university as an institution for disseminating knowledge, and more so for scientific theory, know that it originated with the study of Jewish theses. The first university, established in Prague, included in its program, outside of the study of the astrology and astronomy, the humanities, which meant the study of the historical Bible records. The university has grown, and has outgrown its original basis. It is still growing and will continue to grow, every student hopes, toward the unbiased search for the truth.

Hebrew and the Bible

However, the Bible has fared well in comparison with post-Biblical literature, medieval Jewish history and poetry. How much of the Midrashic beauty, Mishanic precision, is known to Jews and non-Jews? How many of the gems of thought contained in the Jewish philosophic literature, in both its antitheses, philosophy and Kabbalah, are accessible to the student and the public at large?

Hebrew and the Bible are being studied at every university, but as a small part of the humanities. The modern languages have in recent years acquired a vast literature and Bible criticism. Most of these publications were carried on with a purpose. Their appearance coincided with the coming forth of the racial theories in France and Germany, culminating in the Nordicism of America. The study of Jewish literature, both antique and post-Biblical, remained a pending problem, a hoped-for accomplishment.

Harvard is to make the start, through the generosity, vision and idealism of Lucius N. Littauer.

* * *

The simplicity of Amos, the mysteries of Daniel, the chronology of Nehemiah, the vision of Isaiah II, are to be unraveled and presented again to the young mind in their proper historic light; the lyricism of Jehudah Halvey, the speculative sarcasm of Ibn Ezra, the poetic thoughts of Ibn Gabirul, the moralizing of Bachya, the guiding principles of the *Moreh Nebuchim* (the Guide for the Perplexed) and the winning argumentation of the "Kuzari," are to be opened to Harvard students, though the vision and generosity of Lucius N. Littauer.

How did it come to pass?

Lucius N. Littauer – in his youth a friend of Theodore Roosevelt – industrialist, banker, and member of Congress for ten years, is a man of iron principles and steadfast habits who, in his early youth, formed the habit of going to temple. Born in Gloversville, N.Y., in the period of Jewish immigration to America, he received no special Hebrew education except what he was offered in the religious Sunday school. However, the lessons that were impressed upon his youthful mind in those early days remained vividly alive. **In the busy life of the Harvard student of 1878, in the hustle of industry and the bustle of politics during fifty years, he went to temple.**

On a Saturday last May, he listened to a discourse by Dr. H. G. Enelow, Rabbi of Temple Emanu-El, New York, on the needs of higher Jewish education. The discourse of the learned minister impressed the man of affairs sufficiently for him to give the matter his earnest attention. This was in May. In October, A. Laurence Lowell, President of Harvard University, had accepted the offer for the founding of a chair for Jewish literature and philosophy. With the beginning of the new academic year, Profess Harry A. Wolfson was appointed to fill the chair.

The name of Lucius N. Littauer, although he has been active for many years, has not been mentioned frequently in the annals of specific Jewish affairs. Those who studied the recent past know the role that Mr. Littauer, when [a] Congressman, played in the dispatch of John Hay's note to Romania protesting against the persecution of Jews in that country, an act that stands alone in the history of the protection of the minorities. Mr. Littauer, regent of New York University, deeply interested in the humanities, caused no little surprise to his wide circle of friends by his establishment of a special chair for Jewish history, literature and philosophy.

Study of Humanities Essential

"The study of the humanities has no doubt been the prime force in the broadening of the human mind, the removing of prejudices and the creation of social conditions that are in truth humane. I observe that the Jewish part in the humanities has been undeveloped. It is my contention that inasmuch as intelligence can remove prejudices, the establishment of a chair for Jewish studies will accomplish something in that direction. The span of a man's active life ranges from thirty to fifty years. If one student gains this knowledge, it can be multiplied by that number and also by the number of those who are under his influence or his instruction," Mr. Littauer modestly explains.

The foundation is to carry the name of Nathan Littauer. He was one of the early Jewish immigrants from Germany, and was born in Breslau in 1829. Lucius' mother came from a family that moved to Breslau from Lithuania, a family that had a lineage of rabbis in its tradition. One of the pioneers of the glove industry, Nathan Littauer left a name that is held in memory by his fellow citizens. A hospital in Gloversville was dedicated to him.

The grandson of the family of Lithuanian rabbis, when leaving the House of Representatives and insisting upon retiring from public life, was given the following testimonial by the House.

"Your service has been notable for untiring industry, for conspicuous ability, for integrity of purpose, for accuracy of judgment, for wondrous quickness of perception and for volume of accomplishment. That you possess in large measure the most admirable traits of mind and heart, each day's intercourse with you has made more apparent. Your service has been of great value to your country. The going out of no man from our 'inner circle' could produce a more poignant pant of regret. We admire you, we respect you, we have for you a strong affection and we wish you to take with you to private life this assurance of our esteem and our regret that you have voluntarily severed the ties of an association that will ever abide with us as among the most pleasurable memories of Congressional life."

A year before the lapse of 50 years since he graduated from Harvard, Lucius N. Littauer establishes a chair for Jewish history, philosophy and literature in the perpetual memory of his father.

The epic does not end. It begins.

"Josef Pilsudski, Poland's Strong Man"
The Jewish Tribune, May 21, 1926

With breathless expectation, Eastern and Western Europe, as well as millions in America, have watched the development of the last fortnight on the Vistula, for many generations the scene of battles that initiated world events.

Situated between the Union of Soviet Socialist Republics on the east and Germany on the west, the resurrected Republic of Poland, in its eight years of existence, has hardly succeeded in emerging from its formation period, made more difficult by the sharp conflict of class differences, modern influences and ancient traditions, national minorities' problems, cultures and adjustment, financial and economic difficulties and handicaps.

Out of the turmoil there rises again the name of Josef Pilsudski, who accomplished almost a miraculous stroke, which, he claims, is to make Poland "safe for democracy."

Josef Pilsudski is not a new name to those who followed developments in Eastern Europe during the World War. The first Chief of State of the new Polish Republic, when the time came for the election by the National Assembly of the first President of the Republic, Pilsudski declined and, withdrawing into retirement, remained the new Republic's great and puzzling question mark.

Who is the man and what consequences will follow his successful *coup d'état*? What may be the effects on the welfare of the Republic in general and its Jewish community of three millions?

Much of what is known of Pilsudski is connected with his ascent, following the conclusion of the Armistice and the formation of the Polish State.

A Most Romantic Career

The career of Josef Pilsudski is perhaps one of the most romantic that any of the European statesmen claim. His was a life of dreams and idealism, dire need, suffering and daring action. One must wonder where the poetry in Pilsudski's life ceases and where reality begins.

Born in 1867 in Polish Lithuania, near Vilna, two years after the last of the participants in the Polish Rebellion against Russia in 1863 died on the gallows, under the administration of "General Murawieff, the hangman," imbued with the spirit of prophetic verses of his countryman, Adam Mickiewicz, Pilsudski, a son of a landed Polish family, grew up under the influences that were permeated with the experiences and recollections of the defeated Polish Rebellion against Russia. Many of his relatives, in fact, his father and his aunts, were victims of "Murawieff, the hangman."

While at the University of Charkoff, where he was enrolled in the medical college, Josef Pilsudski soon became the object of the Czarist persecutions and was excluded from the university for participating in the students' movement. A year later, back at home, in Vilna, Pilsudski was accused of having some sort of connection with the attempt on the life of Czar Alexander III and, as a young man of 20, was sentenced to five years' exile in Siberia.

In these five years on the cold and silent snows of the distant Siberia, Pilsudski laid the foundation for his future career, learning there the greatest of all arts: the art of self-control. "To govern others one must first learn to govern oneself" has since become the favorite saying of Pilsudski. When he returned from his five years of exile, his family urged him to return to the medical college and offered him its connections and assistance in order that he might continue his studies. Pilsudski, however, imbued with a spirit of Polish patriotism, with a feeling of revenge against the obnoxious Czarism and influenced by the social and economic tendencies then dominating his youth, decided that his mission lay not in administering to individual sufferers, but in administering to his people, whom he considered thoroughly "sick" while under foreign domination.

Pilsudski with a small group joined in the formation of the Polish Socialist Party and became its theoretician and exponent. For the six years from 1894 to 1900, Pilsudski, under the eyes of the Russian gendarmerie and secret-service men in Poland, was the editor of the *Robotnik*, the illegal paper of the party. He was not only the editor, but also the typesetter, circulation manager, everything. All he had at his disposal was a portable printing plant, the innumerable names under which he operated, an exceptional calmness of mind, and ability to wander from town to town and from lodging to lodging, persecuted by the Russian gendarmes, nevertheless always escaping, despite the fact that the Russian government had offered large sums for his head. About this time he acquired as assistant editor the cooperation of Stanislaw Wojoiechowski, the president of the Polish Republic whom he has now compelled to resign.

Once Pilsudski lost his vigilance. In Lodz, in 1900, he was suddenly besieged by the Russian gendarmes, arrested and put into the Tenth Pavilion of the Warsaw Citadel, the chamber of horrors for many a Polish and Jewish youth in those story years.

When captured, he at once decided that the best way would be to simulate insanity in the hope that he might be transferred to the hospital for the insane at Tworki where he might have a chance of escape. He simulated insanity to perfection and the Russian officials were compelled to send him to an insane asylum.

By a strange coincidence, one of the doctors of the St. Petersburg asylum happened at that time to be Dr. Wladyslaw Mazurkiewicz, a Pole who was also a member of the party of which Pilsudski was the leader. Coming to examine Pilsudski, he brought in his bag civilian clothes in which the "insane" man dressed himself and walked out of the asylum with the doctor.

Soon Pilsudski left Russia and transferred his activities to Galicia, where the Poles enjoyed a sort of local autonomy and greater freedom to develop their cultural activities. Instead of conducting his activities underground, he decided to come out in the open and lay the foundations for a Polish military youth movement. He made frequent excursions to Congress Poland under assumed names, organized secret fighting groups of the Polish Socialist Party, which engaged frequently the Russian authorities in Poland. During the period, he traveled to Western Europe, visiting Switzerland, Belgium, Germany and England, studying the international situation, having one dream in mind: a free, resurrected Poland, the testament of Tadeusz Kosciusko. A member of the Polish Socialist Party, fighting for social justice, he always laid emphasis on Polish independence as a condition *sine qua non* to the fulfillment of the party's other social program. His socialism was more in the way of an approach than a task in itself.

His Mission to Tokyo

During the Russo-Japanese War, Pilsudski urged his countrymen to refuse to respond to the call of the Russian government's mobilization and instead to rise against Russia. Opposed and even ridiculed by the majority of Polish groups and parties, Pilsudski undertook a new mission. He went to Tokyo with the hope of influencing the Mikado to take up as an issue of the Russo-Japanese War the question of Poland's independence. The Japanese government was willing to give assistance to a movement that would make trouble for Russia at home, but was too distant to appreciate Pilsudski's arguments in favor of an independent Poland.

Disappointed, Pilsudski returned to Poland and renewed his work of organizing the *Strzelcy* (the Shooter) in Galicia and the secret groups in Congress Poland, leading many a spectacular fight during the revolutionary period, in the hope of awakening the will of the Polish people to what he termed "action."

The majority, however, of the Polish groups and parties, particularly those of the landed classes and the townsmen, were afraid of the risk. The National Democrats, the strongest party that then developed the anti-Semitic edge of its program, became Pilsudski's bitter opponent. It believed in cooperation with the Czarist government. So did many others. Pilsudski alone persisted and when the World War broke out on Aug. 5, 1914, on the night of Aug. 6, he moved his loose forces in an independent and hopeless effort into the territory of Russian Poland.

Against the opposition of the cool-minded Polish official leaders, who flirted with the Czarist government, Pilsudski organized his legion that marched together with the Austrian Army, although it never was recognized as a part of that Army. When Poland was occupied by the Austrian and German armies, Pilsudski turned against the occupants of his country and started to organize the Polska Organizacjia Wojskowa, the Polish military organization, which was an open challenge to the plans that the Germans had prepared for Poland's future.

At the orders of the German Governor General of Warsaw, von Beseler, Pilsudski was arrested on July 20, 1917 and jailed in the Fortress of Magdeburg.

When the Armistice was signed and the revolution broke out in Germany, Pilsudski, released from the Fortress, came to Warsaw where he immediately assumed supreme power and set the Polish Republic in motion, much to the displeasure of the leaders of the National Democratic Party and the other groups who could not see Pilsudski in this role.

It was during the period of his command, when a democratic government was organized, the Sejm called, the constitution adopted and the first president elected, continuously exercising the power that he acquired in distant Siberia: to govern himself before governing others. He mastered himself into declining to run for election as the first president of the Republic, his opponents bestowing upon him, instead, the proud but empty title of first and only Marshal of the Republic.

When Gabriel Narutowicz, the first duly elected president of the Republic, was murdered at the hand of Niewiadomski, a partisan of the anti-Semitic nationalistic party, because of the fact that, in the majority by which Narutowicz was elected, the votes of Jewish deputies were included, Pilsudski broke his silence and in a striking book poured out his wrath on those Polish "patriots" who could go to the length of murdering their president because of the participation of Jewish deputies in his election. He stated at that time that the task which Narutowicz faced was that of internal consolidation and curing the people of the "after effects" of foreign domination.

Having contributed as no other man in Poland toward creating and strengthening Poland's independence, striking now to make liberated Poland safe for democracy, will the one-time medical student apply himself to curing the "after effects" also with regard to the Jewish question?

"Builders of American Cities:
Isaac Meister, Founder of American Venice"
The Sentinel, July 2, 1926[4]

The road of civilization as developed by the inhabitants of this globe is, on the surface, a short one. Originating in the caves, it proceeded to the village, from the village to the town, from the town to the city and – in its present form – from the city to the residential section.

Life is probably the same as it was when it started; it is new forms, added comforts and increased beauty that history has accomplished.

In the early records of this process of building, usually laconic, the ancients never failed to add to the record of this or that hero that he "lived . . . had children and 'Va liven Iir' (and he built a city)."

The building of a city was a milestone in the progress of this globe's population.

The Jewish people in Palestine, as well as in their later wanderings over the various continents, have been builders, if not of cities, which they were not often permitted to engage in, then at least neighborhoods, later to be known as ghettos, of synagogues and of commercial enterprises and industries. This circumstance resulted in an impression, which was quickly picked up by the anti-Semites, that the quality of the Jew is not in creating or in building, but in making use of things already built.

The latest chapter in Jewish history, which is unfolding before our eyes today, [that is to say] the achievements of American Jews, is a striking example of the lack of foundation of such an opinion. The record of the achievements of many Jewish men in the development of American sections and cities, investing huge capital in improving land properties and turning forests and the wilderness into places of habitation, awaits intensive study and an able pen. It beggars description.

---

[4] Attributed to Z. Alroy.

The charge that was forwarded against Jews in general has been stressed in particular against East European Jewry. This prejudice found expression not only in the Immigration Act of the United States, but also in several undeveloped countries that have set up barriers against those immigrants who are not, as the Secretary of Labor recently termed it, of the "beaver type."

A testimony to just this "beaver type" is the life story of Isaac Meister, builder of American Venice.

The treasurer of the Zionist Organization of America began his career in a manner similar to that of tens of thousands of his people. Born in Teplik, in the dark Ukraine, where he grew to manhood, in a vicinity where brick houses are rare and well-paved roads are not to be trodden upon, where elementary education was the privilege of the few, Isaac Meister, a young man, attracted by tales of America, went, unaccompanied, to the new world.

Singlehanded, he made his way in the new environment. Starting as a laborer and jewelry peddler, he soon discovered America for himself and, without jewels to finance his project, but equipped with powers of observation, enterprise, and honesty of purpose, he concentrated on that which many previous generations had been kept from, on developing and building.

Many a high structure that supports the symmetry of New York's skyline, many a virgin forest in which the traces of the Indian tribes were still discernible, were transformed into places of habitation through the efforts of Isaac Meister.

Trading in real estate in the United States today is no longer a new enterprise. Projects for development and opening up new districts for the branching out of the urban population is common. While serving, no doubt, a necessary need and creating new values highly desirable from the communities' viewpoint, they do not contribute anything substantially new. The builders of the old cities had this distinction that they were comprehensively planned and each locality was given a peculiar touch of its own in conformity with the geological and ethnological conditions, so the structures that were raised on the new sites represented a new style or followed a particular shade of an old style in architecture, thus creating new values in art and beauty, in addition to utility.

Isaac Meister had a new idea. It was not enough for him to open up a district or to erect a new skyscraper. He looked for a development with an idea of its own.

On his way to Palestine, he stopped off in Italy. For centuries the saying "See Venice and die" has been quoted. Meister, headed for Palestine, went to see Venice with not the slightest intention of dying. He wanted to see Venice and live and not only live himself but to let others live in Venice. There the idea came to his mind: why not an American Venice?

Venice, the beautiful, was the result of its own geographical situation. How could there be an American Venice without a similar situation? The enterprising Meister is not afraid of geography. Zionism is a fight against geography, Dr. Weizmann has said. Why cannot a Zionist builder fight geography on Long Island?

The corner strip of land on Long Island on the shores of South Bay presented the opportunity to him. Water was on two sides of the site of the future city. All that was necessary was an investment of millions of dollars, the making of canals similar to those in Venice, the erection of bridges in Venetian style, the placing of Venetian gondolas in the canals. With thirty years of experience in developing American land, with directness of purpose and constructive ability, Isaac Meister proceeded to the task. American Venice is now a reality.

Some have been fond of referring to the Jew with a hint at *The Merchant of Venice*. They will have to change. Here is the builder of American Venice.

"Announcement of the Observance of the Fiftieth Anniversary of Prof. Albert Einstein"
Jewish National Fund, 1929

It was shortly before Albert Einstein submitted to the Prussian Academy of Sciences his newest discovery of the identity of the laws of gravitation and electro-magnetism. The great event had already cast its shadow before it. Again, as in 1919, when Einstein's prediction that rays of starlight passing close to the sun will be found deflected was verified, and his Theory of Relativity confirmed, the entire world was stirred by interest and curiosity.

Reporters and correspondents of newspapers throughout the world were conducting a regular siege upon the modest and defenseless scientist. What did it matter to them that neither they nor their readers could possibly understand his formulae and deductions? They begged for interviews, they demanded elucidations, they clamored for his latest treatise in order to cable it – Greek and all – to America. The wizard had waved his wand again and, without comprehending his magic, the world was stirred by a new vision of the marvelous.

It was then that Albert Einstein issued a statement. Instead, however, of speaking of his new discovery, he spoke of his people – the Jewish people – of their problems and hopes. In this statement, given to the Jewish Telegraphic Agency, Einstein said:

"Jewry is like an organism that was beheaded 2,000 years ago. Jerusalem with its Temple was its head. It was God's miracle that it remained alive for so long a period without a head. A second miracle occurred when the body, grown formless, decided several scores of years ago that it must have a head, and has already formed a little head in Palestine. However, this head is still too small, and too weak for such a huge body. See to it that it grows into a full-sized head as befits the body."

Thus, the man whose vision embraces the sweep of stars and universes, whose keen gaze has penetrated into some of their deepest secrets, proclaims the hope and faith that is the daily food of his spirit. Not even Einstein the cosmic scientist can suppress Einstein the Jew and Zionist. He dreams dreams and he sees visions. And perhaps the most ardent of his dreams, the most glowing of his visions, is the dream and the vision of his people restored to a wholesome and creative life in Palestine.

In his hour of world triumph, he chooses, with apparent irrelevancy, to proclaim his kinship with the Jewish people and his allegiance to its highest aspirations. When, in 1921, Einstein visited this country, he was also much more ready to talk of Zionism and Palestine than of his scientific achievements. Is there not in this proud proclamation of his Jewishness an indirect, perhaps unconscious, rebuke against those Jews who nervously cover up their Jewishness as soon as the world has given them a little recognition?

And now comes the announcement that this meek and retiring searcher of truth, this mild and gentle brooder over the secrets of heaven and earth, who fears and dislikes publicity, has nevertheless consented that his Fiftieth Anniversary should be publicly observed the world over by the Jewish National Fund.

All Jews, and certainly all Zionists, will participate in the celebration of the event with happiness and pride. The pride is entirely pardonable. What people would not feel its stature exalted if it gave an Einstein to the world? For Einstein is not only the fascinating legend, the fabulous necromancer, which he is to the popular fancy, the supermind who has risen above time and space, who stands on the threshold of penetrating the ultimate mystery of existence. Einstein is more. Einstein has received the acclaim and the homage of the scientific world, which has classed him with the foremost pathfinders in the sphere of human knowledge. The leading scientists have paid chivalrous tribute to the special character of his discoveries and to the revolutionary implications of his Theory of Relativity. Sir Joseph J. Thomson, President of the Royal Society of England, one of the greatest living physicists, said in 1919, shortly after Einstein's prediction had been verified by observations made by two British scientist expeditions during an eclipse of the sun:

"If his theory is right, it makes us take an entirely new view of gravitation. If it is sustained that Einstein's reasoning holds good – and it has sustained two very severe tests in connection with the perihelion of Mercury and the present eclipse – then it is the result of one of the highest achievements in human thought."

Another world-famous scientist, Sir Oliver Lodge, wrote of Einstein's discovery:

"Einstein's theory will dominate all higher physics and the next generation of mathematical physicists will have a terrible time of it. Sooner or later the Einstein physics cannot fail to influence every intelligent man."

The outstanding physicist, Prof. Planck, who in 1920 was awarded the Nobel Prize, has said of Einstein's theory:

"It surpasses in boldness everything previously suggested in speculative natural philosophy and even in the philosophical theories of knowledge. Non-Euclidean geometry is child's play in comparison. The revolution introduced into the physical conception of the world by this theory is only to be compared in extent and depth with that brought by the Copernican system of the Universe."

The Jews of America have good reason, therefore, to celebrate with pride and joy the Fiftieth Anniversary of the birth of Albert Einstein, the peerless scientist, the noble spirit, the great Jew, the champion of his people's restoration in Palestine. In accord with his wishes, the observances will be held under the sponsorship of the Jewish National Fund, the basic instrument of the restoration, the redeemer of Palestine's soil for the Jewish people.

The scientific mind is primarily the realistic type of mind. Einstein cannot help recognizing the fundamental reality of the rebirth of the Jewish people: the soil of Palestine. The greatest scientific minds have also been touched with the urge and passion of idealism. The Jewish National Fund makes a particular appeal to the gift of idealism in the mind of Einstein.

Those Jews to whom the progress of Jewish destiny is indissolubly linked with Palestine require no sanction for a conviction that moves them with the force of a primal instinct. Nevertheless, there is something reassuring and uplifting about the adhesion of a spirit like Einstein's to that conviction. The restoration of the Jewish people becomes, as it were, a note in the cosmic harmony; it rises above all particularism to universal proportions. Einstein, moreover, is moved by a fervent social idealism that, though embracing humanity in its scope, is nourished by the vital idealistic impulse that animates the Jewish restoration in Palestine. And of this idealism the chief repository is the Jewish National Fund.

A tangible mode for the expression of our admiration and affection for Albert Einstein has been sought and found in the opportunity afforded by the Golden Book of the Jewish National Fund. It has become a noble custom to inscribe in this Book the names of those whom we esteem and cherish. Such an inscription confers a distinguished honor upon him whose name is entered, and, at the same time, the National Fund is provided with additional means to bring nearer its great goal, the redemption of the soil of Palestine as the inalienable possession of the Jewish people.

As a part, therefore, of the observance of Einstein's Fiftieth Anniversary, groups and individuals throughout America will inscribe his name in the Golden Book of the Jewish National Fund. It is proposed to present Prof. Einstein with an artistically bound volume of the certificates of inscription, an "Einstein Golden Book." The Jewish National Fund is persuaded that no more appropriate and welcome token of affection and esteem could be presented to Albert Einstein by the Jews of America.

The worth of a people may be measured by the stature and achievements of its greatest sons. The vitality and solidarity of a people are revealed by its readiness to give honor and recognition to its great sons. In honoring Albert Einstein the Jewish people honors itself.

Albert Einstein: Biography

Born at Ulm, in the Kingdom of Wurttemberg in 1879, Albert Einstein spent his boyhood in Munich, and when, in 1894, his family migrated to Italy, Albert continued his education in Switzerland, of which he eventually became a citizen. It is amusing how, in later years, when Einstein became one of the most famous of living personages, the newspapers vied with each other in confusing his racial origin. In an article in the *London Times*, Einstein discusses this matter in a rather whimsical manner:

"The description of me and my circumstances in the *Times* shows an amusing feat of imagination on the part of the writer. By an application of the theory of relativity to the taste of readers, I am today called in Germany a German man of science and in England I am represented as a Swiss Jew. . . . If I should come to regarded as a *bete noire*, the descriptions of me will be reversed, and I shall become a Swiss Jew for the Germans, and a German man of science for the English."

Einstein's first scientific monographs made such an impression that in 1909 he was made extraordinary professor of mathematical physics at the University of Zurich. His reputation continued to grow until, in 1914, shortly before the outbreak of the World War, he was called to the Royal Academy for Research in Berlin to succeed the celebrated Dutch physicist Van't Hoff. This post gave him the leisure and means to carry on his research. He had announced his Special Theory of Relativity in 1905, and in 1915 came the publication of his General Theory of Relativity. He has made important contributions to atomic as well as celestial physics. Einstein is a member of many scientific societies and the recipient of degrees from many universities in different countries.

Einstein visited the United States in 1921 as one of the members of the Zionist Commission that included also Dr. Chaim Weizmann and M. M. Ussishkin, Chairman of the Board of Directors of the Jewish National Fund in Palestine. He has also visited Palestine where he lectured in the Hebrew University on Mount Scopus.

"The Jew on the Stage and Screen"[5]
B'Nai B'rith Magazine, January, 1929

Bread and amusement, the cry of the Roman populace, is still eagerly sought in the life of the world as it is rolling along down the years. The prosperity that the industrial age

---

[5] It would appear that this was intended to be the first in a series of columns on this subject.

is providing for ever-growing strata, particularly within these United States, stimulates in its progress an ever-growing need for the other inseparable half-amusement.

A seat in the movies or in the theatre for every workingman, a political slogan recently, is possible and within reach only with the standardization and mass production of bread and amusement. So we are living in an age of wholesale products and [the mass] consumption of bread and amusement, regardless of the variety in quality and substance. The beautiful things in life that were available only to the few are now offered at standard prices to the mass that is affluent or carefree enough to enjoy life while living.

An amused and happy humanity would naturally seem to be a better humanity. It has not, however, always been the case. Too often amusement is being sought at the expense and discomfort of others. The danger that lies in mass production and consumption of amusement has been recognized only of late. A motion picture or a play shown on Broadway is likely to be seen by countless numbers in every part of the country. Opinions, habits, and, not the least, prejudices, that many, in previous times, have been imparted to a few are [now] dispensed to the many who are even more certain to be susceptible to the opinion-forming and prejudice-instilling amusement. Nothing enters the soul more swiftly than the word or the picture that is received with accompanying pleasure.

It was, it seems, the Anti-Defamation League of the [Independent Order] B'nai B'rith that first drew attention to this phase of the entertainment problem. It is quite natural that the Jew, having been trained by centuries of observation and persecution, should be more apt to sense danger while it is still invisible. The observations made by the Anti-Defamation League have since been vigorously supported by others in a more direct manner. A play or a picture must necessarily have a villain. With the growth of sensitivity, more and more groups, classes and people are objecting to being conspicuously depicted as the villain or as the stock that produced villains. The Italians, the Germans, the French, and even the English have objected to films where they were depicted in a light they considered untrue or unfair. The danger of generalization is rightly feared.

To tell of the Jew's constructive contribution to the stage and screen and of the plays and motion pictures in which the Jew's life and character are depicted or touched upon will be the purpose of this reviewer's observations along the Great White Way.

* * *

The talents of two outstanding Jews, a Hungarian and an American, Ferenc Molnar and David Belasco, have combined to produce what might properly be described as this season's outstanding play.

It is the drama of the industrial age, which witnesses the struggle of machine against man, of invention against soul.

Mima, the American adaptation of "The Red Mill" by Ferenc Molnar, does not deal with trivial incidents in a man's life. It does not even play on the much-abused triangle theme. It deals with the triangle of humanity, in the fundamentals of life on earth as it unfolds today.

The events take place in hell. It is a demonstration before His Majesty, Satan, and his court, by the Magister, an inventor of a man-destroying machine. Playing on the Bible motifs of temptation and salvation, Ferenc Molnar passes in review the diversified types of mankind in all walks of life. The Magister, putting up a telescope toward earth, is in search of a model man upon whom he can test the efficiency of his machine, which can bring that man to the lowest depths of degradation in an hour, "what takes New York twenty years to accomplish." Think, what a saving of time! None of those reviewed is considered a good enough candidate for the man-destroying machine, as each belongs, His Satanic Majesty decrees, to inferno anyhow.

The choice falls upon a forester who is a model son and a model husband. When the wicked countess of his vicinity tried to tempt him, he hid himself in the top of a tree. He is kidnapped and brought down to inferno where he is put into the machine. Mima, the creation of inferno's great inventor, given life by devilish rays, the woman who is beauty and temptation to perfection, the woman with two hearts that beat equally strong with love and hatred, good and evil, is the vehicle. Leonore Ulric, the star of the production, plays the role magnificently.

The forester goes the whole gamut of vice and degradation. The path leads through forbidden love, corrupt finance, swearing and lying, politics and blackmail. The machine registers faithfully each crime committed. Finally, when the lowest depth is reached and the former model man is about to murder the woman for whom he committed all his deeds, something goes wrong with the machine and instead of carrying out his determination to kill her, he is overwhelmed by his feeling of mercy and forgiveness. The man-destroying machine yields to the strength of the grain of good that still remains. The machine collapses and the manikins, human beings, who were held in the clutches of the infernal structure of iron and steel, are free. Light from the earth descends, as the forester ascends the ladder to return to his forsaken wife and child. Mima, broken and repentant, becomes the object of pity of her creator, the infernal inventor.

The Red Mill, the Faust of the age of iron and steel, is in more than one way a biting satire, a crushing indictment, a warning and the holding out of a hope.

The play was produced first in Vienna where it was hailed as a masterpiece. It is doubtful, however, whether it could convey its full meaning and beauty without the settings of David Belasco. Every device to make hell look like hell, all his ingenuity in stage lighting, for which Belasco is known, and every combination of light and shadow, has been employed in the costly presentation. The Belasco Theatre has been rebuilt; a mass of steel covers the stage. The man-destroying machine is a huge construction of unusual precision and ingenuity. Belasco says the presentation of Molnar's great drama is his greatest achievement in the theatre. He has every reason to be proud of it.

* * *

The proverbial stage Jew who was set up as an exotic exhibit, supposedly representative of the race, whose mere appearance engendered merriment, is becoming more and more a rare guest. It is difficult to determine to whom one is indebted for the change. Possibly it is the justified resentment and possibly a general raising of the artistic standards. This does not mean that what is inherently comic in Jewish characteristics approaches in various situations is or has been barred. But who could object to a hearty laugh when it flows not from malice or prejudice but from the nature of things?

The proverbial stage Jew gave way to a more dignified presentation.

Jewish comedians on the vaudeville stage and in the various musical comedies are still a dominant factor in the entertainment of the Broadway public. They do not, however, appear in such garb or character as to lay emphasis on what might be considered peculiarly Jewish. The disappearance of the stage Jew is being compensated by native Jewish humor and by frequent recourse to Yiddishisms, which, in themselves, are natural and healthy.

* * *

The Jew does not fare so well artistically or otherwise in the specially created Jewish plays. That there is a desire to see Jewish plays produced on Broadway is not to be doubted. The frequency of the products and the comparatively long run they enjoy easily proves it. What one finds difficult to understand is why the producers and actors insist on over-written and over-acted Jews plays.

A case in point is the play *Poppa* produced by H. S. Kraft at the Biltmore Theatre. "Poppa" is supposed to be Yiddish-American for "Papa" and undertakes to present on the stage the "saga of the Schwitzkys." The Schwitzkys, you will readily see, are immigrant Jews who are struggling in their adjustment to the American environment. Their economic plight and their family difficulties, the snobbery they encounter when cupid smiles on their only daughter, the support of the family, Ruth, who falls in love with a Rosenthal, scion of an adjusted American Jewish family, are rich enough ground for an interesting and entertaining tale to be wept over or laughed about, as you please. In *Poppa*, the story, so common in a large section of American Jewish families of recent arrival, is presented with such carelessness and lack of regard for detail or proportion that it is turned into a gross burlesque. The dialogue lives up almost one hundred percent to the Americanese of Milt Gross. Even as gifted an actress as Anna Apple of Yiddish Art Theater renown, and Yechiel Goldsmith, cannot escape the temptation of the lines and transgress fearfully with over-playing and over-intonation. Poppa, Pincus Schwitzky, played by Mr. Goldsmith, the slightly Americanized immigrant father, takes his first lessons in civic duty so seriously and solemnly that he plunges into the political work of the East Side Republican district at the expense of his family's welfare. The penalty that he pays is that, at the time when his only daughter is about to marry, his being a financial failure constitutes an obstacle to her happiness. Then, fortuitously, the district leader cats his eye upon the faithful Schwitzky to nominate him as alderman for the district. He is elected without difficulty and everything seems to be running in best condition. Suddenly, the district leader, for corruption purposes, attempts to put a halt to Schwitzky's enthusiasm for civic betterment. New in the game and idealistic, Schwitzky does not "understand" and refuses to abandon his reform bills. He is framed by the district leader and, incredibly, we find him in jail in the next scene. The authors, however, were good enough to provide, through Herbert, Poppa's ne'er-do-well son, a Dictaphone, which preserved a record of the corrupt politician's "frame-up," and while the feminine part of the Schwitzkys rushes to the license bureau to witness the marriage of a Schwitzky and a Rosenthal, Poppa, not yet cooled off in his civic enthusiasm, hastens away to the Republican district club.

The saga of the Schwitzkys is advertised as a "riotous folk comedy." One is inclined to think that the producers are admitting more than they believe they are.

* * *

George Jessel in *The War Song*, at the National Theatre, a play by Bella and Samuel Spewack and Mr. Jessel, based on a story suggested by E. Richard Scheyer, makes a very sympathetic presentation of a Jewish boy, a singer, viewing the world through tones and musical notes, who is a impossible misfit in an American regiment during the World War. Although, by his artistic temperament, he does not fit, and does not think much of the business of killing, he finds sympathy and understanding even in the stormy days of ferocious warfare. He gains favor by his songs and by entertaining his superiors, telling them witty stories. Incredible though the story may seem, the play has a touch of genuine insight into human emotions and motives. Particularly sympathetic is the character of Mrs. Rosen, the mother of Eddie Rosen (George Jessel), played by Clara Langsner. She portrays the role of a Jewish mother, whose husband gave his life in the Spanish-American war, with real sympathy and understanding. Though she obviously is most unwilling to permit her only son to share the fate of his father, the audience is in sympathy with her motherly concern. Ten years after the World War, a story similar to that told in *The War Song* can find responsive ears. George Jessel, with his resourcefulness and ability, makes the misfit a likable chap. Charles C. Wilson in the role of Captain Conroy, Eddie's superior officer who stands a lot from him, plays the role superbly.

The scene when the misfit singer rushes into the midst of danger during the fighting to apprehend a second lieutenant who had not kept his promise to Eddie's sister touches one keenly.

* * *

David Pinski, the distinguished Yiddish dramatist, was the guest for a while on Broadway. Avrano and Friedman presented his new play, *Three*, in the Edythe Totten Theatre. "Three" is, in reality, four, in Pinski's conception, for whenever two persons do or intend to do anything, there is always the third inseparable factor, chance, which is responsible for the accomplishment or the failure [of the venture]. With this thesis Pinski set out to present – is it a tragedy or a comedy? – three people, two young men and a girl. You will guess that both men, one a painter, the other a sculptor, are in love with the girl. Good friends that they are, they keep no secrets from each other. When they decide to turn their feelings into action, that is, to propose, they are mutually startled by the fact that they are two, and propose simultaneously. Beatrice does not know whom she prefers, Joseph or Robert, and so the matter is to be decided by chance. They throw dice and one wins, but the winner, because of having won, is rejected by Beatrice in favor of the defeated. The defeated, however, feels bound by his vow to accept the decision of chance and turns down the imploring Beatrice. And so Pinski plays with the three as chance will have it. As the curtain falls neither Beatrice nor the audience know who is to be preferred or why.

Not chance alone willed it that the play had a run of less than a week.

* * *

Abie's Irish Rose is back again for a week at the Schubert-Riviera. After a six years' run and presentations in many of the leading American cities, this rather unique conglomeration of what Ann Nichols understood of Jewish life and Irish character is to make another tour of the country, perhaps to the relief of Broadwayites. It is one of the remarkable occurrences in the history of Jewish plays on the stage. Only a few days ago a Berlin audience hailed the play as good humor and critics expressed understanding for its long American run. It was only a minority of the German critics, those writing for the discriminating, who manifested the same amazement as did the leading critics in America and England.

And now *Abie's Irish Rose*, a Paramount picture, is being shown at the Rialto Theatre on Broadway.

* * *

This reviewer was unable to see the Universal production *The Cohens and the Kellys*, which was withdrawn temporarily on account of the suit brought by the author of *Abie's Irish Rose*, claiming that *The Cohens and the Kellys* is a plagiarism of her play. If the court rules, after viewing both, that the charge of plagiarism is sustained, there would be no thrill is seeing *The Cohens and the Kellys*.

* * *

The life and struggle upward of the band of American Jewish singers whose names are renowned throughout the length and breadth of the country, composers of the popular songs and tunes, is a recurrent note in recent movie production. Perhaps the emergence of the "talkies," whose crying need is action combined with sound, is responsible for the coming to the fore of this epic that is one of the important Jewish contributions to present-day American life.

Warner Brothers, who lead in the talking pictures, are now presenting at the Winter Garden two motion pictures that deal with and have been built around the lives of two of these singers. *The Singing Fool,* built around the life of Al Jolson and played by him is in more way than one a thrilling human story. Al Jolson evinces an emotionalism and a sadness of joy that is characteristic of him and of the Jew. The Yiddishisms he cleverly injects into his stirring songs add much to their interest.

* * *

My Man, constructed around the life of the incomparable Fannie Brice and played by her with a strong cast, is put partly in Jewish settings. It promises to be an outstanding feature of the season.

* * *

A significant Jewish contribution to American music is the symphony, *America*, by Ernest Bloch, which had its premiere at the end of the month in Carnegie Hall when it was played by the Philharmonic Orchestra, Walter Damrosch conducting.

On the following day it was simultaneously presented to the American public by the Philharmonic Orchestras of Boston, Philadelphia, Chicago, and San Francisco and again in New York. It will be presented at a later date in other leading American cities.

The symphony, termed by the composer an epic rhapsody, is a unique musical masterpiece. It expresses the past, present and future hopes of America in a score that re-echoes the melodies of early American life, from the time of the Mayflower down to the present jazz age. There are idyllic tones, notes of lyric beauty, of mass reaction, impassioned notes of scorn and visions for the future. It closes with an anthem to be sung by the audience. The composer hopes that the anthem will become representative of America. There is love, there is vision in the score, bordering, as the critic says, on the prophetic, a vein inherent in Ernest Bloch. Not without reason is the symphony called an epic of democracy.

It is characteristic that the noted Jewish composer, a native of Switzerland, who came to the United States in 1916, has produced a symphony that was recognized as most deserving the name America, the land of his adoption. The composer of the *Israel* symphony was the winner in a contest conducted by "Musical America." His symphony entitled *America* was chosen from among 92 scores submitted. It was the unanimous choice of the judges, all noted composers and conductors, who will present it simultaneously through their ten or twelve major symphony orchestras throughout the country. Four years after his arrival in the United States in 1920, Ernest Bloch conceived the idea for his symphony.

The author of *Israel* and *America* has added glory to his name and to the name of his people.

The reception the symphony had in the metropolitan press was not marked, though, by the same enthusiasm all along the line. Notwithstanding the fact that the judges' committee that unanimously chose Ernest Bloch's symphony included Leopold Stokowski, Walter Damrosch, Frederick Stock, Alfred Hertz and Serge Koussevitzky, were voices not lacking among reviewers who termed the symphony "provocative" and at least "debatable." The greatest amount of displeasure on the part of these critics centers around the concluding anthem. One reviewer, writing in the *Telegram*, apparently resents the fact that the composer termed his symphony America "without apologies." References are not missing to the composer's racial origin and his recent arrival. But then, who does not remember the reception accorded by the musical reviewers of the leading composers? Time erased the first-nighter's criticism.

"The Jew on the State and Screen"
B'Nai B'Rith Magazine, February 1929

Of more than passing interest is the drama, *Judas*, written by Walter Ferris and Basil Rathbone, presented at the Longacre Theatre. The events or the legend of the events that occurred in Galilee and Jerusalem some 1900 years ago, giving rise to Christianity, have not yet been historically or psychologically fully ascertained, explained, or understood. When theology mixes with history, the latter is undoubtedly the loser. So it is that, despite the untold volumes written on the subject of the rise of Christianity, its origin and the exact nature of the events that led up to its development are still in the twilight region.

The drama of the crucifixion that has turned out to be, due to the interpretations and the legends springing from it, a Jewish tragedy for the past 1900 years is certainly of a most stirring character. However, the exploitation of this drama outside the realm of the church, and its presentation on the secular stage, is of comparatively recent date. The attempts at the dramatization of this material have in the past followed the official narratives. One of the major characters in this drama is undoubtedly that horrifying and repugnant figure, Judas Iscariot, painted in such dark and unredeeming colors that black is white next to him.

The authors of *Judas*, to their credit, it must be said, have adopted a totally new point of view in the interpretation of his character, faith, and fate. To be sure, the interpretation now given at the Longacre Theatre is not entirely new. It is based on the conclusions of impartial, modern historians, and particularly Jewish scholars who have attempted to reconstruct the story of Jesus of Nazareth on the background of the then-prevailing political conditions in Judea under the Roman yoke. This interpretation, nonetheless, is so radically different from the Orthodox Christian point of view that it will hardly be acceptable to those who are unaware of the research work recently done.

Judas Iscariot, as represented by Basil Rathbone, who plays the part, is not a born betrayer, but a highly dramatic human figure. He did what he did not for ulterior motives, but inspired by patriotic zeal and devotion to his Galilean master in order, as the lines have it, "to save him from himself." It was the impatience of one of the Judean zealots, whose number during the Roman subjugation at that time was legion, and his irrepressible desire to see in Judea the return of the Kingdom of Freedom and Justice, that moved the disciple to force the hand of his master.

Walter Ferris and Basil Rathbone in their play of three acts tell the story of Judas-Brutus with outspoken sympathy and understanding. So conscientious were both in their treatment of the subject that not a single detail recorded in the Christian gospels was omitted or ignored. Surprising, however, as it may be to the uninitiated, these facts when stripped of the bias do not constitute the black indictment that theology has rendered. A human, fighting, and disappointed Judas, driven to an act of desperation, emerges out of Rathbone's interpretation and presents a sincere plea for vindication, although he is aware that the "world will not understand." Even the most indicting detail of the 30 pieces of silver is not omitted, but it really played no role in the act or the motive. Judas agrees to the high priest's suggestion only to "bind the bargain," but when the 30 pieces are thrown to him, he contemptuously lets them drop to the floor, walking away into the darkness to hang himself.

Act One takes place in the courtyard of the house of Simon Ish Kerioth in Judea on Passover in the year 30 of the Christian Era. Act Two takes place in a house in Bethany near Jerusalem on the evening of March 28, the eighth of Nissan in the year 33. The last act takes place in one of the chambers of the Temple in Jerusalem and in the house in Bethany. The figure of the founder of Christianity is not visible but his presence is indicated by a light coming from the garden into the house in Bethany.

Judas, a son of a well-to-do Judean family, a student of the law, is fired with enthusiasm for the redemption of his country. He burns with indignation against the persecutions of the Romans and is most eager for action. He therefore gets into conflict with his pious father. When he is attracted to John the Baptist on the Jordan and meets the Galilean there, he is so absorbed by the hope of redemption for Judea that is to come through direct action and will result in the restoration of the Kingdom of Justice and Freedom that he neglects to return home for the celebration of the Passover and the consummation of his betrothal to Naomi. He has a vision of an empire and thinks that he and the Galilean fulfill each other. He is somewhat impatient with the theory of meekness and of blessing the persecutors, but believes in the powers of his master and in his leadership and hopes to persuade him to [take] action that will grip the people and arouse them against the foreign yoke. When the entry into Jerusalem materializes, he is overcome with disappointment and, when several days in Jerusalem pass without the leader calling for the uprising, he decides to bring it about by forcing his hand to choose between life and death. His leader, he knew, loved life and feared pain, and when confronted by the choice he would assume the leadership. Failure was all that he dreaded. When failure came by failure to act, he hanged himself.

The staging and costumes by Richard Boleslavsky and the settings by Jo Mielziner were chosen with care and skill, with an eye to historical accuracy. Dorothy Cumming in the role of Naomi, to whom Judas sings the Song of Songs, is pleasing to the eye. William Courtleigh in the role of the high priest Caiaphas and also as Simon Ish Kerioth gives a dignified and impressive presentation. Basil Rathbone is the personification of a convincing and sincere Judas pleading for vindication.

It is interesting that some of the reviews in the metropolitan press did not predict a long run for this splendid play, nor are they favorable in their comment. It seems that with theology as an influence, a historical interpretation that sounds plausible and convincing on the face of the facts stands small chance.

Alexander Carr in *Guinea Pig*

Alexander Carr of *Potash and Perlmutter* fame is again starred in the play *The Guinea Pig* at the President Theatre, Forty-Eight Street. The author, Preston Sturges, who had the courage and means to produce his own play, attempted to compress two dramatic conflicts into one. It is difficult to know whether his intention was to present the drama of the theatrical producer, Sam Small (Mr. Carr) or that of the guinea pig, an unsophisticated playwright who happens to be available both emotionally and physically for a novelist, a widow, who has not drunk enough from the cup of emotion to make her love scenes sound genuine on the stage. It doesn't really matter whether the "guinea pig" experiment of the stage playwright is or is not possible, or whether the drama produced on the stage of the President Theatre is in itself a success, but the emotion and talent put by Alexander Carr into the role of Sam Small, the Jewish Broadway producer, is genuine and grips the audience.

Drama Close to Home

A novel idea in stagecraft is the one introduced in *Street Scene*, by Elmer Rice, playing to capacity audiences at the Playhouse, 48th Street. The author, who also directed the staging, demonstrated that for the fundamental drama of life one does not need to travel to exotic corners or to luxurious homes, but right in the streets of modern cities drama looks upon you, enfolds you and haunts you.

In three acts that take place before a tenement house, with only windows, window shades, and the garbage can to indicate the separateness of the families, there passes before you a conglomeration of passion, hatred, deceit and hopeless idealism that, though they sadden, entertain the onlooker.

On a hot night in June the temperaments, dispositions, and lost hopes of the tenement population come into sharp relief after a hard day's work. The crux of the story is, of course, forbidden love, with the milkman, the iceman, the letter carrier, the janitor, and the variety of neighbors of Swedish, Irish, Jewish and other racial stocks as the spectators and participants.

In this realistic drama that one might say is a piece of life put on the stage, vulgar racial antagonism plays no minor role. As the life in the slums vibrates with passion, hope, and resignation, and carefree life, [and] sure enough, leads to fatal results, there is the intellectual and visionary Jew who, though he participates in the medley, keeps on spinning his utopian dreams. The author introduced a new character on the American stage – that of the Jewish radical, the immigrant who still believes that all the evils will be cured if the roots of the evil be "eliminated" from the social order. Abraham Kaplan, a writer, is, of course, a socialist who, though aged and broken, is relentless in his fidelity to the idealism of his youth. His oratorical powers and his intellectual attitude evoke hatred toward him from the under-nourished and ignorant in whose behalf he spins his dreams. Though the neighbors consider him a crank and oft-times a dangerous "Bolshevik," he interrupts his meditations to deliver impassioned addresses on national economy.

The same strain runs in the veins of his son, Samuel Kaplan, who, though liked by the tenement house-dwellers as a sympathetic and promising young man, is hardly sympathized with in his amorous attentions to the daughter of the heroine. Though she admires Sammy, she has as much understanding for him as the rest. Despite her love for Sammy, you will not be surprised to learn that she has accepted the offer of Sammy's rival to move "temporarily" to an apartment, prior to her starring on Broadway. The whispers of the old Irish woman that "to bring a Jew into the family" is, after all, not so desirable, apparently have their effect.

As the street scene closes, after bullets have penetrated the bodies of the sinful, and as other tenants appear to occupy the vacant flat, Abraham Kaplan, with his intellectual calm and resignation, walks off with a bundle of radical papers under his arm to continue to spin his dream for the redemption of humanity.

Leo Bulgakov in the role of Abraham Kaplan gives a true-to-character presentation; so does Horace Braham, as Sammy.

Eddie Cantor in *Whoopee*

Whoopee Ziegfeld's spectacular presentation of the season takes the place of the Follies, with Eddie Cantor as the pillar of a huge structure of beauty, color, melody and the dance. It would, of course, be a great piece of optimism to expect logical sequence in a musical comedy of this kind. The dazzling display and momentary absorption is the thing. However, as much as could be gathered, *Whoopee*, in two acts and ten scenes, tells some kind of story, based upon "The Nervous Wreck," by Owen Davis, of racial difficulties. Eddie Cantor as the singing waiter, as an Indian, as a convalescent patient, and in every imaginable role of a comedian, gets the largest share of laughs in what they are pleased to call "making whoopee."

Marx Brothers in *Animal Crackers*

In the realm where a smile is an investment and a laugh is a fortune, the Marx Brothers in *Animal Crackers* at the 44th Street Theatre takes the front line on the stage. Groucho, Zeppo, Chico, and Harpo Marx, against the background of the various settings, can pleasurably kill any leisure time you may have. The Marx Brothers, on the vaudeville stage for a number of years and lately on Broadway, are playing to capacity audiences that rock with laughter at their antics. Groucho Marx, apparently the first born, is the leader in ingenuity and device.

Besides the Yiddishisms, the Jewish angle is provided as a part of the comedy when the threat is made to one of the characters, who poses as a financier and man of affairs, to disclose that he was formerly "Rabbi Cantor of Czechoslovakia."

Julius Rosenwald in Movietone

The Fox Movietone has persuaded Julius Rosenwald to deliver a talk to the audiences on success and wisdom. "Success and wisdom are not synonymous" is the conclusion of the famous American Jewish philanthropist. Says Mr. Rosenwald through the movietone in a clear, natural voice:

"It was Ingersoll who said, 'I hate a stingy man.' If you have only a dollar in the world and you have to spend it, spend it like a king. I'd rather be a beggar and spend my money like a king than be a king and spend my money like a beggar. Most people believe that because a man has made a fortune his views on any subject are valuable. For my part, I have always believed that most large fortunes are made by men of mediocre ability who tumbled into a lucky opportunity and could not help but get rich, and in most cases others given the same chance would have done far better with it. Hard work and attention to business are necessary, but they rarely result in achieving a large fortune. Do not be fooled into believing that because a man is rich he is necessarily smart. There is ample proof to the contrary."

Talkie Insinuates Nationality

Give and Take, a Universal production presented at the Colony Theatre, is not directly of Jewish interest. It is, one might say, a parody of the industrial-democracy idea and portrays the mischief done by the son of a successful canned-fruits manufacturer who returns from college imbued with the spirit of the times and introduces a "give and take" system. Were the picture entirely a silent drama, it should not find mention in this review.

The trouble, however, is with the sound that one is led to suspect will cause irritation to many ears. In the "talkie" an ordinary conversation seems to the producers to be of no exciting interest unless it conveys a peculiar intonation that characterizes one or another group. In *Give and Take* the manufacturer, sympathetic and respectable member of society that he is, speaks *mit* a German Jewish accent.

"A Prince Has Fallen in Israel"
Canadian Jewish Chronicle, 20 September 1929

A Prince has fallen in Israel!

With the passing of Louis Marshall, American Jewry sustained an irreparable loss that will be mourned not only throughout the United States and Canada, but throughout the world, wherever Jewish communities are to be found. With the death of Louis Marshall, American Jewry lost the greatest, the most gifted and the most influential leader it has ever produced, to whom no Jewish cause was alien.

Though seventy-three years of age, the late leader of American Jewry was active, full of energy and untiring in his devotion for the cause of Judaism, to the very last day, when he was taken ill in Zurich, Switzerland. He was operated upon only a few days after he had steered to a successful conclusion the Jewish Agency conference, when the dream of his life to bring about a union of all Jews, Zionists and non-Zionists alike, for the rebuilding of Palestine as the Jewish National Home, was realized, and the Jewish Agency Council was created with him as chairman of the Council. He literally fulfilled what appears now to have been a prophesy when he said on the occasion of the unostentatious celebration of his seventieth birthday in 1926: "I hope to continue my work. I want to wear out, not rust away."

Leader of International Fame

A leader of international fame, one of the leading constitutional lawyers in the United States, a champion of justice for the oppressed and downtrodden, a fearless warrior for freedom and liberty, he fought many battles for the protection of the rights of Jews everywhere, and proceeded with particular care and devotion to defend in the courts of the United States the rights of racial and religious minorities, including the Japanese, the Negroes, the Hindus, wherever and whenever they were in danger of being curtailed or infringed upon.

As president of the American Jewish Committee since 1912, the late Mr. Marshall became the center of Jewish thought and activity in the United States, spreading his influence and his burning zeal for Jewish causes to almost every part of the globe. As president of the American Jewish Relief Committee, together with Felix M. Warburg, Dr. Cyrus Adler and others, he was the prime force that became instrumental in the creation of the American Jewish Joint Distribution Committee at the beginning of the World War. The Joint Distribution Committee has since that date, under his guidance and inspiration, raised and expended a sum in the neighborhood of $100,000,000, to bring succor and relief to Jews, without regard to group or party affiliation, who suffered economic ruin in the war torn countries. He was the staunchest champion of the American Jewish relief work and of the Jewish colonization work in Soviet Russia in the face of some opposition and of many obstacles.

Responsibility for Unity in Jewish Life

As the outstanding leader of the group of non-Zionists in the United States, he was the man with whom the president of the Zionist World Organization six years ago started the negotiations for the extension of the Jewish Agency to include non-Zionists as well as Zionists. It was due to the late Mr. Marshall's statesmanship, patience, unusual skill, leadership and forbearance, that the exceedingly difficult negotiations were brought to a successful conclusion, resulting in unity in Jewish life.

But alas, like the first leader of the Jewish people, he was permitted only a glimpse of the land of Israel from a distance, but never to enter it.

So greatly was he imbued with the importance of the work facing him in connection with the rebuilding of Palestine under the auspices of the Jewish Agency that, when he awoke from the ether, following his first operation, his first question was, as the cable dispatches reported, "What is the news from Palestine?" During the entire time of his illness, on the orders of his physicians, the news concerning the tragedy in Palestine was withheld from him. Ever unwilling to cross the ocean, he undertook to go to Europe, at his advanced age, this summer, in order to attend the Zurich conference, for the sake of Jewish unity and the rebuilding of Palestine.

Honored by the people of his state and of his country, admired by the members of his profession, and loved and revered by the Jews of America and Europe, Mr. Marshall's life of three score and thirteen was one of the highest idealism and usefulness. A speaker of unusual force, a jurist known for his incisive logic, a writer wielding a clear and convincing pen, a commanding personality radiating strength and goodness, the late Mr. Marshall held a unique position of power and influence in American and in American-Jewish life. During the last decade, as the qualities of his leadership became widely known and respected, his word and decision in Jewish matters were final and universally accepted. Though he exercised his leadership with a firm hand and a strong conviction, he was modest and unassuming to an unusual degree. Very often he could be seen at important Jewish gatherings, in which he played the leading part, occupying one of the back seats until he was called upon to preside.

Born in Syracuse, New York, on December 14, 1856, he was the son of Jacob and Cilli (Strauss) Marshall, Jewish immigrants from Germany. Mr. Marshall was educated in Syracuse High School, graduating with high honors in 1874. While at school, he assisted his father in the hide business. For two years he read law in the office of Nathaniel B. Smith, after which he studied at the Law School of Columbia University, taking the two-year course in one year. He returned to Syracuse and became a clerk in the office of a law firm headed by William C. Ruger, later chief judge of the Court of Appeals. He was admitted to the bar and became a member of the firm. In 1894 he moved to New York City and became a member of the firm of Guggenheimer, Untermyer and Marshall.

First to Sit in Three Consecutive Constitutional Conventions

Mr. Marshall was the first citizen of New York State who sat in three consecutive conventions for the revision of the state constitution, being elected a delegate in 1890, 1894 and 1913.

Held Many Civic Posts

He was appointed by Mayor Seth Low, member of a committee to investigate conditions on New York's East Side in 1902; he was named by Governor Charles E. Hughes as chairman of a State Immigration Commission in 1908; he was counsel for Governor William Sulzer in his impeachment trial in 1913, and for Leo M. Frank before the United States Supreme Court in 1915. He was the mediator who brought about the settlement of the cloak makers' strike in New York in 1910 when he drew up a protocol that was the basis of a great many subsequent strike settlements, and he was a member of the arbitration committee that settled the New York clothing workers' strike in 1919. Mr. Marshall has also appeared before numerous committees of the United States Congress in support of a liberal and humane immigration policy.

Was Constitutional Authority

On difficult and intricate questions involving interpretation of the constitutions of the United States and of the various states. Mr. Marshall's opinion was sought by legist [rest of sentence lost].

President of Temple Emanu-El, New York, Chairman of the Board of Directors of the Jewish Theological Seminary, founder of the Jewish Protectory and Aid Society, director of the Educational Alliance, member of the board of directors of Dropsie College, Philadelphia, trustee of the University of Syracuse, president of the New York State College of Forestry, chairman of the Committee on the Amendment of Law of the New York Bar Association, member of the New York Historical Society, of the Academy of Sciences, of the American Law Institute, of the American Bar Association, of the Zoological Society, of the Phi Beta Kappa (honorary) and of the American Jewish Committee – these are only some of the activities for which the late Mr. Marshall gave of his time, energy and substance.

Though reluctant to receive honors, several degrees of distinction have been conferred upon him. The University of Syracuse, his alma mater, conferred upon him the degree of Ph. LLD. in 1913, and the Hebrew Union College, the institution of Reform Judaism with which he was affiliated, conferred upon him the degree of L.H.D. in 1920.

Leadership Demonstrated In Striking Manner

In two notable cases the late Mr. Marshall demonstrated in a striking manner the qualities of his leadership and ability in defense of Jewish rights.

The first was the fight he conducted as the leader of the movement that brought about in 1911 the abrogation by the United States of the treaty of 1832 with Czaristic Russia, because of that country's refusal to recognize American passports in the hands of Jews who were American citizens.

The second notable contribution to the defense of Jewish rights and to the world's new conception of the rights of minorities was his work in Paris in 1919, when the peace conference was in session following the World War.

Though he was opposed to the idea of a permanent American Jewish Congress, which advocated the enactment of guarantees for the rights of national minorities, he threw himself into the work, proceeded to Europe in 1919 and spent five months in Paris, where as president of the Committee of Jewish Delegations, in conjunction with other Jewish leaders, he drafted the proposals for the protection of national minorities, and succeeded in having these proposals inserted in the text of the treaties between the allied and associated powers and Poland, Romania, Yugoslavia, Czechoslovakia and other countries, safeguarding the rights of racial, linguistic and religious minorities, which were made, under the treaties, obligations of international concern and placed under the guarantee of the League of Nations.

Stressed Need for Jewish Education

Together with Felix M. Warburg, the late Mr. Marshall took an active interest in every major Jewish question that came up for discussion and action during his lifetime. Next to the questions of relief and the upbuilding of Palestine, Mr. Marshall placed foremost the question of Jewish education in the United States and on numerous occasions advocated extensive measures for its furtherance and intensification. He frequently spoke of the necessity of raising at the first opportunity a vast American Jewish fund for Jewish education. Several years ago he declared in a press interview that he had taken the pains to learn Yiddish and expressed his genuine interest and regard for modern Yiddish literature.

On December 14, 1926, when the late Mr. Marshall celebrated his seventieth birthday, he refused to become the object of public praise at a banquet. But a small group of his intimate friends formed a committee, headed by Dr. Cyrus Adler, which presented to him at his home, amidst his family circle, an address that was signed by 7,866 persons, residing in 343 cities in the United States, 425 persons representing 14 institutions of learning and philanthropy with which he was connected, and by 419 representatives of organizations and communities in France, Denmark, Romania, Italy, Switzerland, Austria, Hungary, Yugoslavia, South America, Canada and Cuba.

The late Mr. Marshall's office at 120 Broadway, New York City, where he could be found from early in the morning until late in the evening, was a veritable foreign office for Jewish affairs and Ministry of the Interior for American Jewish matters of importance.

On May 6, 1895 Mr. Marshall was married to Florence Lowenstein of New York who died on May 27, 1916. He is survived by three sons, James, a lawyer; Robert, a physician; George, a forestry expert; one daughter, Ruth, who is Mrs. Jacob Billikopf, and four grandchildren.

May his soul rest in peace.

"Review of an Eventful Year"
B'Nai B'Rith Magazine, October 1929

5689, a short span of time in the annals of the world and the annals of the Jewish people, has been an eventful year. To review it adequately one would have to compress international history for the period into a single chapter, plus the specific repercussions of international and local events in Jewish life.

The politics of Immam Yechia or of Ibn Saul of Arabia had their effects on Jewish life, as did the presidential campaign in the United States. The ignorance of a state trooper in

Massena, New York, had an effect equal to that of the bigotry of the Polish nationalist students in Lemberg; and the political machinations of Josef Stalin, the iron man of Soviet Russia, affected one or more aspects of the life of the Jews in that country, as did the courses chosen by Mussolini in Italy, Pilsudski in Poland and the Grand Mufti of Jerusalem.

The near-action of the legislature of Connecticut in passing an anti-*Schechita* bill, which was killed, would have had a result similar to that in Norway where the Storthing passed a *Schechita* prohibition, overcoming many years of strenuous opposition on the part of enlightened public opinion and the Jewish community.

The decline of the Ku Klux Klan in the United States had its counterpart in the rise of the Iron Wolf in Lithuania and the continuation of anti-Semitic campaigns, accompanied by cemetery desecrations and synagogue invasions, in Germany.

As it has been said of Spain of old times, and the British empire of today, that over their realm the sun never sets, it can equally be said of the periphery of Jewish life, that the sun never sets within it, with the qualification that darkness never passes entirely from its horizon.

Latter Part of Year Darkened

Jewish life in 5689, as [is the case with] the life of humanity of which it is an integral and a most sensitive part, proceeds along its orbit in cycles of light and shadow. And the shadows that have accumulated toward the decline of the period under review are likely to becloud the course for a considerable time.

Sometimes one of those who are affected by the vicissitudes of Jewish life startles the world with his unparalleled discoveries concerning the course of light, announces new conceptions of time and space, enriching the knowledge humanity has gained up to now. Humanity then stops for a moment in admiration of the genius and in celebration of his achievements, but then returns to its normal workaday world, forgetting the people and the tradition that produced him.

Seventy-five years after the emancipation of the Jews in Western Europe and 200 years after the birth of Moses Mendelssohn, the record of 5689 would fit into any chapter of written Jewish history for any known period of our indeed extraordinary people. With equality guaranteed on the statue books by nearly all properly constituted governments of civilized nations, a vigorous fight for real economic, social and legal equality was carried on in the principal countries where Jewish communities in larger numbers are to be found. Whatever may be the form – economic need, cultural or religious problems, questions of immigration or emigration, combating the forces of bigotry that are physically harmless or [make] actual attempts at violence – the Jew's will to live and to adjust himself to the conditions that exist, while striving to improve these conditions by a march toward progress and good will, has manifested itself under the most diverse political conditions in the zigzag march of events.

Anti-Semitism Declines in U.S.

In the United States, notwithstanding the effects of the political campaign, 5689 witnesses a definite decline of anti-Semitism, judging, of course, by the Jewish scale and taking a long view by the method of comparison. Fewer manifestations of anti-Jewish feeling came to the surface and, in the few incidents that were recorded, deplorable as they may have been, they were accompanied by vigorous steps, demonstrating the self-respect of American Jewry and its sound constitutional status, as well as providing a reassuring symptom of the attitude of the enlightened American public. The speedy disposition of the Massena ritual murder tale, the position of the United States Supreme Court in validating the New York State Law against secret societies, aimed at the Klan, as well as the decision of the Supreme Court of Georgia in the attempt to bar Jews from jury duty, showed a trend in a reassuring direction. The announcement of the Federal Council of Churches of Christ in America of its intention to carry on the work of its Committee on Good Will Between Jews and Christians. Notwithstanding the recent controversy, coupled with a new assurance that this work has no ulterior motive of missionary propaganda, is another symptom. The overwhelming sympathy of the American public for the Jewish victims of the Palestine events and the human and friendly attitude of President Hoover, as well as that of the United States government during the Palestine emergency, have been most helpful in a critical moment.

B'Nai B'rith Leads Progressives

Internally American Jewry has continued to make considerable progress in the consolidation and cohesion of Jewish religious and cultural life. Among the agencies that led a vigorous fight for the consummation of this end, the Independent Order of B'nai B'rith added new laurels. New synagogues and temples were built, new school houses were opened, new Hillel foundations began functioning, new centers of Jewish studies were formed, new leaders for the Jewish communities, Reform, Conservative and Orthodox, took their places and of course, the "gentlemen's agreement" to "take care of their own" was more than carried out. Jewish social service agencies for home and abroad continued to work in full swing and the manifold Jewish contributions to American life in all of its phases, economic, cultural and philanthropic, were continued.

The adherence of American non-Zionists to the program of the Jewish Agency for Palestine and the participation of a number of representative American Jews in the first session of the Jewish Agency seems to have ushered in a new era of concerted American Jewish effort on behalf of Palestine. It also holds greater promise for Jewish unity in the United States, and created many possibilities for concerted efforts in the solution of problems that are common to all sections of the community. It paves the way for a joint campaign to continue the colonization work in Russia, the relief work in Europe and the reconstruction work in Palestine. The American Jewish Congress at its last session decided to seek cooperation with the American Jewish Committee, and the two bodies have appointed representative committees to confer on methods of unity.

Jewish leadership, however, suffered an irreparable loss with the death of Louis Marshall. The absence of the President of the American Jewish Committee, beloved and respected as he universally was, and admired for his sterling qualities, will be greatly felt for a long time to come. The grief of American Jewry and of world Jewry at his death was convincing proof of the gratitude of a people that has suffered so much for the lack of outstanding leadership, and was at the same time an encouragement to those who feel the urge to continue championing the cause of Judaism. No less catastrophic was the death of Dr. Boris D. Bogen, great social worker and Secretary of the B'nai B'rith. If one may be permitted to indulge, in a review of the past, in a prediction for the future, there will be no abatement of Jewish activities in the United States in the years to come, but there will undoubtedly occur what might be called an interregnum until a more or less recognized leadership again steps forth.

Year Was Normal in Many Places

In Australia as well as in South Africa, in the British Isles as well as in France and the Netherlands, in Canada as well as South America, 5689 was what might be termed a normal period. Different, however, was the fate of the Jewish communities in Central Europe and in Italy, in Eastern Europe and in Russia, in the Near East and in Palestine.

The hideous face of the ritual murder agitation reappeared with shocking regularity in Poland and in Lithuania, in Yugoslavia and in Germany. Even in Russia under the Communist regime it was not missing. Fortunately it was without serious results, due to the firmness of the authorities in suppressing this medieval libel and the enlightened attitude of some of the Christian clergy as, for instance, the action of the church authorities in Cologne and in Belgrade. Damascus, notorious for its ritual murder case in the 19th century, again witnessed an attempt to awaken this libel that was nipped in the bud by the action of the police. An event of the same class was recorded in Lemberg, Poland, where the medieval charge of mocking the Christian religion was renewed by political intriguers who sought to embarrass the Pilsudski government. The action of the central Polish government in suppressing the riots, in stamping out the libel, and in arresting the perpetrators, was noteworthy.

The general position of the Jews in Poland, two and a half million in number, has slightly improved politically, inasmuch as the government has shown its lack of interest in furthering anti-Jewish sentiment. From this to positive action for improving the Jewish situation there is still a long road to be traveled. Czaristic restrictions, which are annoying if not greatly affecting the population, are still on the statute books, notwithstanding the pressure of the Jewish deputies for their abolition. Overshadowing all the political questions, however, is the economic plight of the largest Jewish community in Europe, which obviously faces the need of mass emigration without a place to emigrate to and without the means to transplant themselves.

In Russia the split in the Communist Party, leading to the exile of Leon Trotsky and to the loss of power of the Trotskyites, is controlled by Jews. The rigors of the Communist government have not been diminished and the campaign of the Jewish section of the Communist Party against the Jewish religion and Jewish forms of cultural life, as it is understood by Jewries outside of Russia, are still in force. In Russia, however, as in Poland, the overtowering question is of an economic nature. The action of the American Jewish Joint Distribution Committee, the Agrojoint and the Rosenwald Fund for helping the settled Jews on the land, has brought succor only to a small number. The Jewish five-year plan for industrialization is still in the state of discussion as is the general Soviet five-year plan for the industrialization and electrification of Soviet Russia. A community that has been largely uprooted and declassed in the process of the social upheaval is still in the throes of a hopeless crisis.

Prejudice Rampant in Russia

The situation is still further aggravated by the emergence, or perhaps continuation, of anti-Semitism that is rampant even in the ranks of the Communist Party, leading frequently to violence and the murder of Jews at the hands of the Communist workers. It must be added, however, that the attitude of the authorities is unmistakably opposed to anti-Semitism and that a vigorous and continuous campaign is being carried out by the Soviet press against this plague.

The Jews of Bessarabia and Lithuania might be compared to the Jews of Russia in that they were exposed to suffering and starvation due to the famine that affected these regions. The Jews of Lithuania suffered in addition by the frequent excesses of the chauvinist elements that ended not without inflicting serious wounds. In Hungary and Romania the wave of militant anti-Semitism seems to have abated. In Hungary the new form of the *numerus clausus* limiting the number of Jewish students in the universities is still being enforced, notwithstanding the official promises made by the government to the League of Nations that it will be abolished. In Romania, where hope was held out with the coming into power of the Maniu government for a real "American era of democracy and prosperity," disappointment is setting in.

Jews throughout the world watched with great interest the developments in Italy as a result of which the Quirinal and the Vatican concluded a treaty of peace. Following which the Catholic Church regained temporal powers in the new state added to the European map, the Vatican City. By the terms of the concordat, the canon law of the Catholic Church has again come into force in Italy in the important field of domestic relations and in the field of education. This created a difficult situation for the Jews of Italy.

Jews in various lands have been active in the movement for international peace. Leading among them was Salmon O. Levinson of Chicago, who was received by President Hoover following the ceremonies attending the putting into effect of the Kellogg-Brian bilateral treaty for the renunciation of war as national policy. Mr. Levinson was credited and honored for his work in this direction, having been the author of the slogan for the outlawry of war and having worked toward its realization. Prominent journals in opinion in America and Europe have urged the award to Mr. Levinson of the Nobel Peace Prize. In Germany, Professor Einstein, together with Rabbi Leo M. Baeck, leader of the German B'nai B'rith lodges, head a recently created body advocating international peace. The body is composed of leading Jews and non-Jews. Among the agencies furthering amity and brotherhood was the Independent Order of B'nai B'rith.

International peace, together with the safeguarding of the fixity of the Sabbath and peaceful reconstruction in Palestine, were the three major questions that have occupied the minds of Jews, regardless of boundary lines. The menace to the fixity of the Sabbath arose with the proposal of the introduction of a 13-month year beginning in 1931, when the first of January will occur on a Sunday. With the introduction of such a plan and the observance of blank days, the fixity of the Sabbath and of Jewish holidays would be affected. American Jews, through the League for the Safeguarding of the Fixity of the Sabbath, as well as Jewish leaders in Great Britain and Europe, have been actively engaged in opposing this plan in representations to a Congress Committee and to a committee functioning on behalf of the League of Nations. An international conference to consider the change of the calendar is still under discussion and the danger to the fixity of the Sabbath has not yet passed.

Arab Outbreak in Palestine

The question of the rebuilding in Palestine of a Jewish National Home toward the end of the year claimed the attention of world Jewry and of the world at large in a degree unparalleled before. While on July 1, 1929, Sir John Chancellor, High Commissioner of Palestine, appeared before the Permanent Mandates Commission of the League of Nations to report that the relations between the Arabs and the Jews were satisfactory, 54 days later the world was aghast at a series of Arab outbreaks, starting in Jerusalem on August 23 and leading to the massacres and atrocities at Hebron, Safed and Motza, where 127 Jews, 87 Muslims and 10 Christians lost their lives, hundreds were wounded and property that was built up with so much energy and zeal during the past quarter of a century was destroyed in the savage attack. A preliminary estimate places the amount of Jewish damages suffered at $5,000,000 and, although the response of American Jewry to the Palestine Emergency Fund has been generous, securing immediate first aid for the victims, reconstruction will now become a serious problem, as will be the continuation and the expansion of the rebuilding work. The reaction of Jews, irrespective of group or party affiliation, Zionist or non-Zionist, has been that violence cannot retard the peaceful reconstruction work. However, the key to the situation lies in the hands of the British government as the Mandatory for Palestine, and although the British Labor cabinet has reassured the public that there is no intention of reopening the question of the Zionist policy, the final word will be uttered not before the parliamentary Commission of Inquiry will have completed its work, which is not expected to be before 1929 is over. In the meantime, a section of the British press that has never been reconciled to the Palestine Mandate has renewed its campaign for the repudiation of the Mandate. The announcement of the British government's intention to bring about a new relationship between her and Iraq, also a British Mandate, on lines similar to the Labor government's settlement of the Egyptian question, has added impetus to this demand concerning Palestine.

The Palestine outbreaks had their origin in the exploitation by various elements of the extremely delicate and aggravated question of the Jewish right of access for worship at the Western Wall, the last relic of the enclosure of the Temple, known as the Wailing Wall. The pavement before the Wall, constituting a narrow alley, is legally the property of the Muslims' religious foundation and although the ground is not sacred to Muslims, its use to any comfortable degree by Jewish worshippers is opposed by a section of the Muslim Arab population of Palestine that finds in the prolonged controversy a vehicle for expression of their opposition to the Zionist policy and for making political capital of it. In this process, the Wailing Wall is being declared a part of the Mosque of Omar and various innuendos and rumors of Jewish designs on the Muslim Holy Places have, without foundation, been given currency among the Muslims of Palestine and the neighboring countries.

Controversy a Year Old

Having started a year ago on the Day of Atonement, September 23, 1928, the controversy has grown deeper and wider, having had resonance throughout the Jewish and the Muslim world and reaching the British government, the Permanent Mandates Commission, and the League of Nations. Just as the Jews in Palestine formed committees for the defense of the Western Wall, so have the Muslim leaders formed groups for the defense of *El Buraq* (the Western Wall) and so far none of the learned and high bodies have attempted or succeeded in cutting this Gordian knot. It is to be hoped that the Parliamentary Commission of Inquiry, whose main purpose it is to determine the cause of the outbreaks, will at least settle the question of the Western Wall in conformity with the dignity of Jewish worship at this Jewish Holy Site and in a manner convincing the Muslims that undisturbed Jewish worship at this place does not encroach upon their rites or involve designs on their Holy Places.

"From Cleveland to Cleveland: American Zionism from 1921 to 1930 in Review"
The New Palestine, June 27, 1930

At a crucial moment in the history of the movement, the Zionists of America will gather in Cleveland, Ohio, on June 29th for their thirty-third annual convention. As in 1921, when American Zionists last met in that city, the session comes after a critical and turbulent period in Palestine and in the movement generally. Now, as then, Jewish immigration to Palestine has been suspended. Now, as then, uncertainty and anxiety are uppermost in the minds of Zionists. Now, as then, readjustment to new conditions and the formulation of a new program of work are the order of the day. Whatever problems pertaining to the movement generally and to the situation in Palestine in particular are to be discussed and determined, the forthcoming Cleveland convention will devote much attention to a specific American Zionist issue – the reorganization and strengthening of the Zionist Organization of America.

In American Zionist parlance the term "Cleveland" has a special connotation. It signifies the rift that occurred in 1921, resulting in the ascension of the administration that has conducted the affairs of the movement in the United States for the last nine years. "From Cleveland to Cleveland" constitutes an important chapter in the annals of the movement. An objective presentation of the major events that transpired since 1921 will be helpful to all concerned.[6]

When the scene opens in 1921, an assembly of several hundred delegates is singing the Hatikvah in acclamation of the new leadership that came into power following a period of severe [internal] strife. Whatever were the issues – the supremacy of the economic character of the Palestine upbuilding work, the place of Jewish nationalism in this work, the founding and development of the Keren Hayesod, the necessity of political work in the Zionist movement, the character of the administrative machinery – the will of the majority of American Zionists was clearly and unmistakably expressed both by the action of the Cleveland convention and the support that the victorious party continued in the main to enjoy throughout the past nine years. By a vote of 153 to 71, the 1921 Cleveland convention passed a resolution withholding approval of the report of the administration that had been in power practically since 1914. A leadership that had great accomplishments to its credit during the war and post-war period found itself at variance with the views then held by the majority of the Zionists of America concerning future policies and methods. Placed in the position of a minority, it resigned and throughout the succeeding period did comparatively little to bring its views before the rank and file and to seek recognition if its program. The field of the American Zionist movement, with a few exceptions, was left clear for those whose views were accepted in 1921.

Engrossed in the battle between the Weizmann and the Brandeis-Mack forces, the Zionists of America at the Cleveland convention acted hesitantly. The mantle of leadership that had fallen from the shoulders of the former leaders was not given to one or two men. An administrative committee was chosen to act as a body. (The committee consisted of the following: Herman Conheim, Abraham Goldberg, Louis Lipsky, Louis Robinson, Bernard A.

---

[6] Note by WZS: the writer finds it necessary to state that he has never been connected with the Zionist Organization of America. He is indebted to the ZOA for permitting him access to the facts and figures that are mentioned here. They are taken from the official records of the Zionist Organization of America.

Rosenblatt, Morris Rothenberg and Peter J. Schweitzer. No officers were chosen. The only designations made were that Mr. Lipsky was to serve as general secretary and the late Mr. Schweitzer as treasurer.) The affairs of the Zionist Organization of America were placed in its charge. Active as the new leaders had been in the Zionist movement for many years previous, devoted to the ideal as they had shown themselves to be, none possessed at the time what might be termed a national reputation outside of the Zionist movement.

This group undertook the steering of the movement in America under most extraordinary circumstances. Principally, the mandate given to them by the 1921 Cleveland convention was a commitment of the Zionist Organization of America to uphold the policies of the World Zionist Congress as expounded by Dr. Chaim Weizmann. This applied in equal measure to the political and economic aspects of the Zionist work. A difficult situation confronted the new administration. The brilliant political success achieved by Dr. Weizmann and his associates in London and by the Zionist Provisional Committee in the United States were followed by the first intimations of trouble. The first foreboding of the Arab anti-Jewish agitation that was to reach its climax in 1929 had found expression in two riots. The Zionist movement, ever since its inception, had to travel along a difficult road. Rooted though it was in the traditions of the synagogue, bound up with the essence of Judaism, inseparably connected with the sentiments and views of the Jewish masses, none the less Zionism had always to seek its way while combating antipathy and indifference and often active hostility on the part of powerful factors in Jewish life.

The phenomenal growth of the movement in the United States during the war and the immediate post-war period was not rooted in solid ground. The enthusiasm of the war period, stimulated by the alluring "self-determination" slogan and the pronunciamento of the Balfour Declaration, was already in the process of cooling off. The hopes that had been kindled when the movement was, by the fortunes of the war, lifted from its narrow and difficult path to the dazzling heights of the international scene and to the intoxicating atmosphere of the Peace Conference were beginning to weaken. The easy satisfaction derived from expressions of sympathy by the powers that were [then extant] began to give way to a searching for plans for the execution of a gigantic task. The Zionist movement had to make a swift turn to the speedy performance of the actual task of reconstruction in Palestine in conformity with the new political conditions that were taking shape. The Mandate for Palestine had not yet been ratified. The jubilation of the so-called "Balfour Zionists" had to be replaced by the constant efforts of the Zionist worker and campaigner. A people that had suffered much during the war, a people of which large sections had been uprooted and shaken out of its economic, political and cultural strongholds, were eager to seize the opportunity it saw for realizing the national aim that had for centuries been the object of its dreams.

Men and money were needed. The situation clearly called for a division of labor. Eastern Europe was ready with its manpower. Economic necessity, combined with the powerful sentiment that had been aroused, recruited an impressive contingent of prospective pioneers. American Jewry, the strongest Jewish community in the world following the war, had shown its leadership by its gigantic accomplishments in the relief furnished [to] the war-sufferers. It was clearly the source from which financial resources for the rebuilding of Palestine was to be drawn.

The unfortunate London 1920 conference failed to bring about unity between the European leaders and the Brandeis regime. The Zionists of America, by their vote at Cleveland, endorsed the London plan for setting up a Keren Hayesod that was to have raised the amount of $25,000,000 for a five-year period. The covering of the Palestine budget through the Keren Hayesod had become the principal concern of Zionists throughout the world and the lion's share had to come from America.

The obligation imposed upon American Zionism by the situation in the world movement was undertaken by the new regime. Most of the Palestine upbuilding work, the political advancement and strengthening of the movement, and its expression in the United States, were thus placed in the hands of the new administration. It is with the record of this work that this review is concerned.

Remittances to Palestine

Since the principal task of the Zionist Organization of America, under the prevailing conditions, was to secure the funds needed for the rebuilding operations as determined by the Zionist Congress and as conducted by the Zionist Executive, it is clear that the results of its work in this field must be considered first. As the parent organization, the Zionist Organization of America was responsible for the organization and conduct of a series of campaigns for Palestine funds waged throughout the country for the past nine years, up to the formation of the Jewish Agency for Palestine. In the face of dissension within the Zionist ranks, the opposition of anti-Zionists and the indifference of many [others], these drives, when judged by their results, may be taken as a barometer of the strength of the movement and of the penetration of the Palestine idea into ever-widening circles. To be sure, the financial results of the nine drives have not always been the same, the response rising and falling with the ebb and flow of the economic status of American Jewry on the one hand, with the reaction to the successes and failures of the upbuilding work in Palestine, on the other.

The records show that under the auspices of the Zionist Organization of America, through the Keren Hayesod and the United Palestine Appeal, the amount of $20,044,160.32 was raised over the period beginning May, 1921 and ending April 30, 1930. Of this sum, the amount of $14,619,527.02 was remitted to Palestine, 26.90% having been expended in the United States on the money-raising apparatus throughout the entire period. During the period beginning August, 1914, and ending May, 1921, the Provisional Zionist Committee and the Palestine Restoration Fund had raised $5,738,998.32 and remitted to Palestine $3,761,279.40, 34.49% having been expended in the United States on the money-raising apparatus throughout that period.

Political Influence

Three major events transpired during the period under review that best express the political influence the Zionist Organization of America exercised in the general field, in the Jewish world and in Zionist affairs, acting in cooperation with the Zionist Organization of America for the furtherance of the ideals and interests of Palestine and the movement.

Its outstanding achievement in the political field was the work that culminated in the passage by the Congress of the United States of the Joint Resolution endorsing the Jewish National Home policy. This was accomplished by the organization in the face of strong hostility on the part of certain Jewish groups that actively opposed the passage of the resolution. Coming as this action of the United States Congress did at a time when opposition to the League of Nations and the general trend towards aloofness from European affairs were at their height in this country, the support of the Jewish National Home policy by Congress was a political event of [the] first international importance. The resolution was passed by the United States Senate on May 3, 1922, and by the House of Representatives on June 30th of that year. It placed the United States government on record as favoring the establishment of the Jewish National Home at a time when the fate of the Mandate was in the balance. This action was greatly instrumental in facilitating the ratification by the Council of the League of Nations of the Mandate for Palestine.

Notable is the achievement of the Zionist Organization of America in its struggle for the consummation of the plan for the extension of the Jewish Agency. Beginning June 18, 1923, and ending with the vote at the Zionist Congress at Zurich in August 1929, the Zionist Organization of America constantly fought for the extension of the Agency. It gave support to the Weizmann policy in the face of numerous difficulties and obstacles often reaching a state of crisis, despite a determined opposition to the plan both at home and abroad. This policy, which has now become a pillar of strength in the upbuilding of Palestine, had first been tested through the Keren Hayesod that the American organization inaugurated and through which it strove to attract non-Zionists as well as Zionists.

In the councils of the world Zionist movement, the Zionist Organization of America held a leading position. Represented on the Executive Committee in London and in the Zionist General Council, it had a leading part in shaping the policies of the movement. American Zionists served on the London and Jerusalem Executives. It was the influence of the American delegation to the 1927 Congress that was responsible for bringing about the "consolidation policy" that had then become necessary.

Propaganda

Propaganda is admittedly the main function of a movement such as Zionism, which strives to embrace within its fold the majority of the people whose national ideals and dreams it set out to realize. The Zionist Organization, in the conception of its founders, was principally to act as the spokesman of the Jewish people in relation to Palestine, while making every effort to enlist the sympathy and active support of the people for that purpose to which the active minority had pledged its energies.

Even after the issuance of the Balfour Declaration and the ratification of the Mandate, the Zionist movement was still a force that had to make continuous conquests in order to maintain its position and to create such conditions as would accelerate the realization of its program. The membership of the Zionist Organization, even at its height, never represented the full strength of the sentiment that lay behind it. No matter how many Zionists were enlisted in the Organization, the number of sympathizers, prospective members and workers was always vastly greater. The field for Zionist propaganda was limited only by the size of the Jewish population. With the advent of the period of active work in Palestine, these limits had to be extended. Zionist enlightenment had to be carried into the non-Jewish field as well. The raising of funds that had to be undertaken created wider and greater opportunities in that direction.

During the period under review, the work of the Zionist Organization of America in this field reached an unparalleled scope. Whereas previously sporadic Zionist publications brought the message of the movement to a limited number of readers, the ZOA during the past nine years maintained a continuous stream of Zionist information and enlightenment through these channels. The first was that of its weekly publications, *The New Palestine, Dos Yiddishe Folk*, and, for some time, the *Palestine Pictorial*. For nine years *The New Palestine* and *Dos Yiddishe Folk* appeared every week, reaching at times in the case of *The New Palestine* as many as 60,000 Jewish families and, in the case of *Dos Yiddishe Folk*, about

10,000. On these publications the Zionist Organization of America expended for the period an amount close to $800,000. Throughout this period the publications maintained a high standard and some of the issues, such as the University number and the Herzl memorial number, it is universally conceded, have permanent Zionist cultural value.

A powerful factor for spreading Zionist thought and intensifying interest in the upbuilding work in Palestine was the coming to America of distinguished Zionist delegates from Europe. The arrival and departure of the members of these delegations usually coincided with the opening and closing of the Palestine fund drives, but the interest they created and the impression they left were of a stimulating character throughout the entire period.

In addition to Zionist delegations, the Organization, in conjunction with the Keren Hayesod and the United Palestine Appeal, maintained an almost continuous speakers' service that reached nearly every Jewish community in the United States. The number of meetings both in and out of campaign season addressed by Zionist speakers runs into the thousands. Speakers' fees during the period amounted to $92,629.62. There were also the services of volunteers, among them nearly every Jewish public speaker of note.

The immediate result of this propaganda generated by the Zionist Organization through its various channels was the notable widening of the scope of the movement that found its expression both in the amounts of money raised for Palestine and in the number of people whose interest was enlisted in one form or another. The actual membership of the Zionist Organization may have risen and fallen in the succeeding years, but whatever the membership may have been at any given time, one must not fail to take into account the number of contributors to the United Palestine Appeal for the same period. Although the $6 membership never, during the period, exceeded the figure of 30,597 [members], the number of small and large contributors to the Keren Hayesod and the United Palestine Appeal reached as high as 60,000. Some of the contributors to the Palestine funds were still non-Zionists, but there can be but slight doubt that persons who have maintained their interest in the work through continuous annual contributions have been enlisted for the cause.

The outstanding feature of the work of the Zionist organization under the regime that came into power in 1921 was the sweeping conquests it made among the middle classes of American Jewry. Even the Reform Rabbinate, which previously had been a leading source from which opposition to the movement emanated, had become in many cases predominantly Zionistic. The cultural values and the interests of a living Palestine seemed to bring new Jewish content to the Reform congregations. Previously, active interest in Zionism and in the Palestine work was primarily centered in the upper-middle class and among the Jewish intelligentsia. To raise huge funds it was necessary to enlist larger numbers in the work. This was accomplished through the Keren Hayesod and the United Palestine Appeal. By drawing in the middle class, the organization succeeded in opening up a vast field whose resources and capacities have not yet been fully exploited. Advantageous as this has been for the cause of Palestine and for the movement as a whole, it brought with it certain features that may not be pleasant. The Zionist whose imagination was wholly captured by the ideal of the movement and who entered into the work for the sake of the cause alone now found as his companions many who, though they subscribed to the purpose of the movement, saw in that work, as usual in popular movements, a vehicle for local purposes as well. Zionist work as it developed with the aid of the large middle class became in some cases a stepping stone for individual ambitions. Zionism, which set out to bring national values into Jewish life, to bring about a renaissance of Jewish culture, had been unavoidably caught in the wheels of American Jewish adjustment. The large number of men and women who were drawn into the service in various local and national committees in all parts of the country naturally brought with them standards and ways expressive of the classes and communities to which they belonged. However, when the advantages and disadvantages are weighed in the scale of accomplishment, the gain is on the side of the services performed and the results achieved.

One of the impressive results of this development is the fact that toward the middle of the period, even before the Jewish Agency extension began to assume concrete form, rabid anti-Zionism, with which the movement had had to contend, was stamped out in the United States. Hardly an organ of public opinion or a Jewish leader of prominence, in lay or religious life, could be found to be engaged in active anti-Zionist propaganda.

Membership and Strength of Movement

The membership of the Zionist Organization, since the $6 [membership] basis was adopted, rose and fell. When the new administration came in into power, the membership, including women, showed an enrollment of 30,579 for the period October 1, 1920 to December 31, 1921. The new regime, however, entered into an arrangement by which the Hadassah, the Women's Zionist Organization, though it remained an integral part of the ZOA, was given an opportunity for autonomous development along lines of work that were regarded by the women's leaders as best suited to drawing in large numbers of women as members. Beginning with 1922, the membership of the Zionist Organization, unlike the procedure followed in other countries, was strictly divided according to the sexes.

With attention concentrated on the Palestine fund drives, with the $6 membership fee as a basis, the enthusiasm of the war period subsiding and with the conception in the minds of many contributors to the Palestine funds that their subscriptions expressed their affiliation with the movement, the struggle for maintaining and increasing the actual membership of the Zionist Organization was naturally one of great difficulty. Thus, the organization ended the year 1929 with an enrollment of 18,031 [and an annual income from the membership of $144,850].

The full strength of Zionist Organization of America, however, would be greatly underestimated if one's judgment would rest only on the foregoing figures. The total strength of the Zionist Organization in the United States can best be estimated when the situation is reviewed as a whole and when the total number of its supporters of various types and in various forms is considered, as seen in the following figures:

ZOA district members in good standing: 18,181
ZOA district members in arrears: 7,565
Order [of the] Sons of Zion: 3,200
Roll Call Registrars, December 1929: 45,200
Shekel Payers (non-members): 2,068
Histadruth Ivrith: 1,815
Avukah: 1,000
Young Judaea: 11,300
Hadassah: 35,195
Junior Hadassah: 8,500
United Palestine Appeal contributors: 60,606

The Administration

The administration of the Zionist Organization of America for the past nine years was carried mainly by the impetus that had its origin in the events of 1921. However, it would be inaccurate to maintain that it produced a one-pattern leadership. An examination of the personnel of the important committees and the lists of honorary and active officers who functioned during the period suffices to demonstrate the multiplicity of characters, viewpoints and energies that went into the making of the leadership that carried on. The not-infrequent cases of friction, which found expression in the several opposition groups within the administration, groups that which stormed the administration fortress toward the end of the period, and the various changes that were made, clearly prove the point.

The administration succeeded in drawing in a considerable number of co-workers both in the administrative tasks as well as in the development of the campaigns for Palestine funds. Although the attempt made at the 1922 convention to bring about a reconciliation with the previous leadership brought no result, time seemed to be healing the breach and members of the Mack-Brandeis group lent their cooperation in one form or another to the administration. Notable were the services rendered by Dr. Stephen S. Wise as national chairman of the 1925 United Palestine Appeal, coming as it did during the period of controversy over the Russian colonization plan, and of Judge Julian W. Mack, who served as honorary vice-chairman of the United Palestine Appeal in 1928. Messers. Rosensohn and Berenson, and the late Mr. Lindheim, who might be regarded as representatives of the group, were a part of the administration elected at the 1927 convention.

Yeoman service was rendered in the early organization and conduct of the Keren Hayesod and the United Palestine Appeal by Mr. Emanuel Neumann, in various executive capacities, by Morris Rothenberg, as Chairman of the Board of Directors of the United Palestine Appeal, and by Judge William M. Lewis, of Philadelphia, as National UPA Chairman.

Notwithstanding the changes and transformations through which the administration passed, the man whose leadership held sway and whose mental energies vitalized the movement was Louis Lipsky. However, the leadership was not conferred upon him by one stroke. One of the seven elected to the administrative committee in 1921, his elevation to the presidency of the Zionist Organization of America did not occur until June, 1926, he having acted before in the capacity of chairman of the national executive committee and chairman of the administrative committee. The services he rendered to the Zionist movement for a period of thirty years and the qualities he displayed so impressed themselves upon the majority of the rank and file of the movement that, notwithstanding the fierce attacks made by the various opposition groups at the 1927 convention in Atlantic City and the 1928 convention in Pittsburgh, his leadership was upheld.

For the purpose of conducting the work of the Zionist movement in the United States, the Zionist Organization of America received a total of $1,786,645.65 over the nine-year period. Of this amount $1,123,190.31 came from membership dues. An amount of $167,927.71 was refunded to the districts for local administrative and propaganda work. Out of the membership income received by the administration and $28,506.18 received from shekel prayers, $209,267.72 was remitted to the Zionist Organization as the American federation's membership fee to the world organization for the maintenance of the international headquarters in London.

From the total net income of $1,779,059.10, the amount of $931,606.80 was expended for general administration purposes. The amount of $791,967.58 was expended on the publication of the Zionist weeklies, *The New Palestine* and *Dos Yiddishe Folk*. It must be noted that the periodicals had an income of $617,609.31, part of which, $409,434, was derived from subventions given them by the Keren Hayesod and the United Palestine Appeal for services rendered to the various campaigns. The amount of $206,321.70 was paid by the Zionist Organization of America to subventions to the Young Judaea, the Avukah, the *Hadoar*, a Hebrew weekly, the *Hatoren*, a Hebrew journal, and other bodies engaged in furthering Jewish cultural aims. Against the net income of $1,779,059.10, the total expenditure amounted to $1,930,096.08, leaving a deficit of $151,036.98.

The Deficit

Deficits are not uncommon in organizations whose purpose is not financial profit but rather service to a cause. The figures of the Zionist Organization of America for the period July 14, 1918, to October 31, 1920, under the former regime, show a deficit in the organization department amounting to $144,743.29. This deficit was covered from other sources than membership income. The deficit of the Zionist Organization of America on May 31, 1929, stood at $130,374.90. By a resolution of the 1929 convention, the organization took over the deficit of Young Judaea amounting to $16,000, bringing the deficit as of June 1st to $146, 374.90.

Since 1923 the question of the deficit was being grappled with and periodic attempts to wipe it out were made.

It will be noted that the amount of $206,321.70 paid in subventions exceeds the deficit.

Solution of the Amzic Problem in Sight

Greater than the troubles of the deficit were the difficulties that beset the organization on account of the entanglement of the American Zion Commonwealth. It must be stated that the difficulties of the American Zion Commonwealth were due to the economic crisis that enveloped Palestine after the collapse of the Fourth Aliyah, but it is likewise conceded that the Commonwealth found itself in difficulties because of its methods of financing and management.

The Commonwealth was organized in 1914 and had the moral backing of the Zionist Organization both prior to and after 1921. The Organization recognized its moral responsibility to the American purchasers of land and, in cooperation with the Zionist authorities in London and Jerusalem, made every effort to help the Commonwealth disentangle its affairs and see to it that the land stretches that came into Jewish possession should remain in Jewish hands. It was for this purpose that the United Palestine Appeal loaned the Commonwealth $523,699.33 that will be returned to the Keren Hayesod when the assets of the company will again become liquid.

According to a statement by Mr. S. A. Van Vriesland, who was appointed by the Palestine courts as the representative of the interests involved in the disentanglement of the Zion Commonwealth affairs, a successful solution of the problem is at last within sight.

Readjustment to New Conditions

Again the Zionist Organization of America stands on the threshold of readjustment. The conditions that imposed grave responsibilities upon the Zionist movement in 1921 have basically not changed, with the exception that the task of raising funds required for the

Palestine upbuilding work is now being shared by the new forces that joined in the work of the [Jewish] Agency for Palestine.

The Zionist Organization of America no longer shoulders the responsibility alone for the Palestine funds. A part of its energy has thus been freed for the tasks that are peculiar to Zionism, and the Organization, which since 1921 has been compelled to devote most of its time and effort to the raising of funds, can now undertake the work of strengthening its ranks so that it may discharge its functions as a strong and influential factor in the life of American Jewry, in the affairs of the world Zionist movement and in the enterprises of the Jewish Agency for Palestine that came into being due mainly to the continuous battles fought by the Zionist Organization of America for its realization.

In this readjustment, the purity of Zionist ideology, the strengthening of the movement in the United States and abroad, the safeguarding of the positions in Palestine, and the lessons learned during the past decade must be taken into account.

"The Scramble for 'Elbow-Room': International Drama Centering Around The Soil Question"
The Jewish Standard, November 14, 1930

Palestine has been the subject of a fierce battle during the past year. It culminated with the ill-starred Passfield 'White Paper.' A fictitious scramble for 'elbow room' was staged in order to justify the Arab riots of 1929 and the Passfield statement of policy in 1930. In the following article, written specially for *The Jewish Standard*, Mr. Spiegelman, noted journalist and former editor of the *Jewish Daily Bulletin*, delves into official documents and explodes the land-shortage myth. – The Editor.

It all developed because of the "elbow-room" question.

In the year 1930 of the Christian Era, 13 years after the issuance of the Balfour Declaration, and after a decade of active Jewish settlement work in Palestine, the question was suddenly put to a confused and astounded world: "Is there enough elbow-room in Palestine for the Jews and Arabs to dwell together in peace?"

The awaited report of Sir John Hope is expected to shed much light on this perplexing problem, although many are by now convinced that the raising of the issue was an unfortunate move used to divert attention of the gazing public opinion of the world from the real dark spots in Palestine, inquiries into which might have exposed the seat of real responsibility for the Palestine bloodshed of a year ago.

Any traveler from the Western world who visited Palestine, be it only for a short while, must have carried away with him the impression that the country had been sadly neglected for many centuries, and that the territory west of the Jordan is both underpopulated and underdeveloped. The impression that any observer must gain even from a flying [airplane] visit to the country is that Palestine can indeed stand a great deal of improvement in regard to its agricultural, industrial and commercial growth. This impression gains particular strength from the fact that in Palestine, as nowhere else, the desert is so infrequently found in close proximity with civilization, and native neglect is so strikingly contrasted by modern Jewish culture in all the fields where sanitation, production and personal industry pave the road for the march of Western civilization. There, as perhaps nowhere else, the desert and civilization are engaged in a combat of man against nature, the like of which has not been seen since the days of the American Covered Wagon.

To the utter surprise and bewilderment of the world, the British Commission of Inquiry sent to investigate the cause of last year's riots returned no indictment against any one in particular. It whitewashed wherever and whomever it could, and for the rest it brought back the discovery that the reason for all that happened was the fear of the Arabs that there is not sufficient elbow-room for Jews and Arabs in the country.

To be sure, the now discredited Shaw report did not say in so many words that Palestine cannot absorb any further Jewish immigration; it sought, instead, to convey the impression by the subtle art of implication. "When the facts are against you, speak about the law; when the law is against you, speak of the facts; when both the law and the facts are against you, belittle your opponent." This eminent advice of a sophisticated lawyer to his new associate was apparently the guiding principle of those who drafted the chapter in the Shaw report dealing with the land problem in Palestine. They have made no study of the land problem of Palestine as such. They have not, so far as is known, called for the testimony of Col. E. R. Sawer, the Director of the Agricultural Department of the Palestine Government. He is known to have a favorable opinion, based on facts and many years of observation on the spot. They have merely reiterated the opinions and the "fears" of the Arab politicians without expressing their own opinion as to the reliability or the accuracy of the statements and allegations made. They preferred to belittle the absorption capacity and the possibilities of Palestine, and thus find a convenient "cause" for the outbreaks. The Palestine administration was obviously found wanting, but once fear is conceded to have been the cause of the Arab outbreak, it is an easy matter to explain. No government is in a position to know when "fear" may seize any section of the population and be properly prepared for it. The drafters of the chapter on the Palestine land problem in the Shaw report have become so engrossed in their "fear" complex that they extended it not only to the present Arab population, but even to the unborn Arab generations.

It is remarkable that the "elbow-room" question, as presented by implication in the Shaw report, has never been viewed in such a light before. It is curious that the entire question had not occurred to any of the experts who carried out an extensive survey of Palestine and its possibilities in 1927 under the auspices of the Joint Palestine Commission, which included such eminent experts as Dr. Elwood Mead, Commissioner of Reclamation of the United States Department of the Interior; Dr. J. G. Lippman, Director of the Agricultural Experiment Station of the New Jersey College of Agriculture; Mr. A. T. Strahorn, Soil Technologist of the United States Department of Agriculture; Professor Frank Adams of the University of California; Mr. Knowles A. Ryerson, Horticulturist, Agricultural Experiment Station, Haiti; Mr. C. Q. Henriques, Irrigation Engineer of the Zionist Organization in Palestine; Sir John Campbell; and Sir E. J. Russell. These experts dealt with the specific [technical] problems of the development of Palestine's agriculture, commerce and industry, and apparently entertained no fear that the country, with a total area of 8,000 square miles or 5,683,200 acres of land, is about to reach its saturation point at a time when the population is below the one million mark. They were satisfied that the exploitable land of Palestine is 4.5 million acres, of which approximately 2.75 million acres are considered as cultivable. They were even inclined to accept the opinion that out of the uncultivable 1.75 million acres a considerable area may be wrested for settlement purposes by the development of certain swamps and sand dunes, and by the extension of dry farming into the Negev.

The Shaw Commission, however, was so overwhelmed by its duty of reciting the Arab "fears" as an excuse for the bloodshed that it expressed a view that the "position seems to be that, taking Palestine as a whole, the country cannot absorb a larger agricultural population than it at present carries unless methods of farming undergo a radical change." It therefore recommended a scientific inquiry into the prospects of introducing improved methods of cultivation in Palestine. The Commission hastened to express another fear that the native Arab population may not always be equipped or fit for improved methods of cultivation. Without apparently committing itself to any view, the Shaw Commission labored to create by implication the "elbow-room" question in Palestine. The issue having been raised, and the Labor Government agreeing that it is necessary to institute such an inquiry, and undertaking it through Sir John Hope Simpson, the suspension of Jewish immigration and the rest that followed seems quite a "natural" course of events.

Of course, it was quite obvious that this way of attack that took the form of raising the "elbow-room" question was directed primarily against the Jewish National Fund, the agency of the Zionist movement for the acquisition of land in Palestine as the property of the Jewish people. The land purchases of the Fund in the Valley of Jezreel and at Wadi Hawareth figured prominently in the hearings of the Shaw Commission, and in the unfounded assertions about "evictions" of tenants made by the Arab spokesmen during the inquiry, although even the Arab spokesmen were compelled to admit, as did the Shaw Commission, that the land transactions of the Jewish National Fund have been completed not only in full compliance with the prevailing Palestine land rules, but with every principle of equity and fairness. The Jewish National Fund has always, as did the other Jewish land purchasing agencies, sought to compensate the Arab squatters, and to help them settle on other land, at considerable expense beyond the price to the landlord, and beyond the extremist demands of the laws governing the transfer of land.

That this "elbow-room" question was but a myth that owed its origin to juggling with figures is now clearly established. This juggling with figures was exposed in the memorandum of the Jewish Agency, prepared by Dr. Leonard Stein, which was submitted to the Permanent Mandates Commission that carried the day in Geneva. This is a highly interesting story in itself and the reader will be greatly interested to follow the figures for a while.

The Shaw Commission supported the impression it sought to convey that there is no more room in Palestine by the following argument: the land available in non-Jewish ownership in Palestine is now approximately 10,100,000 dunams,[7] the Commission stated. Taking the Arab rural population of Palestine, exclusive of the Bedouins, who occupy the desert area of the Southeast of Palestine, to be approximately 460,000 [people], and assuming that the average Arab family consists of five persons, there are 92,000 Arab families in Palestine "who depend upon the soil for their sustenance." Assuming further that to obtain a living from the soil, an Arab family would need an area varying from 100 to 150 dunams of land; now, dividing the 10,100,000 dunams by 92,000, it would seem that, after taking care of the present Arab agricultural population alone, there would be no more room left. And what about the unborn Arabs, that is, the natural increase that is certain to come?

Mr. Stein rendered a real service to the cause of Palestine and of accuracy by his critical analysis. He showed very clearly that what the Shaw Commission sought to do was merely to indulge in generalizations without regard to accuracy or to the facts as they are known from everyday life. First, the figure 460,000 for the rural Arab population is quite uncertain in the light of official Government reports. Secondly, that even if the figure of

---

[7] A dunam equals one-quarter of an acre.

460,000 is more than a guess, it is unreasonable to assume that all of these 92,000 families consist of cultivators of the soil. It is obvious that not every Arab who lives in rural areas is a cultivator of the soil. According to a Palestine Government report, approximately 50 percent of the rural population is engaged in other occupations than cultivating the soil. Furthermore, the 100-150 dunams that the Commission assumes is necessary for each family are needed only when the farmer is engaged in growing cereals. How did the Commission gets its information that the entire Arab farming population intends to engage in the growing of cereals?

It is on such mathematics that the Shaw Commission based its contention that there is no room for Jews in Palestine without displacing Arabs. On this point, causing some confusion in certain liberal quarters, the Shaw Commission suggested the charge that through the Jewish settlement work a great number of Arab tenants have been "evicted." The Shaw Commission hastened, it is true, to absolve the Jewish organizations from any moral or other responsibility, adding that they completed their transactions in the most proper manner, with the consent of the government, and that furthermore, in all cases, they have compensated the tenants with money, even though the prevailing law did not require this of them. Again by implication the Shaw Commission expressed the fear of the Arabs that continued land purchases might tend to create a "landless proletariat." The Commission reiterated the allegation that "many Arabs" were "evicted" from the land that they had been cultivating under agreement with Arab landlords. This obviously was intended to heighten the impression of the acuteness of the "elbow-room" question in Palestine.

This assertion was, however, totally exploded when it was closely examined by the Permanent Mandates Commission of the League of Nations. It is curious that in this regard the British representatives on the Mandates Commission did not prove the fallacy of the assertion. The minutes of the sessions of the Permanent Mandates Commission show that it was Lord Lugard, the British member, who directed point-blank to Dr. Drummond Shiels, the Under-Secretary of State for the Colonies, the question as to whether he could give the Commission more definite information as to the dispossession of tenants in the Valley of Jezreel. Dr. Shiels was compelled to state that "he was unable to give these figures because no records were available."

Thus the "elbow-room" question stood exploded in the light of an impartial examination.

"At the Mayflower: A Jewish National Home in Palestine"
Jewish Telegraphic Agency, January 29, 1932

Alfred, the headwaiter of the Mayflower, one of the official hotels in Washington, D.C., was obviously bewildered. The caterer, and so to say, Sergeant of Arms at many distinguished Washington gatherings, a gentleman with the accent of a distinguisher foreigner and the mannerisms that would make him a walking book of etiquette, he has seen many a dazzling party in his day. He knows the preferences of every important personage. He is an expert on interpreting the whims, likes and dislikes of the ladies and gentlemen who make the life of Washington what it is reputed to be. He knows the purpose and the inner motive of almost anything that transpires after 6:00 pm. That evening he was at the end of his wits.

The exquisite Chinese room of the Mayflower, the private residence of the Vice-President of the United States, was open at seven o'clock sharp for the entertainment of a select group of seventy-five men and women, mostly men at this time. Several days before the Vice President himself had shown keen interest in the arrangements for that evening. The menu had been specially approved. No seating list however had been prepared and no question of social precedence had been solved. Who will occupy the distinguished seats at the rather short head table, and who will grace the ten round tables distributed rather sparsely over the inviting floor of the Chinese room?

Alfred's bewilderment grew stronger and more confusing from minute to minute. Here is the Secretary of Agriculture, Arthur M. Hyde, followed by Senator Thomas E. Watson, Republican majority leader; here is the interesting figure of Henry T. Rainey, Democratic Congressman from Illinois and House majority leader. Here is the Chairman of the House Foreign Affairs Committee, two personal secretaries to President Hoover, the Solicitor of the U.S. State Department, the Assistant U.S. Attorney General, and here is Ruth Bryan Owen, daughter of the late Wm. J. Bryan and the most brilliant representative of American womanhood in the Congress of the United States, and several score of Senators, Congressmen, high officials, and leaders of public opinion. The mere presence of any of the guests, if announced in advance, would be sufficient to fill a Carnegie Hall. At any rate, the oratorical capacity of these guests could easily consume a sizable issue of the Congressional Record.

Still, no flow of oratory or even political argument was heard. The seven dishes composing the menu were served in a rather rapid succession and disposed with rather easily. In the center of the head table there was the amiable and impressive figure of the Vice President, whose attitude would convey the impression of being both host and guest of honor, seated next to Senator Wm. H. King, coming from the Mormon state of Utah, the only place in the world where Jews are Gentiles and Christians are Israelites. At the end of the head table one could see the striking countenance of that youngish figure of the fiery Senator from Wisconsin, Robert M. Follette, a man in his thirties, rapidly rising to a dominant position of national leadership. At the opposite end of the table, almost as a contrast, one had to observe the distinguished appearance of a rather pale-faced equally youngish man and similarly rising in prominence in the Zionist movement – Emanuel Neumann. Next to him there were the pointed features of that intellectual phenomenon who is known in American legal writings and in liberal circles as Felix Frankfurter.

Congressmen and Senators, Republicans, Democrats and Progressives, Supreme Court Justices and high government officials were mingled together, engaging in conversation across the dinner table. Was it reparations? Foreign securities? World War debts? Remedies for the current depression? Presidential candidacies? Fragments of the views exchanged seemed to show that none of these weighty matters were under discussion. The strange names of biblical localities that one heard long ago in Sunday School or came across while reading the Holy Scriptures frequently recurred: Jordan, Plain of Esdrealon, Sharon, Jerusalem, Haifa, Dead Sea, Galilee....

Soon the orators turned listeners, the statesmen shaping the policies of a mighty nation and the destiny of the world postponed for an evening the weighty matters, for the consideration of "The Palestine Situation and its International Aspect." The American Palestine Committee, [designed] to create an organized form for the sentiment of the American people and of American public opinion, for the furtherance of the Jewish National Home in Palestine, was to be born. A message from President Hoover, succinctly giving expression to that sentiment, read by Senator King as Toast Master, met with the approval of Democrats and Republicans alike. Expressions of approval from Governors of many states, noted writers and men of affairs, were coached in even warmer and more direct language. Even without further evidence it was clear that enlightened American public opinion is clearly in favor of Zionist aims and wishes to see a Jewish National Home in Palestine speedily realized.

The Israelite from Utah presented the case for the land of Israel with a warmth and sincerity of conviction of an enrolled Zionist. He yielded the floor to the guest of honor, the Vice President. A man of few words, he supported the pending "resolution" by revealing for the first time publicly that it was he, at the request of an orthodox Rabbi, Rabbi Simon Glazer, formerly of Kansas City, who was the actual author of the Zionist Joint Resolution (designated in the Congressional Record as the Lodge Resolution), which was passed by both houses of Congress in 1922, just at a propitious moment, when the fate of the Palestine Mandate hung in the balance. There was majestic simplicity and the makings of nearly a legend in the tale of Rabbi and statesman working for the restoration of the Holy Land.

Felix Frankfurter startled his distinguished audience with his flow of direct argument and matchless frankness. In nearly an hour he succeeded in sketching in sharp lines the tragedy of the Jew in the post-emancipation era, and the promise beckoning to him from a restored national home in Palestine. Anti-Semitism in the United States is a social and economic fact and was perhaps for the first time discussed in the presence of so distinguished a gathering in Washington. Jewish law students in Boston and New York, the two cities he knows best, find the doors of non-Jewish law offices shut in their faces, Professor Frankfurter related. The United States has a Jewish population larger than any to be found in any other country. The questions of Palestine and Jewry do, as they must, find their way into the U.S. State Department. Even regardless of America's part in the framing of the Balfour Declaration and in the adoption of the Joint Resolution and the special convention between the United States and Great Britain regarding Palestine, there is the concern of a large body of American citizens who have made considerable investments in the mandated territory and who are deeply concerned over its fate and progress along the lines of the internationally approved Mandate.

Only two other speakers were to be heard: Dr. Albert Mead, U.S. Commissioner of Reclamation, who was a member of the Palestine Joint Serving Commission and who spoke of personal experience, and Emanuel Neumann, American member of the World Zionist Executive.

"The achievements of the Jewish colonists," said Dr. Mead, "deserve the grateful recognition of the world. They have been wrought under hard and discouraging conditions. Instead of being an injury to the Arab, in many ways he has been an immense gainer. In a hundred ways Jewish settlement has brought modern civilization into all parts of Palestine, transformed poverty-stricken areas into places of opulent vegetation, and multiplied manifold the wealth and opportunities of the country."

For years the leaders of Zionism have been toying with the idea of finding a way for crystallizing American public opinion in favor of the idea, in a manner similar to that which was followed in England, France and Germany, where pro-Palestine committees have been established and have rendered valuable services to the cause. It was left to the vision and sagacity of Emanuel Neumann, whose name is identical with an important chapter in the annals of American Zionism during the past decade, to translate this idea into a reality as his first important act as a member of the World Zionist Executive. In twenty-five minutes, in sentences as clear as they were brief, in facts as lucidly presented as the figures he quoted were telling, he presented what one might rightly describe as the case for Zionism.

"I am a professing Jew," he declared.

"The Man Who 'Desired Life'"
The Jewish Spectator, September 1933

Death wrote *finis* to the life of a sage and a saint in Jewry. The Chofetz Chaim, who became a legendary figure during his lifetime, passed away.

When Poland lost her last tragic struggle for independence, in 1863, he was already in the prime of his life.

When the first Jewish pioneers left imperial Russia in 1882, to lay what has since become the cornerstone of the Jewish National Home in Palestine, he was no longer a young man.

When Nicholas II ascended the throne of the Romanoffs, he had already become a saintly and venerable figure, revered and looked at with awe by Jews of all shades of opinion.

On Friday, September 15th, a brief news dispatch, originating in an obscure Polish village, announced his death. Few people knew his real name, yet his fame was so widespread and respect and veneration for him was so deep-seated, that the parenthetic explanation ("Chofetz Chaim") following in the obituary notice the proper and family name of the deceased, that of Rabbi Israel Meri Ha'Cohen, was sufficient to cause deep consternation and genuine mourning.

In no "Who's Who" would his name be found. In no lexicon of writers, essayists, poets or philosophers would you find any biographical data concerning him. If one were to be guided by the strict rules of accuracy, even the title "Rabbi" in the brief news dispatch must be regarded as slightly inaccurate, for the Chofetz Chaim did not occupy the position of Rabbi either at the time of his death or long before. It would be a safe guess to assume that were Rabbi Israel Meir Ha'Cohen to have left his place of residence, Radyn, near Wilno, and travel, not incognito, but under his own name, that name, when announced to the average Jew in Europe or in America, would not have evoked any particular interest. What a profound change, however, would have occurred in the attitude of that average Jew were someone to whisper into his ear, "That is the 'Chofetz Chaim.'"

A mere recital of the life story of Rabbi Israel Meir Ha'Cohen of Raydn would hardly suffice to convey to the Western reader the greatness of that unique figure who dominated the scene of traditional Jewish life and learning for nearly a century. Particularly must a pen-picture prove inadequate in depicting the background of majestic simplicity and peculiarly Jewish moral strength that was embodied in that intellectual and moral giant who became known to Jew and non-Jew alike by the unpronounceable description Chofetz Chaim. Perhaps one sentence may provide the canvas upon which the lineaments may be sketched: He made a book on ethics a bestseller.

For the name and the fame of the Chofetz Chaim have had their origin in the title of a book he wrote and published in 1873. In Psalm 34:13, there is a passage running as follows: "Who is the man that desireth life (*He'Chofetz Chaim*)? Guard your tongue from evil and your lips from guile." This passage, familiar to many, served him as the text for three volumes on human behavior and on character-building methods.

"Gossip is the spice of life" is a popular dictum in many climes and languages. Lawsuits involving slander and libel are most difficult to win in the best-regulated courts.

But gossip is a factor most destructive of ethical and moral life, and slander a most damaging engagement before the court of conscience. It is a high tribute to the Jewish life that was [in the past] that the three volumes of the Chofetz Chaim, first in Rabbinic Hebrew and later in Yiddish, without the benefit of high-pressure salesmanship and without the stimulus of modern press agency, had a distribution of more than 400,000 copies. It is an indication of the moral strength of authentic Jewish life that these books, even today, have a reading public that is larger than some of the latest bestsellers could ever hope to reach.

But the influence of the man was even greater than that of this particular book or of his other books in the field of Halachah. Great as he undoubtedly was as a Talmudic scholar and commentator, he never aspired to dazzling brilliance in this domain. In the latter part of the 19th century and the first decades of the 20th, over which his long and useful life has extended, there appeared in Jewish life in Eastern Europe and elsewhere Talmudic scholars who were equally as great, if not greater, than he. As a moralist and champion of loyalty to Jewish tradition, he was never aggressive or a belligerent reformer. His strength lay rather in the integral simplicity and inviting directness of the example that he has furnished by his own life.

From January 11, 1839, when he was born in the village of Zhetil near Slonim, Government of Grodno, to September 15, 1933, there stretches a span of nearly a century's length. During this eventful period the whole order and outlook of life have changed many a time. Attitude, behavior, views, habits, fashions and modes have come and gone; science has undergone a most radical change; philosophy has taken on new and newer aspects and garbs; inventions have transformed the face of the earth; mighty Empires, at the peak of their glory on the day when the unknown Polish-Lithuanian was born, have crumbled into oblivion; peoples that have been suppressed and oppressed during the major part of his lifetime have gained new strength and life. Even in Jewish life itself the whole scene had radically changed. The Haskalah movement has come and gone. Zionism has emerged on the road to realization. Trends of thought, viewpoints, parties and groups of which no one dreamed during his boyhood and manhood have come to the fore. The Chofetz Chaim remained unshaken in his faith and exacting loyalty. In an age of storm and stress, of transition, of adjustment, of many compromises, he stood out as a rock. He steadfastly held high the ethical standard of Jewish life and the banner of loyalty to Jewish principle, thought and the Orthodox way of life.

In the stormy seas through which Jewish life has drifted during the past 50 years, the Chofetz Chaim has been looked up to by Jews of all shades of opinion as a tower of light and strength. The ship could not have drifted too far out of the course of historic continuity as long as he was there. The stream of Jewish life in the capitals of the world could not have traveled too far from its source as long as the sage of the obscure village of Raydn, modestly, passively but powerfully, continued to weave the traditions of Rabbi Akiba, Maimonides, the Ramo and the Gaono of Wilno.

The saga of the Chofetz Chaim is quite extensive. The many legends that have grown up about this unique figure deal principally with his uniform reactions to his constantly changing environment. The dominant note in these stories is a command: conform. The simple facts, however, are that, after marrying at the age of 18 into a well-to-do family in Radyn, his father-in-law had intended him to become the Rabbi of the town. He preferred, however, to instruct little children rather than to assume the duties of a Rabbi. When he had saved up 50 rubles from the tuition fees he had been receiving, he established a grocery in the village, leaving the business in charge of his wife and devoting most of his time to his studies. A misfortune then beset him: his business was too successful. He became aware of the fact that the community patronized his store more than anyone else's. The Chofetz

Chaim rapidly liquidated the establishment, declaring that he did not wish to have an advantage over his competitors. Around that time his book had become very popular and he thought that he could derive his livelihood from its sale.

One day a delegation of Baale Batim called upon him, insisting that he become the Rabbi of the community. He flatly refused this offer. When they persisted, he finally agreed to accept the post on the condition that no salary be attached to it. He further stipulated that he would remain in office as long as his decision would be obeyed. Shortly afterwards, two local businessmen came to him for a decision in a business dispute. The Chofetz Chaim rendered his decision, but one of the parties hesitated to abide. Immediately Rabbi Israel Meir Ha'Cohen resigned from the Rabbinate to remain "just a member" of the community until his last day.

Ephraim Caplan, the well-known Yiddish essayist and champion of traditional Judaism, related to the writer an interesting dialogue he had with the Chofetz Chaim several years ago in Radyn. The American visitor had asked the Chofetz Chaim for his definition of a Jew's duties in daily life. The aged saint expostulated at length, demanding complete and constant observation of all Shulchan Aruch regulations in minutest detail.

"Rabbi," said the American visitor, "judging by this standard many millions of Jews living today would have to be declared as non-observant."

"My dear friend," replied the Chofetz Chaim, "when one asks for spirits of 93 degrees in strength, the vendor must give you the genuine article. Dilution, if the purchaser should desire it, is his own concern."

"The Year's Events in Diaspora Jewry:
A Review of the Highlights of 5696"
The New Palestine, September 11, 1936

The division of time into convenient spans for the purposes of review is, historically, a strictly Jewish concept. The New Year of the Hebrew calendar is not, as is well known, an occasion for hilarious celebration, but a day of judgment. The Auditor on High opens on Rosh Ha'Shanah the *Sofer Hazichronoth*. Solemnly and fearfully "all creatures pass in review" before their Creator. Their record of achievement or of failure, within the period under review, is the basis for the award of merit or the infliction of punishment. Individually, the Jew has thus been trained to a knowledge of the facts affecting his own life, to a rigorous discipline of strict accountability in relation to God and fellow man. Diaspora life has made this system of meticulous accounting almost imperative with regard to the acts, facts and conditions affecting Jewry as a whole. Too frequently the view and review have been localized and narrow.

It is to the birth of our national movement and to Zionism in particular that we owe the habit – instituted by Max Nordau at an early Zionist Congress – of assembling the facts of Jewish life from all four corners of the globe and of preparing Jewry's national balance sheet. For this purpose, the totality of the Jewish scene, as reflected in the events within a given time, had to be studied and reviewed. At the turn of the century and for decades afterwards – how incredibly good those "good old days" now appear by comparison! – the world would hear from the platform of the Zionist Congress a detailed account of events affecting Jewry everywhere. With a penetrating analysis and in lucid accents, the unforgettable Nordau would, on the stones of Jewish misery, hew in relief what the immortal Herzl had diagnosed in brief as the *Juden-not*. On the basis of the facts he would make a presentment before the bar of public opinion, which, in every detail, constituted a true indictment of humanity's inhumanities to the Jew. Charging the Jewish will to survive with new energy for self-aid and redemption through a national rebirth, his word-picture of the Jewish scene would simultaneously carry with it a ringing challenge to the conscience of a civilized world.

The reviewer of events in 5696, no matter how tenaciously optimistic his belief may be in the ultimate triumph of right, cannot delude himself with the hope that his reader will, however indirectly, derive a measure of dubious comfort that usually fills the heart of the aggrieved in relation to the wrongdoer. The defendant before the bar of public opinion does not deny his guilt; on the contrary, he boasts of it. In a world that cherished liberty, still clinging to the ideals proclaimed by the American and French Revolutions and pretending to be guided by them, there was comfort as well as hope in an appeal to its conscience, although that "conscience" reacted hesitatingly and rather grudgingly to an appeal for right that was not buttressed by might. What comfort or hope, it may seem, can there be found in a world that is driven by fear, consumed by hatred and guided by madness on a road that leads to certain disaster unless the unforeseeable and the miraculous happen? Where is the ray of light to be found on a horizon that is dominated by the nightmare of a Nazism apparently triumphant?

He who contemplates the 5696 scene is not, however, without cheer. That cheer has its origin in the reassurance – call it faith or life instinct – that resides in a people that looks at the world and its history from the height of 5696: a people that has a recorded history of three thousand years, having survived and triumphed over oppression and tyrannies in preceding dark ages.

Nazism Spreads Out

The events that cast their shadow over the 5696 scene may thus be reviewed and understood in their proper relation if the scene is divided into two distinct zones: the areas that have been infested or affected by the Nazi disease; and that fortunately larger part of the globe where quarantine measures, taken in time, have been successful in keeping out or at least in preventing the spread of the plague. From the outset it may be stated that the year under review witnessed a series of amazingly successful moves on the part of the Hitler machine to spread out its tentacles far beyond the frontiers of the Third Reich. Having established itself on a firmer basis within the Reich, Hitlerism put an abrupt end to the gains of the emancipation era obtained by German Jewry after a long struggle. The legal, cultural and economic status of the Jew in Germany has been completely destroyed.

The year opened with the enactment of the infamous Nuremberg Laws, which virtually transported German Jewry back to the dark ages. In September, the Reichstag, convening in that ancient German city, "affirmed" Adolph Hitler's decree that deprives the Jews of their citizenship, excludes them from the army, forbids what has been described as "race shame" (any relations between a Jew and an Aryan), prohibits the employment by Jewish housewives of Aryan female servants up to an advanced age, and imposes numerous other restrictions, all of which have as their purpose the degradation of the Jew to the status of a pariah.

Although it was stated at the time that legislation as to the economic position of the Reich's Jewry was being postponed to a later date (presumably until after the Olympic

Games), a ruthless and relentless process of "liquation" (synonymous in present-day German with practical confiscation) of Jewish business enterprises in various fields was going on throughout the year. Particularly was this process severe in the smaller towns and cities, where the eyes of foreign observers could not easily penetrate. True enough, the Olympic games that Hitler was anxious to retain in the face of a strong opposition abroad, and particularly in the U.S., have served a humanitarian purpose. They provided the bleeding Jews of the Reich with a comparative breathing spell from more drastic measures.

As it was, the pressure upon German Jewry was of such crushing force that, according to a reliable estimate, 100,000 Jews (35,000 of whom settled in Palestine) left the Reich since the advent of Hitlerism. Within the same time, the number of Jewish deaths exceeded the number of Jewish births in the Reich by 25,000. The problem of the 400,000 Jews still remaining in the Reich was thus reduced to the terrifying formula: emigration or extinction. Coupled with this process was the systematic cultural segregation of German Jewry that now lives in a virtual ghetto. A separate Jewish school system has been established to which a majority of Jewish children have been transferred.

These conditions led the Hon. James G. McDonald, the outstanding American publicist and statesman, to resign from his post as League of Nations High Commissioner for Refugees (Jewish and Other) from Germany. His letter of resignation, addressed to the League Council, contained a scathing denunciation of Nazi barbarities and appealed for the League's intercession. This unprecedented persecution aroused the warmest compassion of Jews throughout the world for their kinsmen. It also led to two acts of violence: an assassination and a suicide. David Frankfurter, a Jewish student, shot and killed Wilhelm Gustloff, chief Nazi propandist in Switzerland. This occurred in February at Gustloff's home in Davos, Switzerland. Frankfurter is to be tried for murder by a Swiss court in October. In July, a Jewish newspaperman from Czechoslovakia committed suicide while attending a public session of the League as a means – according to a note left by him – of drawing the attention of the assembled statesmen to the bitter fate of German Jewry.

But the Nazi regime has not remained satisfied with its successes within the Reich. Parallel with its violations of international treaties and the revival of the old dream of a *Mittel-Europa* under the German heel, a gigantic Nazi propaganda machine has been working overtime on all fronts. Seeking its own political ends and exerting its vilest influence to entangle its near and distant neighbors in its design for conquest and world domination, the Nazi machine used its "exemplary" solution of its Jewish problem as the most effective bait as well as screen. First in the line of the attack came the countries with comparatively compact Jewish populations, where anti-Semitism has had a fertile field even without the example of instigation by the Nazi.

Clouds over the Vistula

Heavy clouds hung over the misty skies on the banks of the Vistula as the Republic of Poland, which had sprung into existence by the magic of President Wilson's fourteen points, continued its dangerous flirtation with Nazi Germany. While it was doubtful whether the fraternity between Poles and "Szwabs" would withstand the first clash of interests or arms (within the past fortnight Poland has returned to the embrace of its former ally, France), this fraternizing between Warsaw and Berlin has had a most salutary effect on the mood of the Polish urban [masses] as well as [the] rural masses in regard to the three and one-half million Jews of the Republic.

The heirs and successors to the power and glory of the late Marshal Pilsudski cannot be accused of instigating anti-Semitism in a vulgar or wild form. They cannot, however, be exonerated of the charge that governmental policies, often taking the shape of legislation, are directly aimed at destroying the economic foundations of the country's Jewish population. Nor can they be credited with willingness or ability to enforce law and order – they are somehow very effective when other interests are at stake – when the safety of Jews is being menaced.

And so the year opened with a strong movement in government circles to prohibit the *Shechitah* in the Republic. A bill to this effect had been introduced in the Sejm by no less a personage than the wife of the speaker of the Polish Senate. A day of fast[ing] and prayer was declared by the Rabbinate of Poland. A wave of indignation and protest against this unjustifiable attack on the Jewish religion swept over the Western world. Suddenly, those interested in the prevention of cruelty dropped their tender feelings for Polish animals. They remained satisfied with passing a law restricting the volume of Kosher slaughtering with the result that a great many Jewish families lost their means of gaining a livelihood.

Political and economic pressure on the Jews of Poland has become so heavy that this vast population, which has had its deep roots in the country since the middle of the 9th century [Christian Era], is literally in a state of a bottled-up exodus. The economic misery of Polish Jewry simply cries to heaven for relief. And while Polish statesmen are not at all adverse to manifesting sympathetic interest in the matter on the international arena (they are preparing now to raised the issue of Jewish emigration at the September session of the League Assembly; incidentally, this may place in their hands an additional powerful argument in support of Poland's demand for oversea colonies), the authorities that exercise power in the country have done little, if anything, either to alleviate the oppressive conditions or to curb the organized attempts at intimidation, which often take on the character of an anti-Jewish terror.

Illustrative of these conditions, which are particularly acute in the smaller towns, were the events that took place in March in the small town of Przytyk, Poland. Following the prolonged agitation among the local peasantry, a mob attacked the Jewish community in broad daylight. With unusual ferocity, Jewish homes were ransacked, two Jews brutally murdered and scores wounded. The Jewish population throughout the Republic declared a one-day strike in protest against the Government's failure to prevent the attack or to hold the mob in check. Non-Jewish labor groups joined in the protest. Subsequently, 14 Jews and 43 Poles were tried on charges arising out of the Przytyk events. What ensued cannot be regarded in any other manner but as a mockery of justice, for the Polish judge saw fit to free the murderers of the two Jewish victims while a Przytyk Jew who shot and killed one of the attackers in self-defense was sentenced to death. Stale falsehoods against the Talmud, long disproved, were aired in court by counsel for the defense.

Under the Swastika

The shadow of the Swastika fell gloomily and menacingly on the Jewish communities of Austria, Romania, Hungary and Czechoslovakia.

Austrian Jewry lived through a year of high tension intensified by the unfriendly and discriminatory attitude of the Schussing government as the Fascist but not officially Nazified regime carried on its zigzag policy of swaying now toward Rome, now toward Berlin. The near future does not appear too bright, now that Berlin and Vienna have become closely linked through the recently concluded pact.

Romania, whose Cuzists and anti-Semites of many varieties have never ceased to engage in the daily task of annoying and harassing its Jewish population of one million, has welcomed a new addition to the anti-Semitic family: the Iron Guard. The Nazi parentage of this new Romanian offspring is clearly discernible. The country, long an ally of France, has during the past year been torn between two powerful blocks: the pro-French and the pro-German. After a year of extensive Nazi propaganda in which Jew-hatred a la Hitler played no small part, the pro-French forces, headed by the former foreign minister, Titulescu, were pushed into the background. Romania, governed by a new Cabinet in which the Titulescu party has no influence, may definitely be placed in the Nazi column. What this means to the safety and status of Romanian Jewry needs hardly to be pointed out.

In Czechoslovakia, whose government under that truly great statesman, Edouard Benes, maintains the friendliest attitude toward Jews and Jewish problems, the Nazi menace assumed considerable proportions. The Henlein party, professing to represent eight million Germans in the Republic, with irredentist leanings, scored a great victory at the polls in the last general elections. But here, the Jews are not alone, as the growth of the danger is an equal menace to the existence of the Republic [itself].

The saddening picture presented by the state of affairs in the countries enumerated above has its happy contrast in conditions on the Balkan Peninsula. The Balkans, once the powder keg of Europe, are now in close economic connection with Nazi Germany. Bulgaria, Yugoslavia, Greece and Turkey are Germany's best buyers. Germany is also their best customer. And yet quiet prevailed on the Balkan front, except for a minor anti-Jewish disturbance in Yugoslavia and the decree issued by the Greek government prohibiting the teaching of Modern Hebrew in the Jewish community school for some unexplainable reason.

Turkey absorbed a considerable number of Jewish scientists, refugees from Germany, making room for them on the faculties of its institutions of learning.

Interest in Zionism and emigration to Palestine have grown considerably in Yugoslavia, Greece and Turkey, even though the country of which Palestine was formerly a province still looks with disfavor on the Zionist movement. The Turkish government is placing great obstacles in the way of those Turkish Jews who immigrate to the Jewish National Home.

On the other hand, it should be noted that the tentacles of Nazism have reached as far as South Africa, where Hitler's agents carried on extensive propaganda in the former German colonies. Nazi influences were also rampant in Shanghai, China, where a strong pro-German and anti-Jewish movement was noticeable in certain press organs.

In the South African Union, where Jews enjoyed tranquility and prosperity, the government officially took a stand against the boycott of Nazi goods and services fostered by Jews. There was also on foot a strong movement pushed by the nationalists to close the Union's gates to the small stream of refugees from Germany that had been trickling in.

Democracy Stands Guard

Democracy stood guard over its cherished liberties, refusing to fall for the Nazi bait of anti-Semitism in the expansive English-speaking world, in France, in Holland, in Belgium, and in the Scandinavian countries.

In the United States, a marked decline was noted in the public activities of the Nazi societies among the German Americans. Our country was also the battleground for the most energetic fight against the participation of American athletes in the Olympics. This gallant fight, led by the Hon. Jeremiah T. Mahoney, although it failed of its purpose, has served as an occasion as well as an indicator for the abhorrence in which the overwhelming majority of the American people hold the Nazi practices.

While the undercover attempts to inject anti-Semitism as an issue in the current presidential campaign may be ascribed to the usual eruptions of the political volcano and may be expected to evaporate after November, considerable concern has been aroused by the emergence of what seems to be a native American anti-Semitic movement with a strong Hitler tinge. Interest is centered in the influence of the none-too-friendly, although only indirectly anti-Jewish radio-priest, [Father] Coughlin. Secret terroristic bands, of which the Black Legion, recently exposed and suppressed in Michigan, have also made their appearance in what may rightfully be described as the anti-Semitic underworld.

British Jewry, too, has had for the first time in decades to take special measures of defense against anti-Semitic agitation and attempts at violence inspired by Fascists. Mosley's Black Shirts and kindred groups developed a propaganda of growing extent. Attacks on Jewish passersby in the East End of London have had their repercussions in the House of Congress. The ritual-murder accusation was revived and made use of by one of the Jew-baiting journals.

The world watches with the greatest interest the developments in France, where Leo Blum, Socialist and Jew, rose to power as Prime Minister of the Popular Front Government. It is the irony of history that the year that witnessed some of Hitler's great impudences should be coincidental with the period of the rise of Leon Blum as France's leading statesman and defender. On the success of the Blum "new deal" policies depend not only the fate of democracy in France, but also the lot of French Jewry. The first Jew to occupy this high position, Blum has been the target of attack on the part of reactionary forces in the country where De La Roque's "Croix de Feux" had previously developed a not inconsiderable later of anti-Jewish feeling.

The fate of some 30,000 Jews in Spain and in North African positions is bound up with the outcome of the civil war now raging in the country. Tragically enough, some of the Jews in Spain now awaiting with anxiety the outcome have but recently left the land of the Nazis.

U.S.S.R.

In Soviet Russia, where anti-Jewish hooliganism of the old type seems indeed to have been stamped out, the cultural and religious disintegration of a once-virile Jewry continued under the Communist dictatorship. Safe in body, the spirit of Russian Jewry as known for centuries is slowly but surely taking on a new aspect.

Much expectation was aroused by the avowed intention of the Stalin regime to implement a new Soviet Constitution under which freedom of religious worship will be guaranteed. This, it was thought, may possibly lead to the lifting of the severe restrictions on the instruction of Hebrew and to the repeal of prohibitions on Zionism. It was also hoped that under a more liberal procedure the Zionist exiles would be allowed to return home from their internment in the Solovetzky Islands. But the new fundamental law has not yet been implemented and what course events will take is merely a matter of speculation.

Biro-Bidjan, which is now a Jewish Autonomous Region and is slated to become a Jewish Republic within the Soviet Union, if and when its population growth and upbuilding progress warrant it, has only a population of 50,000 souls. Of these, 15,000 are Jews. A considerable number of the first pioneers who could not adjust themselves to their new environment returned to their native towns and villages in the other parts of the Union. Negotiations were, however, under way between the Moscow authorities and Jewish groups abroad with a view to allowing and encouraging the immigration to Biro-Bidjan of non-Soviet Jews.

The swift executions that followed the Zinovieff-Kameneff trial, and the ensuing mass arrests of Trotskyites among whom many Jews were to be found, gave rise to an opinion in some quarters that the Stalin regime is determined to "purge" the party of the influence of its Jewish members.

Constructive Defense

Under the impact of the attack on the status of the Jew, and under the pressure of swiftly occurring events, Jewish life in 5696 took on the aspect of a people fighting with its back to the wall, but exerting every effort for defense of its position. Parallel with the defensive action, there were numerous efforts at reconstruction: relief in the Diaspora countries and constructive upbuilding work in Eretz Israel.

Outstanding on the defense front was the event that took place in the month of August in Geneva, Switzerland. There the first session of the World Jewish Congress was held with the participation of about 300 delegates representing five to six million Jews who reside in 32 countries. The World Jewish Congress, an idea and ideal that occupied the thought of Jewish democracy for several decades and became the subject of bitter controversy, particularly in the United States, was finally fashioned, under the leadership of Dr. Stephen S. Wise and Louis Lipsky, into an authoritative agency for the defense of Jewish rights and the protection of the Jewish position. The sessions, which were held in the League of Nations Assembly Hall and were conducted on a high and dignified level, attracted world-wide attention and resulted in the formulation of constructive plans and the establishment of an apparatus that, it is hoped, will soon be fully equipped to cope with the great responsibilities entrusted to it.

The various plans to cope with the problem of German Jewry through coordinated emigration – a subject that had impelled Sir Herbert Samuel, Lord Bearsfed and Simon Marks to undertake a special trip to the United States for the purpose of conferring with leaders of American Jewry – have finally crystallized into the creation of a Council for German Jewry with Sir Herbert as Chairman of the British section and Felix M. Warburg as Chairman of the American section. The Council is to undertake the gigantic task of transferring 100,000 Jews, up to the age of 35, from Germany to Palestine and other lands. Fifty percent of that number is to be directed to Palestine. A revolving fund of $15,000,000, to be contributed by British and American Jewry, is to be placed at the disposal of the Council.

Plans for extending the scope of Jewish emigration from Eastern and Central Europe have also been formulated and special steps taken to extend immigrant aid service at the HIAS-ICA Emigration Association Conference held in the early part of July in Paris. Representatives of emigrant and immigrant aid societies from 30 countries attended this conference, which marked the 10th anniversary of the establishment of the HICEM, a partnership in service to the cause of the Jewish wanderer between American Jewry's HIAS and the Jewish Colonization Association.

The American Jewish Joint Distribution Committee, which has a distinguished record of service in the field of philanthropic aid to Jewish communities in many parts of the world, has continued its work during the year under review.

The boycott on Nazi goods and services, adopted by numerous Jewish organizations in cooperation with labor and liberal groups, as a measure of defense against Hitlerism, has continued. Valuable services have been rendered in this field by the Non-Sectarian League, the Boycott Committee of the American Jewish Congress,[8] the Jewish Labor Committee, and the American Federation of Labor. It should be recorded that in the past year the prosecution of the boycott has met with growing difficulties in many countries caused by the political maneuvers of the respective governments.

The American Jewish Committee, the Alliance Israelite Universelle and a number of other organizations have drafted and submitted to the League of Nations a document of international importance relative to the status of German Jewry under the Nazi regime. The document, which bears the form of a petition, urges the intervention of the League and it is expected that one of the leading European powers will sponsor this move at the forthcoming session of the League Council.

Zionism Gains Momentum

Zionism, as the expression of the Jewish people's will to live, has scored even greater gains during the past year, notwithstanding the disquieting and even alarming reports coming out of Eretz Israel since April 19th, the beginning of the Arab terror.

In the United States, Zionist fundraising agencies have been consolidated into the United Palestine Appeal, which, seeking to raise the amount of $3,500,000, has presented to American Jewry the elevation of Eretz Israel to a position of parity in the planning of Jewish communal budgets. Notable has also been the progress made by the Jewish National Fund [in America],[9] which attained an income unprecedented since the peak year of the prosperity period. Corresponding gains have also been recorded by the Keren Hayesod [Colonization Department] and Keren Kayemeth [the Jewish National Fund] in their fundraising activities in all [the other] parts of the world.

A notable event in the annals of American Zionism was the 39th Annual Convention, held in Providence, Rhode Island, which resulted in the election by acclamation of Dr. Stephen S. Wise as the President of the Zionist Organization of America.

The unshakable faith of Jewry in the Zionist ideal and in the ultimate attainment of the Zionist goal in Eretz Israel, notwithstanding temporary difficulties and setbacks, was demonstrated in the attitude of the Jewish communities toward the events in Palestine during the progress of the Arab campaigns of terror. Admiration for the strength of the Yishuv in the face of provocation-protest against the vacillating policy of the Palestine Government and a demand upon the Mandatory Government to live up to the letter and spirit of the Mandate have been the notes, sounded with confidence, courage and hope, in the mighty echo that has vibrated throughout Diaspora Jewry in response to the events in Eretz Israel.

"America's Response to a Vital Appeal"
The New Palestine, October 8, 1936

The fiscal period, which concluded on October 1, was a record year in the fundraising history of the Jewish National Fund of America. Within that period, American contributions for Palestine land redemption, raised through the traditional methods of the Keren Kayemeth, as well as through its participation in the current United Palestine Appeal,

---

[8] William Z. Spiegelman was the head of the American Jewish Congress' Boycott Committee in 1934.

[9] William Z. Spiegelman had been the head of the JNF's publicity campaigns in the U.S. since 1930.

amounted to more than \$700,000, the highest sum ever contributed within a single year. As the JNF 35th anniversary draws to a close, the total of America's participation in the fundamental work of providing a national land foundation for the Jewish renaissance in Palestine stands at \$5,700,000.

* * *

The American branch of the Jewish National Fund is the oldest national agency of American Jewry for other than local purposes. In point of nationwide operation and contact with the basic phase of the Jewish problem, it antedates any of the other instrumentalities through which American Jewry sought in the pre-war as well as the post-war periods to discharge its responsibilities of participation and leadership. Its history is indeed the record of a popular and spontaneous response to the call of a pure idealism that is motivated by a great national vision, the compelling reality and strength of which has not always been grasped by those who had the means to make it come true but who were lacking in appreciation of history in the making.

* * *

The graph showing the annual totals of American Jewish contributions to the Jewish National Fund over a period of 26 years, published here,[10] tells the story of the present-day total. But beneath it spread the record of the triumphs and failures of Zionism as a movement, and of the strange paradoxes of American Jewish life. To evaluate properly this record, it is necessary to divide the 35 years into the three different periods that they embrace: (1) the premier period, when Zionism and Jewish life in America were still in their infancy, (2) the war and post-war period, when American Jewry and Zionism grew to their full stature, and (3) the era of the Jewish National Home, when the realities of Jewish life in the Diaspora and of Palestine came into bold relief.

When the first Zionist Congress [convened] in December 1901, announced to the Jewish world its decision to establish a Jewish National Fund, the Jewish population in the United States stood at a figure of approximately 1,250,000 souls. The gates of immigration to the United States were wide open. Every month witnessed a new influx of Jewish immigrants from Eastern Europe to these shores. The idea of the Keren Kayemeth and the devotion to its purpose came on the crest of this wave. When the Zionist Congress decided on an issue of Blue-White Stamps as a fundraising method for the Keren Kayemeth, and set the price for the various countries that were represented in the Congress, the price for the sale of these stamps in the United States was fixed at one cent per stamp. These stamps found circulation among the new arrivals to these shores. Few and far between were the native American or Americanized sympathizers. An occasional contribution to the Keren Kayemeth through the use of a Blue-White Stamp on one's private letter or a synagogue ticket, or a donation when one called to the Torah in the synagogue, was a good Zionist "deed." An inscription, on the basis of a \$50 contribution, in the Golden Book of the Keren Kayemeth was a generous bit of support for a sacred but distant ideal. Zionism in its pre-war period was a relatively calm and unruffled stream. The Federation of American Zionists in the East and the Order [of the] Knights of Zion in the mid-West were the channels through which it flowed.

---

[10] The graph hasn't been reprinted here, but the information it contained has been integrated into the text.

It was, in the main, a spontaneous response of the poor and humble, who, having just emerged from the depths of the ghetto, carried in their hearts the vision of a new life that would come through the processes of national redemption. Herzl's challenge rang in their ears: "We shall prove to the world that a poor people can provide greater sums for the restoration of its Homeland than the wealthiest millionaires!" Whatever the Zionist in this prehistoric era contributed himself or raised from among his intimate friends, he remitted to his Zionist society or to one of the two national federations – the Federation of American Zionists and the Order [of the] Knights of Zion.

May, 1910, was a turning point in the progress of this effort. Sensing that the growing American Jewish community was destined to play a leading part, Keren Kayemeth headquarters, then in Cologne, Germany, under the vigorous direction of Dr. Max F. Bodenheimer, undertook special efforts to organize the American branch of the Fund on a centralized basis. It was in this year that the Jewish National Fund bureau for America was established. From this point on, the history of its effort is recorded. A maintenance budget was provided by the Cologne headquarters for the American bureau. Gifted organizers and propagandists were dispatched to the American scene. The fruitful field, plowed by an unnamed legion of enthusiasts and zealots for the Keren Kayemeth idea, started to yield fruit. With the fiscal year May, 1910, to May, 1911, when the total of contributions reached $20,149.25, the upward trend began.

David H. Lieberman, a businessman and an ardent Zionist, known mainly to the small band of Zionists on Manhattan's East Side, was chosen to the presidency of the American branch, an office that he occupied during the period 1910-1912. He was succeeded by Senior Abel, one of the early Zionists, [a] Maskil and [a] writer, who occupied the office of president from 1912-1924. What they lacked in quantity they made up in quality. To whatever extent they were deprived of worldly riches, they were compensated in ardor and idealistic devotion. Immigration to Palestine was only trickling in. Land purchase on a large scale was hardly possible and not even contemplated. But any day the great event may happen. A charter will be obtained from the Sultan of Turkey or some other miracle may come about as a result of the World War conflagration. In the meantime the national chest of redemption must be filled up. A cent must be added to a nickel and a nickel to a dime and a dime to a quarter and quarters to dollars, for soon the National Fund may have an opportunity to act, to redeem the soil of Eretz Israel!

It is no exaggeration to say that long before the modern methods of mass action were being applied, the band of Zionist devotees who directed and were engaged in the operations of the JNF in the United States devised and applied methods that had the same purpose in mind and in the use of which they obtained a comparatively high measure of success. The "man in the street," that unfathomed figure, whose sentiment and opinion and readiness for action are of decisive importance in all political movements, had his say in shaping the early course of the JNF. Hundreds and thousands of men and women volunteered their services several times a year for consecutive mass enterprises on behalf of the National Fund. They consecrated their leisure time to distribute boxes, to visit synagogues, to solicit donations, to sell a flower or a miniature Zion flag in a series of activities that punctuated the calendar all year round. Their ceaseless efforts were instrumental in evoking a response of scores of thousands of small-coin donors. No other American Jewish institution can boast of equally as large a number of friends and supports as can the National Fund. This assertion will be substantiated when it is realized that the bulk of the annual totals that have been contributed to the Jewish National Fund were made up of small contributions made on occasions such as Flag Day, Flower Day, box clearance, synagogue collections and appeals by mail.

If, however, the effort of this corps of JNF volunteers and Zionist propagandists were fruitful in propagating Zionism by bringing it into the homes of large numbers of American Jews, the monetary results could not, in the nature of things, measure up to the need. Other and more productive methods had to be applied to attain the larger end. In this direction the successors to Lieberman and Abel in the persons of Judge Bernard A. Rosenblatt (who occupied the office of president during 1934-36), Dr. Joseph Krimsky (who occupied the same office in 1937) and the late Joseph Barondess (who in 1938, shortly before his death, occupied the presidency of the JNF), impelled by a realization of the need for mustering from American Jewry a much greater measure of support for this vital cause, sought new ways and new methods.

The figures shown in the graph[11] for the corresponding years give an indication of the strenuous efforts made along those lines. But to the reviewer of the record there looms here a strange paradox. During the administration of Bernard A. Rosenblatt, when the American branch was incorporated under the laws of the State of New York, the nonpartisan status of the Keren Kayemeth was acknowledged. There was then evolved an elaborate system of representation under which Jewish National Fund work in the United States was to be stimulated, supervised and directed by a union of all [the] Zionist forces. The articles of incorporation stipulated that the governing bodies of the JNF are to contain representatives of all Zionist parties and groups.

And yet the very triumph of the Zionist cause and the growing response of American Jewry to its appeal in the 1920s served to dampen zeal and obscure vision insofar as the lead problem of Palestine was concerned. The major part of Zionist energies were concentrated upon the Keren Kayemeth, which from its birth in 1920 to date has raised in the United States a sum exceeding $14,000,000, out of a world total of $31,000,000. In devoting its greatest attention to the Keren Kayemeth, the Zionist leadership acted under the pressure of the tasks that fell upon the Zionist Executive in connection with the biennial budgets for immigration, education, etc., voted then by the successive Congresses. A feeling seemed to have prevailed that the task of the Keren Kayemeth was a long-range program for which there will be ample time when the other needs will be less pressing.

But the other needs of Palestine never were less pressing and the call upon American support was never less urgent. More aggressive insistence on the prior urgency of the JNF appeal was called into play through the administration that was presided over by Emanuel Neumann (1928-1931),[12] when the then-unprecedented figure of $418,226.35 was recorded for the fiscal year 1929-1930. Similar were the plans of the administration over which Nelson Ruttenberg presided (1931-1933). But then the great economic depression descended upon the American scene. The effect of the depression was reflected in the alarming decline recorded for the fiscal year 1932-1933, when the JNF income from the United States amounted to $144,278. The urgent appeal of Menachem Ussishkin [which was made] during his visit to the United States in 1931 for a $5,000,000 commitment by American Jewry for the acquisition of a specific and strategically important land tract to be accomplished over a five-year period found an echo but led to no tangible results in an America economically depressed. The five-year plan that had been inaugurated after the 1930 crash fell by the wayside.

---

[11] The graph hasn't been reprinted here, but the information it contained has been integrated into the text.

[12] According to Max Rudensky's obituary for William Z. Spiegelman, reproduced elsewhere in this volume, Emanuel Neumann was the one was who hired WZS to be the JNF's Director of Public Relations.

A new surging forward made itself felt with the vigorous leadership of the cause by Dr. Israel Goldstein, who assumed the office of president of the American branch of the JNF in the winter of 1933. With the improvement of economic conditions in the United States and due to the application of an energetic system of stabilization, planning and extension, both in the traditional fundraising as well as in the special campaigns, a gradual but constant growth appears on the peaks of the graph[13] leading up to the record figure for the fiscal year that has just ended.

"Brandeis Looks at Us: His Analysis of and Approach to the Jewish Problem and Zionism Show Incisive Logic and Breadth of Vision; An Interview with Brandeis On-Record"
The New Palestine, November 13, 1936

The nation that has on November 3rd spoken through the ballot (an America based on economic as well as political democracy and liberty) pauses to hail its major prophet of economic liberty and industrial democracy – Louis D. Brandeis, Associate Justice of the Supreme Court of the United States, who attains today his 80th birthday.

Twenty years have elapsed since his elevation to the bench. Much water has flowed under the bridges over the Potomac. The face of America's social and economic life has undergone tremendous changes since the "People's Attorney" has become a member of that group of nine learned jurists whose prerogative is to interpret the fundamental law of the land and to weigh in the scale of their exclusive judgment whether or not any given measure that has been enacted into law is in conformity with the spirit of America as embodied in the Constitution.

What Mr. Justice Brandeis thought about this country's most acute problems and its efforts to cope with them by way of legislation is written largely by [the man] himself in what Felix Frankfurter, his closest disciple, is fond of describing as Mr. Brandeis' "severe autobiography." This autobiography is a unique and inspiring record. It is a record that occupies, now, more than ever before, the minds not alone of the legal profession. America's electorate has evidenced its interest in it on November 3rd last. It is contained in those austere volumes containing the cases adjudged since the October term 1916 (242 U.S. –).

And yet a host of newspaper men will gather today at the modest apartment of the "Sage of Washington" in an attempt to obtain an expression of opinion from the "great dissenter" as to how America and the world appear to him on the morning when he enters, according to Biblical view, the "Age of Strength."

An Unusual Interview

Brandeis has never been the delight of interviewers. Unlike many celebrities of our time, he is not an overly generous friend of the working newspapermen. As the "People's Attorney," even before his elevation to the Supreme Court bench, Mr. Brandeis was described by one interviewer as a difficult subject. "It's hard to interview Brandeis. He

---

[13] The graph hasn't been reprinted here, but the information it contained has been integrated into the text.

wastes your time interviewing you," the writer reported. So the chances are that very few words, if any, that may have come from the lips of Justice Brandeis will be found between quotation marks in the American press of today or tomorrow.

But there is another phase to the personality of America's great jurist and champion of industrial democracy: his deep and abiding interest in the problems of his people; his spiritual leadership in the cause of Zionism and Palestine that have become his consuming passion since the autumn of 1914, at the age of 58. To obtain from L.D.B. – as he is not infrequently called in Zionist intimate circles – on the occasion of his 80th birthday, a formulation of his analysis of the Jewish problem and of his approach to Zionism and Palestine, the writer received an assignment from *The New Palestine*. Unlike his unfortunately situated colleagues, who will have to be content with the forbidding silence that surrounds the Supreme Court bench or with the alternative of penetrating the maze of the austere volumes beginning with the October term 1916, this writer has selected for himself the refreshing privilege of spending a number of hours with Louis D. Brandeis in the library – an interview, as it were, with Brandeis on-record.[14] Brandeis, himself, has consistently given preference to the written over the oral form of presentation and motivation. What he has formulated, expounded or urged in his papers, composed or delivered over a period of twenty-two years, may be taken as describing his view and as stating his approach to the problems of Jewish life and Zionism, in which his interest and his leadership is as potent today as it was then. Here [in printed letters] the prevailing restrictions of reticence have been lifted. Here the directness and succinctness of expression equal the depth of his analysis and the breadth of his clear vision. Here the realities of Jewish life are weighed, not in the scales of emotion, but measured by the yardstick of life embracing judgment.

But in sifting the views and utterances of a man of the stature of Brandeis, whether by the direct or indirect method of interviewing, a sixth sense of discernment must be in control. As in Jewish law, a line of demarcation must be drawn between the fundamental and the transitory, between the statutory enactment and the provisional ordinance – in this case, a policy, a plan or a method of procedure – which may have been enunciated, as the Talmud puts it, *Leshaatah*, for the moment, and may have been subject to revision. From this vantage point and with the preference for leaving to the future historian the determination of the question as to what might have happened if this or that controversial point had been approached in a different spirit and determined differently than it had been, our interview with Brandeis on-record proceeded smoothly and dealt with the fundamentals that determined for him and explained to us the outcome of his analysis and the manner of his approach to the problems of Jewish life and Zionism.

Appraisal of Jewish Values

The inherent craving of Jews for education and their readiness to bring all sacrifices in order to attain it, a trait observed by Brandeis among Russian Jewish immigrants, furnished him with the key to the basic character of the Jew. For Brandeis sees that:

"Our intellectual capacity was developed by the almost continuous training of the mind throughout twenty-five centuries. The Torah led the 'Prophet of the Book' to intellectual pursuits at times when most of the Aryan peoples were illiterate. Religion imposed the use of the mind upon the Jews, indirectly, as well as directly. It demanded of the Jew not merely the love, but also the understanding of God. This necessarily involved a

---

[14] The interview was conducted via exchanged letters.

study of the Law. The conditions under which the Jews were compelled to live during the last two thousand years promoted study in a people among whom there was already considerable intellectual attainment. Throughout the centuries of persecution [in which] practically the only life open to the Jew that could give satisfaction were the intellectual pursuits, their mental capacity gradually developed. And as men delight in that which they do well, there was an ever-widening appreciation of things intellectual."

Noblesse Oblige

In addition to these qualities that Brandeis discovered as being, in combination, characteristic of Jews, he finds three other traits that make the Jewish inheritance a treasure worthy of being transmitted, unimpaired if not augmented, to coming generations. Contrary to the widely spread opinion that the Jew is an individualist (he asserts that such view is a misleading half-truth), he sees among Jews a developed community sense, a longing for truth and a passion for justice. Upon these he places a precious value, a value that is the foundation of twentieth century civilization.

"Is it not a striking fact," Brandeis asks, "that a people coming from Russia, the most autocratic of countries, to America, the most democratic of countries, come here, not as to a strange land, but as to a home? The ability of the Russian Jew to adjust himself to America's essentially democratic conditions is not to be explained by Jewish adaptability. The explanation lies mainly in the fact that the twentieth century ideals of America have been the ideals of the Jew for more than twenty centuries. We have inherited these ideals of democracy and of social justice as we have the qualities of mind, body and character."

Jewish assimilation is tantamount to death, and death – Brandeis argues – is not a solution to the problem of life. With such an inheritance, with an estate so held by us in trust, it is unthinkable for Jews of self-respect to shirk the responsibility of solving their problem rather than to "end it by ignoble suicide."

Approach to Zionism

The Jewish problem and Zionism as its solution have been stated and formulated innumerable times. Pinsker viewed it from the inner-Jewish angle as a problem of auto-emancipation; Herzl lifted it on the wings of his inspired vision from the depth of a *Juden-not* to the height of international thought and diplomacy; Achad Ha'am saw it from the sanctum of Jewish culture and from the necessity of salvaging "Judaism" as a valuable pattern in the fabric of the world's culture. The Kentucky-bred and Boston-raised Louis D. Brandeis, a descendant of the Dembitzes of Poland and the Brandeises of Bohemia, of stock that produced rebellious spirits who took up arms for the liberation of peoples under oppression, formulated Zionism as a cause of liberty, [which is] a growth that has its deep roots in the story as well as in the example of American democracy. He approached the problem of Zionism, as he put it, "through Americanism" which, in his interpretation, is equivalent to the very core and the basic foundation of Western civilization.

"Our teaching of brotherhood and righteousness," Brandeis tells us, "has, under the name of democracy and social justice, become the twentieth century striving of America and Western Europe. Our conception of laws is embodied in the American Constitution that proclaims this to be a 'government of laws and not of men.'

"America's fundamental law seeks to make real the brotherhood of man. That brotherhood became the Jewish fundamental law more than twenty-five hundred years ago. America's insistent demand in the twentieth century is for social justice. That also has been the Jews' striving for ages. Their affliction as well as their religion has prepared the Jews for effective democracy. Persecution broadened their sympathies. It trained them in patient endurance, in self-control, and in sacrifice. It made them think, as well as suffer. It deepened the[ir] passion for righteousness."

Problem's Cause and Extent

Brandeis found that "the whole world longs for the solution of the Jewish problem." Nearly twenty years before Hitlerism and the now thoroughly apparent bankruptcy of the "emancipation," he diagnosed anti-Semitism as a disease that is "universal and endemic," its prevalence varying only in degree and not in kind. Even America of the World War period was not altogether immune to it.

The cause of Jewish misery lies in the fact that even under the influence of the liberal movement of the nineteenth and early twentieth centuries, the world has remained half free and half slave. Liberalism had granted individual equality before the law but failed to recognize the equality of whole peoples or nationalities. "Not until these principles of nationalism, like those of democracy, are generally accepted, will liberty be fully attained," he declares.

An American Approach

Out of the American experience and doctrines that made possible the growth and development of these United States, out of the principles embodied in the American Constitution, Brandeis fashioned an argument that is irresistible because of the strength and inspiration inherent in the vigorous example of American democracy. The Jew as an individual cannot be free as long as his people, his nationality, remains enslaved. A nation is largely the work of man[kind]; nationality is a fact of nature. "The false doctrine that nation and nationality must be made co-extensive is the cause of some of our greatest tragedies," he teaches. In the education of children we recognize that the aim is to develop each child's own individuality, not to make him an imitator, not assimilate him to others. Shall we fail to recognize this truth when applied to all peoples, and what people in the world has shown greater individuality than the Jews? Has any a nobler past?" he asks.

A Method Most Promising Success

The Jewish nationality, Brandeis continued his argument, has not only a right but the duty to survive and develop. Persuaded that the Jewish people should be preserved, he finds that "it is our duty to pursue that method of saving that most promises success." And Palestine – as the object of Zionism – promises most success because within a generation the "Jewish pilgrim fathers" – such is his appellation for the BILUs and Chalutzim – have succeeded in establishing two fundamental propositions. First, that Palestine is fit for the modern Jew and, second, that the modern Jew is fit for Palestine. Zionism is, in Brandeis' view, the method of saving that most promises success because "there only (in Palestine) can Jewish life be fully protected from the forces of disintegration; that there alone can the Jewish spirit reach its full and natural development, and that by securing for those Jews who wish to settle in Palestine the opportunity to do so, not only those Jews, but all other Jews will be benefited, and that the long perplexing Jewish problem will, at last, find solution."

That this solution is entirely feasible and can be accomplished within a reasonable time he is persuaded by the lessons of recent world history. "The position of the Jew is not entirely unique. The history of the Bohemians, Poles and several other Slavic races as well as the Armenians provides remarkable parallels." We have but to lead the way and "we may be sure of ample cooperation from non-Jews."

The translation of the Zionist ideal into a reality makes necessary, in Brandeis' view, the accomplishment of two tasks. One is a very definite and material objective: "Our task is to bring into Palestine, as rapidly as we can, as many persons as we can. That really comprises the whole work before us," he says. The other lies in the realm of the spirit and culture – Hebrew culture. This he defines in one comprehensive sentence: "Zionism has given a new significance to the traditional Jewish duties of truth and knowledge as the basis of faith and practice."

Unity Versus Oneness

Having accepted, interpreted and amplified the doctrine of political Zionism, Brandeis drew the logical consequences from such acceptance. He is fond of referring to Zionism as "the democracy of the Jewish people." In complete accord with the Herzlian principle that the emancipation of the Jews can come only through themselves, he interprets it as meaning "by democratic means." The recognition of this principle he extends to the periphery of Jewish life everywhere and draws a marked line of distinction between oneness and unity. "Unity means not oneness in opinion, but oneness in action." Unity maybe achieved only if it is arrived at on the basis of democracy, which allows for full and open discussion, and there cannot be unity of action of a free people unless "the decision is the act of that people participating through its properly constituted representatives." That was Brandeis' argument that carried the day when the idea of organizing Jewish life in America on a democratic basis was first broached through the launching of the American Jewish Congress Movement.

In the Light of Palestine Realities

The charge has frequently been leveled that in planning the realization of the Zionist ideal, Zionist leaders, in the early stages of Palestine's development, had lost sight of the Arab problem. This does not hold true of Brandeis, for numerous references to the Arabs and to the difficulties that are likely to be encountered in the solution of the problem, are frequently found in Brandeis' utterances.

The 1929 events impelled him to break a silence that he had maintained for a number of years in order to give renewed expression to his faith in the ability of Zionism to smoothen out the sharp edges of this formidable problem. As early as 1918, the "Pittsburgh program," penned by him, was built on a plank of a comprehensive social justice program that, in its broad sweep, included a commitment to discharge obligations with regard to "existing rights."

However, he remained undismayed and undeterred from the Zionist purpose when confronted with the Arab outbreaks of 1929. In an address delivered on November 24th, 1929, in Washington, D.C., Brandeis finds that Jews going to Palestine will "make Palestine perhaps – all things considered – the safest place in the world."

"Dr. Thon, Philosopher and Political Realist"
The New Palestine, November 20, 1936

It happened in the late fall of 1918. One of Woodrow Wilson's Fourteen Points jumped out of the sphere of idealistic aspiration and political speculation into stark reality. As if by magic, the resurrection of Poland, for 150 years a wish of patriots and a dream of poets, came to pass.

But no sooner was Poland given her independence than sad tidings began pouring in from various parts of the Republic then in process of formation. The oppressed and downtrodden Poles "celebrated" their freedom by committing what their leaders were pleased to describe only as "excesses" upon another oppressed and downtrodden people, the Jews, who had shared in the suffering and in the struggle for "your and our freedom." Krakow, the ancient capital, distinguished itself with the duration and severity of its "excesses" against its Jewish population. Great was the shock. Warsaw was disconcerted and even alarmed. A group of newspapermen, including the writer, were prompted by all sorts of communications from the scene of the excesses to investigate and to report. After an exhausting effort that lasted throughout a night and a day, and following a fierce struggle with the military censor to allow as much of the truth as was possible to be rescued from his "supervision" over the telegraph office, your war correspondent felt he was entitled to a night's rest. However, there was no room in Krakow, all hotel rooms having been requisitioned for military use, and the bewildered citizens were frightened and suspicious of strangers.

In that critical moment, my acquaintance with Modern Hebrew literature came to my rescue. I recalled that Krakow, in addition to being the capital of the ancient Polish Kings, the site of the Wawel, a seat of learning and a scene of anti-Jewish excesses, was also distinguished by the residence in it of Osias Thon, the Hebrew essayist and philosopher, the Zionist theoretician and expounder of the Kantian philosophy.

I rang the bell of Dr. Thon's comfortable apartment and, presenting to him my strange request to be taken under his roof for this night, I obtained unexpectedly a close-up of a unique figure in Polish Jewry. Dr. Thon's apartment, too, happened to have been overcrowded, but having seen my credentials and learning the purpose of my mission, he graciously placed at my disposal his library room.

"Here you may rest, or, rather, spend a restless night, if you are one of those fellows who cannot remain comfortable in the presence of valuable folios," he said, ushering me in.

But after having bidden goodnight, Dr. Thon returned. Apologetically he explained that having learned of the work I had done during the day, he could not retire without getting a full picture of the extent of the excesses. With that ingratiating charm for which he was known, he intimated that a mere perusal of the copy of the wire I had dispatched to Warsaw would not do; he was anxious to know the situation in minute detail. A sleepless night in the library ensued.

Dr. Thon's feelings alternated. In the deep, long hours of the night his emotions changed from sadness to gladness as he permitted his unexpected guest to listen to his thinking aloud.

* * *

[Dr. Thon said:] "Sad, sad, my friend. 'When a slave becomes king.' These excesses, brutal and unpardonable, are the remnants of the slavery that had enmeshed a people that was once free. Painful as they are, and deeply disappointing, these events are perhaps only the birth pains of the new freedom. Patience, forbearance, tact and understanding must be our conduct."

* * *

"It's a sad moment in the history of Poland when the hour of its freedom is marred by brutality toward the Jew. It's a happy moment in the history of the world. Mind you, a dream has come true. They [the Poles], whose tragedy has been so analogous to ours, must tread the path of freedom. It's a moment for which generations of men had prayed and waited. If their hour arrived, ours will arrive, too. Zionism and the National Renaissance of Jewish [words lost] is no longer a distant aspiration."

Born in 1870 in Lemberg, and educated in the University of Berlin and the Berlin College of Jewish Studies, Dr. Thon was an outstanding product of the post-Haskalah period. In him there was achieved an ideal blend of cultural patterns. In him Western methodology served as a handmaid to Eastern content. Accepted in 1897 as Chief Rabbi of the Krakow community, he was neither a pietist in the sense of the East nor a reformer in the fashion of the West. Better than any other description, the title *Rav*, in its original Hebrew meaning of "Master," fitted him. By training, equipment and scholarly temperament he was primarily a master of science, of learning and of thought. The great Jewish communities on the European continent have to their credit what is distinctly a great virtue in Jewish leadership. Unlike their brethren across the ocean, they do not insist on clothing their spiritual leaders with the robes of priesthood in which a predilection to eloquence rather than to substance and a "holier than thou" attitude seems to be the dominant features. Instead they give preference to leaders who serve their people in the broader fields of the intellect rather than in the parochial functions of the parish. For such was the capacity in which Dr. Thon functioned, not only in his community of Western Galicia but in Polish Jewry as a whole and in the Zionist movement in general.

He was a member of that intellectual quartet whose three other members – Dr. David Neumark, Mordecai Ehrenpreis, and Micah Joseph Berditchevsky – have made lasting contributions to Modern Hebrew and Jewish literature in the fields of philosophy, *belles lettres*, sociology and the reformulation of Jewish values. His own entrance into Hebrew literature was effected via a critical analysis of Herbert Spencer and a fundamental contribution to the philosophical foundations of Zionism. It was his ambition – so he confessed in later years – to erect, with the aid of the science of sociology, a thought structure that would prove to be "the scientific basis of Zionism." Caught in the whirlwind of rapid events, Thon was too frequently compelled to leave his study for the performance of urgent functions in the social and political fields. Thus the great thought structure that he had striven to raise to full height has not gone up. But the essays that he wrote bear a close resemblance, in form if not in content, to that style of precision and logic of which Achad Ha'am was the originator and master in modern Hebrew literature. They may well serve as a foundation for a structure that may be reared by succeeding thinkers. Thus we see him devote his intellectual strength to a discussion of themes like "The Essence of Judaism," "Construction and Destruction," "National Literature," "Nationalism and Zionism," "Cause and Purpose," "Laws of History," "*A Priori* and *Post Priori*," and "Party and People." In all these essays, a thorough-going effort is being made to bring into accord the essence of Jewish national thought with the essence of the humanities, as formulated in Western Europe toward the close of the 19th and the beginning of the 20th century.

His generation differed from the preceding in the respect that it sought enlightenment not for the attainment of general non-Jewish culture but knowledge for the attainment of Jewish culture. The humanization of Judaism or the Judaization of the humanities is the goal of his intellectual search. An admirer and disciple of Achad Ha'am, he did not hesitate to lead the revolt in Modern Hebrew literature against Achad Ha'am. He demanded what he described as an "extension of the frontiers" outlined by Achad Ha'am for the Hebrew renaissance. He accepted Achad Ha'am's basic principle of [rest of sentence lost]. [Beginning of sentence lost] but he himself went much further. "The essence of Jewish content in the future and the expression of our national soul in a distant age are unpredictable," he contended.

Paying tribute to Achad Ha'am for his introduction of exactitude of expression and the application of scientific methods, he denied that Achad Ha'am succeeded in creating an "Achad Ha'amistic" school of thought. More particularly did he object to that Achad Ha'amistic concept of the Jewish aim in Palestine that gained wide currency, the famous formula of the "Spiritual Center." He agreed that Palestine must and will become a center of Jewry, but not of the Jewish spirit. That he was unwilling to confine to Palestine alone. Diaspora Jewry, too, will continue to play its part in Jewry's intellectual development. Yes, Eretz Israel must and will become a center of Jewish strength (not a *Merkaz Ha'ruach*, but a *Merkaz Ha'Koach*).

The depth of the spiritual significance that he regarded as the source of the Jewish National Renaissance is perhaps best determined by his charge that Zionism, after all its political successes and practical achievements in the post-war era, has not as yet been taken seriously either by the world's political factors or by the Jewish people themselves. The President of the Zionist organization in Western Galicia, and a member of the Zionist Actions Committee, [Dr. Thon] in his introduction to his collected works boldly says, "I have not discovered in any of the events and happenings, including the very encouraging issuance of the Balfour Declaration and the San Remo Decision, even one single figure of that deep earnestness with which the world is accustomed and compelled to regard a truly great and strong national movement."

* * *

Dr. Thon wrote these words in the early '20s. How startlingly correct is their meaning towards the close of 1936, when the depth of Jewish desperation in Poland produces a Jewish Legion movement for the launching of a mad march to Palestine by hundreds if not thousands of young men without passports, visas, means of transportation or the slightest hope of reaching their destination or being admitted into their only [words missing]. These words assume prophetic significance when, against this background, British high officials in London and in Jerusalem formulate plans to so curtail Jewish immigration that it never exceeds the natural increase of the Arab population within any given year.

Easily may we trace the source of Dr. Thon's prognosis. To him Zionism, intellectually as well as physically, was "a historic necessity" from which neither the Jewish people nor the world can find an escape. He knew well that there is no escape, for he knew thoroughly the groundlessness of Jewish existence and the extent of Jewish misery in Poland.

As a member of Poland's Constituent Legislative Body, the First Sejm, and as a frequently elected deputy from Western Galicia, as Chairman of the Polish-Jewish "Kolo," the Club of Jewish Deputies, as the spokesman of the "Kolo" on major parliamentary occasions, as one of the moving spirits in the formation of the Jewish National Council in Poland, as a member of the Polish-Jewish delegation to the Versailles Conference and as one of the few authoritative voices of Zionism in the new Republic, Dr. Thon touched Jewish life at all angles and knew the extent of the problem and the extraordinary powers required for [words missing]. [Beginning of sentence lost] and bombastic leaders of Polish Jewry, he was not fond of the catchphrase that may for the moment help to excite an audience, but does lasting harm to the cause one seeks to serve. To him there were no "surplus Jews" in Poland. Not a million, not a thousand, not even a single Jew, economically suppressed and politically degraded, could with his blessing be delivered into the hands of political manipulators in the Polish Foreign Office for bickering and bargaining in the arena of national politics.

Dr. Thon's method was different. His way was that of broad vision, of tactful negotiation, of persuasive argument, of organized action. In the midst of his vision for a new Jewish renaissance and in the harness of labor for its realization, he passed, at the age of 66, into history.

"A Century in Retrospect: Survey of Trends and Events in the Course of the Hebrew Calendar Century Closing on Rosh Hashanah"
The New Palestine, September 12, 1939

When the sun sets on September 13th, the people that counts time from Creation will mark the end of a hundred years in its history. The eighth century in the sixth millennium of the Hebrew calendar will begin.

The history of mankind, examined from the point of view of its progress, is only the story of the periods between natural catastrophes or those catastrophes that mankind brings upon itself through hate and war. The century that has now come to an end (the period between 1839 and 1939), although heralded as the period of enlightenment and progress, did not essentially differ from the centuries that preceded it. Many armed conflicts and large-scale wars ravaged the earth and consumed life and treasure. In fact, this span of time has the dubious distinction of having been the period within which the first World War was fought and the second World War was begun. What will follow may be the subject of speculation but since the past is a preparation for the present, the future cannot be expected to be more than an extension of the latter. One could not indeed derive much comfort from this prospect were it not to be modified by the recognition that at least the present and future are subject to the dynamics of the human will, and to the powers of the human mind at its best, if and when these factors come into play.

The story of the seventh century in the sixth millennium in retrospect would indeed to a monotonous tale of man's inhumanity to man – not unlike the story of Jewish life of preceding centuries of exile and persecution – were it not for the dynamics of the Jewish will to live and of its proved ability to survive after seemingly crushing blows and to carry on along the path that started, four millennia ago, at Ur of the Chaldees. It is on this dynamic aspect of the past and the guidance that it provided for the future that our interest centers.

Light From America

As the drama of the seventh century in the sixth millennium opened, the scene was illuminated by the powerful rays of the light that was kindled in 1775 by the American Revolution. Derived from Hebraic sources, the proposition that "all men were created equal" hardened into a principle that was incorporated into the Constitution of the United States thirteen years later. Only an insignificant number of Jews who had trickled across the great expanses of the Atlantic came under the beneficent rays of this light. When, however, the French Revolution burst forth and the cry of "Liberty, Equality, Fraternity" resounded from the banks of the Seine to tyrant-ridden Europe, the most martyred of all members of the human family – the dispersed, oppressed and despised Jew – was emboldened to hope that for him, too, the era of enlightenment and progress would bring deliverance.

The fifty years that elapsed between the French Revolution and the beginning of the Seventh Century (1839) brought, however, only partial relief and proved the Great Hope to have been largely illusory for the Jews of Europe. The Jewish communities were teeming with excitement and expectancy. There was strife between the "enlighteners" [partisans of *Haskalah*] who believed that all that their brethren would have to do to gain the desired emancipation would be only to shed a part of their ancient culture and "improve" the forms of their religious worship, and the "reactionaries" who were equally desirous of obtaining their natural rights but insisted on maintaining the loyalty that sustained their people for so long and bitter a period. But even the enthusiastic "enlighteners" were destined to recognize that at best Emancipation meant only a constant struggle for equal rights.

The Inquisition in Spain was officially revoked as late as 1834. The abolition of the legal disabilities against the Jews in the various Kingdoms and Provinces of Germany was not officially decreed until 1869 (to last only until April 1st, 1933 – 64 years!). Even in England, it was not until 1858 that Parliament passed the Jews Disability Bill. Baron Lionel de Rothschild was the first Jew to take a seat in Parliament, in the same year, without taking the oath "On the true faith of a Christian," which was customary until then.

The light that was kindled in Independence Hall, Philadelphia and flamed into a mighty torch in the French Revolution required more than half a century before its rays reached in 1848 the plateaus of Central Europe. A popular movement for freedom then reached a temporary zenith followed by swift reaction. Even so, Emancipation of the Jews, in a civic and economic sense, never crossed the Vistula River into the lands of the Russian Czars. True, under the guidance of Benjamin Disraeli, the first statesman of Jewish origin to become Prime Minister in England, the Berlin Congress, with the approval of Bismarck, took action to guarantee, by means of an international agreement, the civil and religious rights of Jewish minorities in Serbia, Bulgaria and Romania. But these "guarantees" were never taken seriously by any of the signatories. Romania, which long rivaled Russia in the art of Jew-hatred, has found it easy to evade its international obligations up to this day.

Origins of Hitlerism

The Seventh Century will be known in the history of our people as the span of time in which the most despicable figure that ever trod God's earth made his appearance among the human species: the anti-Semite.

Not that hatred and persecution of the Jew were unknown or unpracticed before his arrival. Almost everything that the anti-Semite said and did with regard to Jews was said and done many times before. His contribution lay in the fact that he, the anti-Semite, made a "science" and, more often than not, a lucrative profession out of his hatred. Hitlerism, against which England and France have now declared war, and against which the sympathies and cooperation of all civilized men are now so fervently invoked, rode into power, unchecked, on the Trojan horse of anti-Semitism. No one could or should have been deluded for the thing was not new. It was conceived and practiced and developed into a political science long before the Hitlerian pestilence made its appearance. It was "made in Germany" and bears the imprint of [19th century] German politics.

Adolf Stoecker (1835-1909), chaplain at the Emperor's Court, founder and leader of the "Christian Socialist" Party, was the true forerunner of Adolf Hitler. The term anti-Semite made its appearance in German letters in 1879, when – the irony of history! – Wilhelm Marr, an apostate and former Social Democrat, bewailed the "victory of Judaism over Germanism" in a pamphlet of that name. He founded in Berlin the first "Society of Anti-Semites." Heinrich von Treitschte (1834-1896), a professor of history at the University of Berlin, was the first German scholar to formulate the foundations of "scientific anti-Semitism." It suited the politics of Bismarck to employ anti-Semitism in his fight against the progressive elements and particularly against the Social Democrats in Germany, among whom Lasker, Edward Bernstein and Lassalle played a leading part.

The slush fund fittingly described in those days as the "Reptiles Fund," at the disposal of the German Chancellor, unleashed a flood of "scientific anti-Semitism," which became in 1880, and for many years after, the leading issue not only in Germany but also in Central Europe and elsewhere. The poisonous gases, foreshadowing Hitlerism, infected wide areas all over the Continent and embittered the lives of [several] generations of Jews.

It never required much argument or persuasion to whip anti-Jewish feeling into fury. In 1840, the first year of the century saw the revival of the ritual-murder accusation. The celebrated Damascus case necessitated the journeys of Sir Moses Montefiore and Adolph Cremieux to the Orient and the unfolding of many efforts before the falsity of the accusation was established. The anti-Semitic agitation under the slogan (Hitler has not been original!), "the Jews are our misfortune," resulted in reviving ritual-murder accusations in Xanten and in Konic, Prussia, and opened up a series of ritual-murder accusations against Jews in other lands, beginning with the famous Hilsner Affair (1899), in which the late Thomas Masaryk, founder and first President of Czechoslovakia, played a leading part as a defender of the Jewish name, and ending with the Beillis affair in Kiev, Russia, in 1913.

Under the Czars

In Czarist Russia where the largest segment of European Jewry was herded into the "Pale of Settlement,"[15] the drama of Jewish survival against overwhelming odds was enacted during the major part of the century. The several Romanoffs differed only in degree of severity with which they carried through their programs of legalized oppression, forcible "enlightenment," and outright curtailment of elementary rights of a Jewish population of nearly 6,000,000 souls. The height of cruelty was reached, however, with the anti-Jewish decrees and riots of 1880 that had their sequel in the regime of Nicholas II, the last of the Czars. His ignominious defeat in the World War and death at the hands of the Bolsheviki closed the saddest chapter in the history of Jewry.

---

[15] In Russian, *pale* means demarcation line. To be "beyond the *pale*" meant outside of the Jewish-only area, and thus in danger. Because the English word "pale" connotes an absence of color, and thus ghastliness, the phrase has come to mean someone or something that is offensive, intolerable, or beyond help.

It was within the crowded cities of the Pales of Settlement and on the steppes of Russia that Jewish vitality and ability to withstand the heaviest pressure was most severely tested and found not wanting. For Russo-Polish Jewry, yearning as it did for Emancipation and equal rights and persisting in its struggle for them, kept aloft the torch of Jewish loyalty and, unlike its more fortunate but Jewishly less sturdy brethren in Western Europe, it was never willing to attain its coveted Emancipation at a price like that paid by the upper stratum of French Jewry or so eagerly offered by some sections of German Jewry. East European Jewry, far from being ready to denounce its ancient culture and national characteristics, absorbed the ideas and ideals of the modernized West but constantly strove, through various means, to evolve a solution that would not conflict with its past or inner self. To be sure, no unanimity was ever achieved. Various schools of thought, flourishing under the impact of world events and the ideas for social and economic justice that arose in the West in the wake of the industrial revolution, warred with each other for dominance over the Jewish scene. However, the bulk of Russo-Polish Jewry, long the reservoir of Jewish tradition and intellectual strength, remained an immovable rock of Jewish loyalty, acting as a stabilizing and restraining influence on the flight from Judaism in the West.

It was precisely here that the dynamics of the Jewish will to live – and not only to live *ad loco*, but to seek release through initiative and through daring thought and unflinching action – flourished.

In the West

The flight from Judaism in the West, too, was by far incomplete. The constant remainder of Jewish misery in the East and the recurring pressure in the lands of full or partial Emancipation activated the best elements in Western Jewry. With the new wealth and influence that accrued to an ever-widening circle in France, England and parts of Germany, Western Jewry was in a position to undertake remedial action that was formerly not possible. Thus, the century witnessed the organization and development of Jewish organizations like the Alliance Israelite Universelle (established in 1860) and the Hilfsverein of German Jewry, the Foundation of Baron Maurice de Hirsch, which, after the death of the philanthropist, developed into the Jewish Colonization Association. These instruments of philanthropy rendered, indeed, great service to the masses of Jews in helping to solve some of the acutest problems of the day. Some of these instruments also served as vehicles for diplomatic action at special occasions and under particular circumstances. The first and the last mentioned also acted as disseminators of modern education and European culture, but they never went beyond the philanthropic gesture.

The "poor brethren" had ideas of their own. Drawing from the wells of Jewish yearning for justice, of loyalty to its national tradition and culture, of the ever-present memory of a Homeland lost but to be regained, and of the invaluable treasures of an original and unique culture, East European Jewry – fructified, to be sure, by the seeds of progress and enlightenment from the West – labored hard and steadfastly along the paths of creativeness to bring about its deliverance.

Sources of Hope

First in this development during the century was the revival of Hebrew letters. Taking its cue from the "enlighteners" of the West, East European Jewry avidly began the process of the Hebrew Renaissance, which culminated in a Modern Hebrew literature in which thinkers of the stature of Achad Ha'am and poets of the sweeping vision of Chaim Nachman Bialik came to the fore, a growth that flowered in the revival of Hebrew as a spoken language and in the cultural fabric that is now the foundation of the new Jewish life in Eretz Israel. Parallel to this process went the development of what was known in the middle of the century as "jargon" into Yiddish, in which a galaxy of gifted novelists, poets and essayists gave expression to their creative genius and established vital and intimate contact between the Jewish masses and the thought and the feeling of the age. A powerful Yiddish press in the United States and in Eastern Europe arose to serve the Jew in his search for freedom at home or in his endeavor to find liberty and opportunity at more hospitable shores overseas and – last but not least – to advocate the realization of the vision of Zion, which he had been cherishing so long in the depths of his soul.

Religious Changes

In the field of religion, the century witnessed a mighty struggle against the alienating influences of the extreme forms of Reform Judaism, which in the early part of the Nineteenth Century threatened, if unchecked, to bring about disintegration of Jewry. As the period opened, a great champion of traditional Judaism appeared in Germany, the birthplace of its new rival, in the person of Samson Raphael Hirsch (1808-1888). As the century rolled into eternity, the desire for adjustment to the outside world through shedding as much as possible of the original forms of Jewish religious observance was definitely checked in Europe [only] to be transplanted – on the crest of the German-Jewish immigration that followed the year 1848 – into the United States, where it was to arise as "American Judaism."

Untouched by this struggle in the West, the stream of Jewish piety and learning continued in the East, and brought to the fore such outstanding and widely recognized authorities on Jewish religious law as Rabbi Chaim Soloveitchcik of Brest-Litovsk; Rabbi Israel Salanter, who enriched the seats of traditional earning with his *Mussar* (Ethics); Rabbi Samuel Mohilever (1824-1898), who was one of the first sponsors and leaders of the Chovevei Zion; and Rabbi Abraham Ha'cohen Kook, who became the first Ashkenazi Chief Rabbi in Palestine during the Mandate era.

Cultural Advances

Of Jewish contributions to civilization and the welfare of mankind, the century saw an abundance that can hardly be matched even by more numerous and firmly established peoples. Ever since the seats of learning were opened to Jews with freedom of thought and expression, Jewish men of genius have left their imprint on nearly all branches of human thought. But three names need be mentioned: Albert Einstein, in physical science; Karl Marx in political science; [and] Sigmund Freud in psychology.

In the field of Jewish culture the outstanding contribution of the century is the development of what has been loosely called the "Science of Judaism," but that actually represents a scientific evaluation and appraisal of the history of the Jewish people and the literary and cultural heritage of its ancient and medieval periods. The People of the Book, prolific and fruitful in the fields of religion and culture, somehow in the Diaspora lost their aptitude for the systematic recording of their history. This, too, has been remedied in the period under review. Within the century, there arose Jewish historians of note: Heinrich Graetz and Simon Dubnow, whose monumental works, complementing each other, made it possible for the scholar as well as the lay reader to familiarize himself with the authenticated history of the Jewish people.

Searching for a Solution

But more important and more interesting contributions towards a solution of the Jewish problem along three lines originated during the century and still are progressing with full impetus and vitality. These three developments burst forth into life almost simultaneously and stemmed from the same sources: the plight of the Jewish masses, the crying need for their deliverance, and the dynamics of the Jewish will to survive. The developments were (a) the emergence of American Jewry as the most numerous and powerful Jewish community in the world; (b) the formulation and partial fulfillment of Zionism; and (c) the birth of an organized Jewish labor class.

All three developments received their impetus from the 1880s, when "scientific anti-Semitism" raised its head in Germany and had its repercussion in the form of anti-Jewish violence in Russia and severe decrees of expulsion and persecution. The recently erected juridical structure of Emancipation in Central and Western Europe began to crack. The palliatives of Jewish philanthropic endeavor already then began to show their futility. Organization, based on an inspiring ideal and on self-help, was clearly the need, but recognition of this truth was slow in coming.

Origins of Zionism

Two rival thoughts strove for supremacy as lines of guidance for a mass of people caught in the maelstrom of history. The one – vaguely described as "love of Zion" – played on the strings of the Jewish heart and held out a distant hope for a Homeland that was never forgotten; the other, nurtured by the revolutionary ideas of an emerging proletariat, held out the promise of liberation through the ultimate Social Revolution. The first had just made its initial step on the sand dunes of Palestine under the yoke of the Turks. It had kindled the imagination of Orthodox Rabbis like Mohilever and Kalisher, on the one hand, and intellectuals and students, on the other hand, to whom the clear analyses of Moses Hess (1812-1875)[, author of] "Rome and Jerusalem" and Leo Pinsker's "Auto-Emancipation" made a strong appeal. "Love of Zion" made its entry into the students' circles of the Russian universities and into the study rooms of Orthodox Rabbis and Hebrew writers, but it had yet to be equipped with the organization and the power to cope with the problem at hand. The promise of deliverance with the arrival of the social revolution was no less enchanting to the intellectual youth but it, too, required a long and slow struggle that involved many sacrifices and acts of heroism in collaboration with the slowly maturing non-Jewish proletariat before it could attain an initial success. The bulk of East European Jewry, whether in Russia or in Romania, or in the Austrian-Hungarian Empire, was in dire distress and was, except for occasional philanthropic aid, unaided and unguided as it embarked on the great exodus to the Western hemisphere, to the sidewalks of New York, Baltimore and Philadelphia.

U.S. Jewry Emerges

Up to 1880, the Jewish population in the U.S. of America did not exceed 250,000 souls. The exodus that continued almost uninterruptedly from 1880 to a few months prior to the World War brought in its wake the great mass that now composes American Jewry, by now fully integrated into the economic, cultural and political fabric of these United States, and thus capable of demonstrating its great worth in an atmosphere of freedom.

The emergence of American Jewry is one of the greatest epics in the history of the Jewish people. This event remained not unrelated to the other two methods of salvation for the Jewish masses. When Herzl appeared in 1897 at the first World Zionist Congress and evolved the idea of political Zionism, he found a warm echo in American Jewry. When the Jewish labor movement began, first in the form of the Bund and several years later in Labor Zionism (the Poale Zion Party was established in 1901), they found their adherents among the Jews of America.

At this stage, the two trends merged, producing the most remarkable and admirable figure in the Jewish life of the century – the *Chalutz*, the Palestine pioneer.

A Jewish Homeland

It was American Jewry that coalesced into a united body when, towards the end and after the close of the World War, the need for political and relief action for war-stricken European Jewry and on behalf of the Jewish National Home in Palestine arose. It was American Jewry that clothed men like Louis Marshal and Felix M. Warburg in authority and strength to undertake and carry though a gigantic war and post-war relief program that followed, in ever-increasing measure, the leadership of Zionism, as exemplified by Louis D. Brandeis, Chaim Weizmann, Stephen S. Wise, Louis Lipsky and others, to further the realization of Zionism.

The outcome of the first World War, insofar as the Jewish people is concerned, was expressed in two acts of international scope and importance: (a) the insertion of clauses into the peace treaties with the newly established States, guaranteeing minority rights for the Jewish population; and (b) the issuance of the Balfour Declaration and the promulgation, under the aegis of the League of Nations, of the Mandate for Palestine. Of the first, hardly a shred has remained. Of the second, the present Yishuv, 500,000 strong, has emerged as an immovable reality that, for the first time since the destruction of Judaea, raised the issue of a Jewish State in the Land of Israel.

As the seventh century in the sixth millennium of the Hebrew calendar comes to a close, and as the second World War gets under way, the fate of the Jewish people and of Eretz Israel is again at stake. Again it is on American Jewry that the responsibility for timely, wise and effective action devolves.

"Land for Victory"
The Jewish Post, September 25, 1941[16]

A thorough evaluation of the year 5701 in Palestine must include a study of the development of agricultural settlement – the basis for any permanent

---

[16] Attributed to Z. Alroy.

economic existence in a country. Z. Alroy bases this interpretive picture of Palestine on the achievements of the Jewish National Fund, which is preparing to celebrate the 40th anniversary of its land-purchasing operations in Palestine and which last year alone provided the land for eight new agricultural settlements. – The Editor.

What fate does the future hold in store for Palestine? If and when the cause of the democracies prevails [in World War II], will Palestine (a) become incorporated in a Federation of Middle Eastern or Arab States? (b) be set up as a bi-national state in which Jews and Arabs will hold political parity? (c) be partitioned into two states, one Arab and the other Jewish? (d) remain mandated territory, as heretofore, and administered by Great Britain? or (e) be admitted into the British Commonwealth of Nations as the Seventh Dominion?

These and similar questions occupy the minds of publicists, political analysts, contact men, negotiators and statesmen, as the second year of World War II, coinciding with the Hebrew year 5701, has drawn to a close. In Cairo, negotiations are said to be going on with Arab leaders regarding the shape of things to come in the Arab world. Political thought, after a self-imposed prolonged silence on the part of Zionist leadership, is also beginning to stir in London, in Jerusalem, in New York and in Washington, D.C.

All this is, of course, predicated on the conviction that the Axis powers will be ultimately defeated, and that the new order that will be established after the war will be determined, not by the proponents of the "might is right" principle, but by the victorious adherence of individual liberty and national freedom. Of the three parties that are interested in the present and future of Palestine – the British, the Jews, and the Arabs – only the first two cling to this hopeful assumption. The Arabs still retain an open mind on the question. Actually, insofar as the Jewish National Home in Palestine is concerned, the *status quo ante bellum* still prevails. The restrictions in respect to Jewish immigration and land purchase, promulgated in the MacDonald White Paper before the outbreak of the war, when Chamberlainian appeasement was at its height, are still the law of the land. Moreover, these restrictions that violate the very essence of the Balfour Declaration and the League of Nations Mandate do injury to the country's most vital economic interests that have been and are being implemented by the Palestine Government.

And yet, the objective reviewer of the Palestine scene in the second year of the war is pleasantly surprised at the conclusion that the facts seem to warrant. Considered against the background of the tragedy, chaos and misery that have swept over the Axis conquered and dominated lands, and the catastrophe that has come over the Jewish communities in these lands, the story of the Jewish National Home at war constitutes a remarkable epic of progress and achievement. It is the one bright spot in the Jewish sector of the worldwide Battle for Freedom on which not only no position has been lost, but new bastions of strength[17] have been gained and are being held firmly as a preparation for and a promise of the future. The story is most objectively and, simultaneously, most graphically told in the facts and figures pertaining to the operations of the Jewish National Fund during the Hebrew year 5701. The Fund is one of the two major instruments of the Zionist movement through which national resources are being mobilized and made available for upbuilding and strengthening the Jewish National Home. Its special task is the acquisition of "land," as national and inalienable property, for current and future needs.

---

[17] Cf. *Bastions of Jewish Strength and Hope*, elsewhere in this volume.

What is the sense of buying land in wartime? Is the application of public funds for such a purpose a "wise" investment? Is there no danger that the land might fall into the hands of the invader? These and similarly "optimistic" questions have been hurled at the leadership of the Jewish National Fund since the collapse of France and the entry of Italy into the war. It is characteristic that these questions came from the "prudent" lips of those who were far removed from the danger zone themselves. The Jews of Palestine, where the danger of invasion seemed imminent several times during the year, entertained no such misgivings or fears. For them – and this occurred long before the psychological "V for Victory" campaign was launched for the benefit of the subjugated or threatened lands – there was only one orientation: Ultimate victory.

The months of anxiety have only served to stimulate greater exertions, with the result that since September 1939, up to August 1941, the continuity of Jewish constructive as well as defensive efforts has remained unbroken in Palestine. Vision, determination and unshakeable faith in ultimate victory have borne fruit. After two years of war, in which the country experienced a number of air attacks by Fascist and Nazi bombers, and faced the dangers of invasion from the North, East and South, the Jewish National Home stands on a firmer "land" foundation, has a greater locally-grown food supply, and houses a larger number of agricultural settlers rooted in the soil than it had at the outbreak of hostilities. The same progressive trend has come to the fore in the other parts of the Jewish National Home structure. In these paragraphs, however, the reviewer limits his observations to the progress in land acquisition because land is fundamental to the entire development and expresses more than any other thing the long-range view and the fundamental faith in the future. The fruit that this faith has yielded took on the shape of very tangible "facts" which were of extraordinary importance for the Yishuv struggling with an acute food-supply problem, and will prove of equal, if not greater, importance in the future when the fate of the country will be decided. Let's look at the facts.

The War and After

The second World War uprooted 6,000,000 Jews in Europe. Of these 3,500,000 are in the territories conquered by the Nazis or are under Nazi influence. About 2,500,000 Jews lived in the eastern part of Poland and the western part of Russia, which became the scene of bloody battle as a result of the Nazi invasion. The problem of Jewish immigration will persist even after German rule in Europe will have been brought to an end. There will obviously be no solution until immigration is directed towards such countries where Jewish agricultural settlement – the basis for any permanent economic existence – is possible.

Palestine is the only country that holds out promise of large-scale and stable immigration, for the bigger the Jewish agricultural population of a country, the more easily can it absorb additional agricultural settlers. Palestine, which had a Jewish agricultural population of 30,000 in 1933, was able to absorb an additional 30,000 into agriculture during the years 1933-1941, in contrast with the several scores of refugees from Germany who managed to find a place for themselves in agriculture in other countries.

Palestine Agriculture Progresses

In the first 18 months of the war, Jewish agriculture in Palestine has made considerable progress. The national land area has been extended, since September 1939, by more than 60,000 dunams of soil. Nor have the restrictions placed upon land purchase in the MacDonald White Paper proved to be a serious obstacle. In the first year following the promulgation of the White Paper, March 1940 to February 28, 1941, the Jewish National Fund has been able to acquire 33,270 dunams of land. Of this number, 12,300 were acquired in the Free Zone; 11,770 dunams in Zone B, where land purchase could be effective with the consent of the government; 9,200 dunams were acquired in Zone A, where the transfer of land by an Arab to a Jew was prohibited.

In the first ten months of the Hebrew year (October 1, 1940 to August 1, 1941), the Jewish National Fund in Palestine acquired an additional area of 22,869 dunams; 9,000 dunams have been acquired in Judaea; 5,000 dunams in the Valley of Jezreel; 2,000 dunams in the Sharon Valley; and approximately 200 in the Upper Galilee. The other parts of the Jewish reclamation program have not been neglected. Since the beginning of the war, the Jewish National Fund has been able to continue its reforestation work, having planted during the period an additional 350,000 trees in the various agricultural settlements and afforestation zones.

In terms of human lives, this development made possible the absorption into Jewish agriculture an additional number of 7,500 men and women who, whether native born or refugees, found their land-settlement opportunities in the Kibbutzim and Moshvei Ovdim, the collectives and the smallholders settlements, located on the land of the Jewish National Fund. Eight new agricultural settlements were established on JNF land since September 1939.

"Menachem Ussishkin"
Pittsburgh Tri-State Pinkas, 1947[18]

Within Menachem Ussishkin's life span (1863-1941) many dramatic events and profound revolutionary changes occurred in the world. From the historian's angle, these turbulent 78 years have witnessed a remarkable upward trend in the scientific, cultural, economic and political progress of the peoples that were the players in the world's drama. Only one member of the human family has not benefited from the new development that was under way before the advent of Nazism: Jewry. Its status has not only not been improved, but has steadily been deteriorating. Two-thirds of the Jewish world population face today physical and spiritual extermination.

When Menachem Ussishkin saw the light of day in Dubrowna, Russia, in the year 1863, Alexander II ruled over All The Russias. Wilhelm I sat on the throne of Prussia. Napoleon III reigned over France. Victoria was Queen of England and the Dominions beyond the seas. Abraham Lincoln, having freed the Negroes, fought the Civil War for the principles of Emancipation. In Palestine, under the Sultan's sovereignty, there lived but a handful of old and pious Jews who had come to the Holy Land to die there. In the United States the Jewish community numbered less than 250,000 souls.

The era of the Isms was then in its mere infancy. Only fifteen years had elapsed since Karl Marx and his associates had issued their *Communist Manifesto*. But in Germany, the land of Goethe and Schiller, Kant and Hegel, anti-Semitism, the forerunner of Aryanism and Hitlerism, began to raise its head in the garb of "scientific anti-Semitism." The upper strata of West European Jewry, which had striven hard to persuade itself that the Emancipation,

---

[18] Attributed to Z. Alroy.

which had come painfully and slowly, really wrote *finis* to the Jewish Question, began to wonder whether this was really so.

In Eastern Europe the Poles were rising against the oppression of Czarist Russia. In Russia proper the Nihilists and the social revolutionaries were busily engaged in surreptitiously setting the stage for that process of revolt that culminated in the revolutions of 1905 and 1917. Russian Jewry, 6,000,000 strong and a reservoir of Jewish life, tradition and culture, was in the throes of an inner severe crisis that resulted from the struggle between the traditionalists and the adherents of the *Haskalah* (Enlightenment). It was yet to experience the pogroms, the humiliations and the oppressions of the decades that were to follow. Its confinement to an official Czarist Pale of Settlement was yet to be enacted.

It was not a happy world into which Menachem Ussishkin was born and in which he grew to manhood. So oppressive was the life of the Jewish masses on the steppes of Russia and in the adjacent lands that the misery and hopefulness that hung over it produced among the more thoughtful and forward-looking leaders of the older generation a feverish desire for a radical change. Some joined the forces of the revolution that promised release. Others sought release through national revival in accordance with a pattern that had its living roots in the deep-seated traditions of the Jewish masses and its incentive in the ancient glories of Israel.

As a youth of 18 – then a student in the Moscow Technical Institute from which he later graduated as an engineer – Ussishkin was already engaged in founding a branch of the *Chovevei Zion* (Lovers of Zion), the Palestine colonization movement that preceded Theodor Herzl's Political Zionism. Stirred to the depth of his soul by the anti-Jewish pogroms of 1882 in Russia, he joined the BILU (abbreviated Hebraic description of those who issued the slogan "House of Jacob, come, let us go!"), the first group of Russian Jewish students who abandoned their careers to take up the life of agricultural pioneers on the malaria-ridden swamps of Judea. To be admitted into the group it was necessary for Ussishkin to pay into its treasury an amount of 450 rubles. He pawned his gold watch to make the first payment but, when the day of departure arrived, the leaders of the group found that only seven members could embark. There was not sufficient money to cover the traveling expenses from Odessa to Jaffa. Ussishkin, together with his schoolmate Tchlenow, who subsequently played an outstanding role as a leader of Russian Zionism, were left behind.

Thereafter Menachem Ussishkin's life was wrapped up in ceaseless work for the realization of his Zionist idea. From 1891, when he paid his first visit to Palestine, to October 2, 1941, the day of his death, he was a vital factor in and a living symbol of Zionism and Eretz Israel. It is difficult, almost impossible, to conceive and to describe the development of Jewish and Zionist life in Europe and in Palestine without a full appreciation of Ussishkin's predominant part in it. The saga of his labors, struggles, setbacks and achievements in the five decades is, indeed, inseparable from the story of Zionism and the upbuilding of Eretz Israel. His single-minded devotion to the cause and his unswerving loyalty to it have been universally recognized by friend and adversary alike. Admirer and opponent alike have concurred in conferring upon him the title of Zionism's Man of Iron, a label that expressed the affection of his supporters and the respect of his opponents.

His was a simple faith in Israel and in the Land of Israel. Yet no man's faith could be more profound. So deeply rooted was it that no storm could shake it, much less uproot it. In the annals of Zionism, there are many interesting stories about his lifetime, all of which would involve one in writing a condensed history of Zionism and Palestinian development during fifty years. The man became a legend even during his lifetime. There is the story about his rallying to the call of Theodor Herzl and then bitterly opposing him on the issue of Uganda versus Palestine. There is the epic of his struggle, together with Weizmann, for a

Hebrew University idea; there is the intricate story of the relationship between Ussishkin and Weizmann; there is the epic of his great influence upon the masses of Russian Jewry prior to and during the World War; there is the dramatic scene of Ussishkin's plea in Hebrew before the Supreme Council of the Peace Conference in Paris; there is the interesting and instructive part played by Ussishkin in the controversy of national versus private capital of 1921; and there is the story of his determined fight against the partition plan. But, above all, there is the epic of Menachem Ussishkin's everlasting contribution to the resettlement of Eretz Israel – the contribution that he made as the World President of the Keren Kayemeth Leisrael (the Jewish National Fund).

In the twenty years during which he presided over the Keren Kayemeth in Jerusalem and directed the activities of our Palestine Land Fund, Menachem Ussishkin became the Keren Kayemeth of the Keren Kayemeth. After a fruitful, long and stormy Zionist career, he had been chosen at the age of 60 to head and direct that instrumentality for Palestine Land Redemption that Theodor Herzl created at the Fifth Zionist Congress and that had made but meager progress up to that date. We of the Jewish National Fund who had the great privilege of close and intimate collaboration with Menachem Ussishkin for, alas, too brief a period, are perhaps able to appreciate more fully the true significance of his contribution and the sterling qualities of his inspiring leadership.

In retrospect it appears that the twenty years that had elapsed between the founding of the Keren Kayemeth and the assumption of its leadership by Menachem Ussishkin were merely a preliminary measure for the new advance that was to follow.

The stage for the new advance was set at the London Conference of 1920, which restored to the Keren Kayemeth its original character as that of a Palestine Land Fund designed to collaborate with its sister fund, the Keren Hayesod, which was entrusted with the task of serving as the fiscal instrument of the Jewish Agency for Palestine and the colonization fund of the Zionist movement.

How great is the progress that has been made since that turning point? Great as it was, it was not satisfactory enough for Menachem Ussishkin. The extent of the advance must be measured, however, against the background of the events that crowded that eventful twenty-year period between the San Remo decision to award the Mandate over Palestine to Great Britain and the outbreak of World War II. The entire development of the Jewish National Home in the course of the two decades is inconceivable without the land foundation that Ussishkin and the Keren Kayemeth laid. His first large-scale accomplishment for Geulath Ha-aretz – a purpose to which he had been singularly devoted even while other phases of the movement occupied his attention and energies – was the purchase of the first extensive land tract in the Valley of Jezreel. It was a venturesome enterprise that was opposed by some but that has been proved in the light of history as the act of a great man of vision and action.

Superficially, it may appear that the task that was entrusted to Menachem Ussishkin when he was called to the presidency of the Palestine Land Fund was a job calling for administrative skills only. Actually, the implementation of the Geulath Ha'aretz program, as a national enterprise that is based upon the principles of national land ownership and social justice, is predicted upon considerations of much greater scope than ordinary real estate transactions, which are based on business and financial considerations alone. In the truest meaning of the term, the task was that of nation- and homeland-building, requiring high talent and inexhaustible energies in properly evaluating and coping with the historical, political, strategic and psychological elements and phases of the complex Palestine problem. Only a man of great stature, whose roots have struck deep into the core of the Jewish soul and soil, could be equal to the task. Ussishkin proved his great capacity to perform the historic mission that he undertook at an age when most people might be inclined – and justifiably so – to rest on the laurels of their past achievements.

The Jewish people in all parts of the world, including our own United States, have instinctively sensed the intrinsic value of the great leader and the urgency of his mission. Responding to his exhortations, pleadings and demands, the broad mass of our people have contributed in ever-increasing measure to the Jewish National Fund. Under his administration, the Keren Kayemeth was entrusted with new resources amounting to LP 5,100,000 or approximately $25,000,000. The bulk of this amount has not been the gift of the well-to-do, but the mite of those who have not been blessed with too much of worldly goods.

What has Menachem Ussishkin accomplished with the resources that the Jewish masses have placed in his trust? Although the epic of Keren Kayemeth's achievements during the past two decades is pretty well-known in a general way, it will be refreshing to glance here at but a few figures. When he took the helm, the Keren Kayemeth's world income amounted to LP 667,000 or approximately $3,335,000. At the same time our national land holdings in Palestine stood at 19,000 dunams. Only a score of agricultural settlements existed on National Fund land at that time. On October 3, 1941, when Ussishkin's mortal remains were carried for burial in Nicano's Cave, Mt. Scopus, Jerusalem, the national land possessions had been brought by the Jewish National Fund to the formidable height of 550,000 dunams, and on these strategically located land tracts in Palestine's four principal valleys there stood 81 Moshavim and Moshavoth, 70 Kibbutzim, 57 workers' camps, 15 rural quarters, 16 urban quarters and 12 agricultural schools – the very backbone of the Jewish National Home and its bastions of strength and hope.[19] This is not the record of a mere administrator's job, but the achievement and the life work of a trailblazer, a man of vision and action, a statesman, a nation-builder whose memory will long be cherished.

What was the driving power behind this man of vision and action? His simple but unshakable faith; his long historic memory of what Eretz Israel meant to the Jewish people in the past and what it will mean in the future; his deep human sympathy for the suffering of the broad mass of Jewry and the recognition that the pattern offered by the Zionist idea is a way of salvation; and his anxiety for progress before it is too late. One need not delve into the numerous essays, programs, exhortations and reminiscences that this man of action wrote, although he was not a writer, to appreciate the magnitude of the force that drove him on. The key to his mind is found in the 38 recorded epigrams that were uttered by Ussishkin at critical periods in the life of the movement and of Palestine. They embody his testament to his people. He said:

> "Do not say 'we shall buy land in Palestine tomorrow'; tomorrow may be too late."
> "If the soil of Palestine will be ours a dozen (Lord) Passfields will not prevail against us; if not – a dozen Balfours will not help us."
> "Jewish capital may redeem the land of our fathers; Jewish intellect may build the Jewish homeland; but only Jewish labor has it within its power to make the land the permanent possession of the Jewish people."
> "When the People of Israel will redeem the Land of Israel, the Land of Israel will redeem the People of Israel."

---

[19] Cf. *Bastions of Jewish Strength and Hope*, elsewhere in this volume.

"When Eretz Israel went up in flames, the Jewish people went into Diaspora; when [the] Diaspora goes up in flames, the Jewish people must return to Eretz Israel."

"I once told Professor Einstein: it is much easier for the Jewish people to produce a dozen Einsteins than a single genuine and efficient farmer."

"Sentiment and reason are often at variance; Will is, however, supreme over both. There is nothing that stands in the way of the Will."

Contrasted with the Jewish tragedy of 1941 and with the problems of Jewish homelessness that will confront Jewish leadership even after Nazism will have been crushed, the sufferings of Jews in the 19th century and in the first three decades of the 20th appear to have been relatively tolerable. When the practical phases of the Zionist program were being formulated by Ussishkin and his colleagues, the Jewish people needed a homeland but it could still count on a margin of safety in the Diaspora. Today, with two-thirds of the Jewish population of the world either homeless wanderers or slowing starving to death behind the barbed wires of the concentration camps and the ghetto walls, the vision of a Homeland is not an answer to a nostalgic prayer, but a stark and urgent necessity.

Because Menachem Ussishkin lived as he did, labored, fought and achieved as he did, the answer to the call of distress of the Jewish people can be given not in terms of a theory or an idealist's exhortation, but as a practical method of salvation. This method rests on the firm foundation of an experience of sixty years of successful colonization and on the tangible assets of land and colonies. These colonies and the Jewish National Home that they compose have served as a laboratory for colonization and social progress and, in a world that is to be reconstructed on the basis of individual liberty and national freedom, will serve as an example of a modern design for Jewish living.

"Four Decades of *Geulath Ha'Aretz*: Program, Achievements and History of the Jewish National Fund Briefly Described"
Pittsburgh Tri-State Pinkas, 1947

JEWISH NATIONAL FUND (English name for the Keren Kayemeth Le Israel), Palestine land-purchasing agency of the Zionist World Organization. Headquarters: Keren Kayemeth Building, Jerusalem, Palestine.

AIMS: (1) To acquire the soil of Palestine as national and inalienable property; (2) To carry on drainage work on the land it has acquired; (3) To carry on afforestation; (4) To install in the settlements modern water-supply systems; (5) To give the soil under 49-year hereditary leases for cultivation to settlers as individuals or as collective groups.

PRINCIPLES: Underlying the work of the Jewish National Fund since its inception was the urge of the Zionist movement to reestablish the union between the People and the

Land of Israel. Concepts of social justice were woven into the Jewish National Fund program. These concepts found their most tangible expression in a set of principles adopted for the development of a national land-acquisition program. The principle of the Mosaic Law ("And ye shall grant redemption to the land" – Leviticus, XXV: 24) governing the transfer of land to its original owners after each fifty-year cycle, lent a continuity and the halo of ancient tradition to the advanced doctrine. These principles were adopted not merely because it is obviously right that land bought with money raised through popular contributions should remain national property, but also because it represented the best way for preventing abuses that often arise out of private land ownership.

The national capital was employed in a manner that benefited not merely the individuals settling upon the soil, but the community. Hence the decision to apply the funds for the purchase of land that shall forever remain the inalienable property of the Jewish people. Out of these principles flow the conditions under which the Fund places its land holdings at the disposal of settlers, to wit: (1) The settler receives the land on hereditary lease only, and has not, in any way, either direct or indirect, to refund the value of his holding. He is given the land in usufruct alone. (2) The settler is expected, after the expiration of the first five years from the date of his release, to pay the Fund an annual rental equivalent to 1 to 2 percent of the assessed value of the land he occupies. At the end of fifteen years, the land is reappraised and the rent adjusted to the then-current value. (3) The lessee is obliged to reside in the holding and to cultivate it regularly. (4) The lessee is obliged to execute, with Jewish labor only, all works in connection with the cultivation of the land.

ACHIEVEMENTS: Up to January 1, 1944, the Jewish National Fund acquired 670,400 dunams of land (a dunam equals one-quarter of an acre) in all parts of Palestine. Of these, 197,600 dunams were acquired during the war years (since September, 1939). Upon the Fund's land there have been established by the Keren Hayesod, the Palestine Foundation Fund, and by individual settlers and groups, 190 agricultural settlements, comprising 68 percent (of a total of 276 Jewish agricultural settlements) of the number of Jewish villages in the country. Thirty-three settlements were founded on the land of the Jewish National Fund since the beginning of the war. The colonies established on the land of the Jewish National Fund are either (a) Kvutzoth or Kibbutzim, communal or collective villages; or (b) Moshevi Ovdim, smallholders' settlements.

In the 42 years of its operations, the Fund has invested about LP 7,000,000 in land redemption. By draining swamps, the Fund reclaimed more than 300,000 dunams of land and transformed them into fertile areas. The Fund has reforested more than 14,000 dunams by planting thereon over 3,000,000 trees.

In the settlements established on the land of the Jewish National Fund there live and work 72,500 men, women and children. Fifty-one thousand, constituting 44 percent of the Jewish rural population and 66 percent of the actual agricultural working population of the country, live in the settlements on Jewish National Fund land. 21,500 people live in urban and suburban residential quarters on the land of the Fund. Settlements on Keren Kayemeth land provide 63 percent of all the Jewish output of milk, 73 percent of poultry and eggs, 62 percent of cereals, 75 percent of vegetables, and 82 percent of potatoes. All the land acquired by the Jewish National Fund during the war has been put under cultivation and has thus served to increase the production of food in the country. Before the war, Jewish agriculture provided 34 percent of the Yishub's requirements for milk; today it supplies 58 percent. Its egg production has risen from 37 percent to 64 percent, and vegetable production from 44 percent to 63 percent of consumption. Jewish production of potatoes, a crop that was introduced only on the eve of the war, now satisfies 55 percent of the Yishub's needs.

The Fund has also installed modern water-supply systems in 57 agricultural settlements and provided the sites for the Hebrew University on Mt. Scopus, for hospitals, synagogues and schools. Fifty industrial enterprises have been founded on the land belonging to the Fund.

By reason of its land policies and achievements in the field of colonization, the Jewish National Fund is regarded as the backbone of the structure of the Jewish National Home that was reared in Palestine in the era following World War I, and on the basis of the Balfour Declaration of November 2, 1917 and the League of Nations Mandate of July 24, 1922.

FINANCIAL OPERATIONS: The Jewish National Fund, conceived and fashioned as one of the two (the other is the Keren Hayesod) financial instruments to translate into reality the Zionist program in Palestine, has enlisted the support of large numbers of Jews in all parts of the world. A variety of popular fundraising methods and special campaigns have been put into operation since the Fund's inception forty years ago. Up to October 1, 1943, a total of LP 7,812,800 was contributed by the Jewish communities toward the Jewish National Fund. Before September, 1939, branches or committees, manned and directed by representatives of the public at large, were engaged in raising funds for the Jewish National Fund in fifty-two countries. Following the outbreak of World War II, the major part of the financial support became the responsibility of US Jewry, the Jewish communities in the British Empire and Palestine Jewry itself.

These funds that are raised under the slogan *Geulath Ha'aretz* (the Redemption of the Soil) have been and are being obtained largely through the medium of popular methods that are calculated to obtain the cooperation of all classes within Jewry. Chief among these are the widely known Jewish National Fund methods: (1) Stamps; (2) Blue-White Boxes; (3) The Golden Book; (4) Sefer Ha'Yeled; (5) Tree Planting; (6) Semi-annual street collections known as Flower Day and Flag Day; (7) Dunam Land Contributions; (8) Bequests and Living Legacies; (9) Nachloth – the acquisition of a specifically delineated tract of land for the establishment of colonies bearing the names of outstanding personalities or of geographical units.

HISTORY: The idea of a Jewish National Fund was first conceived by Dr. Herman Schapira, Professor of Mathematics at the University of Heidelberg, Germany. He proposed its establishment in a telegram dispatched to the first conference of Chovevei Zion that met in Kattowitz on November 6, 1884, but no action was taken. He proposed it again to the First Zionist Congress convoked by Dr. Theodor Herzl at Basle, Switzerland, in the summer of 1897. But it was not until December 1901, when the Fifth Zionist Congress met at Basle, Switzerland, that the proposal was adopted on the recommendation of Johann Kremenezky of Vienna and Dr. Theodor Herzl, the President of the Congress. The Jewish National Fund was incorporated in England, as a Limited Liability Company under the Companies' Act, complete and permanent control over it being vested in the World Zionist Congress. The Fund is being administered by a Board of Directors of nine members who are elected by the Actions Committee (General Council) of the Zionist Organization, which is in turn elected bi-annually by the Zionist World Congress. One-third of the Directors resign each year in rotation.

During Dr. Herzl's presidency of the Zionist Organization, when the administration of the Zionist movement had its seat in Vienna, the head office of the Jewish National Fund was also located in that city, with Johann Kremenezky as President of its Board of Directors. In 1905, when David Wolffsohn succeeded Theodor Herzl as President of the Zionist

Organization, Zionist headquarters, including the head office of the Jewish National Fund, were moved to Cologne, Germany, with Dr. Max Bodenheimer as President of the Board of Directors. Upon the outbreak of the World War in 1914, the Jewish National Fund headquarters were moved to The Hague, Holland. Nehemiah de Lieme, an outstanding Dutch Zionist, became the Fund's President. At the close of the war, the head office was moved to London, England, which then became the headquarters of the World Zionist Organization. In 1921, at the Zionist World Conference held in London, England, a new Board of Directors was chosen with Menachem Ussishkin as President, a post he held until his death in October, 1941. In 1922, the head office of the Jewish National Fund was transferred to Jerusalem, and on May 6, 1930, it moved into its own home, which is now a part of the group of Jewish Agency buildings in Jerusalem. Ussishkin's assumption of the leadership of the Fund inaugurated a new era in the Fund's fundraising and land-acquisition activity. Under his guidance, the Fund's resources grew from $4,177,000 in 1921, to $29,825,000 in 1941, and from its meager land holdings of 19,000 dunams in 1921 to 550,000 dunams in 1941. Since Menachem Ussishkin's death, the affairs of the Keren Kayemeth Le Israel have been administered by a Presidium of three, namely, Dr. A. Granovsky, Rabbi Meyer Berlin and Berl Katznelson. The world income for the last fiscal year that ended on September 30, 1943, amounted to LP 1,145,500.

A recent tabulation of disbursements shows that the Fund's receipts were expended in the following ratios: 72 percent on land for rural settlement; 7 percent for afforestation; 7 percent on drainage of swamps; and 6 percent on water supply.

"High Noon at Kfar Etzion: Leaves from a Palestine Traveler's Notebook"
Land and Life, February 1948

We left Jerusalem early in the morning.[20] The sun that rose over the horizon seemed to throw knowing glances on the hill slopes over which bullets buzzed and fear stalked only a few hours ago, during the dusk-to-dawn curfew.

We were cautioned that the trip southward was not too safe. A visit to Hebron, nest of rabid Husseinism since the 1929 massacre, and even passing through Christian Bethlehem were, under the prevailing security conditions, out of the question.

To be sure, we were not entirely without cover. Our automobile was manned by one of those almost legendary Egged drivers who are reputed for their mastery of the highways, for their agility in quick maneuvers and effective defense. A young man whose posture indicated familiarity with weapons of defense was also among us and his pockets were rather bulging. Yet caution was the order of the day.

The Jaffa-Tel Aviv skirmishes, with their not-inconsiderable casualties on both sides, were not far behind. Press reports carrying first intimations of the recommendation of the United Nations Palestine Commission for the establishment of a Jewish State had begun to come in. A lull set in, but the few days of relative quiet and the apparently peaceful landscape gave to the observer the foreboding of a storm to come.

---

[20] The letter WZS addressed to Ruth J. Spiegelman on July 23, 1947 (included elsewhere in this volume) suggests that he and his wife, Dora, left for Israel shortly thereafter, while the letter Dora addressed to her children from Jerusalem on August 23, 1947 (not included here) indicates that the tour of Kfar Etzion described in this essay took place in mid-August 1947.

Our last glimpse of the city was a reminder of the virtual state of siege in which Jerusalem had lived through the summer. A detachment of the Seventh Airborne Division, which earned its laurels in World War II, engaged in a task of doubtful heroism. The British lads who played so eminent a part in the Battle of the Bulge were now reduced to performing the unheroic job of identifying and searching – armed to the teeth – the unarmed and non-descript Yemenite vendors in a market on the outskirts of Jerusalem. Our party, too, was halted, identified and searched for the third time since we started from the Hotel Eden only a short while ago.

Travel on the Jerusalem-Hebron highway seemed almost like relaxation after the tenseness of the city atmosphere. One's feeling was akin to that experienced while riding through the mountains of California, not taking into account, of course, the knowledge that here you were rolling along acres of soil upon which ancient and sacred history left its indelible impress.

Suddenly you are shaken out of your complacency. You realize that a strange silence pervades the highway and the surrounding countryside. There is hardly a moving vehicle or a traveler on foot to be seen. By the time we reached Rachel's Tomb – that sanctified spot where one of the world's greatest loves came to an end – we noted that very few of the "children" for whom Mother Rachel has been "weeping" throughout the generations are assembled here to offer the customary prayers.

In normal times, we are told, this Biblical shrine, which was repaired and preserved for posterity by Sir Moses Montefiore, draws large throngs of worshippers and tourists during this season of the year. Today we discovered inside the enclosure of Rachel's Tomb a lone aged Yemenite who, prostrate on the stone bench, was reciting Psalms with a piercing chant. But he appeared as if he were an immobile and integral part of the ancient site.

The Shamash, whose task it is to explain and minister to the religious needs of the visitors, was surprised not less than pleased to see us on this Elul day.

Yamim Noraim Baim ("Days of Awe are coming") he whispered in a heavy Sephardic accent without making clear whether his words were to be taken literally, as a sort of prophecy in the land of prophets, or figuratively, as a reference to the forthcoming High Holidays.

But Joseph, whom the Keren Kayemeth in Jerusalem had appointed as our guide and mentor of this trip, is a hard taskmaster.

"This is not the time for sentimentalizing about the past or speculating about the political and military consequences of the recommendations of the United Nations Palestine Commission. The boys of Kfar Etzion expect you at noon. We have a great many things to see in this part of the country. We must not keep them waiting," he commands. Some members of our party wished to linger on in meditation. Others, particularly the ladies, eager to complete the purchase of Mezzuzoth, amulets and souvenirs for friends in America and England, did not relish the idea of being hurried.

The mention of Kfar Etzion evokes, however, a responsive chord in the writer's heart. Well did he remember one evening in Manhattan in the winter of 1943 when the war for the Four Freedoms was still being fought. Rabbi Meir Berlin, Mizrachi leader and then acting chairman of the Keren Kayemeth, had come by air from Jerusalem to propose a land-purchase program that would fortify and safeguard the Jewish future of Jerusalem.

"Sooner or later the status of the Holy City will be determined. It is necessary that we undertake now, in the midst of the war, to purchase tracts of land in the hills surrounding Jerusalem to the south and establish a chain of new settlements there," he told his somewhat astonished audience. *Geulath Svivoth Jerusalem* was the slogan he applied to the program that has progressively gained the financial support of Orthodox groups. Kfar

Etzion is one of the hill settlements that was founded as part of this plan.

Twenty-one kilometers due south our automobile turned into a side road in a westward direction. The Judean mountains rise here to a height of approximately thousands of meters above sea level. Faint traces of ancient terraces are still discernible on the slopes. As a whole, the sense unfolding here to the visitor's eye is forbidding barrenness: a bleakness that spreads all around to be punctured, at considerable distances, by low stone and mud houses in small Arab villages clinging to the cliffs.

Centuries ago a thriving vineyard country, these slopes almost audibly cry out against the ruthless and wasteful treatment to which they have been subjected. The only sign of life one sees in entering what has become known as "Kfar Etzion Bloc" is a verdant carob tree that stands as an eloquent survivor of an ancient forest that must have covered this neighborhood once upon a time.

"Honi Ha'maagal, the Hebrew prototype of Rip Van Winkle, must have spent his 70 years asleep under a carob tree like this." The Hebrew scholar of our party attempts to inject a bit of humor into the oppressive mood created by the bleakness of the environment.

"Here are his modern disciples," responds the young Haganah member, pointing to a group of Bedouins who – lo and behold – are resting comfortably under the carob tree, fully protected by its shade from the blazing sun. The noise of the wheels does not disturb them at all.

The speed of the highway gives way to a painful creeping against which the American-made tires protest audibly, threatening at any moment to produce a puncture. The terrain is literally covered with white rocks of all shapes and sizes. Here it seems as if someone, by a malicious and hateful design, had assembled these rocks from all over the universe and strewn this place with them in order to cover the natural fertility and loveliness of these mountain slopes. On second thought, one muses: is it possible that the ancient accounts of this terrain were not too accurate? Do we perhaps see here nature in its original state of rawness?

As if reading our train of thought, Joe interrupts to point out a verdant patch extending over several kilometers on a southern slope, a veritable and magnificent oasis in the desert. . . .

"This is living proof of what this mountainside is capable of producing and looking like. Here is a Russian monastery that was founded about 40 years ago. The Russians, not encountering any opposition, were able to restore the fertility of the soil. Several kilometers beyond we come to our destination: Kfar Etzion. You will see what has been done in a much shorter period."

But before proceeding to the settlements, we ascend the central height from which the full panorama of the Kfar Etzion bloc unfolds: Kfar Etzion to the south; Massuoth Yitzhok to the west; Revadim to the north and En Zurim to the northeast – a veritable ring of outposts of civilization in a stony wilderness.

Surveying the field, one quickly comes to the conclusion that the Keren Kayemeth, in acquiring the land, and the Colonization Department in establishing the settlements, were guided by weighty considerations cooperative efforts for progress and security. Kfar Etzion, the oldest of the group, is almost contiguous to Massuoth Yitzhak, the second of the group, a settlement that bears the name of Palestine's Chief Rabbi, Dr. Isaac Halevi Herzog. The latter is within walking contact with En Zurim, not far from Bethlehem. En Zurim again is linked with Revadim, the youngest of the group that is manned by Hashomer Hatzair settlers. The first three, constituting the core, are occupied by the [Orthodox] religious pioneers of the Hapoel Ha'Mizrachi. Set on the mountain tops to the south, these settlements serve the same purpose that animated the builders of Kiryath Anavim, Maaleh Ha'Chemisha and Nveh

Ilan (situated on the Nachlath Long Island tract) to the west of Jerusalem – outposts of modern cultivation and, if need be, of strategic defense.

We pass through Hirabth Zachariah, an Arab village that is reputed to have in its confines the tomb of the Prophet Zachariah. The place could not possibly win a prize for cleanliness or orderly cultivation of the remnants of ancient grape lanes. Through a winding trail we ascend to the top of the 965-meter height upon which Kfar Etzion nestles.

Joshua, a member of the Kibbutz secretariat, takes us quickly in hand.

He is a walking encyclopedia of facts and figures. One of the original members of Kvutzath Abraham, the group of religious pioneers that settled here, he is eager to share his information with us. An old-timer at Kfar Etzion, he tells us proudly about the twins with which his charming wife recently presented him. The fresh innocence of his blond and blue-eyed children inspires one to fervently believe that the peace of this mountain with its cool breezes and transparent refreshing air will never be disturbed.

"The Jewish National Fund placed this land at our disposal. Our Kvutzah was comprised at that time of about 100 members. During the first year our work was concentrated on clearing the rocks from the land. We soon found that this land, unsuitable for other crops, is excellent for vegetables and good for plantations. During the first year we covered 100 dunams with fruit trees. The second year we extended the area to 200 dunams. Today, with a population of 250, including 60 children, we are deriving our livelihood from cultivating our orchards on which we are growing the best apples in the world, Japanese and European plums, figs, olives, grapes, almonds and cherries. Our clearing work has progressed so much that we can now plan to extend our orchards by another 400 dunams.

"Incidentally, the young trees that you see through the window are the beginning of the Rabbi Meir Berlin Forest planted with the contributions of your friends in the United States."

"Aren't those trees a bit undersized?" we cautiously inquired.

"They are the second set of saplings. The first set was destroyed one night by our neighboring cousins."

"How are the relations with the Arab neighbors?"

"To be sure, the Arabs of Hebron and vicinity did not bring us bread and salt when we arrived here. In the beginning their attitude was not indicative of peaceful intentions, but as time passed we established a cordial relationship with them. We helped them with some of our equipment. On occasion we also exchanged shots in the dark of the night with marauders who, when caught, claimed they came from distant parts. Today, we maintain at Kfar Etzion, as anywhere else in the land, a position of watchful waiting."

"Is there a telephone in this settlement?"

"Well, that would be too much to expect. We did apply to the British authorities for the installation of a telephone 4 years ago, but our request has not yet been acted upon."

"What would you do in case of an attack?"

"We trust in God and rely on our ability to defend ourselves. We were the first but, as you have noticed, we are no longer alone in these mountains. In Massuoth Yitzhok, in En Zurim, and in Rebadim, we have younger brothers whom we can quickly inform by means of our own signaling system. The average age of our adult male population is 27. We have no illusions. We know who we are and what is the value of a Jew's life in the world today. Nearly all of us come from Poland. Most of us have undergone great hardships before we reached Eretz Israel.

"This mountain top on which we are building our own and our people's future is our last retreat. Here we have our Synagogue, our library, our orchards, our stone-cutting industry, our hard-earned foundations for a new life that we dedicated to our ideal. The rocks that are strewn all around us, apparently obstacles to growth and an eyesore to the landscape, we are determined to convert from stumbling blocks into stepping stones. To a considerable degree we have already done so. These stones, which are the raw material for our budding industry, can also be weapons of defense. Here we are and here we are going to stay. From here we shall not budge. So help us God."

It was high noon at Kfar Etzion. The pioneers, medium-sized, brown-faced, of sure and determined step, started to leave their orchard in the direction of the community dining hall. A group of about 30 middle-aged men and women, city dwellers who had come for their vacations to Kfar Etzion's recreation center Beth Ovadiah, walked leisurely in the same direction in response to the gong. The stone cutters, dressed in dust-covered overalls, came marching in almost military formation. Joshua, looking at the sentry who stood guard with the traditional *Kippah* (skullcap) on his head, excused himself. He had important duties to attend to. It was high noon at Kfar Etzion, but dispositions for the time when shadows will fall had to be made.

Sir Leon, a member of our party and an eager chess player, thought the remaining hour offered a good opportunity for a long-delayed engagement to play a game of chess in the cool mountain breeze. When Joshua returned, he threw a penetrating glance at the board and in a matter-of-fact manner observed: "That Rook, having command over the field in all directions, is a powerful means of defense. . . ."

It was not entirely clear whether Joshua's observation was offered as advice for the winning of the chess game, or as an allegory on the strategic importance of Kfar Etzion.

Bastions of Jewish Strength and Hope: Brief Sketches of the Jewish Agricultural Settlements in Palestine: When They Were Founded, Where They Are Located and How They Have Progressed
(Jewish National Fund, 1940)

"Introduction"[1]

While the movement for Jewish agricultural colonies originated at the end of the 18th century, and did not become vigorous until the last quarter of the 19th, it represented the culmination of a Jewish hope that had lain dormant for many centuries. The Jews were originally an agricultural people. From the time of the conquest of Canaan they had been a race of farmers, only gradually taking to artisanry and trade; as late as the 1st century C.E. Josephus was able to write, "We do not delight in merchandise . . . and having a fruitful country for our habitation, we take pains in cultivating that only" (*Against Apion* 1:12). With the loss of Jewish independence in 70 C.E. and the scattering of the greater part of the Jewish population as slaves, many Jews were forced to take up other occupations. However, there were still many Jews who engaged in agriculture, and it was not until the latter part of the Middle Ages, as the result of attacks that made it necessary for them to dispose of landed property, as well as of decrees that forbade them to own land, that they finally abandoned the cultivation of the soil.

With the new spirit of toleration that arose at the end of the 18th century, there was a removal of the restrictions that had been imposed upon the Jews, and a movement for return to the land. Both Jews and non-Jews realized that it was important to change the occupations of many of the Jews, to release them from the confines of the ghetto and its narrow forms of livelihood. Sometimes the motive for the support of the movement was self-interested, as when governments encouraged Jewish colonization to build up newly acquired territories; sometimes it was assimilative, an attempt to wean away large groups of Jews from the traditional ways; and sometimes it was theoretical, based on the ideas of the dignity of labor or plans for a cooperative community. In the latter part of the 19th century, the movement tended to become national; Jewish colonization was envisioned as becoming the broad base for the recreated Jewish nation. In the 20th century, the movement has been expanded to take care of the refugees from Europe where thousands of Jews, deprived of their livelihoods by governmental decrees, have been compelled to take up new vocations.

The early attempts at Jewish colonization were seldom successful. Their proponents failed to realize the tremendous difficulties that inhere in the problem of returning a population that was town-bred for centuries back to the soil. Governments miscalculated the amount of money and preparation needed, and willing Jewish colonists were met with a lack of proper provisions for their needs. After 1881 more permanent settlements were established. On the whole, it can be said that even with its failures, the Jewish movement for colonization was more successful than any other attempts of the 19th and 20th centuries to

---

[1] When *Bastions of Strength and Hope* was reprinted in the *Universal Jewish Encyclopedia*, Vol. 3 (1941) under the heading "Colonies, Agricultural: Palestine," it was supplemented by three new paragraphs, which appeared at the text's very beginning. Those paragraphs are included here, as well.

go back to the soil. The dogged determination of the Jewish colonists, their ability to learn by their mistakes, and the spur of persecutions from 1881 and after, finally succeeded in returning hundreds of thousands of Jews to the cultivation of the soil, their first occupation in the time of their independence. In 1940 there were far-flung Jewish agricultural settlements in Palestine, Asia, Eastern Europe, Canada, the United States, South America and Australia.

Of the more than 500,000 Jews now living in Palestine, 125,000 persons are engaged in farming and incognate agricultural pursuits. The Jewish farming population is settled in 250 agricultural colonies of varying types and sizes.

Three distinct categories, each of which is described and known by a different Hebrew name, are discernible in the development that has taken place between 1878 and 1940. A Jewish agricultural settlement in Palestine may have the character of (a) Moshava, (b) Moshav Ovdim, or (c) Kvutza or Kibbutz.

A Moshava is a settlement of freeholders: independent farmers who own their land as their private property.

A Moshav Ovdim is a settlement of smallholders who do not own the land as their private property but who hold it under a hereditary lease. The land, belonging to the Jewish National Fund, is national property leased to the settler for a 49-year period. Each settler in a Moshav Ovdim has the land tilled by him and his family clearly delimited. He enjoys full property rights in regard to the plantation, livestock, buildings and farm equipment. The settlers practice cooperation in all matters affecting the colony as a whole such as the purchase of livestock, seed and necessities, and in the sale of the produce, as well as in the maintenance of the necessary institutions.

A Kvutza is a communal settlement established on nationally owned land (belonging to the Jewish National Fund). The land is granted to the settlers as a group under the terms of the Jewish National Fund lease. The estate is worked in common. All property is owned by the community. A Kvutza comprises the land under cultivation, the living quarters, the buildings and the public institutions.

The principles of the Kvutza also apply to a communal settlement of a similar name: Kibbutz. The Kibbutz differs from the Kvutza only in its size or scale of operations. A Kibbutz is a settlement that has a larger land area and a greater number of members.

The term Kibbutzim is also applied in describing groups of agricultural workers that cultivate nationally owned land but have not yet been permanently settled on a definite piece of land. The Kibbutz lives in temporary quarters and is largely dependent for its maintenance on the wages earned by its members outside of their settlement. Nearly all Kvutzoth (plural of Kvutza) existing in Palestine today began as Kibbutzim (plural of Kibbutz).

The history of the Jewish agricultural resettlement of Palestine may be conveniently divided into time periods.

(a) Preliminary Period. In 1859 the Alliance Israelite Universelle of Paris, France, founded Mikveh Israel as the first Jewish agricultural training school in Palestine on an area of 2,600 dunams situated four kilometers southeast of Jaffa. Charles Netter, general secretary of the Alliance Israelite Universelle, is credited with the initiative of establishing the first Jewish agricultural settlement in Palestine in modern times. The Alliance obtained the land from the Turkish government on the basis of a lease of 49 years, renewable thereafter. In 1878 a group of Jerusalem Jews made the first attempt to establish the first agricultural settlement that they named Potach Tikvah (Gate of Hope). This attempt was not successful.

(b) The Hovevei Zion Period, which began in the years 1880-1883, when he first wave of immigration from Russia brought a number of settlers, including the idealistic pioneers who went under the name of BILU (initials for the Hebrew sciences: Beth Iaacov Loohu U'Nolchah – "House of Jacob, Come, Let Us Go," Isaiah II.5). Aided by the Hovevei Zion, these settlers laid the foundations for the colonies Petach Tikvah, Rishon le Zion, Zichron Yaakov, and Rosh Pinah.

(c) The Rothschild Period, which covers the span between 1883 and 1899. Baron Edmond de Rothschild of Paris, France, known in the annals of Palestinian colonization as the Nadiv Hayadua (famous philanthropist), reorganized the Hovevei Zion villages, converted them into vine-growing settlements and established at Rishon Le Zion the famous wine cellars bearing his name.

(d) The Jewish Colonization Association (JCA) Period, which covers the span between 1899 and 1907. In 1899 the administration of the Rothschild colonies was taken over by the JCA under whose auspices new settlements, on a cereal-growing basis, were founded in lower Galilee.

(e) The Zionist Period, which covers the span between 1905 to 1940.

The difference in the type and character of the various agricultural settlements may largely be traced to the dates and characteristics surrounding their establishment. Those colonies that were founded in the first three periods in the history of Palestine colonization were in most cases founded on the private ownership principle. Those establishments in the subsequent development, both prior to the issuance of the Balfour Declaration on November 22, 1917 and after, were in most cases founded with the funds supplied by the Zionist movement and with the land provided by the Jewish National Fund, on the collective principle.

The Fifth Zionist Congress held in Basel, Switzerland, in December, 1901, established the Keren Kayemeth Leisrael (Jewish National Fund) as the instrument of the Zionist movement for the acquisition of land in Palestine as national and inalienable property. The first settlement established on Jewish National Fund land was that of Degania on the Trans-Jordan side of Lake Kinnereth. Degania was founded in 1909. It is known as the "Mother" or as the first of the Kvutzoth. The Kvutza system was subsequently found to be the most effective and suitable for the settlement of larger numbers of agricultural workers. The system was evolved largely in accordance with a plan recommended in 1910 by Dr. Franz Oppenheimer, a German-Jewish agricultural expert who made the first experiment at the colony Merhavya in the valley of Jezreel.

All Kvutzoth are organized as cooperative societies functioning under the Cooperative Societies' Ordinance promulgated by the Palestine administration in 1933. All Kvutzoth function on the basis of a written constitution, common to all. The constitution lays down, broadly, the following principles: (a) the government of the Kvutza is vested in the general meeting of all members of the Kvutza; (b) general meetings must be held annually and whenever required by not less than one-third of the members of the Kvutza; (c) members have one vote each, which is expressed by show of hands [rest of sentence illegible]; (d) a simple majority of votes at a general meeting binds all members of the Kvutza; and (e) a committee of management is elected by the general meeting for one year.

The Committee of Management, commonly known as the Secretariat, is composed of three or more members and usually meets once a week. No official status is accorded to the chairman of the committee.

Each member of the Committee of Management has different duties. One member is usually secretary-treasurer; one is the labor organizer and a third is the Mukhtar, who deals with external affairs relating to the government and the neighboring Arab villages. In the larger Kvutzoth there are other Secretariat members who deal with the purchase and distribution of supplies. The Committee of Management is usually assisted by a number of small standing committees elected by the general meeting: household management, farm management, labor, education and culture. Although any working member can be elected to the Secretariat, it is usually the more experienced men and women who are elected and reelected to these posts.

Of the approximately 250 colonies and settlements that exist in Palestine at the present time, 150 have been established on the land belonging to the Jewish National Fund under a leasehold that aims at attaining the following objectives: (a) the settler who has little or no money obtains land for a farm without incurring heavy debts. The ground rent is fixed for a period of many years, so that he is protected against arbitrary increases. (b) The system assures that farms will be kept at a normal size, because the holdings can be neither enlarged nor broken up into smaller units. The soil is protected against undue exploitation. A limit is set to the farmer's indebtedness. (c) The land remains Jewish in perpetuity since it cannot be transferred to non-Jews. (d) The national interests are safeguarded in connection with the settlement project. One of the main advantages is that the fundamental principle of Jewish labor is safeguarded. (e) It provides for a just division of the increase on the value of the land. The settler receives that part of the increase which has been created through his efforts, while the balance goes to the Jewish people as the owner of the land. (f) It is a means of combating land speculation and usury.

As the site for a new settlement is chosen or when the colony is established, an appropriate Hebrew name is selected. The national settlements, built by the Keren Hayesod on the land of the Keren Kayemeth, have been given their names by a Place Names Committee that functions as the headquarters of the Jewish National Fund in Jerusalem and is comprised of representatives of the Keren Kayemeth Lesisrael, the Zionist Executive and the Keren Hayseod, the [illegible] Le'Umi, the Federation of Agricultural Workers, Hebrew University and the Jewish Society for the Exploration of Palestine and its Antiquities. The names are derived either from names known in the ancient history of Palestine or from local place names. In some cases they embody allusions to the topographical conditions of the environment. In other cases the settlements bear the names of generous donors who made possible the acquisition of the land or [the names] of the men and women who gained distinction in the leadership of the Zionist movement.

Mary Fels: A Study in Jewish Womanhood (1927)
Chapter I

It was one of the young German writers of the Nineteenth Century who uttered the paradox: the Jewish question and the woman question are identical. Both are eternal, both are complicated and both are almost unsolvable. Strangely enough, the author in whose mind this paradox was born was, at the same time, an anti-feminist and, although not an anti-Semite, was certainly not a friend of the Jews. Unwittingly, he paid a compliment to both.

Half of humanity – one might be surprised to realize the literal meaning of this statement – half of humanity is feminine. It is hard to realize this in a man's world. The difference between man and woman, economically, culturally, politically and even linguistically, has been so striking in the course of mankind's history that this fact has not only been ignored, but almost forgotten. A study of the lore and culture of antiquity would reveal the fact that this fundamental principle in God's creation has been persistently overlooked to the injustice of the fair sex and to the harm of the race in general.

Beginning with Greece, where the Spartan law required that newborn girls be killed, through pre-Christian Rome, where the woman did not appear as an individual, to the time of Christianity, when the woman, although recognized as a factor for the upbuilding of the church, was denied her natural privileges, not to mention the age-old traditions and customs of China, Japan and Tibet, this attitude was maintained.

Strange indeed are the ways of history.

The early recorders of Christian tradition definitely state the attitude of the founder of the Christian church toward his mother. When, surrounded by his disciples, announcing the arrival of the Kingdom of Heaven, he was informed that his mother was waiting outside, he declared harshly: "Who is my mother?" Pointing to his disciples, "You are my mother, brothers and sisters." He refused to see his mother. The realization, on the other hand, of the doctrines of the Galilean teacher, with all its accompanying features, created a contrasting fact. The Galilean woman whose son refused to see her was elevated to the height of the Madonna, the inspiring personality of the Catholic church, the object of adoration and exaltation, standing out as a symbol throughout the ages to millions of men, as if intended to be a compensation for the wrong and injustice done her and her sisters since the time of Eve.

A single exception must be recorded. It occurred within that tribe or tribes that were the antecedents of what later became known as Semites and, subsequently, Jews. In contradistinction to many Aryan languages, "man" and "woman" in the Semitic dialects are not two different words, but merely the masculine and feminine forms, respectively, of one root: *Ish*, a man; *Ishah*, a woman. This is not an accident. Students of early philology know that the sounds that later formed words were not accidents, but were direct results of the emotions and feelings of the primitive human being. The beautiful legend of Genesis that has remained unparalleled ever since in any lore of any people bears testimony to this observation. The Bible distinctly declares that "This will be called Ishah because she was taken from Ish."

Even that part of the description that remained in the minds of many as the lasting burden upon the woman, giving birth to the theory of sin in the mind of the tribe that created it, has a redeeming feature. The "sin" committed by Eve was nothing more than a striving for knowledge.

Apparently there is a fundamental difference in the conception and in the attitude toward the woman. The paradox of the German writer of the relation between the Jewish question and the woman question has, therefore, a deeper significance.

What has been the status of the Jewish woman? What of her achievements? Her struggles? Her privileges? Her disabilities? Her continuous progress and her particular distinctions?

I became deeply interested in the question when by chance of fate I was privileged to know the singularly brilliant and striking personality of one American Jewish woman: Mary Fels. Her life story runs through the romance of America's industrial, social, cultural, and political life. Out of the midst of industrial success, out of the victory of material advantage, Mary Fels succeeded in plunging across the cleavage that existed between materialism and the spirit. With a deep devotion, with an unlimited kindliness and charm, with a mind penetrative of problems affecting not only the social group in which she was reared, but of those affecting the rest of humanity, the life story of Mary Fels could be told to any group and in any language with a similar appeal.

What was the background that was favorable to the development of such a personality? What were the traditions that could nourish the kindliness of such a heart? What were the arteries that supplied the strength to this world-embracing mind? What was the racial stock that furnished the mental energy and vision required to grapple with the problems of the world?

The gallery of Biblical women and those Jewish women who followed throughout the history of the race furnish the background. No racial group can count in its national history as many heroines who are held in reverence, not only by their own race, but by humanity as a whole, as can the Jewish race. This distinction made itself felt even in that part of the lore that might be called Jewish mythology. In contradistinction to the heroines of Greek mythology, Diana, Athena, Rhea, Artemis, Aphrodite, and Leto – who were considered at least as demigods – the heroines of the Jewish race were and were considered purely human. Their being humans and their being a part of humanity was given expression by their having conferred upon them the "Motherhood of the Nation." Jewish lore invokes simultaneously the fatherhood of Abraham, Isaac and Jacob, and the motherhood of Sarah, Rebecca, Leah and Rachel.

The tradition was continued throughout the ages. Of the western nations, France holds the distinction of having as her heroine the canonized Jeanne d'Arc. Jewish tradition knows more than one. As a symbol of motherly devotion, unassailable by danger, we are told of Yocheved, the mother of Moses. As a symbol of sisterly attachment and prudence, we retain the picture of Miriam, Moses' sister, who knew to "stand at a distance."

As a singer of national unity and victory, there is heard through the ages the song of Deborah, flowing like the ancient river Kishon, which inspired her. As examples of self-sacrificing heroism in time of war, shining from afar, are the prophetesses Chuldah and the beautiful daughter of Zion, Judish. As a suffering, devoted and faithful wife in the time of famine, there stands out Naomi, the sweet. The story of Ruth attracts us an idyll. As saviors from persecution emerge the graceful Esther and her legendary double, Estherke, the wife of Kazimierz the Great in Poland. As the helpful mate of the scholar there appears Brurya, the wife of Rabbi Meir. As a leader in letters stands the daughter of Rashi in Twelfth Century France, and, as a leader of men, stands Eidel, the daughter of the Baal Shem, when the foundations of the Hassidic movement were laid.

Unmentioned, but well known, is the legion of Jewish women who, in times of oppression and danger, took upon their shoulders the protection of their families. Familiar is the picture of the Jewish woman, still to be found, who, in order to enable her husband and sons to acquire the culture of the race, undertakes the burden of the provider.

Whenever Jewish life was at a crossroad, the Jewish woman made her appearance. When the epoch of enlightenment dawned, following the long period of Middle Age darkness and lawlessness, the Jewish woman in the *aufklaerungs* [enlightenment] epoch took her position in the vanguard. When Jewish life began to develop in the new world, an intellectually and emotionally strong group of Jewish women attended the birth of the new community.

Where lies the cause for this difference?

It lies, first, in the outlook on the world that grew out of the race psychology and in the lore, customs and laws that regulated the life of the Jewish woman.

One of the most ancient documents concerning the rights of women, the popular *Ketubah*, which enumerates in the marriage contract the rights and privileges of the bride-to-be, contains a significant clause: *K'orach Gavrin Yehudain* ("as is the custom of Jewish men"). It is on that custom that the background for this phenomenon is based. To understand the conditions that produced this attitude toward the Jewish woman, to fully appreciate the background as well as the achievements, and to tell the life story of Mary Fels, this volume will be dedicated.

Chapter II

What was the status of the Jewish woman in Jewish lore, Jewish law, Jewish society and the Jewish home?

Of all the revelations that mankind's history has regarded as divine, the revelation at Mount Sinai has made its strongest impression on the human mind.

Out of the thunder and storm, mankind received what is usually termed the Ten Commandments through the Hebrew channel. Much of the cultural, political and economic conditions that underlie the structure of organized society rests upon the principles of these Commandments, the necessity of which now appears self-evident.

"Thou shalt not kill. Thou shalt not steal and thou shalt not covet" have assumed universal significance.

It was, and still is, different with the Commandment, "Thou shalt honor they father and thy mother." This Commandment was indeed a commandment to be obeyed and drilled into ancient society. The status of woman in pagan antiquity, and even into Christian medieval times, was little different from that of property and slaves. Not to mention the status of women in the Sumerian, Babylonian and Egyptian civilizations; as late as the Roman Empire, the conception of family as consisting of man, wife and child, as individuals with equal rights, duties and privileges, did not exist. The Latin expression *famulum* meant nothing more than "property."

With this commandment, the liberation of the Jewish woman and, ultimately, women in general, began.

Varied indeed has been the situation of the Jewish woman throughout the recorded ages. In accordance with the conditions of the time and environment, it underwent the necessary changes.

The note, however, struck in the fourth Commandment remained as a tremendous influence in formulating the attitude, the status, the condition and the appreciation of the Jewish woman.

Faced by the environment of the cave man's world, the ancient custom of the Israelite tribes did not entirely abolish the dependence of woman. It merely went to the extent of limiting this dependence. The father was the master of his daughter. He had, indeed, the right to sell her. This right, however, was limited to six years and with the understanding that the future master, or his son, would marry her. Should he fail to do so at the expiration of the period, the girl was freed for "he has dealt with her deceitfully." This was only applicable to the daughter who had not attained majority, that is, twelve and a half years. If the daughter reached this age in her father's home, she could not be sold. The father had the right to betroth his daughter before her majority, with the understanding, however, that the engagement could be canceled should she, upon attaining her majority, not desire to marry her betrothed. The choice of Isaac by Rebecca is an example that has been followed.

When Abraham's emissary came from Palestine to Mesopotamia to his relatives to ask for the hand of Rebecca for his son, Isaac, the girl's parents immediately declared: "We will call the damsel and inquire at her mouth," a privilege that was not granted to sons.

"The price of the virgins," the old established payment of the bridegroom to the bride's father, was soon changed into the dowry. As early as the time of Solomon, this institution of dowry brought by the bride into her husband's family was, it seems, well established. The position of the married woman naturally improved when she brought her husband a dower instead of being purchased by him.

The Hebrew word *Shilluchim*, which literally means "the dismissal," was soon out of taste. The dismissal dowry was soon substituted by the Babylonian word *Nedunyia*, which was meant to be the father's bestowing on the daughter such gifts as would inure to the husband's benefit. In Jewish life, it early became customary for the father to return to the husband the "price" that he obtained from the bridegroom. The "price" gradually developed into the dowry. The dowry became the wife's "insurance policy," strangely enough the first social insurance, which was to be returned to her in the event of her husband's death, prior to every other obligation his estate might have incurred. This "policy" was also to be paid in case of divorce. This clause made divorce difficult and often impractical, although the Jewish conception of marriage was far from adhering to the principle "What God has joined together let no man put asunder."

Another distinction must be noted. It found expression in the popular definition of marriage.

"Before the law was given, a man could have walked along in the marketplace and met a woman. If he desired to take her, and if she agreed, he could bring her to his home and she became his wife by mutual agreement. Since the law was given, the Jews were ordered that if a Jewish man wants to take a woman, he must purchase her first before witnesses, and afterward she would become his wife."

In these few words, Maimonides, the Twelfth Century codifier of Jewish law, expresses the difference between common-law marriage and Jewish marriage. Simultaneously, a new word came into use for the marriage ceremony. It was no longer a "taking" but a sanctification: *Kiddushin*.

One sixth of the collection of Jewish laws in the Mishna and Talmud are devoted to the subject of marriage and women's rights. The forms of marriage were treated in a special tractate named *Kiddushin*. This treatment of marriage as a sanctification, the rights and the respect accorded to the mother, the right of choice to the daughter, led to the creation of a wholesome family life within Jewry. A bride groom was, according to ancient law, to be released from military service for one year. The priests, who were prohibited from attending funerals or remaining under the same roof with the unburied dead, were not only allowed, but were instructed to attend the funerals of their wives, although they became, in accordance with the priestly law, tainted.

Numerous are the songs in world literature devoted to the description and admiration of woman. Poetry, modern poetry in particular, had its inspiration in woman. Her beauty, her charm, have been the object of poets' and artists' adoration. Unparalleled, however, remains the ancient Jewish ode to woman that, while appreciating her beauty and charm, proclaims that "charm is deceitful and beauty is vain."

This ode, which dates back to almost a primitive stage of civilization,[1] repeated for centuries in Jewish homes on every Friday evening by the husband as part of the ritual in honor of the "Sabbath princess," stands alone in its tribute to woman:

Who can find a virtuous woman
For her price is far above rubies.
The Heart of her husband safely trusts in her
So that he shall have no need of spoil.
She will do him good and not evil
All the days of her life.
She seeks wool and flax,
Works willingly with her hands
She is like the merchants' ships
She brings her food from afar.
She rises with the dawn
Gives meat to her household
And a portion to her maidens.
She sees a field and buys it.
With the fruit of her hands she plants a vineyard
She girds her loins with strength
And strengthens her arms.
She perceives that her merchandise is good
Her candle goeth not out by night
She lays her hand to the spindle
And her hands hold the distaff.
She stretches out her hand to the poor
Yea, she reaches forth her hands to the needy
Not afraid of the snow for her household
For all her household are clothed with scarlet.
She makes coverings of tapestry
Her clothing is silk and purple.
Her husband is known in the gates
He sits among the elders of the land.
She makes fine linen and sells it,
Delivers girdles unto the merchant.
Strength and honor are her clothes.
She will rejoice in time to come.

She opens her mouth with wisdom
And her tongue is the law of kindness.
She looks well to the ways of her household
And eats not the bread of idleness.
Her children rise and call her blessed,
Her husband also praises her

---

[1] Proverbs 3:15.

Many daughters have done well
But you excel them all.
Deceitful is charm and vain is beauty,
But a woman that fears the lord
She will be praised.
Give her the fruit of her hands
And let her work praise her in the gates.

Polygamy, which was not prohibited in the original law, was not, it seems, generally practiced during the second Commonwealth. In all the records of the rabbis and leaders who shaped the fate of the nation, polygamy is never mentioned.

The wives of the leaders and rabbis are held in almost equal reverence with them. Frequently they are mentioned as participating in the work of their distinguished husbands. "His house – that means his wife" was an interpretation reached by the Talmudists, not only in their method of exegesis, but in the way of life, as well. The Biblical definition of the woman ("a help against him") was interpreted in Jewish tradition to mean that the choice is offered: if he is worthy, he has the privilege of her being a help to him. If he is not worthy, she is against him. To establish on firm foundations the rights and privileges of woman, so that she should be a help for the man, Jewish tradition has missed no occasion. Both in the laws of marriage and in the laws of inheritance, property division, economic participation and social position, the interests of the woman were zealously guarded. The "Ketubah," one of the most ancient forms of contract, is a document of which the liberality, foresight and precision has not been surpassed.

The six hundred and thirteen ordinances that were intended to regulate the life of the individual Jew and that created a discipline and formed the hardiness of the Jewish character do not, it is true, apply to the Jewish woman. Of the six hundred and thirteen, only three were assigned as her immediate obligation. They were the lighting of candles, the purity of family life, and the dedication of the family bread – three essential conditions for the growth and fostering of a healthy atmosphere in the home and the development of a strong generation.

"Women are merciful" is a saying that goes through all Jewish literature. "For the sake of the righteous women our forefathers were liberated from Egypt" is another. "Treat the woman gently for her tears grow hot" is another. "If your wife is of small statue, bow when you speak to her" is an oft-repeated command of gallantry. "Let each man honor his wife as himself and love her more than himself." "The custom of the man is to court the woman." These are only a few of the gems of the gallantry with which the woman in the family was honored.

This treatment had its effect. It created proverbial Jewish family life, unadulterated and unassailed, even by the forces of danger. The records of the Inquisition, the documents of the Crusader period, contain the names of as many women as men who preferred death at their own hands or at the hands of their oppressors to betrayal of their family faith and culture.

Chapter III: The Beginning of a Romance

It was the second half of the nineteenth century. Leading minds in European culture were being rapidly emancipated from the rationalist doctrine that undertook to solve all the puzzles of mankind by the application of pure reason. An age of ferment and doubt followed the years of certainty and dictatorship. While in the eighteenth century the French school of rationalists dominated the intellectual world and kept the huge mass of humanity in a stagnant position, the middle of the nineteenth century saw the world preparing for its new age.

Inquiry, instead of ready-made opinions, doubt instead of disbelief, in the world of the intellect, was murmuring beneath the surface that rapidly expressed itself in open ferment and revolt in the field of politics.

Aged Europe, which had just emerged from the dark Middle Ages, quickly entangled itself in various holy and unholy alliances, which culminated in the World War.

Driven by intellectual unrest, economic need and the everlasting search for the unknown, great masses of Europe's population transplanted themselves to the New World.

The New World, with its vast territory, rich resources and virgin soil, entered into the great day of its promise. Sailing vessels, in a fight against the elements, brought shiploads of the best of Europe's human material, the most capable, the most promising and the best fit, because they were dissatisfied and daring.

Into the components of the new republic, cemented by "Hebrew mortar," a small stream of Hebrew element flowed.

This element had not an easy task before it.

Fleeing from political oppression, which followed the Prussian Revolution of 1848, uprooted by the economic destruction that followed it, driven by the doubt of the future, the handful of Jewish refugees from Germany found themselves bewildered. The small group of Dutch, Spanish and Portuguese refugees who preceded them, extended, indeed, its hospitality to the newcomers. However, this hospitality corresponded with their means. But backed by an age-old tradition, with an innate love for freedom, desire for education, hardiness of stock and eagerness for hard work, the newcomers soon adapted themselves to the new world.

The command of Jeremiah given to the exiles in Babylon ("Build houses and take unto yourselves wives and pray for the peace of the city") was speedily carried out.

The Jewish refugees from the western countries who filtered in sought their opportunity for freedom and reconstruction on the wide, open, unbuilt spaces of the new republic.

On one of those sailing vessels a Jewish family from Sembach, Germany, was brought to the shores of America. A member of this family was the three-year-old Mary Fels.

The Fels family found in the new country an environment that, although it was full of ferment similar to that which they had left behind, had the distinction that the principle of liberty had already triumphed.

The effects of the Civil War, which had been concluded a year before, were beginning to be felt. For the first time in the history of mankind, slavery was abolished by the proclamation of Abraham Lincoln, giving rise to similar steps all over the world. The economic results of the Civil War were dreadful. However, with the vigor characteristic of the new republic that came into its full meaning by the decision of the Civil War, substituting the form of a federation of states by "one nation, indivisible, with liberty and justice for all," developed a strong economic and intellectual activity.

Out of the misery of the war, the foundations for greater prosperity were emerging. Liberty and equality were the slogans of the day, privileges appreciated and enjoyed with eagerness and enthusiasm by the Hebrew element.

The Fels family joined the stream of those young men and women who went west. Soon they were established in the State of Iowa, the fertile plain that grew rapidly. Its economic growth was accompanied by the growth of educational facilities.

In the town of Keokuk, on the banks of the Mississippi and the Des Moines, on the wide, fertile plain, Mary Fels was reared.

America was on the eve of its great day as a leader of mankind. In these days, Mary Fels, as a pupil of the Keokuk high school, from which she graduated at the age of 16, and as a student of St. Mary's Academy, Notre Dame, Indiana, chose her own way. While still a child, Mary Fels differed from her environment and went along the untrodden road. From the bluffs of the Mississippi banks, looking toward the fertile plains of Iowa, Mary had visions of the future. On the fertile plains of Iowa, with no mountains to obstruct the view, the girl dreamed and had her visions of America, of her people, of mankind.

Naturally, her Prince Charming would come across these plains.

And it came to pass.

A young man, twenty years of age, born and reared in this new country, a son of one of the first families who settled in the South, traveled in the Southern and Mid-Western cities to sell the products of a coffee firm in whose employ he was. He was a pleasant and likable chap. As a pupil in the public school he had left his mark early. His father, however, decided that the best field for the lad was commerce. Joseph Fels was the name of the boy.

Swift of motion, a pleasant conversationalist, an excellent salesman, he sold not only the goods of his firm, but his personality as well. His circle of friends grew with every town he visited.

One day in 1872 he passed through Keokuk, Iowa. Conversing with one of his customers, after the usual courtesies had been exchanged, the buyer, learning the young man's name, hastened to inform him that there was a Jewish family in the town bearing the same name – Fels.

With the family love peculiar to the Jewish race, Joseph left his business and his prospects, and hastened to visit the house and to get acquainted with these people who were, perhaps, members of his family.

When he reached the door of the house and pulled the knocker, a charming little girl came out to open the door and usher him [in] to her father and mother.

He was twenty; she was nine. His name was Joseph Fels; her name, Mary Fels. They became acquainted.

The child remained in her room, busy with her school books and probably dreams of that young prince who would some day come and take her to his castle. No one could foresee that the results of this meeting would be important not only to the pair, but would perhaps constitute one step forward in the social order of humanity.

The young man spoke to her parents about the topics of the day – it was an important epoch in the history of the country. When he departed, he promised to return in due time. However, every year the young traveler came back to Keokuk, with the regularity of a clock. When he came, he did not fail to visit the house of Mary. Nine years he came and went and then, on November 16, 1881, the two were married.

"When I saw that little girl I decided that she would some day be my wife," Joseph Fels testified after many years.

Thus began the beautiful romance on the banks of the Mississippi.

Conclusion[2]

There is a distinct difference between the literature of the ancient Greeks and the ancient Hebrews. While the Greeks indulged in indefinite meditation over abstract

---

[2] Though not titled or numbered, this chapter reads like it was intended to be the book's last.

questions that resulted in the creation of the philosophic schools, the Hebrews, indulging in meditation, had for their theme the way of life. The Jewish thinkers in the early ages strove not to create systems of philosophy but a system of life. This trait was responsible for the production of the typically Hebrew wisdom literature, instead of a literature of philosophy. It is, instead of a literature of philosophy, a philosophical literature.

It is characteristic that, while the names of the early Greeks who laid the foundations of Greek philosophy, civics and art, were preserved and handed down through the generations, the Hebrew wisdom literature, with only a few exceptions, is anonymous. It is the task that scientific workers have taken upon themselves, to discover [rest of this paragraph lost].

[Beginning of this paragraph lost] philosophy of the individual's life, but with his way of life. *U'vacharta Bachaim* – "and thou shall choose life."

Thus, it became possible that the wisdom literature of the race carried not the names but sayings, and not books but thoughts. Obadiah, a simple peasant of the plain who "heard a rumor from the Lord," has become a messenger and his single chaptered work found its place within the people's sacred literature. A saying of only a few words by the wise was cherished and preserved.

The life and the work of each individual constitute a hymn to the Creator, says the Hassidic doctrine. However, not all hymns are expressed. It is the quality of the hymn that brings about its expression and it is its tone that creates its resonance. Not all hymns have been sung, not all are being sung, because not all are of the proper quality.

The life and work of Mary Fels, as depicted, constituted a rising song, which is in itself expressive enough and resounding.

Mary Fels, however, has done more than mere living; she has, in addition to creating an example in achievements and in addition to stimulating the broadminded vision of others, reached that degree of expression that is innate only in the few. From the height of her exemplary life, experience in all climates and contact with the best circles of living humanity, Mary Fels lived, observed and thought about the eternal problems of God, religion, love, [word lost], justice, the fate of the Jewish race, Palestine and their destinies.[3]

In our daily life with its numerous activities, attending lectures and banquets, going to religious services and taking up University courses, we slip into the habit of thinking that we know God and that we serve Him. Yet most of us are restless, excitable, full of yearning, and all the time a vague sense of dissatisfaction gnaws in us to the very depths of our soul. It is the urge toward God. For this is certain: we are not living in harmony with Him, nor are we even near Him. Hence the soul's prodding to keep us in the quest for, and in harmony with, God. In this quest two great obstacles stand in mankind's way. One is the alien attitude of science. How absurd this attitude, how unthinking! For, what is science but man's mind on the trail of God's laws? Every discovery is a perception of the working of His laws. One set of sciences follows this working in the world of mind and spirit; another seeks clue after clue in the material universe; both try to know and understand and utilize, being on the quest for human betterment to the end, consciously or unconsciously, of getting nearer to God.

The other, and greater, obstacle is in the way man obscures God. When Pompey forced his way into the Holy of Holies of the Temple of Jerusalem, he was struck by the complete absence of any image of God. Not even with an image does Israel obscure its God, much less by beings. Its prophets are its prophets, from Abraham to the more recent Son of

---

[3] The rest of this chapter is made up of quotations from Mary Fels' book *Toward the Light* (New York: G. Dobsevage, 1927).

Man. And all are servants of God, adoring Him alone, loving Him "with all thine heart and all thy soul and all thy might," and, impelled by this love for Him, they serve his children by teaching "these words that I command thee," and by love and sympathy and active helpfulness. Every nation has its prophets to the degree of its own degree; the One God is God of all nations. Father of all, and under this Fatherhood all men are brothers.

The One and its unity is a fact simple enough. Truth has always that simplicity. One must, however, be standing in the light to see it. If one admits mists into thought, feeling, and doings, vision becomes obscured, of course. In the light of clear, healthy thinking, one sees that, as the sun is the center of God's material universe, so God in His Oneness is that of his spiritual one. It is this Oneness at the center that puts everything proceeding from it into proper place and brings about true function. We know how true this is in the material universe; why not see how the Law, governing everything everywhere, makes it so in spirit? When one comes into the light and the healthy working of this thinking, then one is on one's way to God. Then one stands in the Light, walks in the Light, works in the Light, and there is no longer stumbling. The spirit is at rest and the heart very happy.

There should be a time every day, when we are all alone, for facing ourselves, feeling the nearness of God. Wise Law, religious Law, sets aside a day a week for this, but every day should provide for it. It would sanctify every day, make it both holy and healthy, for the one brings about the other.

A woman just told me of her "beloved dog" and how she "adored him." The adoration that should go to her God she gives to a dog; the love that should reach out to God and her fellow-men is spent on a dog. What an abomination! She talks about the dog having better qualities than people. Of course, putting the dog in place of man leads to perversion of thought and feeling. She demeans man in the interest of the dog. Her feelings exercise themselves in the world of dog instead of that of man. We should by all means be kind to dogs, to all animals, when they happen to come our way, but to live with them, that is another matter; to love them should be impossible to us. Man only can be our companion, calling out our love and service. No lesser love should satisfy our craving for him.

God's ways are not "inscrutable." It is we who lack light and power for seeing. So we start with wrong premises and end in ignorance and confusion. We talk of the "mystery of the unseen," unmindful of our own inability to see. As if God were not clear as his day if only we did not mar our faculty for clear seeing. We mar it by wrong thinking, perverted feeling and bad living. We are given free will and choice to make or mar, and we mostly mar our lives. Who keeps himself simple, straight-forward, altogether natural? Who lives life in such a way as to keep the sluices of our being open, clean and clear? How to know God save through a pure spirit and its true-to-God thinking? But we are busy all the time obscuring God. We put the tenets of such-and-such church in place of God. We look to mediators instead of to God, Himself. We offer Him formalisms instead of fervent devotion. We do not turn to Him in the depths of our being but say other people's prayers to Him. How can the light from Him enter into us when we do not turn to Him in all our own inmost self? In great silence within and without, all alone, we should stand before the One God, if we would hear and be heard.

As one reads the newspapers and finds page upon page devoted to racing, to contests of so many sorts, one finds them always in the realm of our outer self. Yet it is the inner self that prompts to them. There is an inner urge toward the good, toward God, which impels people, and they make the sad mistake of thinking this outer excitement will meet the inner need. Far from it: the former only leads away from the latter. What is wanting, and so causes the mistake, is self-knowledge and wisdom. "Know thyself," and learn the laws of life, and the true fount of inspiration will open up. When this is released then one enters into true, serene self-direction. When a goodly number have thus arrived, true standards will be set up. Contests will be along the line of inner achievement. Faculties of the soul, not prowess of body, will be the contestants. Deep emulation will take the place of militant rivalry, and States will have cultural patriotism, not cold, cruel, political patriotism.

Take care that your life turns in its own orbit. "Know thyself" and live life true to yourself. Your life-mates should be of your own kind, else it will be with you as with a plant out of its own habitat. Growth will be arrested. Man needs to secure for himself both physical and mental home-atmosphere, else he does not breathe well. The society of his peers is his society. He may, on occasion, meet any other kind of society, and any other kind of person. This he should do for the deepening and lengthening of his horizon, but he must not live there, he must return to his own orbit, there to rotate, to enact life. You do not help, but hinder another by invading his orbit; you injure both yourself and others by being out of place. From your own citadel you can command the situation and can act in the light thus gained.

There are within us possible powers of such clear perception that we cannot only see into and through things, but perceive far forward. These powers are not to be developed by incantations and observances of a particular kind, but by all of life. Purity in life attains this pure vision: purity of body, mind and spirit. Purity of body through not introducing drugs of any sort, and by averting all grossness in either desire or satisfaction of desire. Purity of mind by abstaining from falsehood in thought and act. Purity of spirit by being pure in spirit and living, unfailingly, true to it. Thus the sluices of our being are kept open and clear, and the light shines in, and from, and upon us, and we see accordingly.

Asceticism is not purity. Purity must be spontaneously of the spirit, and not a cult through which rigidly to put ourselves. Asceticism kills spontaneity where there should be constructivity; it induces self consciousness where there should be child-like unconsciousness; it sows distrust to displace trust; and it makes faith a matter of formula instead of a spirited turning to God. It denies the holy passion of love. Asceticism and sensuality confound the latter with the cold lust of passion-apart-from-love. Sensuality especially, having sold its birthright of love for a mess of lust, proceeds to demean the God-given passion.

With purity of life there is always consecration of life. It goes with desire to devote oneself, at one's best, to the service of God, and our fellow-men – God's children. Negative consecration would go with negative purity, and active consecration with real purity. The former is of the darkness of life, the latter is the clear light of life. The one segregates itself, withdraws from life; the other is of life and gives itself to life, to mankind. The one mumbles formulae; the other acts. The latter diligently seeks what and how and where to do; the former has "principles" wherewith to cloak inactivity. One is muddily selfish; the other "thinketh in his heart" constantly.

Hillel, that very good and very wise man, said: "Love of the neighbor is the whole Law." He meant, of course, the neighbor throughout the universe. This love is one with the Fatherhood of God. Realization of the Oneness of God, Father of all, brings with it realization of the brotherhood of man. Each people may have its own great interpreter of God and call him [a] prophet, but they all interpret, try to bring near their fellow-men, the One God. These prophets (which means forth-tellers) are nearer the divine through their love and understanding, but they must not be put in place of God. It is the worst impiety and becomes most confounding. God ceases to be to them the One God, Father of us all, and in this alienation men cease to be brothers.

Deeply inherent in love for God is appreciation and admiration of His natural world. We are moved to prayer by its beauty. Love for our Creator rises powerfully in us as this beauty bursts upon us. So it is with human love. What deep, glowing appreciation we have for every charm of the loved one! It is right that we should have keener eyes for this charm and that it should be transfigured in our sight.

Faith is proof of love. This applies to human love as to the Divine. Faith is evidence of things undefined, rather than of "things unseen." Thus it is witness to great things, those that beggar definition and description. To think to do the latter amounts to a denial – "to define God is to deny Him." And love is the light whereby and wherein one sees clearly, deeply, according to its degree. That explains how it is "he who knows all pardons all," for he sees and knows because he loves, and by virtue of this love he wishes to "pardon all." Like God again who in His love is infinitely forgiving.

In the contests of physical prowess life itself is waged, not to speak of inroads on health, maimed limbs and shattered nerves. What iniquity! Is not this to be counted criminal as we estimate deliberate suicide to be? In the latter case there is more likelihood of sudden or prolonged irresponsibility. There is no such palliative for the former.

One who can speak of religion "as an adventure" has not real religion. For religion is all of life. It is one with every part of life and must be at one with the whole of life. An adventure goes out from life but religion is that to which all life goes out or, rather, goes in. Religion is our relation to God and the right relation of everything in life to this. It is a constant circling around God and gravitation toward Him. So it is in everything we are and everything we do.

Faith is the witness to what is too large to define. By loyalty to this faith we grow toward the larger and thus comes increase of understanding leading to knowledge. Faith in formalisms can have no such growth, for formalisms are ossifications of life.

It is not the earth, earthy feminine, but the "eternal feminine" that leads us onward, upward. We think we see this eternal in beauty and we are right in so expecting: the eternal should express itself in beauty as God does in nature. God's nature is everywhere beautiful, until man comes to mar it, in his stupid materiality. Thus the beauty of human beings is so often marred – by themselves, by society. Then it loses beauty's power and ceases to attract, even to the degree of becoming repulsive.

Real religion entails sacrifice and suffering. One cannot otherwise find God. Not needless suffering but that which comes to sensitive souls in the course of the depths of life. God is all love and beneficence and has provided in our nature that we shall not suffer needlessly. If we are not ready for the lesson of suffering then it is withheld – by our nature, subject to God's laws. Those who may have their prosperity are spared troubles of this life, but what of their inner prosperity, what of [their] capacity for [the] joys of this or any other life? On the way to God is the only true prosperity, the only deep, lasting happiness. So one can suffer and be happy; give up all and have all. But to be intent on what you may gain by your religion is impious. What you may give, how you may get ever-nearer to God, to what service to Him and His children your love for and devotion to God should impel you, this is the way to Him. To count neither cost nor gain but just to offer yourself wholly, gladly, lovingly, as He gives to us. It is the way of true earthly love. The way toward God should be not less but greater, infinitely greater.

"Whosoever drinketh of the water that I shall give him shall never thirst." It is the spirit of God that Jesus offers here. To partake of it is to come home. All cravings are for our home in God. We mistake them for what they are not and thus lose our way. To wander farther and farther out of our way by our mode of life and by departure from truth in our thinking and feeling. There is only one way back to our center: "To worship God in spirit and in truth." But it must be in truth and in spirit. Not by mumbling made-to-order prayers, nor by filling life with formalisms of every sort. Only when we are, spontaneously, on our knees in spirit should we approach God. Only in directing every craving toward God shall we find ourselves near to God. Then all of life will fall into harmony and we are at home.

When we shall worship God in spirit and in truth then we shall serve Him in a living way, by devotion to Him and His children, our fellow men. That living service is all too rare. We fail in it constantly toward our fellow men, living and dead. We have stony hearts toward the living and we erect monuments of stone to the dead. A living memorial is the only kind worthy of living beings, whether they are with us here or have gone Beyond. Better name after him the street in or near which he lived than to erect some obstruction in stone, for the one comes into our life and the other we pass by carelessly. But better set to work the noble ideas that he had and do, as far as we may and can, that which he longed to do. Thus he remains in our lives, the living factor that he was, and the memory of him does not become part of a tombstone or a static statue.

To the good God a deliberate Hell is impossible. We, in our wickedness, fashion one out of our thought and ascribe its creation to Him. Our Hell is here. We make it by our marring of God's world. God's world is altogether good, save where we mar it. We do this by ignorantly and carelessly breaking God's laws. These Laws are so beneficent: they make for goodness, and glory, and consequent happiness. But we break them, and then we suffer, and slowly, through that suffering, we learn. So breaking God's Laws becomes our Hell: the mount of Purgatory down which we fall, and up which, in good time, we climb toward redemption. It is God's Law of growth. The seed goes down into the ground and its fruit pushes its way up out of the earth. So with the spirit; once out of the earth it can look toward the heavens and procede on its struggle God-wards. It must free itself from earth encumbrances, not add to them, as we are so prone to do. And what are such encumbrances? Loving the material rather than the spiritual; frustrating the spirit by meeting it with spirits, alcoholic and narcotic; upsetting the spirit by excitements in place of inspiritings. It is the spirit in us that gives the monitions; the body can only be a sort of interpreter; we must listen with understanding and solicitude. Do we? No, we jump about, we jazz, we smoke, we drink, we overeat. We listen-in to all sorts of sounds, and fail the one Reality, the inner call, "the wee small voice" that comes of the great Dominant Tone.

What about this art of life? It should aim at this: that man and woman should never cease to approach each other with love, reverence, awe. They must guard vigilantly against the commonplace in their relations, and familiarity should be a crime. Familiarity in marriage is indeed a crime, for it kills beautiful, wonderful love. By it love becomes a common thing – it ceases to be love and remains, if at all, as affection. Then the good of marriage is gone; it is no longer the deep inspirer and great creator, but only something more or less comforting, deadening. This cannot be endured by the better man and woman; they get out of it, but alas! only to repeat the same blind experience with another. They will learn in time, after a long time of suffering, but whence and from whom comes light on their path? Not from the novel, which should deal just with this.

One cannot too much stress the importance of after-marriage. The stories lead up to marriage, and there they stop. They spend their force in a long elaboration of the lovemaking about which we all know, but the love-preserving of which we know all too little, they say nothing. These two people with this precious thing stumble along unenlightened by either their own preparation in thought or by experience of others. Who thinks of conserving love? Yet what is more, or nearly as much, worth every care and endeavor? Where does the art of life need to be more solicitously practiced than in preserving that sacred fire, ignited by the fusion of a man and a woman, on which rests the race? on which rests not only mankind in itself, but in his turning towards God?

Reading novels, romances, any long drawn-out fiction, and short stories also, is another way of killing time, and injuring eternity. It leaves no deposit and is far from being an uplift or any kind of inspiration. They may have a part or parts well worth reading, but to get a good effect from them you must cut them out, disassociate them from the long context. Such excellent parts are to be found in George Eliot's books almost more than in any other. Our interest in the life and experience of persons should be directed toward living beings, not used up in reading about fictitious ones. One is reminded at this point of how human emotion when expended on dogs instead of on human beings subjects itself to lamentable perversion. Even if we are quite alone in this world, better, a thousand times better, to long for human love and companionship than fall back on something less. Acceptance of the lower undoes you for the higher. When your love goes out to a dog, your love and sympathy for the human becomes impaired. Be kind to animals but love and live with your fellow creatures, in thought, feeling, act.

Instead of ending in marriage, the novel should begin with it. To be worth reading, books should teach while they interest and entertain. There is dire need on the part of all to learn the conduct of married life and the meaning of marriage. Long ago, I[4] found myself saying, "I would go to the stake for monogamy." I know now, clearly and definitely, what made me say it. Sex-love must be for one only, for it is the love that brings us nearest to God. When we, particles of God, are thrown off to become human beings, it is, one surmises, then that we are divided into male and female. The round of our human life is that search for the other half whereby we are to get back to God. Hence the force and the persistence of the sex craving. It is the noblest desire of our nature, and suffers the worst demeaning, especially in some marriages. There it becomes common in every sense. For we fail to hold ourselves to our highest just where we should be at our best. The art of life ends where marriage begins. Marriage, sex relations, becomes an end in itself, instead of a means to the end of finding God. We should demand that marriage is the meeting of the spirit, and shrink with horror from physical mating that is not the reflex of this. "Our wishes are our prophets." We find the mate by way of love. There must be no sex mating without sex love. The mating accomplished, it must be conserved by everything that is best in us. Beauty, rectitude, wisdom, constantly ready to pay tribute of every sort. If the books portrayed this, how they would lend themselves to the rectitude of life, to the fulfillment of Law, the finding of God – and Heaven.

Our institutions, whether of church or state or society, do not belie us. They express the general. When they no longer do so, there comes a break-up. There are always individuals who run ahead of the average advance, and these make that shining minority whose light and force guide and propel [mankind] into the new order. The longer the change is resisted, the greater the force of the break-up, the worse the pains of travail. For change (growth) being God's Law, and thus inevitable, is irresistible.

Any government that makes for bureaucracy is bad. Governments everywhere should, on the contrary, foster individual initiative. Only through the latter shall we ever attain cooperation, spontaneous cooperation, other than which there is no cooperation. In the field of industry especially is this indispensable. Then in time will the present vicious system of industry be displaced by a virtuous one. Here and there are already indications that this displacement is taking place. Save where willful blinders are in one's thinking, anyone can clearly see that industry depends wholly (capital and all) on the workers, and that accordingly the industry really belongs as much, if not more, to them than to any other or others. What avails brainwork without handwork; what is the latter without the former?

---

[4] Not William Z. Spiegelman, but Mary Fels, here being quoted at great and uninterrupted length.

Thus normally they are always partners. Every industry, from the simplest agriculture to the most intricate commercial enterprise, must recognize this and arrange the business code accordingly. Slavery must cease in business as in every department of life. Employer and employee must be superseded by co-worker.

Whence came disease germs but from disease? Thrown off by the diseased into the general atmosphere. Where do they attach themselves for further propagation but on soil favorable to their life? Thus those diseased or tending to disease are their victims. Accordingly, the more disease in the world the more disease germs are generated. The kind depend on the prevalence of its kind. How urgent then that society in general should protect itself against disease in general, no less than a person should be in good health not only to be immune from bad germs but also not to add any germs himself to the general stock.

How stupid then is society in not taking into its care all of society, in not providing that all of society lives under healthy conditions! It knows very well that food, warmth, air, light and sunshine are essential to health, yet it maintains a state of things wherein the mass of mankind is debarred from these. So those who have government in their hands are not shepherds of their people, nor look properly after their own interests. Thus those who have what they need – and far more than they need – are infected physically by the ill condition of those who have not what they need.

Nor does it stop at physical infection. The soul of the world is sick, both on the part of those who selfishly have and on the part of those who are blighted in mind and spirit through being deprived of what mind and spirit crave. Not only is everywhere catastrophe in consequence of this but there is a constant infection of bad, low spirit, a constant lowering of mind. What might not be the mental and moral status of man if the prevailing mental and moral atmosphere were what it should be: clear and clean, healthy and robust. Let society look to it that conditions are readjusted; that the terrible disparities of life and opportunity are done away with – displaced by equal opportunity for all.

"Your Will: A Potent Factor for Preserving Jewish Learning; A Suggestion to Men of Vision; A Guide for Legal Advisors" (1927)[5]

"In the hour of a man's decease, not silver nor gold nor precious stones and pearls accompany him, but Torah and good works alone, as it is said, 'When thou walkest, it shall lead thee, when thou liest down, it shall watch over thee; and when thou awakest, it shall talk with thee.' 'When thou walkest, it shall lead thee' – in this world. 'When thou liest down, it shall watch over thee' – in the grave. 'And when thou awakest, it shall talk with thee' – in the world to come." (Chapter of R. Meir, *Pirke Abot* 6).

Men and women of vision and understanding do not shirk from stopping in the midst of the hustle and bustle of life, to pause for a moment and think of the ultimate hour. The average man engaged either in securing or in enjoying wealth is too timid and in most cases unwilling to approach a problem that he cannot avoid. This timidity has deplorable consequences in many a case. The ultimate hour, the occurrence of which can never be determined, foretold or delayed, often finds the individual unprepared and many a cause that he cherished, for which he lived and for which he would be ready to die if need be,

---

[5] Cf. letter to WZS from B. Revel, dated October 10, 1927, elsewhere in this volume.

suffers most. The things for which he was most anxious to care in good health and with his appreciation undiminished are often neglected in that awful, short space of time that ends the earthly existence.

To the Jew and to the traditional Jew in particular, who is urged by his religious loyalty to take frequent stock, to measure his deeds, to weigh his means, to divide and to provide for present and future needs, this often-observed timidity and unwillingness to pause is an unnatural state of mind. To the Jew the life Thereafter is no jump into the unknown; it is decidedly a continuation in a form inconceivable to the human mind, unseen by the human eye but felt strongly and commandingly by the human heart.

This command of the Jewish heart that views the universe as a Oneness and life Here and Hereafter as a continuity, the latter depending upon the first, has made its indelible impression on the Jewish mind and has outlined a way and a method for the Jewish individual to pursue for the best interests of his own, his immediate family, and those causes of the Jewish community, of society and mankind at large to which he is bound and which he cherishes.

One of the most distinguishing characteristics of the Jewish mode of thought and life is that recorded of Abraham the Patriarch. The Bible tells us that one of the chief reasons for the Almighty's choice of Abraham to bring before him the Divine Revelation as a Book of Life was the knowledge that the Patriarch would transmit – and thus fortify – this knowledge to his children, that he would leave a will.

"For I have known him, to the end that he may command his children and his household after him, that they may keep the way of the Lord, to do righteousness and justice; to the end that the Lord may bring upon Abraham that which He hath spoken of him." (Genesis 18:19)

Beginning with the Patriarchs, the fathers of the Hebrew race, down through the centuries, it has been an unbreakable custom for Jews to command their children while alive so as to ensure their conduct when their parents are no longer with them. The most stirring scenes that have impressed themselves on the mind of humanity are those depicting the parting hours of the leaders of the Jewish people from their families. Many a permanent ethical thought that has raised the moral standard and has guarded the tradition, the loyalty and the learning of the race, owes its origin to this age-honored and awe-inspiring custom.

Jewish literature, in comparison with the literatures of all the peoples of the world, has the distinction of having a branch all its own. It is the literature of ethical wills. These wills, handed down by parents to their children, in oral or in written form, are indeed the pearls of wisdom based on life experience and are in everlasting testimony to Jewish experience and to Jewish foresight under all possible conditions. In fact, the Hebrew word for will, *Zavash*, means "command," and derives its origin from that Biblical description of Abraham the Patriarch's innate quality "to command his children and his household after him."

A man's life is judged by his will. There is no legal obligation resting upon the individual to make bequests in his last will. There is, however, a moral urge to provide in his will for the needs of his family and for that cause that has been the nearest and dearest to him in his lifetime and to which his loyalty is bound.

Our sages have defined this moral obligation in simple and convincing terms.

"In the hour of a man's decease, not silver nor gold nor precious stones and pearls accompany him, but Torah and good works alone, as it is said, 'When thou walkest, it shall lead thee, when thou liest down, it shall watch over thee; and when thou awakest, it shall talk with thee.' 'When thou walkest, it shall lead thee' – in this world. 'When thou liest down, it shall watch over thee' – in the grave. 'And when thou awakest, it shall talk with thee' – in the world to come." (Chapter of R. Meir, *Pirke Abot* 6).

The collections of Jewish ethical wills, those that are published and those that are still kept in the archives of the world's courthouses and museums, constituting a pride to Jewish tradition and a manifestation of Jewish foresight and generosity, in the majority of cases unfailingly contain clauses providing for bequests to those Jewish institutions that are the chief characteristic of Jewish communal life.

The leading beneficiary in these bequests and the greatest emphasis in the ethical wills that were left by the leaders of the old is the institution of Jewish learning, the Yeshiva, the fortress of the Torah. The Torah, as is obvious, being the background for the distinct Jewish [way of] life, is the foundation and the Giver of Life to all other branches of Jewish activity.

The inclusion of such a clause in one's will makes all the difference in the world. It accentuates the distinction between a technical will and what is rightly termed an ethical will, making it eligible for that precious heritage of Jewish literature.

The institution of the will is a late development among the peoples of the world. But it is not so with the Jewish people. The institution of the will is based on the assumption that the man who lives today has a will of his own, a free will that he is able to exercise. The testament is a legal device to assure the continuity of this exercise of one's will. It has served and is serving as an instrument to maintain and often to strengthen a loyalty and devotion to one's life ideal.

Bequests to charitable institutions are praiseworthy. Hospitals, orphan asylums, and the other institutions caring for the material needs of mankind are necessary and desirable. However, their longevity is limited to locality and durability.

Perpetuation can be assured only by a bequest to that institution in Jewish life upon which the very life of the Jewish people is contingent: the preservation of Jewish learning or the maintenance and expansion of the study of the Torah.

One can find by a perusal of Jewish testamentary documents in all countries for many centuries repeated emphasis of individuals to the executors of their wills that care be given chiefly to the Yeshiva, that perpetual standard-bearer of Jewish learning and Jewish tradition.

American Jews have a particular reason to remember the Yeshiva in their wills.

In the first period of the transplantation of Jewish life to America, the spiritual and cultural needs of the people were neglected, the material requirements being of a pressing nature. The institutions caring for the material needs of the community are at present provided for. The need of the hour and the hope of the future Jewish generations depend on securing the foundation of Jewish learning.

There is an inspiring example in the non-Jewish environment. All the leading American universities, including Yale and Harvard, were founded and owe their development to the generosity of far-visioned individual citizens. The conduct of these universally respected American seats of learning and their continuous expansion is being made possible through large benefactions or through testamentary bequests. Untold millions were left by these men whose appreciation and zeal for learning were high and whose patriotic devotion was unequaled. These funds go for the making of America in the fields of learning and science. Not less than twenty colleges were founded by Catholics in the United States. Greater still is the number of institutions of learning maintained by the various Protestant denominations. These institutions are generously and permanently supported through individual donations and bequests, placing their existence on a secure foundation.

American Jewry, and particularly traditional Jewry, will inscribe itself in the Book of Jewish Life by similarly providing funds for the maintenance and expansion of Jewish learning in this land. Every Jew, by his foresight and devotion, who will add to the funds of the Yeshiva, will inscribe himself and American Jewry in the Book of Jewish Life. Let there be a new addition to the collections of Jewish ethical wills.

The Yeshiva, the Rabbi Isaac Elchanan Theological Seminary, the oldest institution of higher Jewish learning in the United States, is now in the process of expansion through the erection of a series of buildings for the Yeshiva College. It is in need of endowment funds to secure its maintenance today and its continuation in the future. It is in need of large funds for the completion of the Yeshiva College buildings.

American Jews of vision and understanding, of loyalty and devotion to the age-old Jewish tradition of Torah, have an opportunity for accomplishing a great deed for Torah and for Jewry. Simultaneously they have a great opportunity for inscribing themselves perpetually in the Book of Life. An endowment of $10,000 to the Yeshiva will bring interest sufficient to support one senior fellowship at the institution forever. A bequest of $5,000 will provide permanently for the support of a junior student. A contribution of . . . . will secure the naming of a room in the new Yeshiva College building.

A bequest of . . . . will secure the placing of a memorial tablet in the auditorium of the institution. (add propositions)

Those who make possible such a perpetual continuation of Jewish learning will have their names entered in the *Sepher Ha'chaim*, the Book of Life of the Yeshiva, and their *Jahrzeit* will be observed by the students of the Yeshiva.

It does not matter how much or how little you provide in your will. "Bequests for a good cause are diamonds, the small ones are just as true and as precious in the eyes of God, for in them sparkles the faith of the giver, his devotion to God and the eternal idea of the Torah," declared Dr. Bernard Revel, President of the Faculty of the Yeshiva.

In outlining the need of the Yeshiva for bequests, the President of the Faculty stated:

"Depending as it does now upon the sporadic generosity of individuals, struggling continuously for the meager budget that hardly enables it to exist, the Yeshiva expends much of its energy in the very effort to continue its existence, and its work is vitally affected both in scope and in calm of spirit. The Yeshiva must be placed upon a more secure and more dignified financial basis by those who wish Torah-true Judaism and Jewish learning to be perpetuated and advanced.

"As throughout the ages our fathers have always liberally supported our great centers of Torah and learning, which transmit from generation to generation the supreme message of Jewish culture and idealism, maintaining them through years of martyrdom, through all conditions and by every sacrifice keeping alive in its historic home, the light of the Torah, so must those today who bask in the sun of freedom and prosperity in this land remember and maintain in effective power the Torah home in this land today. By contributing to the endowment fund and by remembering it in their wills, they may become partners in the holy work and make possible the continuance of the expansion of the work and the influence of the Yeshiva and its ideals."

A bequest to the Yeshiva either in a separate instrument or in a codicil may be made in the following forms:

(add forms, to be submitted by Mr. Zar)

"A Survey of American Jewry During the Last Five Years" (1930)

Of late, it has become fashionable to divide time into five-year periods. We moderns apparently grew tired of the symbolical setting. So we hear of five-year plans for the future of this or that country, community or enterprise. This survey proposes to deal with an equal period of five years that have gone by in the history of American Jewry. The forthcoming session of the Constitution Grand Lodge of the Independent Order of B'nai B'rith, coming after a five-year intermission, provides an excellent opportunity.

The new five-year period opens under conditions quite different facing American Jews five years ago when the Constitution Grand Lodge adjourned.

President Hoover in a letter just made public, addressed to Felix Warburg, expressed his consent and approval of the observance of April 13th, Jefferson's birthday, as America's Religious Freedom Day. A presidential committee, to be appointed by the chief executive, is to take charge of the nationwide observance of this Religious Freedom Day. It is a thoughtful idea that well signifies the spirit of the age or at least the enlightened leaders' aspirations for it. Passover, Easter and the birthday of Jefferson, author of the ordinance of religious freedom, coinciding on one day, make a remarkable combination.

Quite different were the conditions in America five years ago. When the period opened, the Ku Klux Klan was still a strong factor in the political and social life of wide sections of the country. The agitation for the introduction of religious instruction in the public schools had not yet abated. The Nordic superiority propaganda that culminated in the enactment of the 1924 immigration act was still going strong. Henry Ford's anti-Jewish campaign was at its climax and the *Dearborn Independent* virtually became the depositary for all the nonsensical outpourings of the sickly imagination and European anti-Semites.

It had become increasingly and painfully clear that although eight years had elapsed since the end of the World War, the world had not yet recovered from war hatreds and hysteria. Furthermore, evidence had been accumulated showing that so far as the Jews are concerned, and in particular, those ancient Jewish communities of Eastern and Central Europe, the period of misery, oppression and suffering had just begun. It seemed as if the evils, the mistakes, the hatreds and the passions of a thousand years of European history were erupting in volcanic fashion, pouring their devastating lava on the eternal scapegoat – the Jew.

American Jewry, new in its size and comparative prosperity, had just emerged from a continuous ten-year effort on behalf of war-stricken European Jewry. A fight on a double front, at home and abroad, had become tiresome and exhausting. With the domestic pressure unrelaxed, the pressure from abroad tended to create a new impetus, which found expression in the popular campaign slogan: "Tired of giving? You don't know what it is to be tired."[6]

With the annual communal budget for social, charitable and educational purposes amounting to approximately $60,000,000, the Jews of America, under the leadership of the Joint Distribution Committee, again undertook a $25,000,000 drive for the relief and reconstruction of their brethren abroad. As the five-year period comes to a close, over $21,000,000 of the amount sought was raised and expended for the purposes outlined and particularly for the furtherance of the settlement of Jews on the land in Russia. The Zionist movement, functioning mainly through its financial drives for Palestine purposes, seems to

---

[6] Cf. "Our New York Letter," *The Sentinel*, April 20, 1926, elsewhere in this volume.

be losing its force. Due, however, to what seemed to be a threatening clash with the non-Zionist interests in the Russian colonization, it gained new power, starting a cycle of the so-called United Palestine Appeal drives.

Simultaneously an internal process of consolidation and construction was going on in American Jewry itself. New congregations for the purposes of worship were being formed; old congregations erected new synagogues and temples at an expense ranging between fifteen and twenty-five million dollars annually. The community center, advocated for many years before as the best vehicle for adjustment, came to the fore. Various types and kinds of agencies and institutions were created and renewed. The old problem of the future of the youth or, more specifically, the imparting of a Jewish education to the growing generation, had begun to receive more attention. With the I.O.B.B. [Independent Order of B'nai B'rith] taking the lead, the academic youth now came for its share of the Jewish heritage. A successful Wider-Scope campaign for $2,000,000 was conducted by the I.O.B.B. for putting into operation the plan of the Hillel Foundation in various universities and for kindred Jewish educational purposes.

The three branches of American Judaism, Orthodox, Conservative and Reform, continued to show their determination to survive and gave substantial evidence of their vitality. The Hebrew Union College, inaugurated and successfully concluded its $5,000,000 Endowment Campaign; the Jewish Theological Seminary started the construction of its new buildings, with the assistance of a fund of over a million dollars left by the late Mr. Brush; the Yeshiva College, the institution for the training of Orthodox Rabbis and teachers, raised an amount exceeding $3,000,000, completed the construction of its new magnificent building in Washington Heights, and undertook an unparalleled and daring program of opening, with the charter of New York State University, a college for liberal arts and sciences under Jewish auspices.

While these communal developments were unfolding, a vigilant battle against the forces of prejudice and bigotry had to be continued with the dramatic and memorable recantation by Henry Ford of his charges against the Jewish people in a statement he addressed on June 30, 1927 to the late Louis Marshall. Memorable was also the vigilant fight conducted by the I.O.B.B. against anti-Jewish defamation through the output of the film industry and notably its preventive work in regard to the *King of Kings*.

In the economic field, a notable development was that which took place in the New York needle industries.[7] A large section of the workers came for a while under the influence of the Moscow-minded left wingers, leading to the impoverishment and ruin of many of the workers, the wreckage of the unions and the return of the despicable sweatshop system. The Jewish labor movement, seeing itself menaced and the gains of its struggle for a quarter of a century endangered, gathered new forces. The socialist right-wing waged a severe battle against the Communists and wrestled from their hands the control over the leading labor organizations. The fight against the sweatshop system was renewed and successfully conducted.

The contribution of American Jewry, 3,225,000 strong, to the progress and development of America in the fields of commerce, industry, letters and politics was obviously an impressive one. It is deplorable that the instruments of accurate research, yielding undoubted facts and figures, are not and perhaps cannot be available to draw a complete picture of that contribution. However, the contribution of the Jews to America, so often a topic of discussion, expresses itself primarily in the upbuilding of the life of the country as a whole and secondarily in the upbuilding of the educational, social and welfare

---

[7] Cf. "Our New York Letter," *The Jewish Post*, July 1929, elsewhere in this volume.

institutions that dot the continent from the Atlantic to the Pacific and that throb with vigorous life. The array of Jewish philanthropists establishing vast foundations for general non-sectarian and educational purposes, such as the Rosenwald Foundation, the Ten Million Dollar Fuld Foundation, the several Guggenheim Foundations (for aviation, for advanced studies abroad, for dental clinics) is too numerous for detailed registration in this review.

The contribution of the numerous Jewish writers to the field of American letters, researches leading to new discoveries by men of science like the late Dr. Goldberg, Dr. Falk of Chicago, the veteran Professor A. A. Michelson, the artists and singers, stand out in the public eye.

As the years advance and the eternal processes are consummated, American Jewry seems to be advancing to an unparalleled position. Already now, the leadership of American Jewry in world Jewish affairs, not only in regard to fundraising activities, is conceded. The recent union between the Zionists and non-Zionists in the Jewish Agency for Palestine, with the Americans playing a dominant role in it, places the mantel of leadership of world Jewry on the shoulders of the Jews of America.

"Kosher Food: A Suggestion for Talk On Radio Station WOR's 'Foreign Hour,' Sunday, January 22, 1933 – 3:15 PM"

A traveler who would make a flying [airplane] trip to the capitals of the world and to the lesser centers of population, would, undoubtedly, bring back from his journey one word that is frequently seen and heard almost everywhere. The keen observer would not have failed to notice the three square Hebrew letters *Kof*, *Shin* and *Reish*, which, when transliterated, spell "Kosher," inscribed and displayed in the windows of a variety of establishments and enterprises. These establishments include restaurants, butcher shops, delicatessen stores and groceries. Clearly, Kosher has a close relationship to food.

On the statute books of many states in the Union, there are numerous provisions, enacted by the legislatures of these commonwealths within the past decade, dealing with the problem of Kosher. In the courts of various jurisdictions in this city [New York] and other parts of the country, cases are frequently heard in which the word Kosher figures prominently and is often the basis for determination by judge and jury as to the guilt or innocence, responsibility or freedom from responsibility of the defendant at bar.

Obviously, there is in existence a Kosher food problem of wide ramifications. This problem is of vital and deep concern to consumers and producers alike, to the individual as well as to the community, to the bar as well as to the bench.

Before touching the core of the matter, I believe I will be voicing the sentiment of a vast radio audience within the Metropolitan area as well as in other centers of population when I shall, at the outset, express appreciation and thanks to Station WOR for its courtesy and cooperation in devoting this afternoon's "Foreign Hour" to a factual presentation of the problem and a description of the methods that are being adopted in New York City for its solution.

The primary and principal problem of man, in his struggle for self-preservation, is his daily food. In the early stages of mankind's development, the satisfaction of hunger and the quenching of thirst for the moment were its only concern. When these immediate objectives were attained, man no longer worried. Matters of hygiene, questions of diet, problems of selection and care for health did not enter into consideration, except, perhaps, for the dictates of instinct and preference of taste. As knowledge widened and experience accumulated, and especially since the day when the Commandments of revealed religion have become a potent and regulatory factor, man could no longer be governed only by his desire to eat. He learned that before satisfying his hunger, he had to stop and think what and how to eat. Sets of rules and regulations, evolved in the course of experience, came into being. Hence the origin and the basis for hygiene and laws of diet that, although not as yet developed to such perfection as to secure man's sustained enjoyment of health and happiness, are, perhaps, the very foundation of the life of the human species.

The first recorded doctrine of hygiene and certainly the earliest code of dietary laws, now a subject of immense interest to present-day science in this field, is contained in the sacred Books of the Bible. When the people of Israel came upon the scene of recorded history, they had the manifold blessings and sustaining advantage of a system of dietary laws, carefully and minutely drawn. This system, a gift of revealed religion, sanctified by custom and practice for thousands of years, expounded and carefully guarded by Rabbinic tradition and interpretation, has been one of the principle factors that have contributed towards the survival and preservation of the vigor of an ancient race, compelled by historic circumstances to live under unfavorable conditions.

This system is symbolized by the word *Kosher*, which means "fit for consumption," "properly prepared" in accordance with the rules and regulations of the biblical dietary laws and under the supervision of Rabbinic authority.

For the information of that part of the radio audience who may not be familiar with the background, it perhaps will not be amiss to spend a few seconds on several explanations that will afford the listener a glimpse into the complicated and arduous tasks that must be performed in pursuance of the dietary laws before meat and meat-products, as well as poultry, may be regarded as Kosher.

In the first place, the animal or fowl must be slaughtered through a specific humane method known as *Shechitah*. The *Shechitah* maybe performed only by a *Schochet* or a ritual slaughterer who must be well versed in the ritual law and properly accredited and certified by Rabbinical authority. The duties of the *Schochet* are manifold. Not only must he be able to perform the act of slaughtering in accordance with the many rules, swiftly and humanely, but he must also be thoroughly familiar with the anatomy of the animal. He must conduct a careful inspection of the lungs to ascertain whether they are sound. A defect in the lungs disqualifies the meat and makes it non-Kosher. Other defects and conditions discovered in other parts of the carcass render it non-Kosher. The carcass found to be Kosher must be so marked and stamped with the word Kosher. The stamp must bear the date when the animal was slaughtered. The hind part of the carcass is not Kosher. Certain veins and certain fatty parts are not allowed for use. They must be removed. Meat cuts preserved in the icebox must be washed at certain intervals in accordance with the minute provisions of the dietary laws.

These and many other details must be attended to before Kosher products may be offered for sale as Kosher. It will be seen that an elaborate checking system, a method of supervision, must be constantly employed to insure strict compliance. The maintenance of such machinery as is necessary to produce Kosher products involves an expense that is not attendant upon the production of non-Kosher products, hence the marked difference in prices that the public consuming Kosher products – and this public does not consist of Jews alone – is willing to pay and is paying for Kosher articles.

Here is where the Kosher food problem begins. The divergence in prices offers great temptation to unscrupulous dealers. To gain but a superficial understanding of the magnitude and extent of the problem, it is necessary to recall that numerous industries have sprung up and are functioning for the express purpose of satisfying the needs of the Kosher market. Limiting our consideration at this time to the Kosher meat and poultry market alone, it will be interesting to quote here the figures of the Bureau of Agricultural Economics of the U.S. Department of Agriculture for the year 1930. According to these figures, 159,673,975 lbs of beef, veal and mutton were consumed by the Kosher trade in that year in the United States. According to the figures of the same department, published in May, 1929, 12,000 carloads of live poultry, having a retail value of more than $100,000,000, reach New York terminals annually, most of which is being shipped to meet the needs of the Kosher trade in this city. Limiting our view to the City of New York alone, it has been estimated that the weekly consumption by the Kosher trade in the city amounts to 3,000,000 lbs. of meat and 4,000,000 lbs. of poultry. It has further been estimated that the Kosher trade in New York City takes in, annually, an amount of approximately $200,000,000 and that approximately $25,000,000 is being paid by the Kosher consumer in excess of the normal value of the articles because of his belief that the article sold to him is Kosher.

For decades this has been a perplexing problem to the Kosher-products-consuming public and to the religious leaders of the Jewish communities. Those insisting on complying with the dictates of their conscience and with the dietary habits of their race could never feel sure that the food they were buying and paying for in excess of its normal value was actually Kosher. A gigantic problem that affects not only religious faith and practice but also the moral standard of the community as a whole has thus a reason to perplex and plague the mind and conscience of religious authorities, leaders of public opinion, legislators and courts. The necessity of guarding the public against misrepresentation and fraud led the legislature of the State of New York to enact special provisions in the Penal Code of the State, making the sale of non-Kosher foodstuffs as Kosher a misdemeanor punishable by fine and prison. The validity of these provisions, the so-called Kosher Law, was contested and upheld by a decision of the United States Supreme Court.

Still, the evils and abuses have not, as yet, been eliminated. The absence of an effective system of supervision to prevent misrepresentation and abuses necessarily left the eradication of the Evil to chance. Occasionally, a violator of the law was apprehended and brought to the bar of justice. The basic condition, however, remained deplorable. Lack of unity within the Orthodox Rabbinate itself, the authority that alone has the power to determine matters of *Kashruth*, was another contributing factor.

It should be a source of gratification to the community as a whole and to the consumers as well as the producers of Kosher food to be informed that the movement to secure the condition and create order out of chaos in so vital a field is on the road to success.

The Kashruth Association of Greater New York, under whose auspices and on behalf of which it affords me great pleasure to speak this afternoon, has evolved and is putting into effect throughout the Metropolitan area an extensive plan that holds out great promise to remedy the conditions I described before. Under the aegis of the Kashruth Association have united 228 Rabbis in the City of New York and many leaders prominent in all walks of life, to give strength and support to a community supervision of Kosher food production. Under the leadership of its able and indefatigable President, Mr. Samuel Rottenberg, the entire field has been surveyed and plans have been laid to assure the consuming public that high standard to which it is entitled. The President of the Kashruth Association, who will follow me, will, I am sure, acquaint you with many facts and details that will be of interest to the public. As one who is familiar with the deplorable conditions that have been existing in the Kosher trade for many years, as one who is frequently seen, at close range, the necessity for remedial community action in this field, I wish the Kashruth Association of Greater New York the fullest success and bespeak for it the support and [word lost] of the public.

"I Saw *The Eternal Road* Ten Times:
A Review of Audience Reactions to the Themes and Characters in Reinhardt's Production of Werfel's Biblical Drama and Spectacle" (1937)[8]

Last Saturday night *The Eternal Road* reached its 100th performance on the stage of the Manhattan Opera House. At least a quarter of a million persons of the metropolitan area's cosmopolitan population passed through the box office, paid approximately four hundred thousand dollars for the privilege of enjoying the great biblical drama on the preparation and staging of which Meyer W. Weisgal devoted three years.

Since its opening performance on January 7th, *The Eternal Road* has been the subject of enthusiastic acclaim. Critics and reviewers have devoted hundreds of thousands of pounds of newsprint to describe its dramatic grandeur and to sing the praise of this great spectacle. The literary value of Franz Werfel's text, of Kurt Weill's musical score, Bel Geddes' settings, Max Reinhardt's direction and Benjamin Zemach's dance compositions have been subjected to minute scrutiny and found to be "perfect and without flaw" from the respective points of view.

But what of the audience? After all, it is the audience, the man not on the street but on the theatre seat, who is the final judge and arbiter. What is his reaction to and appreciation of all the things that go into the making of this unprecedented stage play? The answer to this question is priceless information not only to the producers but the student of mass psychology and reaction. This is particularly interesting to one who would seek to determine non-Jewish reactions to plays and public presentations of such eminently Jewish topics as the biblical history depicted on the upper levels and present-day Jewish reality enacted in the pit of the stage in the Manhattan Opera House.

The first and perhaps most reliable bit of evidence this reviewer is in a position to offer is of course his own experience. Without fear of contradiction or challenge he wishes to preface this review of audience reactions by the veritable statement that he saw *The Eternal Road* ten times. This fact alone is sufficient to dispel any doubt as to the capability of the performance to gain and to hold the onlooker's attention and absorption. Even without the element of surprise and expectancy (after the fourth or the fifth attendance, this reviewer knew almost all the lines by heart and could well visualize in advance the imminence of the next gesture and setting), the scenes in Reinhardt's production of *The Eternal Road* are full of the dramatic grip. Familiarity with subject, line or setting is far from producing self-satisfying knowledge. On the contrary, the more intimately this reviewer got to know the scenes in the absorbing drama, the greater grew his curiosity for the discovery each time of new meanings in the spoken lines and experiencing newer thrills from the dramatic accentuations of the groupings and the acting, as well as the musical accompaniment in each of the scores of scenes that follow each other in perfect harmony.

During those ten performances this reviewer has had as fellow spectators ten variously composed audiences of the average numerical strength of twenty-five hundred persons per audience. The reaction and the behavior of these audiences, as far as they can

---

[8] Attributed to Z. Alroy.

possibly be judged on the surface, probably represent the sum total of human emotions provoked in the minds and hearts of twenty-five thousand theatergoers, fifty percent of whom – at least – were non-Jews. A cross-section of public sentiment has thus impressed itself upon this reviewer's mind. He is willing to share his impressions with his readers unless they, parts of the same audiences, are ready to come forward with contradictory observations. The first and most potent impression one carries away from his contact with audiences at *The Eternal Road* is the feeling that the principal subject – biblical history – is generally familiar to the Jew or Gentile in the house. Very little reference to the explanatory synopsis is seen or observed in the audience. Apparently New York Jews – notwithstanding plaintive notes from the Rabbinical pulpits to the contrary – know their *Chumish*. The same may be presumed for the non-Jewish part of the audience. Apparently biblical influences still cement the foundations of Protestant Anglo-Saxon culture. Abraham, Isaac, Jacob, Joseph, Moses, David and Solomon are familiar figures, but this is the kind of familiarity that is coupled with a reverential and affectionate attitude, an attitude that adds rather than subtracts interest in the flesh-and-blood presentation. There is no heaviness or heavenliness in the Reinhardt portrayal of these revered figures of the Bible. The audience feels at one with these characters of historic posture. Stepping forth from the pages of the Book, they bear the characteristics of the Book that impressed their image and grandeur upon mankind's mind. The sacred halo does not obscure their significantly human characteristics, their struggles, trials and tribulations. Yes, these were the heroes of a distant and sacred past and this is how they may have appeared and acted in actual life. There is a stamp of genuineness upon the Reinhardt characterizations that do not minimize and certainly do not offend the most orthodox conception. On the contrary, these characterizations tend to increase their plausibility. The dramatic qualities of the play as it emerges from Werfel's lines and sequences are easily traceable to the portraits handed down in the biblical text, which as literary critics have long ago observed, is deeply human by its unmitigated simplicity and directness.

There are certain stages in the progress of *The Eternal Road*'s settings and actions that produce invariably a salvo of hearty and enthusiastic applause. The plaudits, as the surest expression of the reaction of the audience, here take on an additional significance. The average man applauds in the theatre the action or the statement with which he is in agreement. The statements, the supplications, and the actions of figures like those of the Bible obviously do not require approval. The audience invariably abstains from expressions of such approval. The applause rings high at moments when neither the actions nor the statements of the characters but their characterizations and settings come to light in a dazzling and grandiose manner and in arrangements of scene and position that make the action plausible. Thus when the first effects of the brilliancy of the Heavenly Hosts come to full view in the Covenant conclusion scene, the audience's approval of the artistic conception and the play of light burst forth. The man in the theatre seat loses control of his emotion; he is carried away by the grandeur of the picture. He gives loud expression to his approval. Similar is the invariable reaction of the audience to the brilliantly-lit scene that brings out in what appears to be a plausible and accurate manner the enslavement of the Israelites in the bondage of Egypt and the appearance of Moses on the scene of World History. Text, sound and light blend into one. You actually see, hear and feel the immense suffering of enslaved Israel who awaits his liberator.

The dance around the Golden Calf is no less brilliant, both from the point of view of the light effect as well as the plausibility of the intense action. And yet, hardly if ever does the hushed audience stir. Here one may observe applause in reverse. The effect produced by this scene, which winds up with the breaking of the Tablets by Moses, is so profound that all senses are absorbed. No active physical expression of approval seems to be necessary or even possible. Similar in nature is the audience's reaction to the enactment of the intense drama of Joseph and his brethren. The very melodious tunes in Kurt Weill's score, and the rhythmic Egyptian dances that fill the ear and the eye when witnessing the scene of the banquet laid out by the exalted ruler of Egypt to the corn-buying visitors from Canaan, incline the onlooker to express his appreciation but the intensity of the drama that follows swiftly stifles this desire into a renewed hush. Again this is the reticence of those who are eyewitnesses to a gripping event. The drama of David and Bath-Sheba keeps the audience in a prolonged suspense that ends only in the succeeding scene when another flash of brilliant effects – in lights, in dance, and in scene arrangement – brings into relief the completion of King Solomon's Temple and calls forth a thunderous applause of approval.

These observations hold true with regard to the audience as a whole including its Jewish as well as non-Jewish component parts. But there is a parallel drama in *The Eternal Road* – the drama that takes place in the synagogue, in the pit of the Manhattan Opera stage. The action there, mirroring as it does the reality in the timeless Jewish community, the death of the Jewish question at a moment of crisis, calls forth quite varying reactions. So essentially patterned after the precariousness of Jewish life in many countries today, the scene in the synagogue is principally a message of courage that is buttressed by the scenes of heroic grandeur on the upper levels. Viewed separately the synagogue scenes carry their message to the Jewish onlooker first of all. The non-Jew can best be expected to bring to the action in the pit a measure of understanding, sympathy and commiseration. Do these scenes call forth such sentiments? Here we enter into the field of speculation.

Werfel in conception and Reinhardt in characterization gave us here a galaxy of types that represent, one might say, a cross-section [entire page missing].

But the spirit of "Remembrance and Law," against which the Adversary so eloquently and effectively rebels, prevails in the congregation under the steadfast guidance of the Rabbi. He emerges in the play as a towering personality who has ready access to the sources of knowledge and faith. Fortified with these he remains detached and stays unafraid. He is not weary of the "dusty roads" and has the steadfastness to bid the congregation to re-embark on these roads when the necessity arises. His is a figure that calls forth respect of the Jewish part and good will of the non-Jewish part of the audiences.

That there are two kinds of applause – one that comes to the fore in the form of thunderous handclapping; the other that imposes upon the audience a hush of absorption – is demonstrated by the reaction of the audiences to the role of the tiny lad who plays the part of the son of the Estranged One. He is the one whom the Rabbi invites at the end of the first act, over the protests of the congregation, to "come to us and listen and watch." Listening and watching, the son of the Estranged One frequently breaks into the action on the upper levels and brings to it a touch of the charms of faith that are inherent in youth. The audience waxes enthusiastic in its applause of the lad's performance in the David and Goliath song scene. But the same audience falls under the spell of a hushed silence when towards the climax the son of the Estranged One rises in Werfel's conception and Reinhardt's characterization to the heights of the Torch Bearer, the idealistic Jewish youth who "longs for Messiah," asks impatient questions and addresses himself to the Spirit of Redemption with words like these:

> Why do you lament . . .
> Are you weary after this night . . .
> I am not weary . . .
> Come Father. . .

Come all of you. . .

[Rest of essay missing.]

"Address to Fellow Members of the American Zionist Guild" (1939)

[First three pages of speech missing.]

B'Kisso, B'Kaasso, U'B'Kosso. I tell you here and now that his [Meyer Weisgal's] gruff appearance is the greatest piece of camouflage. It is totally misleading. It is a false mask that covers a multitude – not of sins – but of virtues. Not the least of these virtues is his deep emotionalism. (Why, he cries like a baby when something serious happens in Palestine or in Jewish life.) His boundless attachment and loyalty to the Zionist cause and to his teachers, colleagues and friends are well known and require no testimony from me.

Yes, it was this emotionalism, this sense of loyalty and duty that moved Meyer Weisgal to play the leading role in the formation of the American Zionist Guild. And he rendered the cause of the Guild and of the Zionist movement an invaluable service. Without his energy and his leadership the Guild would not have come into being. At any rate, it would not have existed more than a month. If the Guild has survived this year, and if we were able to make some initial but greatly promising progress, it is in no small measure due to Weisgal, to whom – I must in all modesty add – I was more than happy to serve as second in command.

Now, only a few words about the Guild.

The Guild, it may be said, is something colossal on a minor scale. Everything that you think, hear and read aloud these days you will find in the progress and purposes of the Guild –

– "Everything that you find on the dry land, you will find in the sea," the ancient Hebrews were fond of saying.

The Democracies are fighting for the sanctity of the human personality – and so are we. The Allies are in need of Victory – so are we. The very keynote of this Festival of Lights – and Chanukah – which we are met to celebrate tonight, has more than something to do with the program of the Guild.

The Maccabean warriors cleansed the Temple by rekindling the lights. We of the American Zionist Guild seek to do likewise. We strive to cleanse the instruments of Jewish salvation and nation-building – the organizations and institutions of the Zionist movement – of the evils that have accumulated over a period of years as a result of [entire page passing.]

The Yishub in the early days of its nation-building work was not slow in recognizing the full worth of human values. Because of that, it has made just, fair and ample provisions for dealing with the human problems in the spirit of our Guild program. We seek to transplant this spirit of Eretz Israel into the councils of the Zionist movement and its institutions in this country. We hope to bring about a happy blend between the spirit of Eretz Israel and the Anglo-Saxon concept of civil service, which has contributed so much toward the smooth functioning of society and government among the free nations of the world.

This is our task. This is our hope. The initiative has come from us, but it will not remain with us alone. We have taken the first step and shall continue to work, argue, persuade and convince all those who still need to be argued with and convinced, until our efforts are crowned with success. Our success will, in the truest meaning of the term, also spell the advancement and success of the most vital interest and glorious future of Zionism and Eretz Israel.

Letters Received

Mr. Wm. Z. Spiegelman
Editor, Jewish Telegraphic Agency
621 Broadway
New York

February 22, 1925
My dear Mr. Spiegelman,

Very many thanks for your letter of the 20th inst. and for the suggestion you make. I am, of course, unable to decide at present whether the musical composition in question would fit in with the arrangements that are being made, but I should like to be given the opportunity of hearing the score if you are able to secure it without too much difficulty.

With thanks in anticipation,
I remain,
Yours sincerely,
Chaim Weizmann[1]

Mr. Wm. Z. Spiegelman
Editor, Jewish Telegraphic Agency
621 Broadway
New York

March 6, 1925
Dear Mr. Spiegelman,

I am much obliged for the very correct way in which my interview has been rendered. I have made only a few slight verbal modifications that do not interfere with the general context.

With very kind regards,
I am,
Yours very sincerely
Chaim Weizmann[2]

---

[1] On the stationary of the Commodore Hotel, 42 Street and Lexington Avenue, New York City.
[2] On the stationary of the Commodore Hotel, 42 Street and Lexington Avenue, New York City.

Mr. William J. [sic] Spiegelman
611 Broadway
New York City

October 10, 1927
Dear Mr. Spiegelman:

I have your suggested booklet on wills for the Yeshiva, and thank you for it and the promptness of its sending.

The central idea is very well expressed and should be effective. I should, however, suggest greater emphasis on the matter of endowments.

Within a few days I shall send you specific suggestions as to certain items in connection with the needs of the Yeshiva, and the costs involved in the endowments of chairs, instructorships and fellowships.

Do you consider it advisable to include in the booklet pictures of the groups of buildings?

With all good wishes,
Sincerely,
B[ernard] Revel[3]

Mr. William Z. Spiegelman
611 Broadway
New York City

Dear Mr. Spiegelman:

I thank you for your letter in which you suggest that I write the preface to the volume by Druck on the Palestine work of Baron Edmund de Rothschild. I am sorry that I cannot do this because I cannot undertake to make a study of the book for the next few weeks.

I have a suggestion to make, however, and, if it can be carried out, it will be far better than having me write the introduction. I think you ought to write a line to Nathan Straus – you may mention my name in connection with it – and ask him whether he would write a few words by way of introduction, he being the man who, next to Baron de Rothschild, has given most to Palestine. I think it would be a most striking thing to have the preface by Nathan Straus. I would be willing – after his birthday celebration is over – to talk to him about this, or else something could be prepared in your office by us together in collaboration with him.

Faithfully yours,
Stephen S. Wise[4]

---

[3] On the stationary of the Rabbi Isaac Elchanan Theological Seminary, New York.
[4] On the stationary of the Free Synagogue, New York.

Mr. William Z. Spiegelman, Editor,
Jewish Telegraphic Agency, Inc.
611 Broadway
New York City

February 28, 1928
My dear Mr. Spiegelman:

I did not receive the letter to which you refer in your favor of February 27th.

I will surely act on your suggestion and write a preface to the volume that will be published on the Palestine work of Baron Edmond de Rothschild.

As I am still very much overwhelmed with work in connection with my eightieth birthday, I would like to know what is the last date on which you can accept this preface.

Very sincerely yours,
Nathan Straus

Mr. William Z. Spiegelman, Editor,
Jewish Telegraphic Agency, Inc.
611 Broadway
New York City

March 2, 1929
My dear Mr. Spiegelman:

There is no more unique press service than the Jewish Telegraphic Agency, Inc. It provides a service that responds to a peculiar need of the widely dispersed Jewish people. It has afforded me real pleasure to note the high standard of impartial journalism that is maintained in the J.T.A. dispatches.

I am happy to send you this message of commendation on your Tenth Anniversary.

Very truly yours,
Robert Wagner[5]

Mr. William Z. Spiegelman, Editor,
Jewish Telegraphic Agency, Inc.
621 Broadway
New York City

March 8, 1929

---

[5] On the stationary of the United States Senate, Washington, D.C.

Dear Mr. Spiegelman:

I am glad that you are bound for California and the West in order to sense the degree of penetration of our work of promoting a thorough knowledge and appreciation of our faiths in opposite groups.

I am thankful for your own personal interest in what we all regard as a task that is the outstanding need of the hour: that is to bring about a more fundamental and better understanding of all faiths and sects to the end that the life of America may reach its pinnacle and may continue to lead the nations of the world in its example of tolerance and brotherhood of man under the inspiration of God.

In this direction your work in the [*Jewish Daily*] *Bulletin* has been helpful in more than one way. I often admire the heights to which you have climbed in presenting facts with so much detachment and fairness as to enable all who are concerned with facts alone, to form their judgment on the basis of the facts as they are.

It requires a deep understanding of human nature to perform such a service and it is for this reason that I have no hesitation in voicing my appreciation of the service that you so ably edit.

Wishing you Godspeed in your mission and with best wishes,
I am,
Very sincerely yours,
Edward L. Hunt, founder and director[6]

Mr. William Z. Spiegelman, Publicity Director
Jewish National Fund of America
111 Fifth Avenue
New York City

December 7, 1931
Dear Mr. Spiegelman:

Thank you very much for letting me know about the broadcast dinner in London today. Unfortunately, I have an important engagement at the time of the broadcast and so I cannot give myself the pleasure of listening to it.

Very sincerely yours,
Cyrus Adler[7]

January 21, 1934
My dear Wm. Spiegelman,

---

[6] On the stationary of America's Good-Will Union, 420 Lexington Avenue, New York City.
[7] On the stationary of Dropsie College for Hebrew and Cognate Learning, Philadelphia.

Thank you for your cordial letter – I am sorry that owing to my intensive work I have been unable to acknowledge your kind efforts.

I am looking forward to meeting you and the gentlemen of the Committee to-morrow Tuesday at five o'clock.

Very sincerely yours,
Arturo Toscanini[8]

Letters Dispatched

July 6, 1928
2137 Cropsey Ave
Brooklyn, N.Y.

My Dear Dora [Spiegelman]:

As I spoke to you over the transcontinental telephone last night I should not write to you tonight, particularly so since in all your letters and telegrams you have not written anything at all.

I mean you have not written the real thing. However, it is Friday evening and I want to make sure that you will get your check for next week in time.

I just came home after having dinner at Buzi's and my ears are full of the WPA and the Convention. You have no doubt read the [*Jewish Daily*] *Bulletin* and know all about the excitement at Pittsburgh and Lipsky's tragic-comic realization. I need a real rest after these trying days.

I do hope that you have already regained your composure, at least that you remember your home address and know the difference between a 6 and a 9. I also do beseech you to please number the pages of your letters so that I am in a position to read them.

Your statement that in the future you "will read every word" of mine may sound well but is not so good. Why? What happened to make you realize it so quickly? And then, is it not of the same category as your similar expression of "this time only"?

I certainly have no intention to interfere with your vacation or pleasure but if you wish to come back sooner than you originally planned, do I have to tell you that you will be welcome? I hope you will admit that I am in no position whatsoever to make the decision for you when I do not know what is the exact position that prompts you to make such a statement. Can you enlighten me on the subject with as many details as you have? I mean bare facts without embellishments.

Why don't you write me about the various entertainments that are being given in honor of the hospitable Eastern matron? How about some gossip, dirt, etc? Take it all in, kid, for this is the "salt of the earth." Pearl writes me (please thank her for her kind letter that I received today; I will write to her and Ike at a latter date) that you have developed intellectually, won't you show me what you can do? But please write the address correctly and, pray, number the pages.

I have already exceeded my usual four [handwritten] pages but we'll continue as I

---

[8] Handwritten on the stationary of the Astor Hotel, New York.

am in a chatty mood and there's no one to talk to. Before I will retire for a much-needed rest I will, therefore, write a few more paragraphs and take up with you a few more matters.

I received today another letter from that girl Jachcia from Jerusalem (don't be jealous! that is the only feminine mail I received so far). I think I told you what Rabbi Gold related to me on behalf of Mrs. Gold who just returned from Jerusalem. It is heartbreaking. What a fine kid she was and what a d––d shame. I also received a letter from her father in Los Angeles. I have written to a fiend of mine in C. Perhaps he may be able to obtain for them a permit. But since you are a Pacific Coast Sponsor, wouldn't you write to her brothers Abe and Sam to do something (in the nature of cash) for them? Mike, as you know, when I spoke to him before your train departed, laughed at the matter. By the way, did he have nothing of interest to say during the entire trip? Did you observe complete discretion?

What is your opinion of the young Mr. Shyer who called on you the other evening together with Mrs. S? He wants to marry a girl via the Yeshiva College and has indicated to me (the letter from the California Jobbing was from him) about his dilemma in a poem in bad Hebrew prose that gave me a pain.

The Yeshiva arrangement will in all probability be renewed but so far Hershel is still bluffing. I will know next week.

How is the rascal's[9] health? Is she growing? Is she enriching her vocabulary? Kiss her a thousand times and double the amount for yourself and do not write but talk on paper.

Yours as ever,
Wolf

[P.S.] Regards and best wishes to all!

Judge Otto A. Rosalsky
January 19, 1933

My dear Judge Rosalsky:

Enclosed is a suggestion (original and copy) for your radio address during the Kashruth Association's program on Sunday, January 22nd, between 3:15 and 4 P.M. in the course of the "Foreign Hour" over station WOR, New York City.

I should appreciate greatly if you will make any corrections or additions you may deem necessary and mail the copy to me in care of this address so that I am in its possession tomorrow morning when I have to send it up to the studio for release to the press on Monday morning. Mr. Samuel Rottenberg, President of the Association, and Rabbi Wolf Gold will be the other speakers. Each speaker will be allowed approximately 14 minutes for his presentation.

Please remember that the broadcast will take place at the New York studios of WOR (not in Newark), located at 1140 Broadway, corner 40th Street, New York City. Mr. Rottenberg and myself will be there to greet you. It is essential that you arrive not later than 3:05 P.M.

Because of the fact that it is a nation-wide hook-up, it was necessary to make the

---

[9] The "rascal" is their daughter, Ruth Joy Spiegelman, then three years old.

address as broad and general as possible, leaving out all sectional references as, undoubtedly, many non-Jews will be listening in.

Faithfully yours,

William Z. Spiegelman
Publicity Director
[Jewish National Fund]

WZS: FW
Encl.

To Ruth Spiegelman
July 18, 1946

Dear Ruth,

Mother and I have been exploring the Land of Oz,* the heritage of the Canadian French, since last Sunday. (*The phrase has its origin in Job 1:1. The Hebrew means: land of woods or land of contemplation.) We spent Monday in Montreal, dinned with the Pietrusluas, arranged for the renovation of Mother's Persian lamb coat, bought two suits for Wolf at very reduced rates, some sweaters and left by bus for the Hotel Vermont, St. Agatha.

Upon arrival (10:30 p.m.) at the Vermont, rediscovered that the hotel has too noisy (Mother, as you know, is a bit fastidious) and, in addition, that the room that has been reserved for us was not available immediately. In the meantime they offered us a tiny enclave (like the territory offered by the British for the Jewish State in Palestine) on the second floor with plenty of steps to climb. Indignant, Mother adamantly rejected the proposal. We got our deposit back and started out in search of a refuge.

With only a small investment in taxi fares we found shelter in a small inn in the center of the village, on the banks of the lake. Contrasted with the heat and humidity of the boiling Metropolis we thought the place was paradise. After a cool and restful night we discovered, at breakfast, that we landed in Galicia on the St. Lawrence. Soup and herring and noise and familiarity galore. Not for this did we leave the truly serene landscape of E. 9th Street, your determined Mother contended. She was right and I agreed.

We strolled to the village again. Mother found that the men of French Canada were good looking but not so smart but the women, well, they are clever and not so charming. With the aid of Mother's French and my "money [is] no object" attitude we secured the services of several taxi drivers who had a holiday (they waited for us a whole year and we could not let them down) taxiing us from one hotel to another until we reached the Lodge. Like the Indians who preceded Mother's folks in her home state, Mother exclaimed: Alabama! So we settled down here (at the rate of $35 per meal per person; very reasonable indeed) and intend to remain until August 4 or 5.

Now, from the point of view of its natural beauty this place truly has no equal. Not in vain did the French, British and American armies fight over it in the dim past before the Atomic Age. Situated at an elevation of 2,500 feet, the landscape is a mosaic of shapely mountains covered by stately [illegible], firs and pines, cut through, as if by a master designer, by an interlocking system of large and small lakes that give fragrance and refreshing coolness to the transparent atmosphere beneath a high-ceiling sky. No trace of humidity here, no suggestion of heat even when the thermostat [*sic*] stands at 90.

How much I (and certainly Mother, who gets lazy at a terrific rate to clean up before going away . . .) was in need of escape from the city you will appreciate from the fact that when I played Saturday afternoon two chess games with Mr. [illegible] I lost both ignominiously. . . . And so I seized the serenity and coolness of this enchanting spot like a weary traveler seizes upon an oasis in the desert.

Since we arrived here on Tuesday afternoon I have been doing nothing but relaxing and it was not an easy task. I had to work hard ,with muscle and will power, to do so. Now, Thursday evening, I feel ready to enjoy our vacation.

Well, that is all I can say about this place. You will note that I said nothing about Mrs. Kaufman's culinary arts (Mother beats her to shreds!) for she feeds her docile thinly Canadianized or Americanized clientele with the scenery. Besides, in matters of diet Mother can – and probably will – do a better job of description.

How have you been getting on? I was glad to hear that your first exam was satisfactory and that you are keeping pace with the program. Getting to know people – judge them correctly – and places is equally as important – and sometimes even more – as book knowledge. This is, however, a task that requires circumspection and experience. That story of your dispute with the Protestant Minister was interesting. You would do better, however, not to discuss Christianity objectively with a Christian Minister. They are not – and cannot be – objective on this point.

Mother is waiting for a game of cards so I will conclude this too long epistle with love and kisses from Mother and Dad.[10]

P.S. Remember the question about two men in the desert? Well, Arthur Koestler has an interesting article on a similar theme in the June [issue of] *Commentary*. You'll perhaps find it at Hillel's.

To Ruth J. Spiegelman
July 23, 1947

Dear Ruth,

Our freighter has been delayed for a day or so. That's why we are able to make it. And so, at 3 p.m. today we are setting sail on this epic journey to Eretz Israel in a most turbulent but entertaining time. Against the doings and curfews of the British we are fortified by my correspondent credentials for the *Nation* for which I have to write a series of articles.

Mother is sending you a letter in a separate envelop. She is thrilled but calm. I do hope that she will prove to be a good sailor and really enjoy seeing the world. Judith has been here since Sunday evening and will return to [Camp] Massad this afternoon after we sail. She was a great help in packing, etc.

Now, darling, I know that I do not have to give you instructions. You know my love and thoughts for you. Bear them in mind. Be well, he happy, make the most of your gifts and talents. Do not worry. Write to us and Judith and David every week. You are the captain! See you[11] on September 24.

---

[10] On the stationary of the Palomino Lodge, Ivry North, Quebec.

Loves and kisses,
Dad[12]

---

[11] Written in Hebrew.
[12] Written on the letterhead of *Land and Life: A National Magazine Devoted to Land Reclamation and Agricultural Development in Palestine and the Middle East*, published by the Jewish National Fund.

"William Z. Spiegelman Appointed Editor of *Jewish Daily Bulletin*"
Jewish Telegraphic Agency, October 30, 1924

William Z. Spiegelman has been appointed editor of the *Jewish Daily Bulletin*. Mr. Spiegelman has had extensive journalistic experience. He started his career in Poland, where he was city editor and parliamentary correspondent of the Warsaw Jewish daily, *Der Moment*. He has been a contributor and collaborator of the *Haolom*, a Hebrew Weekly now published in Berlin, the *Hazefirah*, the Hebrew daily that formerly appeared in Warsaw and many other journals published in English. Polish, Russian, Hebrew and Yiddish. For two years he was editor of the Jewish Telegraphic Agency in London. Mr. Spiegelman has travelled extensively and has an intimate knowledge of Jewish conditions in this country and abroad.

"Better Understanding of Jewish Realities Promoted by *Jewish Daily Bulletin*, says *Dos Yiddishe Folk*"
Jewish Daily Bulletin, December 15, 1924

Dos Yiddishe Folk, organ of the American Zionists, devotes an editorial, in its issue of Dec. 12, to the *Jewish Daily Bulletin*.

"During the past several weeks a small Jewish newspaper, printed in English and called the *Jewish Daily Bulletin*, has been appearing in New York under the editorship of the able, conscientious Jewish journalist, William Spiegelman.

"The paper is small in size but the idea behind it is big," says *Dos Yiddishe Folk*. "It has the purpose of furnishing the American Jews, who do not read the Yiddish press, news of all important Jewish events, couched in the briefest possible form. It also serves as the source from which the general American press secures correct facts about occurrences in the Jewish world. Such an enterprise is worthy of being welcomed not only from the journalistic point of view. It is an important step that may lead to a better understanding of Jewish realities in the circles of American Jewry.

"The *Jewish Daily Bulletin* was successful from its very inception and has been welcomed very warmly in Jewish, as well as non-Jewish circles, because it has proven that it follows the principle of correct information and of decent, responsible, impartial journalism."

"Bialik Greeted by Enthusiastic Thousands on Arrival in New York"
Jewish Telegraphic Agency, February 10, 1926

Thousands of New York Jews waited at Pier A, Battery [Park], for many hours yesterday for the docking of the Mauretania on which Chaim Nachman Bialik arrived from Palestine on his first visit to the United States to assist in the raising of the $5,000,000 sought by the United Palestine Appeal this year.

Louis Lipsky, chairman of the Zionist Organization of America, who was on a short visit to England to confer with the Zionist Executive and Dr. Schmarya Levin of Tel Aviv, also arrived on the steamer.

An enthusiastic reception was accorded the great poet of the Hebrew renaissance and the celebrated leaders of the Zionist movement.

A committee of prominent New Yorkers, writers and Zionist workers, headed by Federal Judge Julian W. Mack and accompanied by city officials, left at nine o'clock in the morning on the Mayor's boat to meet the guests at quarantine. The crowds gathered at the pier, cheered and applauded when the committee introduced Bialik to America.

Bialik, with a simplicity like that of Rabindranath Tagore, the great poet of India, with an un-affected and direct manner, the man who expressed the pain and hope of the Jewish people in a style reminiscent of the prophetic audacity, when interviewed by the representative of the Jewish Telegraphic Agency upon his arrival laconically stated: "I am a man of books. I work for the everlasting things in Hebrew letters. I see my mission in that. However, when I saw the Jewish workmen in Eretz Israel, saw the labor and observed what sacrifices of body and spirit they make and how little support they receive from the Jewish people of the Diaspora, I could not rest among my beloved books without having a sense of guilt toward them."

With a youthful appearance and peasant-like features, with inquisitive eyes, Bialik is a singularly attractive and charming personality who reminds one of a sage: Ezra the Scribe.

"I come to America without any pretensions. I hope my simple words will reach the hearts of American Jews. I am not an orator. I am merely a man of letters. I hope, however, that in my own way I shall succeed in making my fellow Jews appreciate the high values that are being created in Eretz Israel. If they will appreciate the values as I describe them, they will come to know the kind of sacrifices, they, who live under prosperous conditions, ought to make in order that those who labor at the laying of the foundations do not feel abandoned, but receive the strength to go on with their precious work for Eretz Israel," he declared.

"No Jewish leader has ever carried so heavy a burden with such inadequate support as Dr. Weizmann carries upon his poor shoulders. I feel I, too, should be of help to him and our dear cause in this trying time," he concluded.

The reception committee that went on the Mayor's boat consisted of Judge Julian W. Mack, chairman, Professor M. M. Kaplan, Joseph Barondess, Reverend Z. H. Masliansky, Abraham Goldberg, Professor Harry Wolfsohn, Professor H. Chernowitz, Zevi Scharfstein, Maurice Samuel, Samuel Grossman, Joseph Achron, Hillel Bayli, Dr. S. Benderley, I. D. Berkovitch, Rabbi Meyer Berlin, Herman Berstein, John L. Bernstein, Dr. S. Bernstein, Dr. Joshua Bloch, Max Blumberg, S. L. Borowski, Meyer Brown, Dr. S. Buechler, Dr. P. Churgin, Herman Conheim, Dr. A. Coralnick, S. Dingol, S. A. Dorfman, Rabbi Max Drob, E. M. Edelstein, William Edlin, A. Almi, Dr. H. G. Enelow, Joseph Eron, Rabbi L. Finkelstein, Jacob Fishman, Solomon Friedland, L. Z. Frishberg, B. Gingold, Dr. A. Ginsburg, Dr. S. Ginsburg, Jacob Noel, Israel Goldberg, Mrs. Richard Gottheil, Professor Richard Gottheil, Bathsheva Grabelski, Chaim Greenberg, I. Hemlin, Dr. J. T. Hellman, Henry Hurwitz, Dr. I. Kaliski, Professor Horace M. Kallen, Ephraim Kaplan, Dr. Yehudah Kaufman, Israel Kanovitz, Dr. Joseph Krimsky, Mrs. Joseph Krimsky, Sol. Lamport, Jacob Landau, Professor A. Levin, Dr. Israel Levinthal, Abraham Levy, A. Liesin, Leo Liow, Dr. S. Margoshes, Jacob Marinoff, Professor Alexander Marx, Israel Matz, S. B. Maximon, Dr. S. M. Melamed, Emanuel Neumann, Dr. Joshua Neumann, A. S. Orlans, Daniel Persky, S. Yudson, David Piuski, H. Podolski, Dr. David de Sola Pool, Dr. Max Raisin, M. Ribalow, Bernard G. Richards, A. Rosenblatt, S. Rosenfeld, Morris Rothenberg, Z. H. Rubinstein, Harry Sackler, Rabbi Lazar Schoenfeld, Bernard Semel, Bernard Shelvin, Carl Sherman, B. N. Silkiner, Mrs. A. Solomon, Dr. M. Soltes, Dr. I. Sonderling, A. Spicehandler, *W. Z. Spiegelman*, Solomon Suffrin, Henrietta Szold, S. Thau, Mrs. Bernard Traski, Phillip Wattenburg, Meyer W. Weisgal, Rabbi Harry Weis, K.

Whiteman, Peter Wiernik, Benjamin Winter, Dr. Stephen S. Wise, Leo Wolfsohn, Yehoash, M. A. Zeldin, Professor G. Zelikowitch, B, Zuckerman, Dr. A. E. Abramowitz. [emphasis added]

"Vladimir Jabotinsky Will Be Honored at Farewell Dinner by New York Writers and Zionist Friends"
Jewish Telegraphic Agency, March 24, 1926

Vladimir Jabotinsky, noted author and orator and internationally famous Zionist leader, will be honored by New York writers, newspapermen and Zionist followers before his departure from America. Following an extensive lecture tour, in which Mr. Jabotinsky spoke in many cities in the United States and Canada on topical Jewish and Zionist problems, which attracted large audiences, Mr. Jabotinsky will sail for Palestine on April 10.

During his stay in the United States, great interest has been aroused by his lectures and conferences on the present state of affairs in the Zionist movement and in Palestine. His views, which are the essence of the formulated program of the Zionist Revisionists, caused a wide and lively discussion in circles responsible for shaping the Zionist policies.

Mr. Jabotinsky's last address in this country will be delivered at a dinner to be given by a special committee representative of prominent writers, newspapermen and Zionists of all shades of opinion.

The dinner will be given at the Town Hall Club, 123 West 43rd Street, on April 7 at 7 P. M. A select group will be invited to attend the dinner.

The committee sponsoring the dinner are Herman Bernstein, Bat Sheva Grabelsky, Sophie Irene Loeb, Joseph Brainin, Elias Ginsburg, Jacob Landau, William Z. Spiegelman, Chaim Greenberg, Osip I. Posnansky, and Mr. Nagler. Madam Isa Kramer will act as hostess of the evening.

"Conference of United Jewish Campaign Opens in Chicago Tomorrow"
Jewish Daily Bulletin, October 8, 1926

The national conference of the Joint Distribution Committee and the United Jewish Campaign will open here tomorrow night at the Standard Club. The conference will be in session all day Sunday. About a thousand delegates from all parts of the country are expected to attend.

One purpose of the conference is to take stock of what has already been accomplished toward raising the $25,000,000 of the United Jewish Campaign. Another purpose is to hear reports of what has been done in the way of alleviating the distress in Poland, Romania, Galicia, Bessarabia, Hungary and other Eastern and Central European countries, and also the progress and prospects of the Jewish agricultural colonization work fostered in Russia by the Agro-Joint.

The delegates to the conference will hear a report on all countries outside of Russia from Dr. Bernhard Kahn, European director of the Joint Distribution Committee. They will hear reports on Russia from Dr. Joseph A. Rosen, head of the Agro-Joint, and from Dr. A. E. Grower, its legal advisor who drafted the agreement with the Russian government giving the Agro-Joint complete autonomy.

They will hear reports from a number of American Jewish social workers who have visited the countries where relief work is being carried on, including Jacob Billikopf, executive director of the Philadelphia Federation of Jewish Charities; Dr. Maurice Hexter, executive director of the Boston Federation of Jewish Charities; Dr. Ludwig Bernstein, Executive Director of the Pittsburgh Federation of Jewish Charities; Mrs. Rebekah Kohut, honorary president of the Council of Jewish Women, and Miss Irma May and Miss Hortense Breckler.

The conference will hear a report from Felix M. Warburg, detailing what the Joint Distribution Committee has already done and plans to do in the near future for the reconstruction of the life of East European Jewry; from James N. Rosenberg, vice-president of the Joint Distribution Committee, on his observations in Russia, and from David A. Brown, on the campaign. Mr. Louis Marshall is scheduled to deliver the keynote address [...]

A complete telegraphic report of the proceedings of the conference will appear in the Tuesday morning issue of the *Jewish Daily Bulletin*. The conference will be covered for the *Jewish Daily Bulletin* and the Jewish Telegraphic Agency by the editor, William Z. Spiegelman.

"Digest of Public Opinion on Jewish Matters"
Jewish Telegraphic Agency, December 16, 1926

The conviction that the arrival of a spirit of better understanding and unity between the diverse elements in American Jewry is due in large measure to the activities of Louis Marshall is expressed by *The Reform Advocate* of Chicago. Writing on the occasion of the attainment by Mr. Marshall of his seventieth birthday, the paper observes:

"Child of a German Jewish home, Louis Marshall, by his work in the cause of Jewry, has carried over the traditions of one group into the life of another and has in many ways brought the divergent elements of Jewish life into common action. One of these days American Jewry will be a unit. It will have the experience that Russian Jewry had in Russia when it was not originally a unit. There were Portuguese Jews, Italian Jews, German Jews and other Jews besides the Polish Jews in Russia. But as the years went by, Russian Jewry developed with its schools and its community and its united striving – perhaps also strife. There never was a Jewry that was not, if we might coin the phrase, influxy. Italian Jewry had an Ashkenazi group of families. Dutch Jewry had Germans and Portuguese, but in the end they worked together. That will have to happen in American Jewish life sooner or later. But when it happens, the work of Louis Marshall will not be forgotten. Respected and appreciated by the group out of which he came, and admired for his great ability by the other group that came later into American Jewish life, he is in his work a cementing influence in American Jewry."

A parallel between the careers of Louis D. Brandeis and Louis Marshall is drawn by *The Chicago Chronicle*, which writes editorially on the occasion of the attainment of their seventieth birthday by both men.

"The year 1856 saw the birth of two great American Jews, Louis D. Marshall, and Justice Louis D. Brandeis of the United States Supreme Court. The careers of these two great men bear a curious resemblance. Though born in opposite ends of the country, one in the north and the other in the south, both sought and gained fame in the legal profession. Their contributions to the growth of American jurisprudence is both copious and profound," the *Chronicle* says.

Marshall constitutes a perfect synthesis of American and Jew, in the best sense of the two terms, declares Wm. Z. Spiegelman in the "New York Letter" released this week to the American Jewish press by the Jewish Telegraphic Agency.[1]

"If there is any significance in the term 'American Jew,' it applies in the full meaning of the two words to Louis Marshall," we are told. "His Americanism is as much of an ideal as is his Jewishness. As an interpreter of the principles of the American constitution before the bar of justice, he has the recognition of the leading minds of the legal profession. As a champion of justice along the lines of constitutional development, he has demonstrated unusual abilities that have brought benefit to the state and the nation. As a Jew – there was not, in his long and fruitful career, a Jewish matter or question that came up for consideration or that was ripe for action that its fate and course did not depend on the scrutiny of the Marshall mind."

Who's Who in American Jewry 1926
Spiegelman, William Zev

Journalist, editor; b. Aug. 28, 1894, Siedlce, Poland; s. David L. and Eve (Ossinholtz) Spiegelman; ed. Studied at Univ. of Cracow; student of Judaica and Hebraica, pupil of late scholar, Dr. S. A. Poznanski, Chief Rabbi of Warsaw; m. Dora Moreiss, Nov. 29, 1924, Providence, RI.

Started journalistic work on Polish and Jewish newspapers, 1911; city editor, *Fraind*, 1912; translated German books, including Samson Raphael Hirsch's *Nineteen Letters on Judaism*; worked on several Polish newspapers, including *Nasz Przegland*; one of the founders of the Jewish Writers and Journalists Assn. in Poland and served as hon. secy. over three years; parliamentary corr. for Warsaw paper, *Der Moment*; later joined Jewish Telegraphic Agency in London; 1923, exec. sec. Jewish Educational Assn. of San Francisco.

Editor, *Jewish Daily Bulletin*, since its inception, Oct. 15, 1924; editor, Jewish Telegraphic Agency. Author: *History of the Development of Jewish Sects* (mss.) and numerous articles published in Polish, Hebrew, Yiddish, German and English newspaper and periodicals. Member: IOBB; Fed. Of Jewish Philanthropic Societies, NYC. Club: Peretz Writers. Address: 8817 Bay Parkway, Brooklyn, NY.

"American Editors Discuss Palestine Problem with Commander Kenworthy,"
Jewish Telegraphic Agency, January 12, 1927

A group of American journalists and editors engaged in a discussion of the problems facing the reconstruction of the Jewish Homeland in Palestine, at a dinner rendered to Lt. Commander Joseph Montague Kenworthy, M.P., noted British parliamentary leader, at the Hotel Waldorf Astoria, on Monday. The dinner was sponsored by Norman Hapgood, United States Minister to Denmark during the Wilson administration, Herman Bernstein, Editor of *The Jewish Tribune*, and H. V. Kaltenborn, editor of *The Brooklyn Eagle*.

In his introductory address, Mr. Hapgood, who acted as toastmaster, declared: "The doubts long shared by me and other non-Jews as to the possibility of reconciling Jewish nationalism with our international ideals has been dissipated by the remarkable spirit of understanding and goodwill that the Jews of Palestine have brought with them into the country. Enlightened nationalism such as Jewish nationalism is without imperialistic policies and [the fact] that it does not engender a chauvinistic spirit may be regarded of

---

[1] Not included in this volume.

inestimable value to mankind and international peace. This has been thoroughly demonstrated by the present Jewish achievements in Palestine, where Jews live in amity and helpfulness with the Arab population."

Commander Kenworthy in his address declared that not only was the British Labor Party, of which he is a member, giving its fullest support to the carrying out, both in the spirit and in the letter, of the Balfour Declaration, but that both Liberals and Conservatives were also similarly pledged.

"The British people and the Government supporters as well as the enlightened opinion of the civilized world stand squarely behind the Balfour Declaration and nothing can bring about a change in this policy."

In discussing Jewish-Arab relations in Palestine, Commander Kenworthy declared, "relations between the Arabs and Jews are improving from day to day. The Arab population has begun to realize that, with the restoration of the Jewish Homeland, its own standard of living and economic prosperity is being greatly improved.

"It has been proven that one hundred dunams of land, or twenty-five acres, cultivated in an intensive manner is sufficient to support an individual family," he stated. "By careful analysis it becomes clear that the Palestine of today can support an agricultural population of one million. It is reasonable to believe that, with increasing Jewish immigration, the Jewish National Homeland will naturally expand into Transjordan where there are found vast stretches of rich and uncultivated land now left idle. But agriculture is not the only source of livelihood for the Jewish population. Industry and commerce are constantly expanding and, with the improvements and extension of railroads and the construction of the port of Haifa, untold possibilities lie ahead for the Jewish Homeland, which is naturally the key to the entire East."

Among those present at the dinner were Oswald Garrison Villard, editor of *The Nation*; Freda Kirchwey of *The Nation*; Lester Markel of the *New York Times*; William L. Chenery, editor of *Colliers Weekly*; H. Blakeslee of the Associated Press; M. D. Tracy, Assistant General Manager of the United Press; C. R. Hope, General Manager of the Universal Service; Jacob Landau, Managing Editor of the Jewish Telegraphic Agency; George W. Gilmore, Editor of *The Homiletic Magazine*; Sewell Haggard, editor, *Shrine Magazine*; L. S. Richard, editorial writer for *The New York American*; William Z. Spiegelman, editor of the *Jewish Daily Bulletin* [...].

"Jewish Community Leaders Give Unqualified Endorsement of Jewish Telegraphic Agency Work"
Jewish Telegraphic Agency, June 23, 1927

Unqualified support of the work of the Jewish Telegraphic Agency and the *Jewish Daily Bulletin* was given by Louis Marshall, president of the American Jewish Committee, at a round table dinner conference held at the National Republican Club, Sunday night, at which a group of prominent New York Jewish leaders were present.

The dinner was given by a committee consisting of Dr. Cyrus Adler, James N. Rosenberg, Samuel C. Lamport and Harold Korn, in honor of Jacob Landau, managing director of the Jewish Telegraphic Agency and the *Jewish Daily Bulletin*, upon his return from a trip to Europe and Palestine.

James N. Rosenberg, vice-chairman of the American Jewish Joint Distribution Committee, acted as toastmaster. Samuel C. Lamport, Congressman Emanuel Celler, Dr. W. I. Sirovich, Harry Berman, John L. Bernstein and Irving Rosenzweig participated in the discussion that followed a presentation by Mr. Landau of the work of the Jewish Telegraphic Agency and the *Jewish Daily Bulletin*.

In outlining the history of the Agency and the *Bulletin*, Mr. Landau stressed the non-partisan policy and the endeavor to be of service to the Jewish community, to increase the knowledge of Jewish affairs in the Jewish as well as the non-Jewish world.

In his address, Mr. Marshall stated: "Frequent requests have been made for my opinion as to the value and importance of the Jewish Telegraphic Agency and the *Jewish Daily Bulletin*. I wish to say without the slightest mental reservation that it has my unqualified approval. From the time when its reports were issued in mimeograph form down to the present day, I have made constant use of them in the course of my public activities, and have found frequent occasion to refer to its files in dealing with the manifold Jewish problems that clamored for attention. These publications have become increasingly valuable. The news that they gather from every quarter of the globe is presented in clear and concise form, without exaggeration, free from partisanship, and without the tinge of sensationalism. They are reliable and trustworthy and well expressed. So important do I consider them to be that I have no hesitation in saying that, if they did not exist, it would be necessary for the community to create a substitute possessing the same high qualities. With the disappearance of the present organization, that could only be done with much difficulty and at great expense. It is, therefore, the part of wisdom to support and preserve what we now possess. Those connected with it have become familiar with Jewish conditions everywhere and have developed unusual skill in reaching authoritative sources of information.

"The *Jewish Daily Bulletin* is more than a newspaper. It is in reality a publication that not only instructs the lay reader, but affords a fund of information to newspapers and to purveyors of news. Without the service that it assures the press generally, as well as the Jewish public, we would be groping in the dark concerning conditions and movements relating to the Jews throughout the world. This publication has been most helpful in portraying the march of events and in enabling your readers to foresee future developments," Mr. Marshall said.

A resolution moved by Jonah J. Goldstein and seconded by Congressman Celler, expressing appreciation of the work of the Jewish Telegraphic Agency and the *Jewish Daily Bulletin*, was unanimously adopted. The resolution also expressed recognition of the fact that the work carried on by the Agency and the *Bulletin* is of meritorious communal character. Among those present at the dinner were James N. Rosenberg, Irving Rosenzweig. Harry Berman, Jonah J. Goldstein, Morris Eisenman, Harold Korn, John L. Bernstein, Samuel C. Lamport, Emanuel Celler, James Brooke, Dr. William I. Sirovich, Rabbi Israel Goldstein, Joseph D. Bookstaver, William Z. Spiegelman and John Simons.

"Associated Press Testifies to Jewish Telegraphic Agency's Impartiality"
Jewish Telegraphic Agency, February 21, 1928

The Associated Press, through Jackson S. Elliott, Assistant General Manager of the Central Office, 383 Madison Avenue, New York City, forwarded its best wishes and felicitations to the Jewish Telegraphic Agency and the *Jewish Daily Bulletin* on the occasion of the ninth anniversary of the Agency and the one thousandth issue of the *Bulletin*.

The Associated Press, which has cooperated with the Jewish Telegraphic Agency in a most cordial manner, distributing to the hundreds of newspaper subscribers of the

Associated Press the news dispatches of the Jewish Telegraphic Agency pertaining to Jewish events, by declaring that the Associated Press has "in a sense been allied with the Jewish Telegraphic Agency since its inception," pays tribute to the impartiality of the Jewish Telegraphic Agency service.

Recalling the first endeavors in organizing the Jewish Telegraphic Agency to fill the gap in the field of useful service to the Jewish and non-Jewish community, Mr. Elliott writes:

"Representatives came to us saying they wanted to create for the Jewish press a service comparable in public confidence to that of the Associated Press for its membership. We responded in an advisory way, and also tangibly, in that we accepted for distribution to our membership the dispatches relating to Jewish activities that were deemed to be of sufficient general interest to be absorbed in the Associated Press reports. I proposed a change of name and suggested 'Jewish Telegraphic Agency' as one that would be understood by readers, meaning that this organization was bringing dispatches from important Jewish centers throughout the world by cable, wireless, and other prompt means of transmission.

"We have observed the progress of the Jewish Telegraphic Agency with a great deal of satisfaction and, throughout these eight years, have never had occasion to regret the encouragement we gave to your organization and we believe you have sought always to occupy your field by serving to your members news presented impartially."

Editorials lauding the service of the Jewish Telegraphic Agency and the *Jewish Daily Bulletin* were published in all parts of the United States and Canada, served by the Jewish Telegraphic Agency. [...]

[According to] *Hadoar*, [the] only Hebrew weekly in U. S., New York: "The men of the *Jewish Daily Bulletin* have renounced the privilege of a personal opinion and do not seek to impose their views on the reader. They have retreated, sacrificing their individual likes and dislikes in order that we may observe the march of events as they pass before us in review. Limiting themselves to this task, they do not interpret the events, but permit us a glance at what has happened. Having the facts and the understanding, we may form our own opinion.

"To the credit of the *Jewish Daily Bulletin*, one must say that its editor, William Z. Spiegelman, is not only a journalist of exceptional ability, but also a good and devoted Hebraist. It is due to him that much in the field of Hebrew life and literature that other newspapers would overlook or ignore has been given proper expression. Along with our felicitations on the occasion of the thousandth issue of the *Jewish Daily Bulletin*, we would like to express the wish that in future more be done in this direction."

"JTA Sends Representative to Russia in Expansion Program"
Jewish Telegraphic Agency, February 21, 1928

Ben Smolar, editor of the Yiddish service of the Jewish Telegraphic Agency, sailed on the steamer *Republic* on his way to Russia.

Mr. Smolar, who has been connected with the Jewish Telegraphic Agency for the past three years, is being sent by the Agency to act as its correspondent in Moscow in order to secure a continuous and accurate news service from Soviet Russia, in which country the effect of the social upheaval upon Jewish life and the subsequent development in the economic and cultural transformation of a large mass in the Jewish population is of intense interest to Jewish leaders throughout the world.

On the same steamer, Emanuel Aronsberg, contributor to many American magazines, left for London to join the staff of the Jewish Telegraphic Agency there. Mr.

Aronsberg was previously connected with the Foreign Language Information Service and is collaborating in the preparation of a work on the history of Russia in the post war period.

The journeys of Mr. Smolar and Mr. Aronsberg were arranged as a part of a program now being carried out to round out and intensify the news service of the Jewish Telegraphic Agency.

Prior to their departure, a farewell dinner was given in their honor by the staff of the Jewish Telegraphic Agency. S. Dingol, managing editor of *The Day*; H. Kirshenbaum of *The Hebrew Journal*, Toronto; and John Simons, Aleph Katz, Nina Katz and Jacob Kirshenbaum of the *Jewish Morning Journal* were among the speakers. William Z. Spiegelman, editor of the Jewish Telegraphic Agency-*Jewish Daily Bulletin*, acted as toastmaster.[2]

"Readers of *Bulletin*, Jews and Non-Jews, Praise Its 1000th Jubilee Edition"
Jewish Telegraphic Agency, February 28, 1928

Words of appreciation and praise are being received by the *Jewish Daily Bulletin* from its numerous Jewish and non-Jewish readers.

C. B. McAfee of the McCormick Theological Seminary, Chicago, writes: "Let me congratulate you on the one thousandth edition of the *Bulletin*, both for its appearance and the quality of its matter. I am putting it in my files so that I may use its valuable information from time to time as occasion may offer."

The following message was received from E. Tallmage Root, Secretary of the Interchurch Fellowship, Boston: "Congratulations to the *Jewish Daily Bulletin* on its special number to commemorate the one thousandth issue, from the Interchurch Fellowship and the Massachusetts Federation of Churches. The office of the latter receives the *Bulletin* and keeps it on file, and it gives much appreciated information."

The Jewish Voice, Newark, writes: "Observing the great moral and educational success that the little bulletin has met with, and considering how it penetrated the circles of our Jewish leaders and social workers, we feel, and we often expressed this thought openly, that this little bulletin that contains the latest reports and news from Jewish life everywhere proves that something bigger, something more substantial, must be created in the field of Jewish-English information.

"This little paper, which is so full of information from all parts of the world. proves to us what it could do if it had the necessary means and the well-deserved recognition among our intelligent masses as well as among our leaders.

"The same Messrs. Landau and [William Z.] Spiegelman and their co-workers are competent and have all facilities to give us such numbers as this one more often, at least once a week, if the Jewish masses render their support."

"Hebraists to Hold Annual Convention"
Jewish Telegraphic Agency, June 8, 1928

The tenth annual convention of the Histadruth Ivrith of America, with a membership

---

[2] Cf. the "Photographs, Facsimiles and Official Documents" section for a photograph of this event.

of over 5,000 throughout the country, will be held at Paterson, N. J. on Saturday night and Sunday, June 16 and 17. A mass meeting at the auditorium of the Y. M. H. A. will mark the opening of the convention.

One hundred and fifty delegates are expected to attend. Reports on the progress of the Hebrew movement will be submitted by William Z. Spiegelman, and Dr. S. Bernstein. A. Spicehandler will present the treasurer's report and M. Ribalov a report on the progress of *Hadoar*, Hebrew weekly.

"Hebraists Hold 10th Annual Convention,"
Jewish Daily Bulletin, June 19, 1928

Paterson, N. J (JTA) – One hundred delegates representing twelve cities in New York, New Jersey, Pennsylvania and Connecticut attended the tenth annual convention of the Histadruth Ivrith, held here Saturday night and all day Sunday.

The Hebrew movement is advancing both here and abroad, it was reported to the convention by Z. Scharfstein. Dr. Max Raisin welcomed the convention at its opening session.

The progress of the Hebrew schools in Poland, Lithuania, China and the Argentine was reported. Mr. Scharfstein stated that Hebrew culture is spreading in the United States. Fifty Hebrew books have been published during the past year, he declared, urging the extension of the Histadruth publishing company.

The convention authorized the Executive Committee to form a council representing the districts as an advisory body. A budget of $48,000, including $26,000 for the *Hadoar*, a Hebrew weekly, was adopted. Reports were also submitted by Abe Goldberg, William Z. Spiegelman, secretary, and A. Spicehandler, treasurer. The treasurer reported a deficit of $12,000. Abraham Goldberg was elected president and Dr. P. Churgin, vice president. The Executive Committee chosen includes William Z. Spiegelman (chairman), Dr. S. Bernstein, Dr. S. Baron, Dr. M. Katz, Dr. H. M. Gordon, M. Ribalov, M. H. Talner, Dr. M. Einhorn, I. Rivkind, P. Maze, A. Spicehandler, Z. Scharftstein, S. B. Maximon and B. Margolin.

"Current Event and Comment," by H. H. Marlin, D. D.
The United Presbyterian, October 11, 1928

[...] We were led to make amends in the first place [for the brief article "Adherents of Jewish Faith" published in the August 2, 1928 issue of *The United Presbyterian*] because of a beautiful letter that we received from William Z. Spiegelman, editor of the *Jewish Daily Bulletin*, New York City. It was a courteous letter and of a kind spirit. He is a Jew whom we are beginning to love. After we had sent him the amplifying statement requested [by the Jewish Telegraphic Agency] he printed it in his paper in a generous spirit. Moreover he wrote us and said: "It is only human to err, but it is magnificent to admit the error in as frank and courageous manner as you have done."

"United Presbyterian Makes Further Comment"
Jewish Daily Bulletin, October 24, 1928

Further comment was made by the Rev. H. H. Marlin, editor of the page "Current Event and Comment" in *The United Presbyterian* of this city, in a current issue of the magazine, with regards to the editorial that he wrote in the issue of August 2 on "Adherents of Jewish Faith," which drew forth the criticism of Jewish publications because of unfriendly remarks against the Jews that it contained.

Rev. Marlin, in response to a letter of the Jewish Telegraphic Agency, withdrew his unfriendly criticism in a statement he issued for circulation to the Jewish press. In explaining the reasons for the withdrawal of his previous remarks, the Rev. Marlin writes:

"Generally these editorials (criticizing Rev. Marlin for his remarks) were bitter, and some of them were violent. However, we are glad to say that we received some letters relative to this matter that, while criticizing the editorial, breathed the spirit of kindness and courtesy.

"We felt upon reflection that our article was not wholly just and so, in response to a courteous request on the part of the Jewish Telegraphic Agency for an additional statement, we sent a letter frankly stating that we believed we had not been wholly just to the Jewish race and that we were sorry that we had written it. This statement was printed widely in Jewish papers and some of these papers did not treat us fairly nor generously in their comment on our statement. For instance, our article on the Jews may have been somewhat unfortunate, but it certainly was not 'malicious.' In general, also, no recognition was made of the fact that the article of which complaint was made contained sentences that were decidedly laudatory of the Jewish race. Moreover, we were not led to make amends by a 'storm of replies from the Anglo-Jewish press.' When we are convinced we are right, we shall stand unmoved where God places us. Our spirit is Scotch, our blood is Irish and our hair [is] red. And while we do not wish to indulge in any mock heroics, yet we truly seek a portion of the spirit that once filled a great Jew who, conscious of God with Him, and alive to the perils of His every hour, said: 'None of these things move me.'

"We were led to make amends in the first place because of a beautiful letter that we received from William Z. Spiegelman, editor of the *Jewish Daily Bulletin*. It was a courteous letter and of a kind spirit. He is a Jew whom we are beginning to love. After we had sent him the amplifying statement requested, he printed it in his paper in a generous spirit. Moreover he wrote us and said: 'It is only human to err, but it is magnificent to admit the error in as frank and courageous a manner as you have done.' And the second reason for our amplifying statement was, upon serious thought, we were convinced that we had not been wholly just in our article as it appeared in public prints. We were rather surprised to know however that it had 'attracted nation-wide attention,' and naturally we were very sorry that it had occasioned bitterness in the hearts of our Jewish brothers. We read that editorial again, but this time we read it through Jewish eyes and we clearly saw that it was not generous and that it was not wholly fair. Therefore we regretted it. We were sorry it had been written. We were grieved that we had excited bitterness and that we had occasioned wounds. And that is why we gladly stood before the Jewish world to say: 'That article was not wholly fair. It is sincerely regretted.'"

To Whom It May Concern
March 4, 1929[3]

I have known Mr. William Z. Spiegelman for the past seven years and have learned to regard him as a man of high integrity and great journalistic ability. As Editor of the *Jewish Daily Bulletin*, he has achieved perhaps more than any other individual in bringing to the

---

[3] On the letterhead of the Zionist Organization of America.

attention of the world at large a knowledge of Jewish affairs throughout the world, making for an intelligent understanding of Jewish problems and Jewish ideals.

I recommend Mr. Spiegelman not only for his extraordinary abilities as a writer, editor and journalist, and for his wide range of knowledge, but also as a man of fine character and high purpose.

It gives me great pleasure to place these sentiments on record.

Very truly yours
Meyer W. Weisgal
Secretary, National Executive Committee

"Wm. Z. Spiegelman and John Simons Resign from J.T.A. and *J.D.B.*"
Jewish Telegraphic Agency, October 16, 1929

Mr. William Z. Spiegelman has resigned as Editor and Mr. John Simons as Business Manager of the Jewish Telegraphic Agency and the *Jewish Daily Bulletin* in order to engage in the development of the Jewish Biographical Bureau, 51 Madison Avenue, New York, which publishes *Who's Who in American Jewry* and the *Jewish Communal Directory* of the United States.

In making this announcement, Mr. Jacob Landau, Managing Director, gave expression to his appreciation of the many years of service rendered by Mr. Spiegelman and Mr. Simons.

"Mr. Spiegelman as Editor of the *Jewish Daily Bulletin* and the Jewish Telegraphic Agency," Mr. Landau stated, "combined ability with responsibility. In his perseverance, giving unstinted effort to his work, he succeeded in achieving results that are of true value and significance.

"I highly esteem the services that have been rendered by Mr. Simons. With untiring effort he has promoted the business affairs of the Jewish Telegraphic Agency and the *Jewish Daily Bulletin*. Both enterprises owe Mr. Spiegelman and Mr. Simons a debt of gratitude for their work. I sincerely wish Mr. Spiegelman and Mr. Simons success in their new venture."

"50 Years of Jewish Cultural Effort in America to Be Celebrated: Commemoration of Mass Jewish Immigration"
Jewish Telegraphic Agency, March 14, 1932

A public celebration will be held at the Hotel Astor on Sunday, April 10th, to commemorate the 50th anniversary of Jewish cultural and literary activity in America.

Since the beginning of the westward exodus of great masses of European Jewry, the 50th anniversary of which occurred this year, Dr. A. Coralnik, the President of the Jewish Writers' Club of America, under whose auspices the celebration is being arranged, says in a statement that has been issued for the occasion that the Jewish press and literature have played a role of significance in American Jewish life. In the adjustment that followed the Jewish mass migration that began in 1882, they were instrumental not only in fostering among vast masses the feeling of high civic pride, but also in the creation of new literary values that have been specific contributions to America.

Mr. Ab. Cahan, the editor of the *Jewish Daily Forward*, Dr. Coralnik, Mr. Peter

Wiernik, editor of the *Jewish Morning Journal*, Dr. Chaim Zhitlovsky, and Mr. George Zedalie, United States District Attorney, are honorary chairmen of the Committee, Dr. A. J. Rongy is chairman, Mr. Jacob Fishman, managing editor of the *Jewish Morning Journal*, Mr. Louis Lipsky, and Mr. David A. Brown are Vice-Chairmen, Mr. B. C. Vladek, the manager of the *Jewish Daily Forward*, is acting as treasurer, and Mr. W. Z. Spiegelman as secretary.

"Writers and Leaders Honor Ernest Benedikt at Reception Arranged by JTA"
Jewish Telegraphic Agency, October 17, 1932

A reception and tea in honor of Dr. Ernst Benedikt, publisher of the *Neue Freie Presse* of Vienna, leading European paper, noted for its liberal and literary tradition, was held Thursday afternoon at the Hotel Plaza by the Jewish Telegraphic Agency and attended by a number of outstanding journalists in the Jewish and non-Jewish press, as well as leaders in various fields.

Following the reception, Dr. Benedikt left for Albany where he was received by Governor Franklin D. Roosevelt. The distinguished Viennese visitor is in the United States on his first visit to this country, having arrived on the *S. S. Rex*.

Dr. Benedikt will be received by President Hoover this morning at eleven o'clock.

Introduced by Jacob Landau, managing director of the Jewish Telegraphic Agency, Dr. Benedikt made a brief address in which he described conditions in Austria. He expressed the belief that Austria will recover from its present critical state, but that the process will be slow and will be based upon the confidence it is able to inspire from its own citizens and from public opinion abroad.

No recovery is possible, however, without the application of justice and equality to the minorities, he emphasized. The Jewish question is in fact a question of minorities and so is also the problem of Austria as a whole.

The credo of liberalism, Dr. Benedikt stated, had been handed down to him by his father, the late Moritz Benedikt, for forty years the editor of the *Neue Freie Presse*, who died in 1920, and under whose guidance the paper attained its wide repute for liberalism and journalistic and literary excellence.

Mr. Landau, in introducing the guest of honor, referred to the wide reputation that the *Neue Freie Presse* enjoys throughout Europe and in this country as well. He recalled the fact that one of the most distinguished contributors to the paper was Theodore Herzl, founder of political Zionism.

Among those present were Dr. Ernst Benedikt; Jacob Landau, managing director of the Jewish Telegraphic Agency; James H. Furay of the United Press; Louis Wiley, manager of the *New York Times*; Smith Reavis, Foreign News Editor of the Associated Press; Arthur Robb, Editor of *Editor and Publisher*; Simon Lehr, correspondent of the *Vienna Tageblatt*; Dr. Harold Korn, communal worker; his wife, Mrs. Korn; Edward L. Bernays; Dr. Maurice J. Karpf, Executive Director, Graduate School of Jewish Social Service; Simon Bergman; William Z. Spiegelman, Jewish National Fund [...]

"Newark to Plant 5,000 Trees in George Washington Forest"
Jewish Telegraphic Agency, October 28, 1932

An effort will be made to have Newark represented by a section of 5,000 trees in the

George Washington Forest in Palestine, according to a decision at a conference here. Aaron Levinstone, prominent local Zionist, will act as Chairman, and the effort will be guided tentatively by the Jewish National Fund Council of Newark.

Mr. Levinstone will form an Advisory Committee of Communal Leaders immediately after the Community Chest Drive. Max Rudensky and Wm. Z. Spiegelman represented the Washington Forest Committee at the conference.

"Zionists Seek Declaration by Roosevelt on Moral Issues"
Jewish Telegraphic Agency, October 20, 1938

Determined to maintain the American protest movement until all danger of a threatened British sell-out of Zionism vanishes, the Emergency Committee on Palestine announced at a press conference today plans to launch a campaign for one million signatures to a mammoth telegram urging President Roosevelt to make a public statement stressing the moral and humanitarian issues involved in the Palestine problem and requesting Great Britain to abide by its promises to the Jews. It was said there was reason to believe the President would respond to such an appeal.[4]

The campaign will be started in conjunction with the nationwide mass meetings, which begin next Sunday and will continue until Balfour Day, Nov. 2, at which American Jewry's concern over threats to the Jewish National Home will be voiced. Every signature obtained will be appended to the telegram, the signatories paying five cents, the average wiring cost per name from all parts of the country to Washington.

Speakers at the conference pointed out that the protest movement was divided into three phases. The first consisted of the effort to obtain representations from the State Department on the legalistic issues involved, which was culminated by Secretary of State Cordell Hull's statement promising protection of American interests in the event of any change in Palestine's political status. The second will be the appeal to President Roosevelt, and the third will be a demarche directly to Prime Minister Neville Chamberlain.

Speakers at the conference, held at the Hotel Brevoort, included Rabbi Solomon Goldman, Z.O.A. president, Morris Margulies, Louis Lipsky and William Z. Spiegelman, who outlined the petition plan.

Land and Life, June 1947

Behind the Blockade is the name of a new color film produced by the Jewish National Fund. Like the *Land of Hope*, the new film is based upon Palestine scenes and events depicting the heroic struggle of the Yishub.

Narrated by John Carradine, the famous American Shakespearean actor, *Behind the Blockade* tells and shows the absorbing story of Jewish achievements in Palestine despite and behind the blockade of the British Navy and notwithstanding the barbed wire cantonments of the British Army. The narrative is greatly buttressed and enlivened by the Song of the *Ma'apilim* (so-called illegal immigrants) and the Haganah March exquisitely rendered by Richard Tucker, the famous Metropolitan Opera tenor, and a chorus under the

---

[4] Three months previously, and in response to President Franklin D. Roosevelt's role in organizing the Evian Conference on Refugees (July 1938), the Jewish National Fund issued *An Appreciation of the Great Humanitarian Act for the Refugees*, parts of which are reproduced elsewhere in this volume.

direction of Max Helfman.

Behind the Blockade was produced under the direction of William Zimmermann. The script was written by Ruth Zimmermann. William Z. Spiegelman was research editor of the production.

The new color film will be shown in the United States, Palestine, South America, Europe, South Africa and Australia. JNF Councils and committees desiring to show *Behind the Blockade* should place their bookings well in advance by communicating with the national JNF headquarters. A nominal rental fee will be charged.

"William Z. Spiegel Man [sic], Publicity Director of J.N.F., Dies; One-Time Editor of JTA"
Jewish Telegraphic Agency, May 15, 1949

William Z. Spiegelman, director of publicity for the Jewish National Fund for the past 19 years, died here today at the age of 55. The funeral will be held tomorrow. A journalist in Europe for many years, Spiegelman came to the country in 1924 when he joined the Jewish Telegraphic Agency as its editor. He left the JTA to assume the publicity post with the J.N.F.

"W.Z. Spiegelman, With Jewish Fund"
The Brooklyn Eagle, May 16, 1949

William E. [sic] Spiegelman, director of public relations of the Jewish National Fund of America and editor of its magazine, *Land and Life*, died of a heart attack yesterday in his home, 853 E. 9th Street. He was 56 and a native of Poland.

Surviving are his wife, Mrs. Dora Moreiss Spiegelman; two daughters, Ruth and Judith, and a son, David.

Funeral services were held today at the Flatbush Memorial Chapel, 1283 Coney Island Ave.

Unknown Yiddish newspaper
May 16, 1949[5]

Spiegelman (continued from the first page).[6]

with the Yiddish Telegraphic Agency. He worked with the local Yiddish newspapers, in the Hebrew press, and in the English-Yiddish journals. He also participated in [writing] the English-Yiddish Encyclopedia. In his written works in America, Zev Wolf Spiegelman (William Wolf Spiegelman) was dedicated throughout his years to the problems of Zionism and the Land of Israel. He had the great task of spreading and developing the idea of Zionism in Jewish and secular public opinion in America.

Since 1930, the deceased was director of the press department of the Jewish National Fund in America, and redactor of its English-Yiddish Journal, which is published through the Jewish National Fund. On an assignment from the Jewish National Fund, Zev Wolf Spiegelman traveled to Israel some time ago. He took up a directorial position in the

---

[5] Translated by Yaira Singer.
[6] First page lost.

international section of the Jewish National Fund, and recently received an invitation to take over an important office in the Headquarters of the Jewish National Fund in Jerusalem.

Zev Wolf Spiegelman's early death is a heavy loss for the Zionist Movement. He leaves a wife, Mrs. Dora Spiegelman, and three children, Ruth, David, and Judith. The funeral will be held today, Monday, at 11 in the morning, at Funeral Home 1283 Coney Island Avenue, Brooklyn.

"William Zeev Spiegelman," Ernest E. Barbarash
Publication unknown, May 27, 1949

The first time I met the late William Z. Spiegelman was in London in 1921 in the office of the Jewish Telegraphic Agency. It was the day after his arrival from Warsaw where, even at an early age, he was a distinguished member of the editorial staff of the Yiddish daily *Moment*. I was then a youngster and looked upon the "oldster" Spiegelman with a measure of awe and admiration as he dictated a series of articles on Jewish life in Poland. I still vividly recall Spiegelman's dignified demeanor as he sat erect, smoking his cigarette, and with great fluency and ease, punctuated by a constant stream of literary terms, put into shape the articles that later were syndicated throughout the world by the JTA. As assistant to Mr. Spiegelman in the writing of news copy, I was [as a result] the richer in knowledge and experience. In fact, Spiegelman was my first teacher in the realm of journalism.

Language Command

Some months later, Spiegelman left for the United States. Again our paths crossed in 1924 when I worked under him as a member of the editorial staff of the JTA. He was the day editor and I was the night man. I found Spiegelman to be the newspaperman *par excellence*. Steeped in Hebrew and Yiddish literature, Spiegelman possessed a felicity of style, having a thorough command of the Hebrew, Yiddish and English languages. His articles were marked by profoundness and clarity. They were never superficial but were concise and to the point.

Although an introvert by nature, Spiegelman was fired by an inner passion for the ideals that he espoused. A maximalist Zionist, he brooked no compromise in his conviction. He was unyielding where principles were concerned.

He was a prolific writer covering a wide range of subjects. He was a fluent Hebraist and had a thorough knowledge of the Talmud, and his writings were punctuated with Talmudic references. To some, he may have appeared cold and nonchalant, but under his seeming indifference there beat a warm heart that was deeply concerned with the welfare of his fellow men. Thousands and thousands of words flowed from his pen. He spoke and wrote pearls of wisdom. A collection of his writings would constitute a valuable contribution to contemporary Jewish literature.

Press Contributor

William Z. Spiegelman died at the early age of 56. For the last 19 years, he had held the post of Public Relations Director of the Jewish National Fund. In this capacity, Mr. Spiegelman was instrumental in bringing the sacred ideal of Zionism and the purpose of the JNF to the attention of millions of people. He was one of the foremost authorities in his field, but, at the same time, he did not neglect the sphere that was so dear to his heart – the enrichment of contemporary Hebrew literature through his literary contributions to the

Hebrew press in this country, in Israel and abroad. At the time of his death, Mr. Spiegelman served as special correspondent for the Tel Aviv daily *Haboker*. He also translated several books from German and contributed to the *Universal Jewish Encyclopedia*.

Mr. Spiegelman's memory will be cherished eternally in the hearts of the numerous pupils and friends who were privileged to work with him and to know him.

The funeral services for deceased held last Monday were attended by leaders of the JNF, the Zionist Organization of America, United Palestine Appeal, the Yiddish Writers Union and many other Jewish organizations. Judge Morris Rothenberg, president of the JNF, in his eulogy, said that "the passing of Mr. Spiegelman is a great loss to the Zionist cause and the work for the land [rest of article missing]."

"Israel Mourns Spiegelman"
The New Palestine, June 14, 1949

TEL AVIV. – The news of the untimely passing of William Z. Spiegelman, noted journalist and public relations director of the Jewish National Fund in America, was received here with deep sorrow. The Hebrew press carried obituaries extolling his great talents and paying high tribute to his many years of service to the cause of the establishment of the Jewish state.

The Hebrew daily, *Haboker*, to which the deceased was a frequent contributor, in a lengthy eulogy reviewed Mr. Spiegelman's career and contributions both in the literary field and in his capacity as JNF public relations chief.

"Zeev Spiegelman was a Zionist official who embodied the two worlds – old and new – of the Jewish people of Europe and America. Steeped in Hebraic culture from his early childhood in Warsaw, Spiegelman retained his characteristics even after he left to settle in the new world in the West. In New York Spiegelman absorbed all the new American techniques and at the same time retained and applied his rich background of cultural Zionism.

"Spiegelman had a fluent command of the English, Hebrew, Yiddish and German languages, and both as editor of the Jewish Telegraphic Agency and for the past 20 years as public relations head of the JNF in America, he devoted himself with heart and soul to the dissemination of the Zionist ideal and the redemption of the soil as the unalienable property of the [illegible]. He was forever using new approaches and expanded activities. The Jewish National Fund owes him a great deal of gratitude, for he was the author of many plans and ideas in the field of public relations that proved both effective and successful.

"Spiegelman was a devoted *chaver*, a loyal Zionist and energetic worker. His friends and all those who knew him sorrow deeply because today there are not many of his type," *Haboker* said.

"William Zev Spiegelman: A Tribute By Judge Morris Rothenberg, Remarks Delivered At Funeral Service, May 16, 1949"
Land and Life, Summer 1949

The sudden passing away of our friend and colleague William Z. Spiegelman has come as a great shock and sorrow to us all. Those who were close to him knew that he had been in bad health for some time but we were not prepared for this tragic and untimely end.

It is, indeed, as the Psalmist said, "We are like leaves of grass; in the morning we rise up, in the evening we are cut down and wither."

I speak on behalf of the Administration of the Jewish National Fund of America and its staff, and I am sure I voice also the sentiments of the Keren Kayemeth in Israel in paying tribute to the memory of William Spiegelman. He was a gentle, kindly soul, scholarly, steeped in Jewish learning and tradition, and a fine Jew. He was one of the most respected Executives of the Jewish National Fund. As Publicity and Public Relations Director, he brought to his task a profound understanding of Zionist principles, of Zionist history and of Zionist ideals. He was a facile writer in English, in Hebrew and in Yiddish, and he had a wide knowledge of other languages and cultures. He was a man of creative ideas. The literature of the Keren Kayemeth that he produced and edited bears the imprint of his talents and his quiet and dignified personality.

It has been the good fortune of the Zionist Movement that its officials in the manifold branches of its activities were not persons perfunctorily performing the daily routine of their tasks. They were Zionists concerned with the progress and the ultimate success of the Zionist movement.

Spiegelman was an outstanding example of this type of Zionist official. He regarded his work as a form of civil service to the Jewish people and he brought to his labors the devotion and ardor of a life-long Zionist. He followed every happening in Jewish and in Zionist life with breathless interest. He was a proud son and a true servant of his people.

He knew also the art of friendship, and in our country and in Israel there will be many mourners over his untimely death.

To his wife and children, to whom he was so deeply and tenderly attached, I extend the sincere condolences of myself, of the Jewish National Fund of America and of the Keren Kayemeth in Israel.

We shall always remember in kindliness and in the warmth of the good fellowship that existed among us this fine colleague and true Jewish public servant, William Spiegelman, who left us all too soon.

"In Memoriam," by Mendel N. Fisher
Land and Life, Summer 1949

We have lost one of our ablest and most devoted colleagues, whose entire life was dedicated to the service of Israel. As Director of Public Relations and Editor of *Land and Life*, William Z. Spiegelman made a lasting contribution in the dissemination of information on the fundamental ideas of the Jewish National Fund, to which he gave of his great gifts of heart and mind. He served the whole Zionist movement with great effectiveness. His name will be recalled with eternal gratitude. Our loss is irreparable. The JNF staff here, in Jerusalem and in all parts of the world, mourn his passing. We honor his memory.

"William Z. Spiegelman," by Max Rudensky
Land and Life, Summer 1949

William Zev Spiegelman, son of a well-to-do Warsaw merchant and scholar, and – on his mother's side – scion of a Hassidic dynasty, was still a young lad when his father died. His elder stepbrother, a middle-aged man, became his guardian and spiritual mentor. In addition to an intensive Talmudic schooling, Spiegelman was also instructed in Modern Hebrew and Hassidic lore.

After his Bar Mitzvah, Spiegelman went to study at the modernized Yeshiva at Lida, much against the wishes of his stepbrother who wanted to send his young ward to one of the traditional academies. But Spiegelman did not stay long at Lida, being unable to endure his loneliness. He returned to Warsaw where he continued his Jewish and secular studies, at first under private tutors, and later in the special course established by the famous Dr. Posnanski, Rabbi of the Great Synagogue.

The outbreak of World War I interrupted his studies after a few years at Posnanski's courses, and Spiegelman became a journalist working for Yiddish, Hebrew and Polish publications, including the famous daily *Moment.*

When the war ended, Spiegelman – although continuing his journalistic activities – entered the University of Cracow where he spent several years. After the Polish pogroms in 1918-1919, Spiegelman made a tour of the affected localities, investigating the disturbances.

This tour brought him into contact with the late Henry Morgenthau, Sr., who headed a special commission appointed by President Wilson, and with Mr. Jacob Landau, founder of the Jewish Telegraphic Agency.

In 1920, when Spiegelman came to London to the first postwar World Zionist Conference, Landau invited him to serve as news editor of the Jewish Telegraphic Agency. He stayed in London for over a year before coming to the U.S.

For a while he lived in San Francisco, where he had a number of relatives. He studied at the local University and edited the San Francisco Anglo-Jewish weekly. There he met his wife, Dora.

In 1923 he was invited by Jacob Landau, who had now moved to New York, to edit the J.T.A. *Daily Bulletin* and the cable service of the J.T.A.

In 1930 he was invited by Dr. Emanuel Neumann, then President of the Jewish National Fund of America, to assume the position of Director of Public Relations. This post he filled with singular distinction until his death. In the last few years, Spiegelman acted as the New York correspondent of the Tel Aviv daily *Haboker.*

Two years ago, despite a heart ailment from which he had suffered for six years, he undertook a trip to Israel and spent several months in that country. There he was stricken with a heart attack, which he sought to conceal from his family. A few months ago he suffered another grave attack but soon recovered. Then he had another stroke and passed away after a few days on Sunday, May 15th. Besides his wife, the former Dora Moreiss, he leaves three children – Ruth, Judith and David.

"William Zev Spiegelman"
Karnenu, November 1949

The untimely passing of William Zev Spiegelman at the age of 56 has come as a blow to his host of friends throughout the ranks of the Jewish National Fund (J.N.F.). Mr. Spiegelman, who since 1930 served as Public Relations Director of the J.N.F. of America with distinction, left behind him a wealth of journalistic and cultural contributions to the cause of Zionism. Born in Warsaw, Mr. Spiegelman was well versed in modern Hebrew and Hassidic lore and, with his natural love of Jewish tradition, he played an active role in the Zionist Organization from his early youth onwards. Following a year's stay in London after the First World War, Mr. Spiegelman emigrated to the United States where, in 1923, he became an editor of the Jewish Telegraphic Agency. As Public Relations Director of the J.N.F. in New York, Mr. Spiegelman's name was frequently seen over articles in Hebrew and Yiddish as well as English. He will long be remembered as the author of many new and successful projects in the field of public relations, particularly on the subject of land redemption.

"William Zev Spiegelman," Statement by Elias M. Epstein, Director, Overseas Department
Karnenu, November 1949

From the time he entered the service of the Jewish National Fund in America twenty years ago, William Z. Spiegelman devoted himself heart and soul to this institution, and the impress of his personality was deeply felt in every stage of the development of the Land Fund. A son of the last generation, a generation subject to cultural repression, Spiegelman was no rigid traditionalist; he preferred to create, to expand, to change. I particularly remember the discussions we had in Jerusalem prior to the evacuation of the British when it was uncertain whether the United Nations would follow through its resolution about the Jewish State. He took back with him from Israel the feeling that we should declare our independence whatever the odds against the step. William Z. Spiegelman has left behind him a fine record of patriotic service to his people and I am certain that his influence will long remain as inspiration and encouragement to others.

"Remains of William Spiegelman to Be Transferred to Israel for Reburial in Tel Aviv"
Jewish Telegraphic Agency, April 13, 1950

The remains of the late William Z. Spiegelman, public relations director of the Jewish National Fund of America who died last year, will be transported to Israel on the Israel vessel *Akko* next Monday, it was announced here today. Reburial will take place near Tel Aviv. The *Akko* will be met by J.N.F. officials and friends of the deceased. Mr. Spiegelman served as editor of the Jewish Telegraphic Agency before he joined the Jewish National Fund staff some 20 years age.

"W. Z. Spiegelman Buried in Israel"
The New Palestine, 13 April 1950

The body of the late William Z. Spiegelman, veteran Zionist and public relations director of the Jewish National Fund of America, who died in New York more than a year ago, was re-interred in Israel with special ceremonies attended by officials and staff workers of the Keren Kayemeth Leisrael of both Tel Aviv and Jerusalem, members of the Israel Journalists Association, relatives and close personal friends.

The ceremony took place in front of the JNF building in Tel Aviv. Mr. Spiegelman's nephew, who was present with his family and with other members of the Spiegelman family, recited Kaddish as the crowd stood about the blue-and-white draped casket on which lay a wreath of the Keren Kayemeth Leisrael.

At the side of the grave, which is near the graves of those who fell in Israel's war for independence, J. Heftman, on behalf of the Israel Journalists Association and as chief editor of *Haboker*, for which Mr. Spiegelman was correspondent for many years, delivered a moving oration. Eulogies were also delivered by M. Yinnon, of Mossad Bialik, and J.

Yonathan, speaking on behalf of the head office of the Keren Kayemeth Leisrael.

Others who were present included Rabbi J. M. Kovalsky, A. Kamini, who acted as chairman, S. Shulkes, secretary of the Vaad Artzi, and Rav M. D. Gross, of the Mahleket Haharedim.

In memorial services held at the same time in the JNF offices in New York, at which Mordecai Rudensky presided, and Mendel Fisher, JNF executive director, E. Lerner and Sharon Weitz, the latter representing the JNF of Jerusalem, paid deep-felt tribute to their deceased colleague. It was announced that a grove of trees would be planted in his memory in the George Washington Forest.

HaBoker, Tuesday, May 23, 1950[7]

Page 2.[8]

Today, the journalist William Ze'ev will be brought to eternal peace in the homeland soil, after his body was brought in a ship from the United States. Z. Spiegelman was one of the famous and devoted employees of the Jewish National Fund and at one time worked as a writer for the *HaBoker* newspaper in New York.

Before immigrating to America, about thirty years ago, he was a well-known journalist. As a contributor to the *Moment* newspaper, he fulfilled important duties in public reporting, and he was the representative of Jewish Journalists in the Parliamentarian Club of the first Sejm of Poland. In America, Spiegelman first worked at the Jewish Telegraphic Agency and later edited an English newspaper. After an interval, he was handed the marketing department of the Jewish National Fund and accomplished significant achievements in this function. To Zionist marketing, which was infamous for its routine practices, he brought the vision and excitement of a first-class journalist who was always skilled in revealing the interesting and fascinating points in every article that was brought to the public. For twenty years, he was on duty at this office, and managed to successfully introduce the idea of the Jewish National Fund and to have its aspirations and goals be well liked by the public.

He was well liked by all his associates and friends. A man with good conversational skills who, despite of the mountain of work and tasks that he was responsible for while managing the marketing assignments, and despite his burdensome journalist duties, always kept himself quite calm and well-mannered.

His family will find consolation knowing that many share their sorrow, and knowing that his wish to be buried in the homeland soil was fulfilled by the Jewish National Fund, which is appreciative of the virtue of its loyal employee.

---

[7] Translated from the Hebrew by Orly Benun.
[8] First page lost.

In Poland, mid-1910s.

With his mother.

Plowing the soil.

Far left, in New York City.

New York City, circa 1924.

Third from the left, acting as toastmaster, send-off for B. Smolar, Feb 1928.

Third from the right, meeting of unknown group.

Fourth from the left, with Toscanini (far left), February 11, 1934.

At Sde Akiba, Palestine, August 1947. Dora Spiegelman is on his right.

Ruth J. Spiegelman's graduation from college, 1946.
Dora Spiegelman is on the left.

With Dora Spiegelman, date unknown.

Date unknown.

JEWISH DAILY BULLETIN

JEWISH NEWS FROM ALL PARTS OF THE WORLD WITHIN 24 HOURS.

ONLY DAILY REVIEW OF JEWISH EVENTS PRINTED IN ENGLISH.

Vol. I. New York, N. Y., Wednesday, Oct. 15, 1924. Price, 4 Cents. No.

JEWISH MEMBER OF HUNGARIAN PARLIAMENT CHALLENGES ANTI-SEMITIC DEPUTY TO DUEL
Demands Satisfaction for Insulting Remarks in Parliament.

Budapest, Oct. 15. (Special despatch to the Jewish Daily Bulletin)—Stormy scenes which occurred in the Hungarian Parliament last week, during which insulting remarks were hurled at the Jewish member of the House by an anti-Semitic deputy, will find their conclusion, after the medieval fashion, in a duel. The Jewish deputy, Bela Fabian, formerly District Court Judge of Budapest, has challenged Deputy Ulain, who recently came into the limelight again, as defense attorney for the bomb conspirators of Szongrad.

Deputy Ulain, one of the leaders of the anti-Semitic organization known as the Awakening Magyars, appeared in the District Court of Szolnok as counsel for defense of nine members of the Awakening Magyars who, on December 26, 1923, threw a bomb into a hall in Scongrad where a Jewish charity ball was being held. The acquittal of the conspirators by the Szolnok court created great excitement in Hungary, caused the resignation of two members of the Cabinet and was one of the first matters to be taken up by the new session of the Hungarian Parliament. During the session Ulain insulted Fabian, resulting in the removal of the former from the house.

JEWISH NATIONAL COUNCIL, DISPERSED BY POLICE, WILL BE LEGALIZED
Lithuanian Government Reconsiders Its Policy Towards Lithuanian Jews

Kovno, Oct. 15. (Special Despatch to the Jewish Daily Bulletin).—The protest of Lithuanian Jewry against the action of the Lithuanian Government in destroying the last remnants of the previously granted Jewish communal autonomy, has had its effect. The Judicial Committee of the Lithuanian Diet today passed the first reading of a bill calling for the legalisation of the National Rat, the Jewish National Council of Lithuania which was, as will be recollected, recently dispersed by the police.

DR. ROSENBAUM, FORMER MINISTER OF JEWISH AFFAIRS, LEAVES FOR PALESTINE

Kovno, Oct. 15. (Special Despatch to the Jewish Daily Bulletin)—Dr. Rosenbaum, former minister of Jewish affairs in the Lithuanian Cabinet, against whom the Government has recently started proceedings for affixing the title of Minister to his name, is leaving for Palestine, for the purpose of settling there permanently. "I am tired of Lithuanian politics," he stated.

JEWS AND CATHOLICS LEAD IN CHARITY

In a speech delivered last night at Town Hall, George J. Gillepsie, president of the St. Vincent de Paul Society, declared that the Jews and Catholics lead in charity work in New York. In 1923 the Jews collected $3,000,000.

PALESTINIAN NATURALIZATION LAW, READY FOR PUBLICATION, CONFERS CITIZENSHIP ON JEWS AND NON-JEWS ALIKE
Palestine High Commissioner Relates Interesting Details in First Authorized Press Interview.

Jerusalem, Oct. 15. (Jewish Telegraphic Agency)—"The long-expected, new naturalization law of Palestine has finally been worked out and is ready for publication; it will confer Palestinian citizenship on Jews and non-Jews alike, after two years residence in the country", Sir Herbert Samuel, High Commissioner of Palestine declared today in his first formal interview given to press representatives.

"The principles of the Government Ordinance granting autonomy to the Jewish communities of Palestine has been finally approved by the Colonial Office", the High Commissioner further stated. "The going into effect, however, of this Ordinance, may possibly be delayed for some time.

"With regard to the loan proposed by the Palestinian Government for the necessary reconstruction work", the High Commissioner expressed his fear that the "question may be delayed on account of the new Parliament elections in England. It will be impossible to submit the plans before the new Parliament convenes.

"The rumors that Transjordania will be annexed to Palestine are unfounded. Transjordania is a part of the British mandatory area and negotiations are now under way between the Government of Great Britain and Emir Abdullah, ruler of Transjordania, as to the conditions and form of administration of the country", Sir Herbert declared. "My term of office expires next June. The British Government, however, has not considered the question of a successor. One thing is certain: Sir Gilbert Clayton, the Civil Secretary of the Palestinian Government has announced his intention to retire from the Palestinian service next spring."

Sir Herbert will leave tomorrow for Geneva, where he will attend the meeting of the Mandates Commission of the League of Nations, which will receive his report on conditions in Palestine. He will return in three weeks.

ADOLF HITLER, LEADER OF GERMAN ANTI-SEMITES, WILL BE INTERNED IF HE RETURNS TO AUSTRIA
Both Bavaria and Austria Refuse Him Rights of Citizenship.

Vienna, Oct. 15. (Jewish Telegraphic Agency)—Adolf Hitler, leader of the German anti-Semites and defeated general of the Bavarian Beer Revolution, will not be permitted to enter Austria. If he crosses the border he will be interned and held for deportation. Such instructions were issued today by the Austrian Government to the frontier authorities, in view of the fact that Hitler, who is now imprisoned in Bavaria, is to be sent to Austria, his former country.

The Austrian government claims that by reason of Hitler's absence from Austria for 12 years, he has lost his citizenship.

First issue of the *Jewish Daily Bulletin.*

2   JEWISH DAILY BULLETIN   Wednesday, Oct. 15, 1924.

JEWISH DAILY BULLETIN

Published every day in the week except Saturday by the Jewish Daily Bulletin Co., 132 Nassau Street, New York

Jacob Landau, Publisher

Vol. I.   Wednesday, Oct. 15, 1924.   No. 1.

Offices of the Jewish Daily Bulletin

New York ....132 Nassau Street
London ....201a High Holborn
Paris ....7 Rue le Peletier
Berlin ....Hohenzolerndamm 13
Warsaw .... Sp. z Ogr. Odp. Wspolna 9
Jerusalem ....P. O. B. 550

Subscription Rates

	U. S. and Canada	Foreign
One Year	$10.00	$15.00
Six Months	6.00	8.00
One Month	1.00	1.50

Copyrighted

STATEMENT OF PURPOSE

The **Jewish Daily Bulletin** will be the conveyor of the World's Jewish news. It will report impartially, concisely and authentically, all Jewish facts. It will be a connecting link between the Jewish communities of all states in the Union. Today, the Jewish Community of Chicago does not know what the Jews of Boston are doing and the Jews of the West are un-informed of what is happening in Jewish life in the East.

The **Jewish Daily Bulletin** will fill the much felt need of a proper disseminator.

By subscribing to the cable and telegraphic news service of the Jewish Telegraphic Agency, the **Jewish Daily Bulletin** will be enabled to present to its readers accurate reports of Jewish events from all parts of the globe within 24 hours of their occurrence.

The **Jewish Daily Bulletin** will serve as a stimulating guide and will arouse a great many, who are now indifferent, to a larger interest in Jewish affairs.

The **Jewish Daily Bulletin** will be independent. It will not propagate any particular philosophy or theory or tendency. It will limit itself to the presentation of facts, leaving to its readers the forming of their opinion.

The **Jewish Daily Bulletin** will offer its readers a daily survey on Jewish and non-Jewish public opinion throughout the world on Jewish topics.

The **Jewish Daily Bulletin** will be the clarion to the young American Jew, who is growing up uninformed on contemporary Jewish life to proper understanding and consequently consciousness and responsibility to the Jewish community.

The **Jewish Daily Bulletin** will be the Jewish mouthpiece and interpreter.

The **Jewish Daily Bulletin** will acquaint its readers with the manifold activities and undertakings of Jews throughout the world. By giving Jewish news in the right proportions it will enable all thinking non-Jews to perceive Jewish conditions in their true perspective.

The **Jewish Daily Bulletin** will accurately report all developments in Palestine and in the surrounding mid-eastern countries.

DAILY DIGEST OF WORLD PUBLIC OPINION ON JEWISH MATTERS

Mexican Press Opposes Jewish Immigration.

The question of the stranded Jewish refugees in various European ports, as well as those Jews who are compelled to leave their homes and present occupations in a search for new homelands, still holds the attention of the press almost everywhere.

The invitation, extended by President-elect Calles of Mexico in an interview granted to a representative of the Jewish Telegraphic Agency in New York, to the Jewish refugees to come and settle in Mexico caused a storm in many Mexican papers as the Mexican press takes a negative stand on the matter. So, for instance, the Mexican "Excelsior" says editorially, "In spite of the fact that Jews are workers, savers, intelligent and able, we do not consider that this immigration would be the most desirable for this country. They would gain control of industries which today are in our hands; they would receive the support of powerful American and English sources, and there would ensue economic, social and religious conflicts."

Against the Crimean Proposition

The process now going on in Soviet Russia, transforming Jewish city dwellers into land-toilers, and the scheme talked of in connection with this for the creation of a Jewish agricultural settlement in Southern Russia is editorially commented upon by the "Wiener Morgen Zeitung".

"They (the communists) have given permission to Russian Jews to settle in the unpopulated region of South Russia and even to build a Jewish peasant state there! Excellent. They could not be more generous. Only one condition is imposed in connection with this excellent beginning: the Jews themselves bear the expenses of this new State. The Soviet Government does not give one cent for this purpose. Now, the Jews of Russia have to face a peculiar problem. No less than a state is being given to them, after their clothes and shoes were removed; at a time when they do not know whether they will be able to obtain food for their children for the next few hours, how can they know what to do with this territory? It is obvious that every Russian Jew would be ready to sell his share in the proposed State in South Russia for a loaf of bread."

Comments on Refugees Emergency Campaign

The Warsaw "Haint" treats editorially the campaign of the American Committee on Jewish Refugees for half a million dollars for the purpose of helping the stranded refugees and, if possible, affording them an opportunity of going to Palestine.

"Such a plan is within the limits of reality", the paper states. "Were it a question of what to do with 100,000 or more emigrants, the Palestine solution would be insufficient. But 10,000? In the course of the last summer alone, 10,000 Jewish immigrants arrived in Palestine. Why cannot we do the same with another 10,000? Logic sides with the Zionists' solution of the problem. How-

(Continued on Page 4)

First issue of the *Jewish Daily Bulletin.*

Wednesday, Oct. 15, 1924.   JEWISH DAILY BULLETIN

NEWS GATHERING FACILITIES OF THE JEWISH DAILY BULLETIN

The **Jewish Daily Bulletin** will receive daily cable despatches and news letters from its own office in the following centers:

LONDON, PARIS, WARSAW, BERLIN, JERUSALEM, LOS ANGELES, CHICAGO and WASHINGTON.

Among our correspondents are the following: B. Leftwitch, **London**; L. Blumenfeld, **Paris**; Dr. M. Wurmbrandt, **Berlin**; M. Moses, **Warsaw**; S. Schwartz, **Jerusalem**; M. L. Tenenblatt, **Vienna**; Dr. M. Beilinson, **Rome**; Dr. Wolfgang Von Weisl, special traveling correspondent in the Mid-East, (now in Hejas); M. Rosenbaum, **Constantinople**; J. Evin, **Bucharest**; A. Styvel, **Kovno**; L. Sichroni, **Riga**; D. Moskvin, **Moscow**; Dr. Matthew Hindes, traveling European correspondent; Simeon Uschkevitch, **Paris**; J. Nachbin, **Rio de Janiero**; D. Lomonosoff, **Buenos Aires**; Max Rhoade, **Washington**; Ellis Ranen, **Los Angeles**; Eugene B. Block, **San Francisco**; B. Smollnar, **Chicago**; A Rhinewine, **Toronto**; I. Rabinovitch, **Montreal**; Anard Wetstein Littman, **Atlantic City**; N. H. Shoop, **Pittsburgh**; David Soibelman, **Buffalo**; D. Eidelsberg, **Cleveland**; Philip Slomowitz, **Detroit**; Robert S. Ford, **Baltimore**; Robert Reiss, **Philadelphia**; Oscar Leonard, **St. Louis**.

PERCY S. STRAUS PRESIDES AT BANQUET OF NEW YORK JEWISH FEDERATION

Business Men Representing One Billion Dollars Enlist in Campaign for $1,250,000.

Over a billion dollars worth of Merchandising power was represented at a dinner last night at the Hotel Pennsylvania when 150 of the leading resident buyers and their staffs met to form a financial fighting force to help raise the $1,250,000 for which the Federation for the Support of Jewish Philanthropic Societies is making a drive, starting October 26. The Buyer's unit is one of 137 similar units of the Business Men's Council of Federation with ramifications in every industry and profession in the metropolis, each unit having accepted a quota in the drive levied after a careful analysis of its financial status.

Mr. Percy S. Straus presided and among the speakers were Mr. Zion de Frece Bernstein, chairman of the General Campaign Activities of Federation, who urged each of the members to enlarge the organization through the enlistment of $100 subscribers. Speeches were delivered by Dr. Nathan Krass, Mr. Fred Stein, who spoke on the problem of proper hospital service to the public; and Dr. Solomon Lowenstein who outlined the work of the 91 institutions which the Federation supports and controls, of these, 27 are on the East Side.

ATTACKS ON JEWS IN AUSTRIA AND HUNGARY

In Wiener Neustadt, Austria, anti-Semites threw gas bombs into a theatre where a Jewish audience was being shown a moving picture of which the Jew-baiters disapproved, the Jewish Morning Journal reports from Vienna. Similar attacks were made on a synagogue in Shentes, Hungary.

The Hungarian government has refused to allow a large number of Jewish students who wished to go abroad and study permission to leave Hungary on the ground that they are of military age.

OUR FOREIGN NEWS LETTER

Is There A Possibility For Larger Jewish Immigration Into Argentina?

Newcomers face problem of unemployment industry; what are the prospects for settling on the land?

By D. LOMONOSOV, Special Correspondent of the Jewish Daily Bulletin, Buenos Aires.

Argentina, the most industrially and commercially developed republic of South America, is now, after the restriction of immigration to the United States, the next centre of attraction for home seekers.

What are the possibilities for Jewish newcomers in Argentina? Will they, if helped to come here, have the opportunity to enlarge the Jewish community with a new, self-supporting and productive class?

Argentina is not sufficiently developed to be able to receive an immigration of several hundred thousand newcomers yearly. This must be stated emphatically in advance. Due to the increased immigration, a crisis is already beginning to be felt among the workmen. In general there is talk in Argentina of a crisis in industry and commerce, but that is an erroneous impression. Industry and commerce are quite normal; the existing factories operate regularly and with full staffs of workmen. A crisis is noticeable among the workingmen because industry and commerce can not employ the number of hands available, due to the increased immigration. Unlimited immigration into Argentina is possible only for those who wish to devote themselves to agriculture.

Argentina is an agricultural land. Her capacity is large and wide. The more populated provinces are still sparsely settled. There are sections which might be called unpopulated. Their economic and political future depends on their agricultural development. Therefore, while government circles are opposed to an urban immigration, they are sympathetically inclined toward a rural immigration.

Immigrants who intend to engage in farming have two means of reaching their goal: to settle on government property or to form a community on the land of the great land-owners. Jews have still a third way: to become colonists with the help of the "Ica".

The provinces most frequently mentioned as centers of colonization are: Santiago del Estera, Riaco, Chaco and Missiones. All the provinces enumerated (the last two have not a sufficiently large population to be called provinces) are in the south of the Republic. Colonization on private property can take place only in the provinces of Santiago del Estera, Riaco and partly in Missiones. In Chaco one can settle only on government land.

The terms of a typical contract concluded between a landowner and a colonist in the province of Santiago del Estera, are:

The estanciera (landowner) gives the colonist the stated number of acres, work-cattle and all machinery necessary for the work. The colonist also receives seed. The kinds of seed to be sown are determined by a mutual agreement of the colonist and the administration.

The region of Santiago del Estera is arid. Therefore the estanciera udertakes to irrigate the cultivated land. However, he supplies water in

First issue of the *Jewish Daily Bulletin.*

4   JEWISH DAILY BULLETIN   Wednesday, Oct. 15, 1924.

one main canal, from which each colonist must lead pipes to his own farm. The colonist is obliged to clear his ground from trees, roots and weeds.

He is obliged to sow 30 per cent of the land occupied in the first year, 80 per cent in the second year and 100 per cent in the third year. If the colonist fails to fulfill this point of the contract he must pay the landowner the average harvest yield for every unsown acre of land.

After the harvest has been gathered the colonist must return the seed to the landowner. The remainder of the produce is then divided according to the terms of the contract.

The colonist must build his house and stalls for horses and other work-cattle himself. The landowner gives him the place from which to take the needed building material.

The colonist cannot leave his ground for more than three days without the knowledge of the administration. Should he do so, the contract becomes null and void.

Among the Jewish newcomers there is a great problem of unemployment. I asked the president of the Immigration Section of the Central Committee of the People's Relief and Immigrant Aid Society why they did not advise newcomers to settle in the province of Santiago del Estera. In reply, it was pointed out that the province is too far from a Jewish center and for newcomers this is a serious drawback. Secondly, newcomers do not see a future for themselves under the conditions of the contract, usually offered, tending to create a situation from which the colonist can only expect food and never have savings for the purchase of his own piece of ground. Particularly objectionable is the colonists enforced residence on the ground and the area which he may cultivate.

One must also mention the fact that the landowners colonize families exclusively and give the preference to large families. Unmarried men can become colonists only under exceptional circumstances and when they come in groups.

ORTHODOX JEWS IN POLAND FORM COMMITTEES TO SUPERVISE WOMAN'S DRESS

Warsaw, Oct. 15. (Special despatch to the Jewish Daily Bulletin)—The protest issued by the Warsaw Rabbinate and many leading Rabbis in the provincial towns of Poland against the immodesty of woman's dress, is finding support in many orthodox Jewish circles all over the country. In various towns committees of orthodox Jews were formed to supervise woman's dress. In several towns women who appeared in short sleeves were censured and warned against a repetition.

Comments on Refugees Emergency Campaign
(Continued from Page 2)

ever, the Zionists themselves did not venture to think of this.

"Now a report from America states that a campaign for half a million dollars is under way for the purpose of helping these stranded Jews, and, if possible, affording them an opportunity to go to Palestine. This is being done, not by Zionists but by Jews of the type of Louis Marshall and his associates. Palestine is no longer a Zionist Utopia; it is no longer a dream. Should this plan be realized, two things will be accomplished: the emigrants will find a refuge and a home, and Palestine will be looked upon as an affair of practical importance. There are many Jews who have yet to be convinced of this."

COMMITTEE FORMED TO HELP JEWISH REFUGEE PHYSICIANS
Will Raise $25,000.

An organization for the purpose of bringing relief to the large number of physicians who are now stranded in the various European countries, has been formed. Initiative in the matter has been taken by Dr. A. J. Rongy of 590 West End Avenue, New York City, who recently returned from Europe, where he participated in the meetings of the Jewish World Relief Conference recently held in Carlsbad. Under mandate of this Conference, he is authorized to form an American Physicians' Committee for the aid of the physician refugees in Europe. Announcement to this effect was made today by Dr. Rongy. The members of the Committee formed are: Drs. Samuel J. Kopetsky, Henry W. Fraunthel, William Linder, Henry Roth, E. W. Friedman, A. Hymanson, N. Ratnoff, E. Altman and I. S. Hirsch.

Many hundreds of physicians, who, on account of political conditions, were compelled to leave Russia, find themselves in great difficulty, owing to legal restrictions which prohibit them from practicing medicine in their present places of residence. As many as 400 physicians living in Germany, France, Czechoslovakia and Austria are compelled to perform menial work, many of them serving as porters, cabmen and manual laborers, Dr. Rongy reported from personal observation.

The fund which will be collected by the American Physicians' Committee is to be employed to direct these refugee physicians to such countries where they will be permitted to practice their profession and serve the people. Dr. Rongy is chairman of the Committee, Dr. I. W. Held, treasurer, and Dr. A. Saphir, secretary. The Committee will endeavor to raise $25,000.

ALICE C. BRANDEIS, WIFE OF JUSTICE BRANDEIS, DECLARES FOR LA FOLLETTE

In a statement made public at La Follette headquarters in Washington today, Mrs. Alice C. Brandeis, wife of Associate Justice Brandeis, endorsed Senator La Follette's foreign policy, with special reference to American expansion in Latin America.

Mrs. Brandeis, whose husband was considered as La Follette's running mate, declared, "Most of the reforms he has advocated in the course of his long career have become law."

FORMER BROOKLYN RABBI DIES IN JERUSALEM

Rabbi Abraham Eber Hirshowitz, formerly of Borough Park, Brooklyn, died the day after Yom Kippur, according to a cable received by his relatives here. The deceased had lived in the United States some thirty years and was a prominent figure in the rabbinical world. He was rabbi in San Francisco and later in Toledo and Brooklyn, whence he emigrated to Palestine. He is survived by his son, Louis Hirshowitz, and by three daughters, Mrs. Clara Stoll, Mrs. Mendelsohn and Mrs. Sarah Levin.

Pinski-Massel Press, Inc.   84 Bowery, New York

First issue of the *Jewish Daily Bulletin.*

Announcement

of the Observance of the Fiftieth Anniversary of

Prof. ALBERT EINSTEIN

Under the Auspices of the
JEWISH NATIONAL FUND OF AMERICA

T WAS shortly before Albert Einstein submitted to the Prussian Academy of Sciences his newest discovery of the identity of the laws of gravitation and electro-magnetism. The great event had already cast its shadow before it. Again, as in 1919 when Einstein's prediction, that rays of starlight passing close to the sun will be found deflected, was verified, and his Theory of Relativity confirmed, the entire world was stirred by interest and curiosity.

Reporters and correspondents of newspapers throughout the world were conducting a regular siege upon the modest and defenseless scientist. What did it matter to them that neither they nor their readers could possibly understand his formulæ and deductions? They begged for interviews, they demanded elucidations, they clamored for his latest treatise in order to cable it—Greek and all—to America. The wizard had waved his wand again and, without com-

prehending his magic, the world was stirred by a new vision of the marvelous.

It was then that Albert Einstein issued a statement. Instead, however, of speaking of his new discovery, he spoke of his people—the Jewish people—of their problems and hopes. In this statement, given to the Jewish Telegraphic Agency, Einstein said:

"Jewry is like an organism which was beheaded 2,000 years ago. Jerusalem with its Temple was its head. It was God's miracle that it remained alive for so long a period without a head. A second miracle occurred when the body, grown formless, decided several scores of years ago that it must have a head, and has already formed a little head in Palestine. However, this head is still too small, and too weak for such a huge body. See to it that it grows into a full-sized head as befits the body."

THUS, the man whose vision embraces the sweep of stars and universes, whose keen gaze has penetrated into some of their deepest secrets, proclaims the hope and the faith which is the daily food of his spirit. Not even Ein-

Jewish National Fund, 1929.

Jewish National Fund, 1938.

Jewish National Fund, 1938.

Jewish National Fund, 1939-1940.

Tree nursery at Shave Zion, settlement of refugees from Germany.

ה היא
נאולת הארץ?

What is Geulath Ha'-aretz?

1

ה היא
הקרן הקימת לישראל?

What is the Keren Kaye-meth Le'Israel (Jewish National Fund)?

2

Jewish National Fund, 1939-1940.

Jewish National Fund, 1943.

Jewish National Fund, 1943.

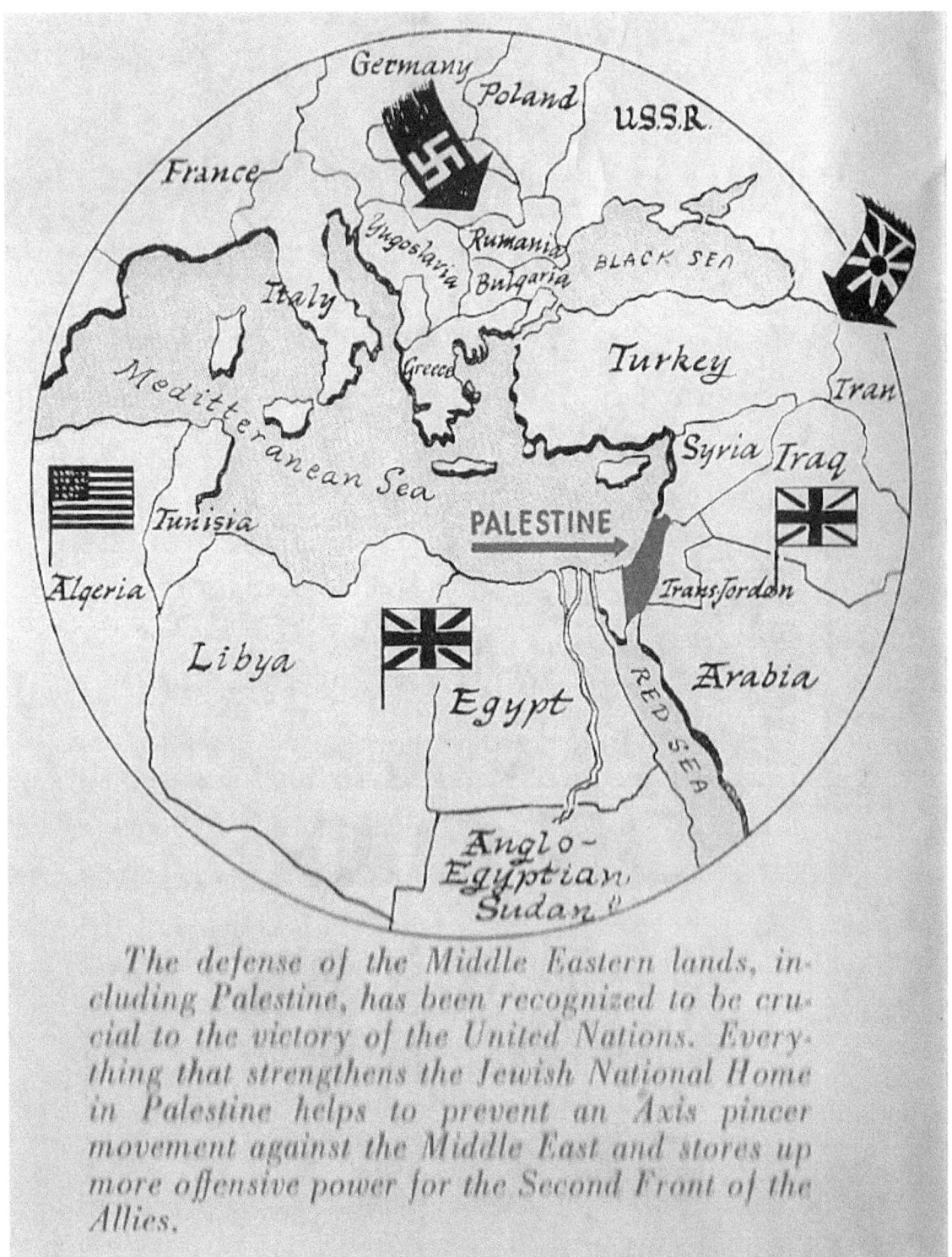

The defense of the Middle Eastern lands, including Palestine, has been recognized to be crucial to the victory of the United Nations. Everything that strengthens the Jewish National Home in Palestine helps to prevent an Axis pincer movement against the Middle East and stores up more offensive power for the Second Front of the Allies.

Jewish National Fund, 1943.

Jewish National Fund, 1948.

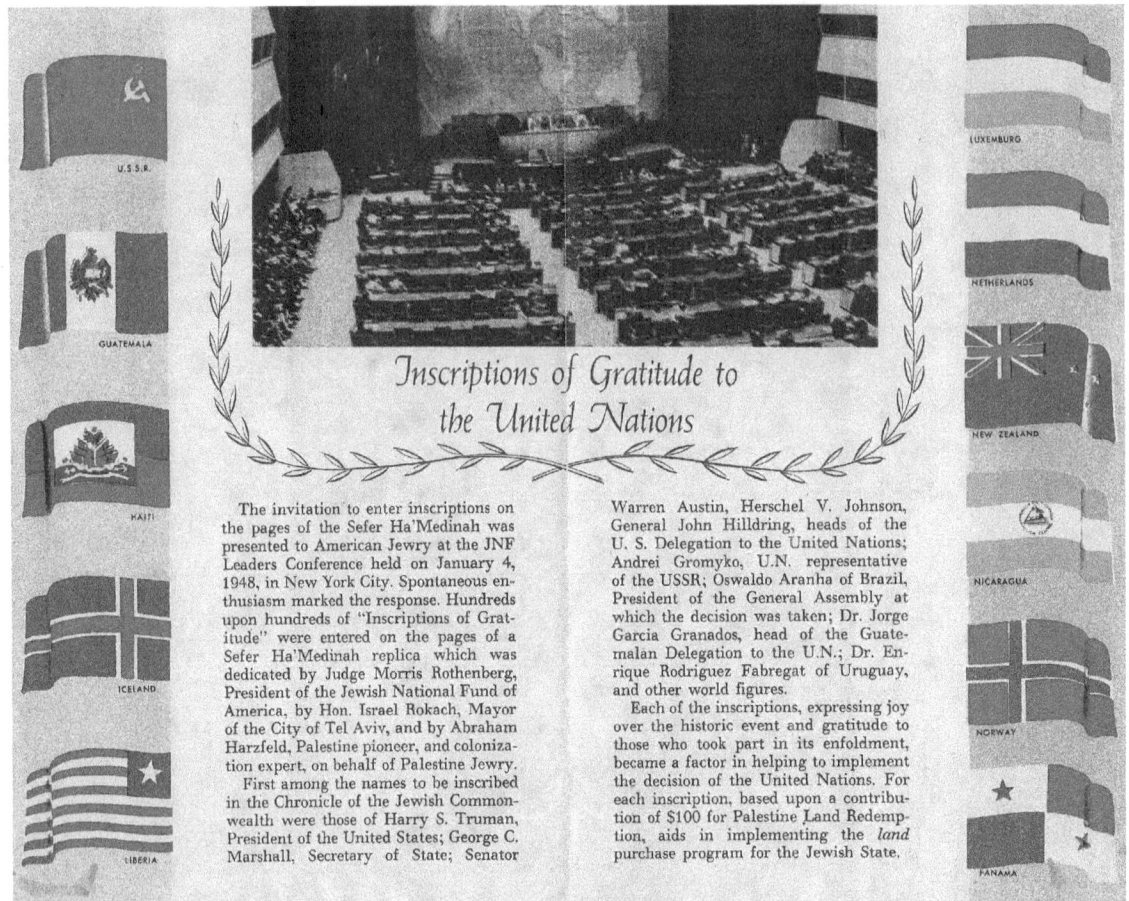

Inscriptions of Gratitude to the United Nations

The invitation to enter inscriptions on the pages of the Sefer Ha'Medinah was presented to American Jewry at the JNF Leaders Conference held on January 4, 1948, in New York City. Spontaneous enthusiasm marked the response. Hundreds upon hundreds of "Inscriptions of Gratitude" were entered on the pages of a Sefer Ha'Medinah replica which was dedicated by Judge Morris Rothenberg, President of the Jewish National Fund of America, by Hon. Israel Rokach, Mayor of the City of Tel Aviv, and by Abraham Harzfeld, Palestine pioneer, and colonization expert, on behalf of Palestine Jewry.

First among the names to be inscribed in the Chronicle of the Jewish Commonwealth were those of Harry S. Truman, President of the United States; George C. Marshall, Secretary of State; Senator Warren Austin, Herschel V. Johnson, General John Hilldring, heads of the U. S. Delegation to the United Nations; Andrei Gromyko, U.N. representative of the USSR; Oswaldo Aranha of Brazil, President of the General Assembly at which the decision was taken; Dr. Jorge Garcia Granados, head of the Guatemalan Delegation to the U.N.; Dr. Enrique Rodriguez Fabregat of Uruguay, and other world figures.

Each of the inscriptions, expressing joy over the historic event and gratitude to those who took part in its enfoldment, became a factor in helping to implement the decision of the United Nations. For each inscription, based upon a contribution of $100 for Palestine Land Redemption, aids in implementing the *land* purchase program for the Jewish State.

Jewish National Fund, 1948.

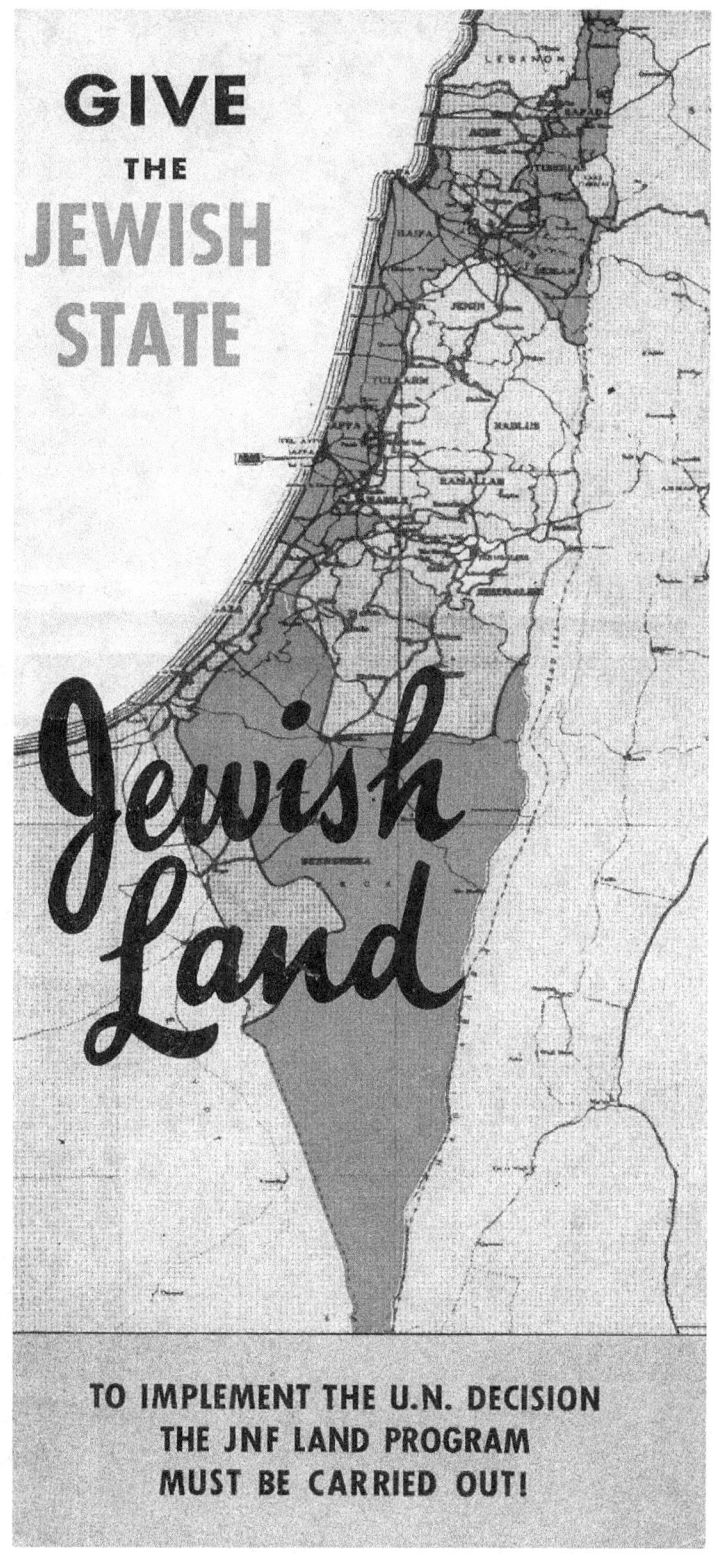

Jewish National Fund, 1948.

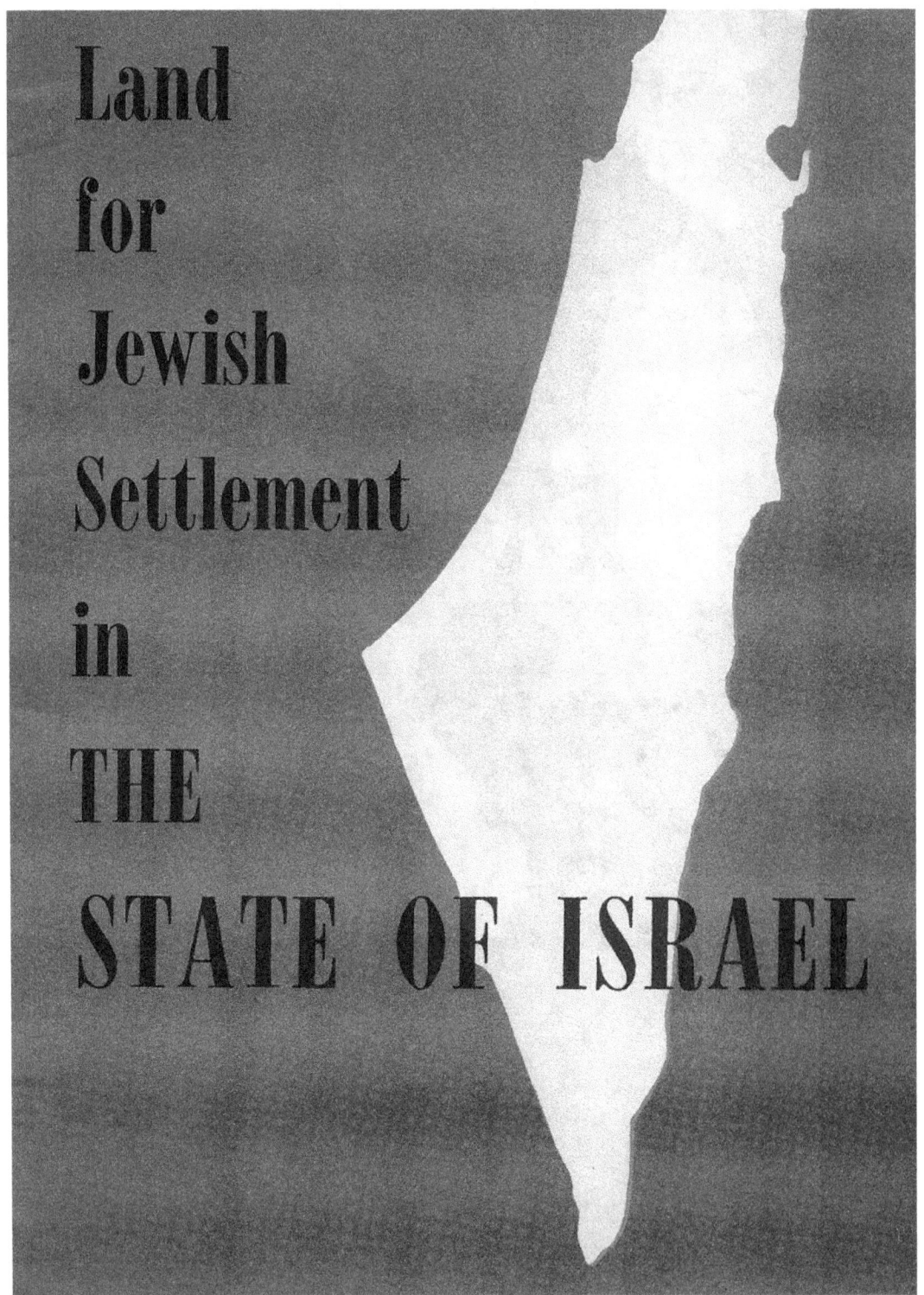

Jewish National Fund, 1948.

Jewish National Fund, 1948.

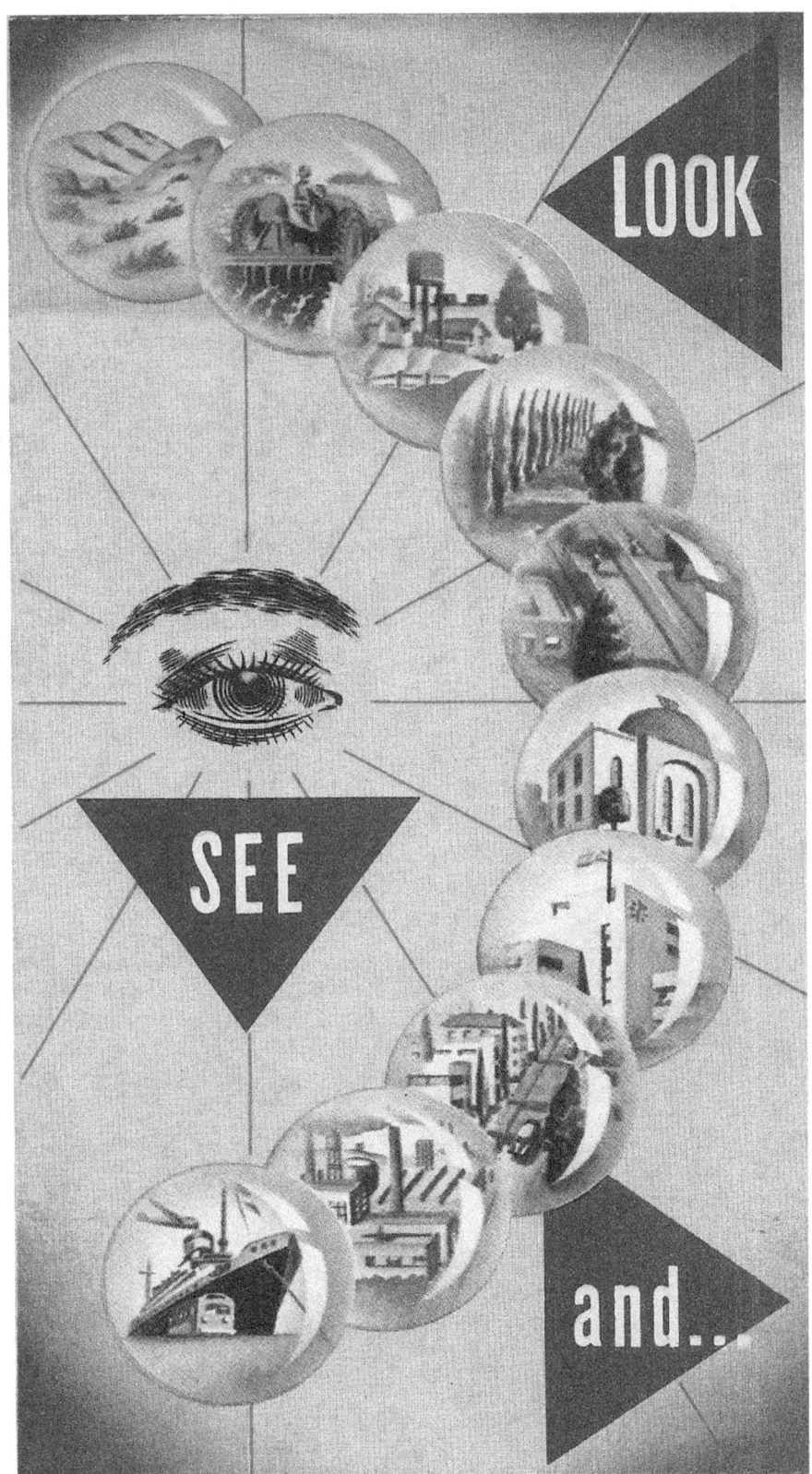

Jewish National Fund, 1949.

Jewish National Fund, 1949.

Jewish National Fund, date unknown.

Jewish National Fund, date unknown.

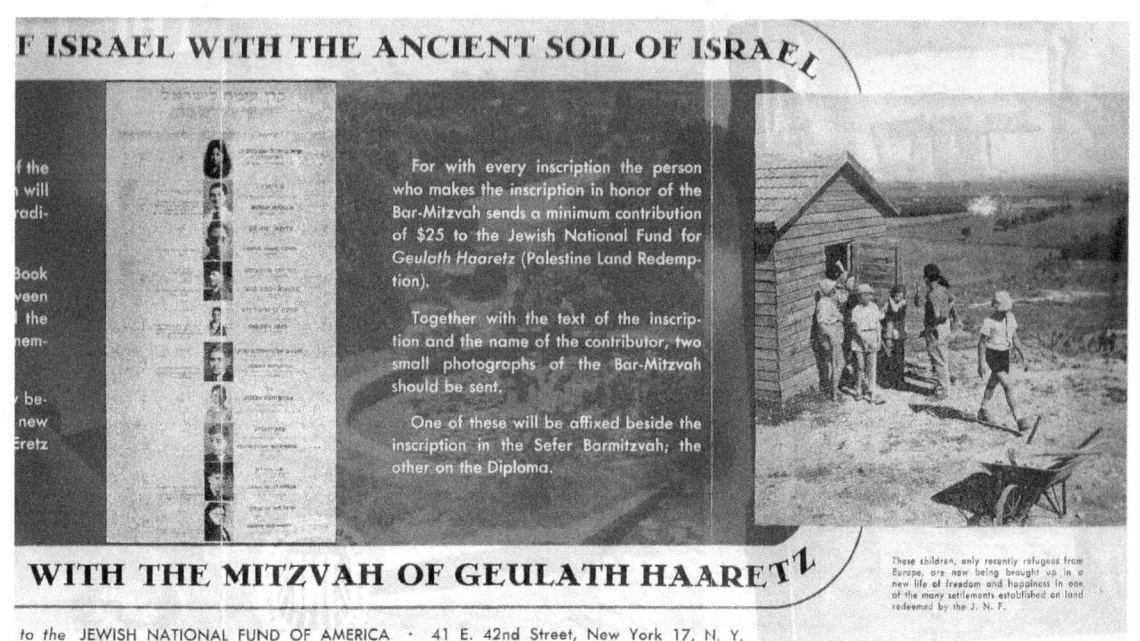

Jewish National Fund, date unknown.

Declaration of Passenger to Canada, June 7, 1921.

DECLARATION OF INTENTION OF MARRIAGE
STATE OF RHODE ISLAND

Full name of Groom *(Expectant.)*

William Zev Spiegelman

Place of Residence Sea Gate N Y

Date of Birth Aug 28 1895 — Age 29

Birthplace Poland Russia — Race or Color W

Occupation Journalist

Father's Name David Spiegelman

Mother's Maiden Name Chava Ossynholtz

Parents' Birthplaces Fa. Poland Russia — Mo. Poland Russia

Father's Occupation Merchant

No. of Marriage 1 — Marriage terminated by Death Date — — Divorce Date — —

Providence, R. I., Nov. 29 1924

I, the expectant groom named in the foregoing declaration, hereby certify that the information given is correct to the best of my knowledge and belief.

William Zev Spiegelman

Signed in the presence of *(Expectant Groom.)*

Full name of Bride *(Expectant.)*

Dora Moraiss

(Maiden Name if Previously Married)

Place of Residence 2024 61st St Brooklyn N Y

Date of Birth Feb 22 1900 — Age 24

Birthplace Lodz Poland — Race or Color W

Occupation At home

Father's Name Jacob Moraiss

Mother's Maiden Name Chava D Spiegelman

Parents' Birthplaces Fa. Poland Russia — Mo. Poland Russia

Father's Occupation Merchant

No. of Marriage 1 — Marriage terminated by Death Date — — Divorce Date —

Providence, R. I., Nov 29 1924

I, the expectant bride named in the foregoing declaration, hereby certify that the information given is correct to the best of my knowledge and belief.

Signed in the presence of *(Expectant Bride.)*

N. B.—State whether the marriage is the 1st, 2d, 3d, &c., marriage of each. State whether white, black, Chinese or Japanese. Give middle names in full.

Declaration of Intention of Marriage, November 22, 1924.

N. J.-N. Y. 9-150-525 191337

ORIGINAL
(To be retained by clerk)

UNITED STATES OF AMERICA
fb **PETITION FOR CITIZENSHIP**

No.

To the Honorable the ____ U S District ____ Court of ____ Eastern District of NY ____ at ____ Brooklyn NY

The petition of ____ William Zev Spiegelman ____, hereby filed, respectfully shows:

(1) My place of residence is ____ 2114 83 Street, Brooklyn, NY ____ (2) My occupation is ____ journalist

(3) I was born in ____ Mordy, Poland ____ on ____ August 28 1893 ____ My race is ____ Hebrew

(4) I declared my intention to become a citizen of the United States on ____ April 8, 1929 ____ in the ____ U S District

Court of ____ Eastern Distri ____, at ____ Brooklyn, NY

(5) I am ____ married. The name of my wife or husband is ____ Dora

we were married on ____ December 5, 1924 ____ at ____ Providence, R. I. ____; he was

born at ____ Lodz, Poland ____ on ____ February 22, 1900 ____; entered the United States

at ____ New York ____ on ____ October 1906 ____ for permanent residence therein, and now

resides at ____ 2114 83 Street, Brooklyn, NY ____ I have ____ children, and the name, date,

and place of birth, and place of residence of each of said children are as follows: ____ Ruth November 5, 1925; Judith ovember

6, 1929 and Samuel August 3, 193?; all born at New York and

reside 2114 83 Street Brooklyn, NY

(6) My last foreign residence was ____ Montreal, Canada ____ I emigrated to the United States of

America from ____ Montreal, Canada ____ My lawful entry for permanent residence in the United States

was at ____ Rouses Pt., NY ____ under the name of ____ William Zev Spiegelman

on ____ March 14, 929 ____, on the vessel ____ Rutland RR #52

(7) I am not a disbeliever in or opposed to organized government or a member of or affiliated with any organization or body of persons teaching disbelief in or opposed to organized government. I am not a polygamist nor a believer in the practice of polygamy. I am attached to the principles of the Constitution of the United States and well disposed to the good order and happiness of the United States. It is my intention to become a citizen of the United States and to renounce absolutely and forever all allegiance and fidelity to any foreign prince, potentate, state, or sovereignty, and particularly to

The State of Russia and or the Republic of Poland

of whom (which) at this time I am a subject (or citizen), and it is my intention to reside permanently in the United States. (8) I am able to speak the English language. (9) I have resided continuously in the United States of America for the term of five years at least immediately preceding the date of this petition, to wit, since

____ March 14, 1929 ____ and in the County of ____ Kings

this State, continuously next preceding the date of this petition, since ____ March 14, 1929 ____, being a residence within said county of at least six months next preceding the date of this petition.

(10) I have ____ not ____ heretofore made petition for citizenship: Number ____, on

at ____ and such petition was denied by that Court for the following reasons and causes, to wit:

and the cause of such denial has since been cured or removed.

Attached hereto and made a part of this, my petition for citizenship, are my declaration of intention to become a citizen of the United States, certificate from the Department of Labor of my said arrival, and the affidavits of the two verifying witnesses required by law.

Wherefore, I, your petitioner, pray that I may be admitted a citizen of the United States of America, and that my name be changed to ____

I, your aforesaid petitioner being duly sworn, depose and say that I have { read / heard read } this petition and know the contents thereof; that the same is true of my own knowledge except as to matters herein stated to be alleged upon information and belief, and that as to those matters I believe it to be true; and that this petition is signed by me with my full, true name.

William Zev Spiegelman
(Complete and true signature of petitioner)

AFFIDAVITS OF WITNESSES

____ Joshua Mark ____, occupation ____ insurance agent ____, and

residing at ____ 50 Bay 26 Street, Brooklyn, NY

____ Nachman Hirsch Ekin ____, occupation ____ rabbi

residing at ____ 36 Bay 26 Street, Brooklyn, NY

each being severally, duly, and respectively sworn, deposes and says that he is a citizen of the United States of America; that he has personally known and has been acquainted in the United States with

____ William Zev Spiegelman ____, the petitioner above mentioned, since ____ March 14, 1929

and that to his personal knowledge the petitioner has resided in the United States continuously preceding the date of filing this petition, of which this affidavit is a part, to wit, since the date last mentioned, and at ____ Brooklyn, NY ____, in the County of ____ Kings

this State, in which the above-entitled petition is made, continuously since ____ Brooklyn 14, 1929 ____ and that he has personal knowledge that the petitioner is and during all such periods has been a person of good moral character, attached to the principles of the Constitution of the United States, and well disposed to the good order and happiness of the United States, and that in his opinion the petitioner is in every way qualified to be admitted a citizen of the United States.

Joshua Mark
(Signature of witness)

Nachman Hirsh Ekin
(Signature of witness)

Subscribed and sworn to before me by the above-named petitioner and witnesses in the office of the Clerk of said Court at ____ Brooklyn, NY

this ____ 21 ____ day of ____ March ____, Anno Domini 19 34. I hereby certify that certificate of arrival No. ____ 275043

from the Department of Labor, showing the lawful entry for permanent residence of the petitioner above named, together with declaration of intention No. ____

____ 176072 ____ of such petitioner, has been by me filed with, attached to, and made a part of this petition on this date.

By *Daniel J. Lyons*
Deputy Clerk.

(SEAL)

No. 67889

Form 2204—L-A

U. S. DEPARTMENT OF LABOR
NATURALIZATION SERVICE

14—2018

Petition for Citizenship, March 21, 1934.

THE UNITED STATES OF AMERICA

TO BE GIVEN TO
THE PERSON NATURALIZED

No. 3831417

CERTIFICATE OF CITIZENSHIP

Petition No. 191337

Personal description of holder as of date of naturalization: Age 40 years; sex Male; color White; complexion Fair; color of eyes Blue; color of hair L-Brown; height 5 feet 5 inches; weight 150 pounds; visible distinctive marks none
Marital status Married race Hebrew former nationality Russian
I certify that the description above given is true, and that the photograph affixed hereto is a likeness of me.

William Zev Spiegelman
(Complete and true signature of holder)

UNITED STATES OF AMERICA } ss:
EASTERN DISTRICT OF NEW YORK }
Be it known that WILLIAM ZEV SPIEGELMAN
then residing at 2114 - 83rd Street, Brooklyn, N.Y.
having petitioned to be admitted a citizen of the United States of America, and at a term of the District Court of The United States held pursuant to law at
Brooklyn on June 26th 19 34
the court having found that the petitioner intends to reside permanently in the United States, had in all respects complied with the Naturalization Laws of the United States in such case applicable and was entitled to be so admitted, the court thereupon ordered that the petitioner be admitted as a citizen of the United States of America.
In testimony whereof the seal of the court is hereunto affixed this 26th day of June in the year of our Lord nineteen hundred and thirty four and of our Independence the one hundred and fifty eighth

Seal

Clerk of the U. S. District Court
By Deputy Clerk

DEPARTMENT OF LABOR

Certificate of Naturalization, June 26, 1934.

Whitestone Hgts.
Spring Valley, N.Y.   No. 3831417

Name ...... SPIEGELMAN, William Zev ....

residing at.......2114 - 83rd St. B'klyn ....

Age.......40.......years. Date of order of admission June 26, 1934.........

Date certificate issued............June 26, 1934................................by the

.....U. S. District.......Court at.......Brooklyn, New York.............

Petition No. ./.9/337

William Spiegelman
(Complete and true signature of holder)

Naturalization Card, June 26, 1934.

REGISTRATION CARD—(Men born on or after April 28, 1877 and on or before February 16, 1897)

SERIAL NUMBER	1. NAME (Print)			ORDER NUMBER
U 1454	William (First)	Z (Middle)	SpiegeLman (Last)	

2. PLACE OF RESIDENCE (Print)
853 East 9th Street   Kings   N.Y.
(Number and street)   (Town, township, village, or city)   (County)   (State)

[THE PLACE OF RESIDENCE GIVEN ON THE LINE ABOVE WILL DETERMINE LOCAL BOARD JURISDICTION; LINE 2 OF REGISTRATION CERTIFICATE WILL BE IDENTICAL]

3. MAILING ADDRESS
853 East 9th Street
[Mailing address if other than place indicated on line 2. If same insert word same]

4. TELEPHONE	5. AGE IN YEARS	6. PLACE OF BIRTH
Navarre 8-1790	49	PoLand (Town or county)
Va. 6-3780	DATE OF BIRTH 8 28 1893	Siedlce
(Exchange) (Number)	(Mo.) (Day) (Yr.)	(State or country)

7. NAME AND ADDRESS OF PERSON WHO WILL ALWAYS KNOW YOUR ADDRESS
Dora Spiegelman   853 East 9 Street

8. EMPLOYER'S NAME AND ADDRESS
Jewish National Fund.

9. PLACE OF EMPLOYMENT OR BUSINESS
41 East 42 Street   New York, N.Y.
(Number and street or R. F. D. number)   (Town)   (County)   (State)

I AFFIRM THAT I HAVE VERIFIED ABOVE ANSWERS AND THAT THEY ARE TRUE.

D. S. S. Form 1   (over)   16—21630-2   William Spiegelman
(Revised 4-1-42)   (Registrant's signature)

Draft Card, 1944.

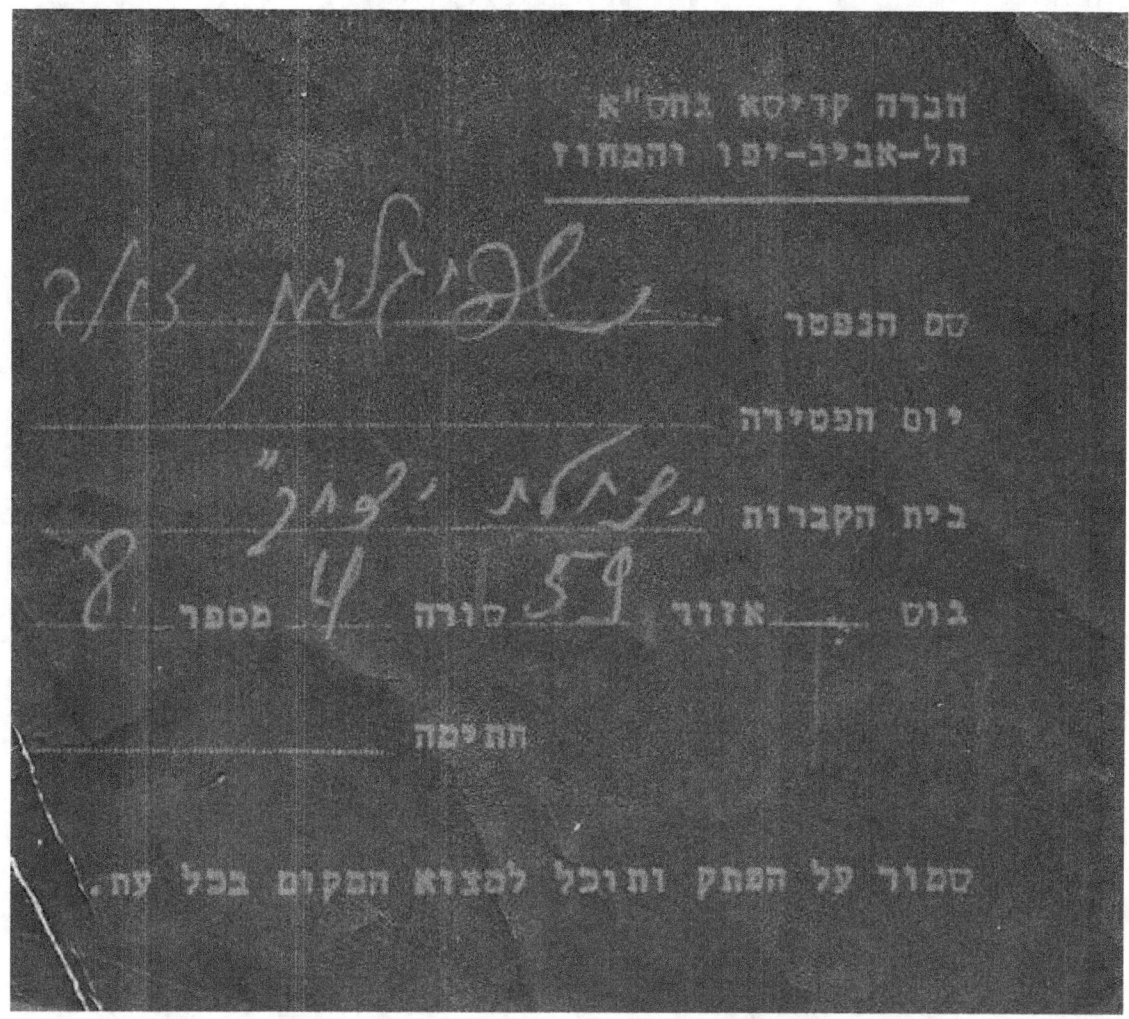

Certificate from Cemetery, Israel, 1950.

Inscription in the Golden Book, 1950. (Note: "Ruth S. Lubin" is Ruth J. Spiegelman, then married to her first husband.)